The City as Target

Bringing together scholars from a diverse range of disciplines, *The City as Target* provides a sustained and critical response to the relationship between the concept of targeting (in its many forms) and notions of understanding, imagining, and shaping the urban.

Among the many spatial and graphic terms used to describe cities in urban studies, the word target is rarely encountered. Though equally spatial, it differs from these others by implying some motive force and, more than that, a force with some intentionality. To target is to aim, to project, and ultimately to impact. It suggests a space of violence, or at least action, or movement resulting in displacement, which most other terms do not. In that sense it is useful, underused, and perhaps revelatory.

Rather than approach the city as simply a site of growth, processes, and developments, the contributors to this volume treat it as the recipient of attentions. The work draws on a wide variety of geographical sites and historic monuments in order to explore this concept, examining and challenging current urban theories. It seeks to highlight both the power of the "global city" and the current vulnerability and fragility of urban culture, exploring the city as a recipient and a culprit in relation to issues including terrorism and urban warfare, the latest cyclical failure of global financial markets, and the relatively new spectre of environmental unsustainability.

Offering a unique and relevant contribution to the literature, this work will be of great interest to scholars of urban theory, international relations, postcolonial politics, and military studies.

Ryan Bishop is Professor of Global Art and Politics, the Winchester School of Art, the University of Southampton.

Gregory K. Clancey is Associate Professor of History at the National University of Singapore, and the Master of Tembusu College.

John Phillips is Associate Professor in the Department of English Language and Literature at the National University of Singapore.

Postcolonial Politics

Pal Ahluwalia, *University of California, San Diego and University of South Australia*, Michael Dutton, *Goldsmiths, University of London*, Leela Gandhi, *University of Chicago*, Sanjay Seth, *Goldsmiths, University of London*

'Postcolonial Politics' is a series that publishes books that lie at the intersection of politics and postcolonial theory. That point of intersection once barely existed; its recent emergence is enabled, first, because a new form of 'politics' is beginning to make its appearance. Intellectual concerns that began life as a (yet unnamed) set of theoretical interventions from scholars largely working within the 'New Humanities' have now begun to migrate into the realm of politics. The result is politics with a difference, with a concern for the everyday, the ephemeral, the serendipitous and the unworldly. Second, postcolonial theory has raised a new set of concerns in relation to understandings of the non-West. At first these concerns and these questions found their home in literary studies, but they were also, always, political. Edward Said's binary of 'Europe and its other' introduced us to a 'style of thought' that was as much political as it was cultural, as much about the politics of knowledge as the production of knowledge, and as much about life on the street as about a philosophy of being. A new, broader and more reflexive understanding of politics, and a new style of thinking about the non-Western world, make it possible to 'think' politics through postcolonial theory, and to 'do' postcolonial theory in a fashion which picks up on its political implications.

Postcolonial Politics attempts to pick up on these myriad trails and disruptive practices. The series aims to help us read culture politically, read 'difference' concretely, and to problematise our ideas of the modern, the rational and the scientific by working at the margins of a knowledge system that is still logocentric and Eurocentric. This is where a postcolonial politics hopes to offer new and fresh visions of both the postcolonial and the political.

The City as Target

**Edited by Ryan Bishop,
Gregory K. Clancey
and John Phillips**

Routledge
Taylor & Francis Group
LONDON AND NEW YORK

First published 2012
by Routledge
2 Park Square, Milton Park, Abingdon, Oxfordshire OX14 4RN

Simultaneously published in the USA and Canada
by Routledge
711 Third Avenue, New York, NY 10017

First issued in paperback 2014

*Routledge is an imprint of the Taylor and Francis Group,
an informa business*

British Library Cataloguing in Publication Data
A catalogue record for this book is available from the British Library

Library of Congress Cataloging in Publication Data
The city as target/edited by Ryan Bishop, Gregory K. Clancey and John Phillips.
p. cm. – (Postcolonial politics; 4)
Includes bibliographical references and index.
1. Cities and towns. 2. Violence. 3. Disasters. 4. Terrorism. 5. City planning.
I. Bishop, Ryan, 1959– II. Clancey, Gregory K. III. Phillips, John, 1956–
HM1101.C58 2011
307.76–dc23
2011022758

ISBN 978-0-415-68722-5 (hbk)
ISBN 978-1-138-85137-5 (pbk)
ISBN 978-0-203-15435-9 (ebk)

Typeset in Times New Roman by Prepress Projects Ltd, Perth, UK.

Contents

Illustrations

Contributors

Pal Ahluwalia is a Pro Vice-Chancellor and Vice-President of the University of South Australia. He was previously Research SA Chair and Professor of Post-Colonial Studies. He was a Professor in the Department of Ethnic Studies at the University of California, San Diego, USA, and Professor at Goldsmiths, University of London. He is co-editor of the Routledge Journals *African Identities*, *Social Identities*, and *Sikh Formations*.

Irina Aristarkhova, PhD, writes and lectures on comparative feminist theory, new media aesthetics, and contemporary art. She is Assistant Professor of Women's Studies and Visual Art at the Pennsylvania State University, University Park and Visiting Professor of Gender Studies at the Media Art History department, Danube University at Krems, Austria.

John Armitage is Associate Dean and Head of the Department of Media at Northumbria University, UK. He is co-editor, with Ryan Bishop and Douglas Kellner, of the Berg journal *Cultural Politics* and the editor of, most recently, *Virilio Now: Current Perspectives in Virilio Studies*, published by Polity.

Ryan Bishop is Associate Professor of English at the National University of Singapore. He is the editor for the Polity series "Theory Now," co-editor of *Cultural Politics* (with John Armitage and Doug Kellner), and is on the *Theory Culture and Society* editorial board. He is co-author with John Phillips of *Modernist Avant-Garde Aesthetics and Contemporary Military Technology: Technicities of Perception* (Edinburgh UP, 2010) and editor of *Baudrillard Now* (Polity, 2009).

Gregory Clancey is an Associate Professor of History at the National University of Singapore. He is also the leader of the STS (Science, Technology, and Society) Research Cluster at the Asia Research Institute (ARI) and the Master of Tembusu College at NUS. He received his PhD in the History and Social Study of Science and Technology from MIT in 1998. His book *Earthquake Nation: The Cultural Politics of Japanese Seismicity* (UC Press, 2006) won the Edelstein Prize from the Society for the History of Technology in 2007.

Verena Andermatt Conley teaches in the Department of Comparative Literature at Harvard. She is the author of many books including *The War against the Beavers* (University of Minnesota Press, 2003), *Ecopolitics: The Environment* *in Poststructuralist Thought* (Routledge, 1996) and *Helen Cixous: Writing the Feminine* (University of Nebraska Press, 1991).

Jordan Crandall is a media artist and theorist based in Los Angeles. He is Associate Professor in the Visual Arts Department at the University of California, San Diego. His video installations have been presented in numerous exhibitions worldwide, including recent group exhibitions at Tate Modern, London and the San Francisco Museum of Modern Art. He writes and lectures regularly and is the founding editor of the new journal *Version*. He is the 2011 winner of the Vilem Flusser Theory Award, given by the Transmediale, Berlin and the Vilem Flusser Archive.

Nick Cullather is the author of *The Hungry World: America's Cold War Battle against Poverty in Asia* (Harvard, 2010) as well as several other books. He teaches history at Indiana University.

Robbie B. H. Goh is Associate Professor in the Department of English Language and Literature, and Vice-Dean of the Faculty of Arts and Social Sciences, National University of Singapore. He works on Asian diasporic literatures and cultures, christianity in Asia, nineteenth-century literature, and popular culture. Recent publications include *Contours of Culture: Space and Social Difference in Singapore* (Hong Kong University Press, 2005); *Christianity in Southeast Asia* (Institute of Southeast Asian Studies, 2005); *Narrating Race: Asia, (Trans)Nationalism, Social Change* (ed., Rodopi, 2011), and articles in *Journal of Commonwealth Literature, Social Semiotics, Journal of Religion and Society, Material Religion, Semiotica, Postsecular Cities* (ed. J. Beaumont and Chris Baker), and elsewhere.

Stephen Graham is Professor of Cities and Society at the Global Urban Research Unit in Newcastle University's School of Architecture, Planning and Landscape. His books include *Telecommunications and the City* (Routledge, 1996), *Splintering Urbanism* (Routledge, 2001), both with Simon Marvin, *The Cybercities Reader* (Routledge, 2004), *Cities, War and Terrorism* (Blackwell, 2004), *Disrupted Cities: When Infrastructures Fail* (Routledge, 2009), and *Cities Under Siege: The New Military Urbanism* (Verso, 2010).

Li Shiqiao is Associate Professor at the School of Architecture, the Chinese University of Hong Kong. He studied architecture at Tsinghua University in Beijing and obtained his PhD from AA School of Architecture and Birkbeck College, University of London. His current research is focused on Chinese cities. His writing has appeared in international journals including *Bauwelt, Domus China, World Architecture, Cultural Politics, Theory Culture & Society, Cultural Studies* (Wenhua Yanjiu), *Journal of Architecture, Journal of Architectural Education, Architectural Theory Review*, and *Journal of the Society of Architectural Historians*, and his books include *Architecture and Modernisation* (*Xiandai sixiang zhongde jianzhu*, China WaterPower Press, 2009) and *Power and Virtue, Architecture and Intellectual Change in England 1650–1730* (Routledge, 2007).

Rajeev S. Patke teaches at the National University of Singapore, and has authored *The Long Poems of Wallace Stevens* (Cambridge University Press, 1985, reprinted 2009) and *Postcolonial Poetry in English* (Oxford University Press, 2006), and co-authored *The Routledge Concise History of Southeast Asian Writing in English* (Routledge, 2009). Co-edited books include *Institutions in Cultures: Theory and Practice* (Rodopi, 1996) and *A Historical Companion to Postcolonial Literatures: Continental Europe and its Empires* (Edinburgh University Press, 2008). He is currently writing a book on *Modernist Literature and Postcolonial Studies* (Edinburgh University Press).

John W. P. Phillips is Associate Professor in the Department of English Language and Literature at the National University of Singapore. He writes on philosophy, literature, critical theory, aesthetics, psychoanalysis, urbanism, and military technology. He is currently researching a project on autoimmunity in biotechnology and political philosophy.

Suzuki Hiroyuki is Professor of Architecture at the University of Tokyo. He has published widely and is the author of *Shuhei Endo: Paramodern Architecture* (Phaidon, 2003) and *Contemporary Architecture of Japan* (Rizzoli, 1991).

Nigel Thrift is Vice-Chancellor of the University of Warwick. His main research interests are in nonrepresentational theory, new forms of the economy, and the nature of cities. His most recent books include *Knowing Capitalism* (Sage, 2005), *Nonrepresentational Theory* (Routledge, 2008), *Shaping the Day* (with Paul Glennie, Oxford University Press, 2009), and *The International Encyclopaedia of Human Geography* (co-edited with Rob Kitchin, Elsevier, 2009). A new book on progressive politics, co-authored with Ash Amin, will be published by Duke University Press in 2012.

Tjebbe van Tijen founded and is curator of the Documentation Center of Modern Social Movements at the University Library of Amsterdam, 1973/98 (now at the International Institute of Social History in Amsterdam). His current research projects are the "literary-psycho-geography" of cities, the mapping of human violence and "unbombing the cities of the world," a centennial commemoration of aerial bombing.

Sharon Traweek is Professor of History and Women's Studies at the University of California, Los Angeles. She is the author of numerous book chapters and articles as well as *Beamtimes and Lifetimes: The World of High Energy Physicists* (Harvard University Press, 1988) and *Doing Science + Culture,* with Roddy Reid (Routlege, 2000).

Eyal Weizman is Director of the Centre of Research Architecture at Goldsmiths. In addition to having many major exhibitions around the world, he is the author of *Lesser Evils* (Verso, 2011), *Hollow Land* (Verso, 2007), and, with Rafi Segal, *A Civilian Occupation* (Verso, 2003).

Acknowledgements

The editors are grateful to a host of individuals and the occasional funding body for logistical, material, and intellectual support in the realization of this project. In addition to the individual contributors, we would also like to thank the Faculty Research Committee of the Faculty of Arts and Social Sciences; Lily Kong, former dean of FASS; Alan Chan, former vice-dean of research at FASS; the Urban Studies Research Project at NUS; our many wonderful colleagues in the departments of Geography, History, English, Sociology, and Architecture at NUS who engaged in conversations formal and informal; John Richardson and Robbie Goh, both former heads of the English department; our many excellent graduate students who worked with us on the development of this project; Pal Ahluwalia and Michael Dutton whose series at Routledge provides an excellent home for the book; Nicola Parkin, our wonderful editor at Routledge; and finally our families and friends near and far without whose support none of this would be possible or meaningful.

1 Cities as targets

Ryan Bishop, Greg Clancey and John Phillips

Among the many spatial and graphic terms used to describe cities in urban studies literature – centers, nodes, nexes, -scapes, densities, etc. – one rarely encounters the word "target." Though equally spatial – invoking an arc, a line, a trajectory – it differs from these others by implying some motive force, and, more than that, a force with some intentionality. To target is of course to aim, to project, and ultimately to impact. It suggests a space of violence, or at least action, or at least movement resulting in displacement, which most of these other terms do not. In that sense it is useful, underused, and perhaps revelatory, which is why we've made it the leitmotif of this book.

Our theme was first broached in an essay entitled "The City as Target," written by Bishop and Clancey just before the attacks on New York City in 2001 and published 2 years later.[1] This initial essay had two goals. One was to point out how oddly rare it was to find the concept of "targeting" in urban literature of any kind despite the unprecedented serial city-killing (real and planned) of the mid- to late twentieth century.[2] That disciplines with "urban" in their titles had largely grown and proliferated in a period of unrestrained urbicide was something that needed to be pointed out if not explained. Second, it examined the analytical usefulness of regarding urban phenomena as the result of various modes of "targeting" rather than simply as "processes," a word ubiquitous in urban literature. The article speculated as to what might happen if a whole series of gradualistic if not somnolent social science terms one normally applies to cities were replaced with action-oriented, sometimes violent words pointing toward, at the very least, responsibility.

Of course the targeting of cities by warfare, conventional and "asymmetrical," had a very long if cyclical history and was, even before the new millennium, coming back into a depressing sort of vogue. The destruction of Beirut in the 1970s had been followed by the bombing or shelling of Tripoli, Panama City, Sarajevo, Grozny, Oklahoma City, Baghdad, Belgrade, and a host of smaller places as the terror-filled twentieth century ratcheted to its finish. Kigali became an urban/suburban killing field on par with Phnom Penh or Warsaw. But the surprise targeting for destruction on live television of very tall and famous buildings in one of the world's major financial and publishing centers had a way of focusing attention on a phenomenon until then associated with places peripheral to global power.

And very soon the Bush administration's "new kind of war" was taken not just to the mountains of Afghanistan and deserts of Iraq (familiar extra-urban theaters for nineteenth- and twentieth-century "conventional" conflict) but to Baghdad, Fallujah, and other cities in the very river valley that gave birth to urbanization, as well as urban conquest and plunder. At the turn of the new millennium, "urban warfare" was suddenly on everyone's lips in a way it hadn't really been since Stalingrad.

The concept of urban targeting has the prospect, in a literal sense, to turn urban studies inside out. Rather than approach the city as a site of "growth, processes, developments," etc., it treats it as the recipient of attentions – which can be characterized along a continuum from benign to terrifying – originating outside its metaphorical walls. This is something different, however, from the externalizing emphasis of globalization theory, whose metaphor is an electronic communications network. The network model is largely a technological upgrading and spatial expansion of the *growth–process–development* one, and is in that sense equally bloodless, and lacking in agency or responsibility. It is particularly limited in describing the relations between cities, nation-states, and the "sudden event" to which both are continually subject. In what sense, for example, was New Orleans "globalized" during the 2005 hurricane season? Was the battle of Fallujah or the horrific multi-sited attacks in Mumbai of the same order as an electronic stock transfer? Or, for that matter, are electronic stock transfers just so much constant global noise, or might they not create huge whooshing or sucking sounds (if sound was generated in the vacuum of electronic commerce) as they collectively target this location or that?

That the concept of "civilization" is so intimately bound up with the idea of cities may be one reason why writers have been historically disinclined to discuss the history, geography, or sociology of urban concentrations in terms that conjure violence, destruction, or mayhem. Although all of these are clearly urban – in fact hyper-urban in micro-manifestation – they still strike us as declensions or exceptions to the rule that cities grow, prosper, transform, and/or sustain themselves like trees or fields of grass. Such ecological/biological metaphors abound in urban description, and the metaphor of the network merely recreates the ecosystem as a benign and cybernetic density of chips and wires. The gradualism built deeply into the way we talk about cities serves the purpose, it often seems, of reassuring us that, despite everything, even aerial carpet-bombing or global economic collapse, the city will survive and might even be better for it, whatever the fates of its inhabitants. This seemed to be the lesson of World War II – or at least the one taught by the post-war planning community for whom *tabula rasa* represented opportunity rather than desolation.

A more mundane reason for the difficulty of seeing targeting at work in cities lies in the way we talk about architecture. In nearly all instances architects and urban planners must destroy – or place themselves in the service of those who do – in order to create. Before there can be a built environment, an existing one must be unbuilt. But great strides are taken to hide the demolition phase from public view – both physically in the form of the tall fences and other barriers ringing "building sites" all over the world, and discursively in the almost complete absence of the demolition site in even the most descriptive and least celebratory works of architectural history. Only in the relatively peripheral literature on historic preservation can we find a hyper-awareness of "normal" urbanity as a destructive spectacle: the City itself, from the perspective of its inhabitants, as a slow-motion mortar attack. Whether one prefers the "before" or "after" is beside the point. Simply to see the violence – and not as *process* toward something but as a series of actions with trajectories and intentions, and with random and contingent results – is the task of the moment, and one that can begin equally well with the aerial reconnaissance images of a pilotless drone or the blueprints for a new urban megaplex.

The City as a site of progress (indeed, its very fount) has such strong sanction in the West that counter-narratives have traditionally been considered in almost every case exceptional, or, if too forcefully insisted upon, politically dangerous. The thesis that democracy, academic freedom, liberal capitalism, etc., began in cities, and remains more naturally at home there than in nation-states or (especially) the countryside, has strongly influenced both the roots and the trajectories of urban-oriented studies. Indeed, the instinct among intellectuals to locate a progressive life force in cities arguably grew stronger in the late twentieth century given the increasing disenchantment with nation-states (at least in the West) following their prosecution of the city-killing World War II. Yet being sensitive to urban targeting need in no sense betray an inclusive and democratic politics. We need to be realistic about the vulnerability and threat posed by concentration – as well as its substantial benefits – if we're to effectively navigate, or simply live in, the urban spaces of the twenty-first century.

If the Western city is obscured by an overly heroic lineage, the post-colonial non-Western city has had a more checkered intellectual career both locally and remotely. It was commonly framed, in the era of nation-state formation, as a site of dangerous, almost malignant growth. That non-Western "primate cities" were often so very large, dense, unplanned, and poor seemed, to many, to be a function of their too-close relations with nation-states – that is, their insufficient city-ness. On the other hand, the fate of Phnom Penh under the Khmer Rouge provided only the most extreme example of a post-colonial state turning against the urban and cosmopolitan in the name of a new, spaceless, de-concentrated purity.

The recent era of the Global City has not really replaced the binary vision of First versus Third World urban development.[3] But it offers up images and discourses that are no longer so identifiable as progressive or retrograde, benign or malevolent. The Global City – when envisioned as one great system of electronically interlinked metropoli – seems in one frame of vision to be in charge of the planet as never before. In another, urban culture is in a condition of heightened awareness of its own vulnerability and fragility, not only through the experience of terrorism and urban warfare, and the latest cyclical failure of global financial markets, but also through the relatively new specter of environmental unsustainability. The City is here both the culprit and the tower from which "the environment" (that which is not the City to its inhabitants) is most visible and real.

In either case, the experience of urban living is increasingly characterized by the *state of emergency*: the sense of the present condition is one of exception; that anything can happen next, and likely will. How does the heroic narrative of the city survive this, or does it need to? The de-urbanization of New Orleans – even if unprecedented in modern times in its completeness – might shake our optimism about urban centers as inherently sustainable. It ought at least to invite further reflection on how vulnerable concentrated populations are to linked forms of violence and displacement, in this case of the natural and state-sponsored kind. A hurricane might have destroyed the engineered infrastructure on which the city depended, but the state and federal governments completed the process by facilitating, if not demanding, complete evacuation down to the city's last inhabitant. In both cases the concept of "targeting" seems to open new interpretive terrain, however vague both Katrina and the Federal Emergency Management Agency (FEMA) were about precisely where their trajectories lay.

All of this suggests that the moment is ripe for writing a different urban history: one that might replace the post-WWII narrative of the City continually re-born and better for it. We need an urban history that will recover the violence of the twentieth (and nascent twenty-first) century in such a way that it is seen to constitute a continuum (in the sense of planning, not ethics) with the post-war displacements, demolitions, and continual re-buildings which continue today. A useful frame is "emergency" itself, a condition that the Western city was subjected to at least as early as 1914, and the colonial city even earlier.

"Emergency" is of course an age-old condition of cities, or walled enclosures, as even the most casual published surveys of urban history demonstrate. The novelty is not to reveal the alignment of emergency with the historic city, but with The Modern City, from which it was supposed to be banished. It is about restoring a sense of historicity to The Modern City, and puncturing the illusion that urban civilization would transform the world into a benign, inter-connected (and thus wall-less) Metropolia. On the other hand, we need to also understand emergency as itself a modern (though not strictly contemporary) condition, which began molding our cities long before September 11, 2001, and in ways not consciously associated with warfare. Mass housing, for example, was often accompanied by mass demolitions, constructions, and mobilizations of populations to evacuate, occupy, and re-occupy. The convergence between the language of modern property development and conquest is not merely rhetorical, but based on a true convergence of landscapes. This and other characteristic twentieth-century urban movements required pre-existing declarations of emergency, and were carried out in haste and (often) violence, though they have hardly been captured in histories of either condition.[4]

Emergency has been the standard state of affairs globally from the moment the first atomic bombs were dropped on Hiroshima and Nagasaki (if not from the beginning of World War II, the Great Depression, or even the outbreak of World War I). The United States, flush with victory and technological achievement, quickly woke to the realization that weapons used on others could be turned against itself. Thus, the last shots fired in World War II were the first shots of the Cold War, and the present age of intensive civil defense emerged.[5] Urbicide might not have had a large presence in urban studies, but it had massive support in the fields of logistics and emergency planning for the refurbishment of the urban built environment and the construction of new infrastructure in city centers. In the

United States and elsewhere, each new facility, from university library to sports field, from hospital to city hall, sported a bomb shelter and provisions intended to survive nuclear attack, as cities came to terms with their new status as perpetual targets. Each "burb" and "burg" had become the frontline, a geography that emerged in any place a mass of citizenry assembled, and the coming emergency of nuclear war pervaded all aspects of planning the urban. Systems analysis and operations research spilled increasingly out of contained military domains to the urban centers and suburban sprawl that were the targets of military strategy and attention. The concentration of material, personnel, and planning on the urban in relation to the Cold War all resulted from the status of each site as a target, while simultaneously, and ironically but inevitably, reinforcing its targeted nature.

The network of surveillance necessitated by "real time" observation of all parts of the world – itself necessitated by geopolitical policies such as the Truman Doctrine – enmeshed cities globally in a technoscientific embrace of targeting by intercontinental ballistic missiles (ICBMs). At the same time, as transnational corporations became increasingly concerned with opening markets to consumer goods, the US ideology of free markets, unhindered capital, consumerism, and democracy became increasingly exported and exportable. The global, as we have come to know it in the latter twentieth and early twenty-first centuries, came into being through a series of inter-related, self-accelerating, and occasionally contradictory set of targeting trajectories. Forecasting and simulation took priority in planning, prognostication, and realization of geopolitical maneuvers; business investment and market expansion; and military considerations. The IT systems used for "real time" surveillance of the globe resulted in the increased de-territorialization and circulation of information, and were mobilized as well for the de-territorialization and circulation of capital. All of these not only shaped the global in specific and profound ways, but also resulted in a leveling of the urban. Cities retained their locality(s) and hierarchies, yet all urban sites were arranged onto a new global grid by virtue of being targeted by a host of forces material and immaterial. As Bishop and Clancey have previously argued, "it is their [cities'] status as targets that renders them, *de facto*, 'global.'"[6]

As broadcast media transformed into nascent IT with the emergence of the digital computer, a discourse of inter-relatedness, co-dependence, and mutual influence blossomed, though belied by realpolitik and real business practice. The network metaphor takes true center stage with the US military's Network Centric Warfare (NCW) agenda, whose tenets read like a précis of urban planning. "Network Centric Warfare is to warfare," claims an executive summary of the program, "what e-business is to business." A "robustly networked force improves information sharing" according to the document, which "enhances . . . shared situational awareness." This in turn "enables collaboration and self-synchronization, and enhances stability and speed of command," all with the aim of "dramatically increase[ing] mission effectiveness" (http://www.dod.mil/nii/NCW/ncw_exec_sum.pdf).

The extension of warfare into the immaterial realm of IT and cyberspace reinforces and affects the material from whence it emerged and for which it was designed. A cybernetic system of feedback and modification serves to create the conditions of possibility that the technology already shapes and determines. We can extrapolate further and say that the immaterial responses to targeting and being targeted have led to an intensification of targeting processes in all domains that operate within and define the urban. The network of Network Centric Warfare is, quite obviously, the network of IT, but it is also that of global capital, forecasting, broadcasting, entertainment, platform-to-platform sharing, surveillance, oversight, defense strategy, and urban planning and daily urban life.

NCW and the shift to both information-based economies and information-based warfare foreground how immaterial conditions of possibility bring forth material ones. The role of the imaginary as it pertains to the urban is not simply the domain of the poet, the urban planner, the politician, or even the general. It is all-pervasive insofar as it entails a targeting inseparable from thinking itself. Sam Weber makes this point at length in his provocative *Targets of Opportunity: On the Militarization of Thinking.*[7] Using the classic example of the archer and target, and working through the etymology of the Greek term *skopos* (something the editors of this volume have pursued elsewhere[8]) as privileging the act of aiming over sighting or surveying, Weber reveals that the term originally indicates both subject and object, both archer and target. In a sense, the act of aiming or targeting entails within itself a type of *techne*, in Aristotle's sense, as something that links subjects and objects and reveals not only their relationship but also the potential residing in each. The *techne,* here the act of targeting in a material or immaterial sense, unfolds the inter-relatedness between subject and object such that each is changed through the interaction. This is a far cry from the type of targeting found in the transitive grammar of English or in technoscience's promise of action-at-a-distance, allowing a subject to manipulate objects through various teletechnologies, without getting his or her hands dirty in the process: a promise just as essential to military targeting as it is to targeting by global capital.

The genesis and structure of the targeted city

The two senses implicit in the concept *target* (scoping out on one hand and striking on the other), when merged with the idea of the city, as well as the historical existence of actual cities, can help shift our sense of what is at stake in urbanism. One question this belies is whether targeted events are functions of the structure and history of the city itself, or in some sense misfortunes that fall upon the city from outside, having no causal principle within the healthy continuity of the site itself.

In 1977 Paul Virilio argued that the city – continuously and from its inception – functions something like a colonial fortress. That is, an agglomeration arises around vectors of movement (the road, the water route) and is marked by the potentials of movement, which it nonetheless attempts to police. He observes:

> It seems we've forgotten that the street is only a road passing through an agglomeration . . . The city is but a stopover, a point on the synoptic path of a trajectory, the ancient military glacis, ridge road, frontier or riverbank,

where the spectator's glance and the vehicle's speed of displacement were instrumentally linked.[9]

Virilio's critical writings are still unusual for their focus on the military basis of social phenomena, a focus that penetrates the martial logic barely hidden beneath historical and contemporary patterns of social organization, including revolution, oppression, and terrorism. Operations that for Virilio typify the military mentality, determining ostensibly non-military kinds of organization, can be regarded as strategies designed to eliminate the accidental, which naturally involves the setting up of defensive borders (frontlines) distinguishing the planned urban structure from the stochastic processes that threaten it in the form of through-passages:

> This military thought that claims by functional planning to eliminate chance (which it considers synonymous with disaster and ruin), becomes totally confused at the end of the *ancien régime* with the thinking of the bourgeois political class, its taste for rational nomenclature, its tireless activity of totalitarian scribe (encyclopaedists), the osmosis taking place at the entrance to the cities (permeable membrane between the highway and the street).[10]

In the logic of Virilio's worldview, the confused displacement historically of an imperial military logic into the post-revolutionary organizations of an urban bourgeoisie will continue to function – catastrophically from time to time – whenever a threat is identified or perceived. And the paradoxical fallout from this situation will involve a targeting intensified in further responses, as the logic of the city begins to take defensive measures against the principles on which it is founded.

In fact we live in such an urbanizing age that *the city* is constantly on the verge of extinction as a meaningful category. The boundaries between the inside and the outside of a city, relatively easy to identify in classical times, have become hopelessly blurred. When a city becomes a target, do we decipher this as an attack on the particular city, a city in its non-exemplary singularity, or an attack on the city as emblematic of a certain urban, cosmopolitan, more or less democratic organization? The situation with the city in the twenty-first century does not allow us to distinguish absolutely between these particularities (the City of London, Southern Beirut, Downtown Mumbai, Paris Centre, Shinjuku, etc.) and the global urban substructure that in some ways justifies an identification of these targets in general as *the city*. Perhaps, if anything, it's the status of these urban sites as *targets* that at once identifies them with and relieves them of their valorized particularity: their unique communities, their uncanny social determinacies, and the geopolitical coordinates that stake out their space on local or global cartographies. Their singular existence disappears with the strike.

In a way, then, the success stories of global urban development and the disasters that remove entire districts function toward the same end, removing anything that one could say did not exemplify the dominant image of the city. But then cities are targeted for diverse reasons. Variously one can identify the wish to remove slums or decaying districts; the wish to strike against the local or global military

industrial complex; the desire to participate in some more or less well-publicized
subterranean struggle; the several motivations in waging armed conflict between
states or over disputed territories; the strategic identification of criminal elements;
operations against security risks; etc. Increased density of populations renders
precise targeting more difficult, so that accidental or collateral damages either are
vaguely calculated within the effect of the strike or become an intrinsic attraction
of the target itself, especially when imagined zones of either cosmopolitanism or
purity are in the cross hairs.

Whether we fix on the local particularities of a site or its emblematic urban
qualities, one thing remains reasonably consistent: the methods and technologies that serve the operational purposes of surveillance and targeting are largely
indistinguishable from the defensive strategies that serve to protect the city from
surveillance and counter-surveillance, targeting and response. The co-implication
suggested in the rubric *city as target* satisfies the sense that the extent to which
a city can be targeted (for surveillance, policing, military operations, destruction, renovation, etc.) is the extent to which it targets and, by so doing, attempts
to protect itself. It is often difficult to distinguish elements that *belong* to the
city from those that are *foreign* to it, or even those which are dangerous to its
continued existence. The circular logic of the *city as target* continues to erupt
from time to time in more or less violent events of conflict and tragedy. There's
nothing inevitable about such events or the contexts in which they occur, but it is
nonetheless possible to strip the dense historical layers of a city back to its origins,
to the inevitably accidental events of its gathering, settling, and self-protection, to
the negotiations that established the city historically and to which, in the various
traumas of targeting, it can once again be reduced. This is the conclusion that Livy
arrives at in his account of the notorious sacking of Rome by the Gauls (*Ab Urbe
Condita* Vol. 5).[11] The upshot (the *apparent* result, in Livy's account, of a series of
unforeseeable disasters) is an eventual improvement in the situation of Rome after
years of increasing neglect and corruption.

The unusual character of this rubric – belying the inexhaustible and continuing
catalogue of events and phenomena it designates – promises to shed new light on
the nature, origins, and structural relations of cities today. Niccolò Machiavelli,
opening his *Discourses on Livy* with a chapter on "The Best Form of Government,"
makes observations about the *origin* of cities, noting that "all cities are built either
by natives of the place in which they are built, or by people from elsewhere."[12]
The importance of this statement has an obscure patina in the twenty-first century
(some way into the historical era of the megacity). Machiavelli's observation has
the virtue of simplicity at least to start with. In the case of the first kind of city
(his examples, in line with the general strategy of forming classical and contemporary parallels, are Athens and Venice), "inhabitants, dispersed in many small
communities, find they cannot enjoy security since no one community of itself,
owing to its position and to the smallness of its numbers, is strong enough to
resist the onslaught of an invader" (p. 100). The city as target is thus implicit
even before the establishment of the city as city. Communities join to become
a city because they are vulnerable to predators. They form a target that is less

vulnerable but obviously more visible. This implicitly suggests that by targeting a city one attempts to reduce it to its pre-civic state of vulnerability. Machiavelli identifies with this kind of city the ideals of civic law that accompany a flexible idea of cosmopolitanism: "without any particular person or prince to give them a constitution, they began to live as a community under laws which seemed to them appropriate for their maintenance" (p. 101). The other kind of foundation involves the colonial gesture of imposing laws. Thus, for Machiavelli, the former kind remains preferable. A city can be maintained only on principles that were present at the level of its foundation.

Machiavelli serves as a reminder that the political question of the city is recurrently motivated, throughout its undoubtedly diverse histories, by the will, as Louis Althusser puts it, "to be *emancipated* from the immutable necessity of the endless cycle of the same revolutions in order to create not a government that is going to degenerate to pave the way for its successor, but a *state that lasts*."[13] Livy's detailed analysis of the weave of Rome's fortunes serves as a catalyst for Machiavelli's attempt to apply a politics of the enduring (durable, robust) popular state to the contemporary context of Italy's warring micro-states. In the same way, political philosophers have since returned to Machiavelli for analogous purposes. G. W. F. Hegel, in the remarkable and early essay, "The German Constitution," observes of Machiavelli that he, "with cool deliberation, grasped the necessary idea of saving Italy by uniting it into a single state."[14] What did Italy, in Hegel's reading, need saving from? "It entrusted its own defense to assassination, poison, and treason, or to hordes of foreign rabble whom their paymasters always found costly and destructive, and often formidable and dangerous; and some of whose leaders rose to the ranks of princes" (p. 79). The Italian city defends itself by employing the very forces that render it most vulnerable to attack. Hegel's extraordinary endeavor – to produce a political theory according to which the interests of the state and those of a diverse people could be made one and the same – begins here with this semi-identification of early nineteenth-century Germany with fifteenth-century Italy:

> Germany shares the fate which Italy once experienced: it has been a theatre of civil wars for many centuries. But it has also been a theatre for the wars of foreign powers; it has been plundered, robbed, vilified, and despised by friends. (p. 83)

The aim of Hegel's politics of right, to establish a single form of political power under which individuals can thrive (today this would be the paradoxical shared sovereignty of a democratic republic), can seem hopeless, undesirable, or repulsive after two centuries of global war-making in the name of universal or egalitarian values (right, justice, freedom, democracy, etc.).

The reference to Machiavelli, however, can help shape our understanding of the situation differently. Hegel draws from Machiavelli the suggestion that a city's modes of *defense* can operate as the chief vehicles of its *destruction*, in which case its chances of survival remain limited. Building on this contradiction he suggests that the situation requires quite radical, perhaps even insurmountable, measures. Machiavelli's always pragmatic and meticulously observed account of the possibility of survival implies a situation demanding frequent renaissance. A city (or a state, a sect, an institution) should regularly be "restored to its original principles [*ritirarla spesso verso il suo principio*]," *Discourses*, p. 385). It should be turned back to its beginnings from time to time: "those are better constituted and have a longer life whose institutions make frequent renovations possible, or which are brought to such a renovation by some event which has nothing to do with their constitution" (p. 385). The principle is exemplified (amongst other diverse examples) by the attack on Rome by the Gauls: "This defeat in a war with outsiders, therefore, came about so that the institutions of this city should be renovated" (p. 386). The effect of an internal or externally produced *event* (Machiavelli lists the catastrophic events recorded by Livy that nonetheless each time lead to the continuing survival-by-renaissance of the Roman constitution) is that a people recall the constitution on which they are founded; and they "review their position" in relation to their founding principles (i.e. their constitution). The best example, in which the city of Rome becomes the vulnerable target of a deliberate militant force, involves destruction on a massive scale; yet for Machiavelli this is literally Rome's most "fortunate" moment: "it plainly appears from Livy's evidence that, in order to make Rome greater and to lead it on to future greatness, fortune decided it was necessary to first chastise it . . . but did not want to ruin it altogether" (p. 371). Livy's carefully slanted historical account of Rome's errors of judgment leading up to the Gauls' assault allows Machiavelli to determine quite precisely the connection between the gradual corruption of the polity and the consequences of this corruption: its capital becoming the target of a warring army. Hegel can in the same way identify the political errors that underlie the dispersion and destruction of the German states at the start of the nineteenth century.

The chapters

Turning to our contributors, the kinds of urban renewal if not actual rebirth examined in Livy, Machiavelli, and Hegel are taken up at the most quotidian levels in Nigel Thrift's chapter on repair and maintenance. Thrift offers a generally hopeful account about the resiliency of cities at the material level, and how repair can provide solace for urban existence. Tempering his optimism, however, is a more dire argument about moral progress finding little advancement despite improvements in material conditions. The political agendas in urban sites, Thrift argues, have become increasingly fragmentary and bereft of larger social visions for inclusionary projects and practices, effacing the presumed cosmopolitanism the city promises. Mobilizing the optimistic dimensions of Ernest Bloch's work on cities, Thrift maintains that the material renewal found daily and ubiquitously can and still does provide the possibility for a "practical utopianism" that reveals how urbanization manifests "a surplus of hope," alongside the abundance of enmity, bespeaking "an unconscious hunger for the future as well as the past."

Hope for larger social change and the imaginary of collective action are themselves the targets of John Armitage's chapter. "The imaginist city" is Armitage's term for the de-territorialized activists and thinkers whose utopian goal is a world without warfare. This urban space of hope and the mind has been targeted, he argues, by the nexus of military–corporate entities behind US geopolitical strategy. Looking at the intellectual history of conservative think tanks and the culmination of their policy recommendations in the wars waged by the Bush administration, Armitage sees the neo-con movement placing the utopian global movement for peace in its cross hairs. This chapter articulates a deep heritage of thought that perceives alternative strategies for being in the world as not just antithetical to the current power structure but threatening it. Of central concern to Armitage's analyses of military elites is their capacity to control electronic media and thus public discourse, making the discursive domain challenging for other voices.

Eyal Weizman's chapter on the Israeli–Palestinian border/barrier explores the impossibilities in the myth of separation that gives birth to barriers, and thus the inevitable defensive moves required as a result of offensive targeting practices. Placing faith in a barrier, an impossible line intended to result in islands and enclaves that safely contain combatants, Israel capitulates to the logic of "emergency" that proposes temporary solutions to extant problems, solutions that historically result in permanent changes in the geographical and political landscape. The website of the Israeli Ministry of Foreign Affairs claims that "the anti-terrorist fence is a passive, *temporary* . . . measure not a permanent border" but the two problems of the Israeli military regime – the consistent presence of violence and the continued presence of political initiatives – mitigate against both the efficacy of the barrier and its temporary status. The Gaza Strip barrier is thus not an actual border, but functions as one in a *post hoc* climate of rationalization, reinforcing the desire to target separation as a viable concept. "Israel and Palestine are not two different places that can be imagined to co-exist side by side, but are in effect different readings of the same place, with overlapping memories and national claims," Weizman argues. Echoing some of Armitage's imaginist city claims, Weizman asserts that "against the endless search for the form and mechanisms of 'perfect' separation comes the realisation that a viable solution does not exist within the realm of territorial design."[15]

Steve Graham's contribution to the volume examines the military–entertainment nexus, focusing on cities built for the purposes of military training and simulation of asymmetrical warfare. Using advanced special effects designed for the movie industry, these cities that appear on no maps – though numbering up to 100 sites globally – extend the long-standing relationship between the entertainment industry in the United States and the military. They constitute in Graham's words "a shadow archipelago of 'cities' that mimic the urbanization of real wars and conflicts around the world." For much of the Cold War, cities were targets for nuclear annihilation but not conventional warfare. The end of the Cold War and its reconstitution as the war on terror, however, has brought cities fully back into military planning and training. Because cities are now perceived as sites that house and hide terrorists, the Israeli model for engaging the Palestinian resistance to the Gaza occupation became the starting point for US and NATO reconsideration of military engagement with urban sites. It is the city itself – its infrastructure and all that allows it to function – that becomes the most explicitly vulnerable and therefore targeted dimension of asymmetrical planning. The use of advanced IT and simulation techniques for this training, Graham argues, re-maps "traditional lines between battlefield and home front" and "forecloses the very possibilities of democratic engagement" that rely on clear divisions between soldiers and civilians. With the help of Universal and Disney Studios, amongst others, the US military has developed a network of cities predicated upon simulation realized in three dimensions, and engaging all of a soldier's senses, to train its troops not only for warfare in cities, but also warfare on them.

Pal Ahluwalia also examines the direct influences of violence on cities and architecture, but in his case it is terrorism that is rescripting the image of the city. Terrorism has arguably supplanted all other global calamities and dangers, replacing them with a single inchoate mass of anxieties that is simultaneously ancient (or tribal) and contemporary. Taking the refugee camp at Kibumba as his site of exploration, Ahulwalia deftly shows the replication of the war-ridden Rwandan nation in the small UN-contained camp, and argues that the impromptu market that emerged there operates as a site where ironically, and in complex interaction with colonial history, a spontaneously emergent Hutu identity can be found. The article considers the site as one of haphazard assembly that moves rapidly from "space" to "place" and from habitable spot to home. The site, the makeshift city or even city-state, was targeted not as refugee space from which to flee, but as protected dwellings (albeit thuggishly in many ways) with a sense of identity and permanence embedded in obviously transitory structures. The materiality of the site has been reinscribed by immateriality of desire bred from despair, creating "a subaltern architecture" of dense configuration. In Ahulwalia's reading, the market becomes a lens through which one can discern a geographic imaginary targeting of improvised space for specific purposes sprung from the historical trajectories. He argues that the easy binarisms operative in colonial architectural practices, and spatial politics in the act of making "home" elsewhere – dependent on denigrating local spatial forms and types – find uncanny resonance in the ways the Hutu use the market in the camp to both replicate and overturn colonial engagements with space.

Following a line of argumentation sympathetic to Nigel Thrift's, and which in fact indirectly answers some of the questions he poses, Verena Andermatt Conley's contribution considers the many valences of the term "target" to argue that the city is a site for potential exploration and innovation in the face of the increasing violence and chaos found in urban environments. Working through a range of contemporary French theorists, not all of whom are necessarily related to urban inquiry, Conley thinks targeting and retargeting through writers as diverse as Baudrillard, Auge, de Certeau, Deleuze, Latour, and Virilio, amongst many others, to consider the ways in which violence, information technologies, and means of surveillance and control actually produce potentially fruitful and challenging opportunities for taking back (retargeting) urban space from a status quo threatening to obliterate social justice and equity. She reminds us that cities have always been sites of contestation, and though the stakes might have been raised in the last half of the twentieth century and the first decade of the twenty-first, the historicity of urban negotiations as elucidated by the host of theorists she engages provides us spurs to action and engagement. "Cities emerge at the intersection of many different networks, images . . . and negotiations," Conley argues. The task of the intellectual is "to continue to retarget today's targeted city, each according to her or his conventions or historical and geographical context."

The indirect targeting of cities by natural disasters is a somewhat contentious point because the initial, commonsensical assumption is that nature does not have volition and is thus incapable of targeting anything. We simply get in the way of nature, which is the point of using the concept of the target to think about natural disasters and emergency generally. Indirect targeting occurs when cities are knowingly built on sites where specific kinds of natural disasters frequently occur, and often built using technologies designed to counter these predictable attacks by nature: the defensive mode of *skopos*. Tokyo is a city that has been targeted by military and natural attacks from its inception, with fires, earthquakes, firebombing, and even development/redevelopment plans making massive changes in the cityscape and the psyches of those who dwell there. Such issues are the concern of renowned Japanese architectural historian Suzuki Hiroyuki in his chapter. Various natural and human-made disasters have been instrumental in the reconstitution of Tokyo's ever-processual urban space. Suzuki is concerned about how planning shifts the priorities of the private sector onto the public, even to the extent of obliterating public interest. The results in the built and lived environment, Suzuki argues, are "island universes" of redevelopment, ill-connected to the city as a whole. This "island" system amounts to an administrative scatter-shooting of private interests that target the urban space in ways that simultaneously isolate buildings and complexes from their immediate environs (here read as the public sphere) and connect them to similarly constructed and developed spaces physically remote from one another. "What is happening," Suzuki argues, "is that the creation of islands of redevelopment is transforming Tokyo from an advanced uni-functional city into a multifunctional cultural metropolis" that nonetheless caters to the specialized interests of corporate entities and elides citizens as residents from being able to live in large parts of the city.

Greg Clancey's chapter starts from the observation that the basis of urban planning from Hausmann to the present is the act of clearance. The ultimate logic of clearance, as manifest in Clancey's mid-twentieth-century America, was to render the city a *tabula rasa*, even evoking the option of its eventual disappearance. Central to Clancey's argument is the new object of "the house" (as opposed to houses or homes) conceived in the inter-war period as a mass-produced and completely abstractable commodity, separable from communal formations and ultimately from urbanism. New Deal housing policies were actually crafted amid widespread and serious discussion of *the house of tomorrow* as a secret economic weapon meant to restore capitalism. Like the automobile before it, however, it promised to radically reconstitute city space. The global financial collapse of the 1930s not only generated "emergency" as a mode of governance, but also invited the strategic targeting of cities to leverage "national" agendas and goals by groups formerly peripheral to city-building. Thus, the US model for urban "renewal" became the clearance of existing cityscapes (both physically and ideologically) and their replacement with the de-territorialized dream of the mass-production dwelling. Clancey's chapter presents a new, more politically informed and urban-conscious origin story for the humble "house" upon which so much of US identity and security, both imperiled and defended, has subsequently hinged.

The full-scale destruction of cities, no matter how horrific, affords the architect and urban planner something each needs: namely the space for a new beginning articulated by Livy, Machiavelli, and Hegel, as well as experienced in Tokyo as argued by Suzuki. The Great Fire of 1666 provided a forum for competing visions of reimagining central London that Li Shiqiao argues exemplified both the culmination of a specific set of historical, intellectual, and aesthetic trajectories in Europe, as well as a catalyst for initiating urban retargeting and change that remains with us into the current moment. In essence, the larger forces of visibility and speed led to an increased softening of the city's edge as walls and moats gave way to tolls and signs as well as electronic networks and grids. The London fire afforded seventeenth-century planners an opportunity to reconsider the exposure of the urban organization that had held the imagination since the Greeks and Romans (filtered through the creative interpretations of the Italian Renaissance) in terms that drew on tradition while envisioning the future. The systemic grids proposed by the surviving London plans indicate a tension between a neo-classical past and a new kind of city predicated upon the advances of science and trade, a tension often articulated in terms of visibility and opacity, networks and closures. Through a sustained reading of the designs, Li details the material, aesthetic, intellectual, and architectural trajectories that manifested themselves in the attempts to revision London in order to unfold those elements of urban formation the plans targeted, and reveal the deep historicity underlying not only the seventeenth-century imaginaries of the city, but also those that remain with us today.

The collective imagination of a nation can be targeted by the general design and logic of its most important urban space, and, for Irina Aristarkhova, it is Moscow's appearance first and foremost as a fortress that has seized the mind of the Russian and the former Soviet citizenry. In a provocatively poetic evocation of the fortress worldview that Moscow embodies, Aristarkhova displays the mentality of defense – an extreme reaction to exposure and targeted attack – that characterizes Russia and the USSR. "In Russia," she writes, "'fortress' has been translated into mythology, into law, into language and culture, into *national identity*: most clearly exemplified by the fortress city, 'Kremlin.'" Aristarkhova argues that the fortress reveals a deep anxiety that pervades Moscow, and metonymically Russia, an anxiety about no longer being desired: for targeting has always had the double valence of vulnerability and desirability.

Exposure and vulnerability, imagination and terror, targeting and defense: these are but some of the themes graphically displayed in the long visual history of aerial bombing found in a staggeringly documented array of artistic and photographic representations evocatively woven together in Tjebbe van Tijen's stunning mural that visualizes a portion of his larger project "Unbombing the World." The mural contains four sections: "primordial air power and God's judgment," "Douhet's bombardment on the will of a nation," "body count and anonymous death," and "making room for multiple truths." The four sections seamlessly flow together in a palimpsest of images charting a shift from the centrality of the gods in antiquity to their replacement by engineers and statistical charts as the prime movers in the devastation of humanity and cities resultant from aerial targeting. van Tiejen's contribution to the volume exemplifies how his "will to archive" offers a dense form of visual argumentation and meditation sorely lacking in academic discussions about the urban.

Rajeev Patke's contribution to the volume similarly considers how the imagination plays a central role in the act of targeting the city by examining the post-colonial poetic imaginary taking aim at London, the metonym for Empire, as something both to shoot for and to shoot at. Drawing upon a large number of Caribbean poets who emigrated to the United Kingdom, Patke explores the diverse forms of migration wrought by colonial/post-colonial relations to argue that their history is "linked by the metaphor of a target, in which the missile also becomes a missive." The vision Patke articulates through the poetic excerpts exemplifies the deeply ambivalent set of ironic historical relations constituted by Empire and its blowback, in which the cosmopolitan center of Empire is forced to live up to its cosmopolitan, Enlightenment ideals through the presence of migrant bodies, minds, and imaginations. London thus becomes a site where missile and target merge in an uneasy but occasionally cozy (and often very funny) set of poetic articulations.

The dream of *terra nullius*, empty land, that drove the colonial project (and thus led to the ironic revenges exacted by the poets Patke discusses) also drives the futural projections of realizing global science cities analyzed by Sharon Traweek. The conversion of empty land into knowledge embodies the ethos, planning, and material aims of the development of science cities and science parks globally. Traweek argues that around the world science cities and science parks are devices for rationalizing land with no meaning, no power: governments appropriate lands of the weak, refiguring the land and the weak into bits of the future. As with the chapters by Suzuki, Clancey, and Li, this chapter takes up acts of targeted and strategic destruction necessary to build urban constructs, the destruction necessary to make *terra* fully *nullius* when it never was but needs to be so for the triumphant tales of progress, development, and science essential to the post-World War II world – stories told in Oak Ridge, Los Alamos, Novosibersk, and Tsukaba, Japan's first science city and the centerpiece for Traweek's analysis. The processes of targeting analyzed by Traweek include specific reiterations of Cold War concerns and values manifested in the expansion of urbanism to rural areas in the form of large R&D university campuses competing in the arena of global science. Although elements of those futural sites have drifted into the past, the predominant trajectories that established them continue to be deployed for both spatial and temporal targeting (i.e. the expansion of the urban into the rural for a greater tomorrow) in the twenty-first century.

Making the case that the military and sports share links back to antiquity, Robbie Goh explores the mobilizing of specific bodies in a hierarchy of geographical sites to feed top rugby teams in major Australian cities, itself an act of targeting as the rugby clubs vie for access to premiership status within the league. Both the military and professional competitive sports target the body in offensive and defensive ways, with technology and global capital being mobilized in the targeting practices and goals. With regard to warfare and sports, Goh argues that the "technological-capitalist targeting of winning bodies is closely associated with the global city." Similarly cities target corporate entities as well as promising recruits to serve the corporate body to engage in a closed circuit of competition within the global marketplace. Goh's deft and complex analysis of the material and immaterial nature of targeting trains its sites variously on individual bodies, labor (in various sectors), the military, competitive sports, cities, capital, corporations, and competition on a largely skewed pitch.

Jordan Crandall's art-based essay turns the problematic of the target into the desire to be absorbed in an assemblage. In this formulation, the purpose of engagement is not possession. Crandall uses his artwork to illustrate and problematize the transitive nature of targeting and thus renders it closer to the analysis provided by the related Greek term "*skopos*," which simultaneously means the watcher or marksman and the object spied or marked. The resulting essay and multi-sensory engagement evokes relinquishment into an assemblage of forces that is not unlike arguments made in new media studies about immersion in mediation versus the illusion of, or desire for, control. Crandall's piece thus offers a phenomenological take on the targeting of cities that operates through an erotics of engagement and erasure of the subject. It is wise to the complexities, levels, and nuances of the semi-planned, semi-emergent capacities of the assemblage, a structure related to but ultimately not reducible to the trajectories of the target.

In much the same way that Traweek's chapter discusses the targeting of the rural by urbanization processes, Nick Cullather's chapter addresses urban technologically driven targeting of rural sites. In his case, however, the site is Vietnam during the American war and the targets are villages. Within US plans for modernization central to winning the hearts and minds on both sides of the Vietnamese civil war, there stood a figure of backward rituals, outmoded technologies, wasteful agrarian practices, anti-cosmopolitan thought, entrenched hierarchy, and resistance to progress, development, and democracy: namely "the village." As the embodiment of all that the United States wished to push aside in its grand sweep to the future during the Cold War, the village was also seen as the natural habitat for – or a site of protection and support for – counter-insurgent anti-US Viet Cong fighters. The US military, therefore, had multiple discursive and material reasons for making the village, not the city, the target of offensive planning. Cullather argues that the same logic and strategies, along with the same rationale, deployed in Vietnam in the 1960s and 1970s underpin the policies for the Iraqi war being waged by the United States in the infinitely amorphous War on Terror, with the battle of Fallujah being a prime example of this thinking and actions predicated upon it. In the final analysis, though, whether urban, suburban, or rural targeting appears to be in the cross hairs, Cullather's title, quoting a Cold War document by agronomists, reveals the real agenda: "the target is the people."

Targeting imaginations

As all the contributions to this volume attest and delineate in their own ways, targeting always shares a confluence of the imaginary and its realization (or failure), as well as the aesthetic and the political. Violence, though, is an inescapable dimension of the city that targeting reveals as something other than an unconscious fetish of civilization; that is, the belief that violence is somehow external to the city rather than being constitutive of it. The aerial aesthetics by which we access cities in cinema or still photography for entertainment or planning purposes – currently articulated forcefully by Google Earth – is, of course, a by-product of aerial warfare and ICBM targeting.[16] Le Corbusier knew this well and wrote an extended paean to the freeing of vision from the pull of gravity afforded by airplanes, and in the form of a manifesto extolling – in fine futurist fashion – the opportunities afforded architects and urban planners by the innovations of the aerial views and aerial warfare.[17] But Google Earth (which is mainly a mapping of the *urban earth*) and Le Corbusier's manifesto are the realization of a geometric imagination, already operating in the early eighteenth century, that allowed for a projected "eye of the Gods."[18] And this projected vision that could target the city from above was the result of the geometrics of war which shifted the perspective for attacking walled cities provided by innovations in ballistics. This geometric vision, in turn, resulted from the innovations of perspectival painting found in Quattrocento art of the Renaissance, itself wrought from the writings on optics by the Islamic scholar Ibn al-Hathim. The complexities of the targeting found in aerial aesthetics manifested by one of its current avatars, Google Earth, proclaim the strongly interconnected trajectories of the imagination and the concrete infused with the aesthetic and the political that reside in targeting itself, especially when its sights are turned on the city.

Ultimately, this volume presents not only "new perspectives" on global urbanism but also the possibility of a true re-thinking, with agency, responsibility, and a greater sensitivity to metaphors and stories foregrounded. To target is to connect with intent, even if the resulting techniques, habitations, and clearances result in a morally ambiguous tableau. The city is almost never "innocent," even when implicated in its own destruction, which is as closely related to its physicality and essence as building and production. But neither does it always deserve its level of violence, and re-centering that phenomenon or quality in "urban studies" may be one contribution in its partial mitigation. If this volume bespeaks a certain ambivalence about urban existence, it is nonetheless a product, like most such work, of scholars intensely engaged with inhabiting their own and others' cities. Neither heroic nor tragic, unique nor convergent, and increasingly not so much an option as an inevitable global condition, urban life has scarcely exhausted itself in the new millennium as a site for new metaphors or novel descriptions. The lived reality of contemporary cities, like the walls that once enclosed them, extends beyond any concept of a traditional frame. Targeting is our contribution to a growing search for a post-Cold War frame of reference, but one that's nonetheless wise to historical continuities, as well as to fantasies of transcending space and time.

Notes

1 The original essay by Bishop and Clancey appeared in Ryan Bishop, John Phillips, and Yeo Wei Wei, eds., *Postcolonial Urbanism* (New York: Routledge, 2003), and was re-published in Stephen Graham's *Cities, War, and Terrorism* (Oxford: Blackwell, 2004).

2 Two notable exceptions to this paucity of material on urban targeting include Mike Davis' *Ecology of Fear* (New York: Vintage, 1999) and Lebbeus Woods' "Everyday War," in Peter Lang's *Mortal City* (Princeton, NJ: Princeton Architectural Press, 1996). See also the other essays in Steve Graham's book, above.

3 The exemplary work on global cities, of course, is that of Saskia Sassen. A number of scholars working from sites that might or might not be labeled global cities have expanded and modified Sassen's work in productive and provocative ways. But one very strong example of this sort of development is the edited collection by Sarah Nuttall and Achille Mbembe entitled *Johannesburg: The Elusive Metropolis* (Durham, NC: Duke University Press, 2008).

4 See Gregory Clancey, "Toward a Spatial History of Emergency: Notes from Singapore," in Ryan Bishop, John Phillips, and Yeo Wei Wei, eds., *Beyond Description: Space, Historicity, Singapore* (London: Taylor & Francis, 2004)

5 See Tracy C. Davis' *Stages of Emergency* (Durham, NC: Duke University Press, 2007) for a detailed analysis of the performative and dramatic element of emergency planning during the Cold War. Also see the writings of RAND theorist/guru Herman Kahn, who made emergency nuclear planning, or Civil Defense, the central site for the United States to consider the possibility of waging a winnable nuclear war.

6 "The City as Target," p. 75. See note 1.

7 New York: Fordham, 2004.

8 See Ryan Bishop, Gregory Clancey and John Phillips' introduction to "Just Targets," a special issue of *Cultural Politics*, vol. 2, no. 1 (2006), and Ryan Bishop and John Phillips' *Modernist Avant-Garde Aesthetics and Contemporary Military Technology: Technicities of Perception* (Edinburgh: Edinburgh University Press, 2011).

9 Paul Virilio, *Speed and Politics: An Essay on Dromology* (New York: Semiotext(e), 1977 [1986]), p. 31.

10 Ibid, p. 43.

11 Livy, *Ab Urbe Condita, Vol. 5*, trans. B. O. Foster (Cambridge, MA: Harvard University Press, 1924).

12 Niccolò Machiavelli, *Discourses on Livy*, ed. Bernard Crick, trans. Leslie J. Walker, rev. Brian Richardson (London: Penguin, 1984), p. 100.

13 Louis Althusser, *Machiavelli and Us*, ed. François Matheron, trans. Gregory Elliot (London: Verso, 1999), p. 41.

14 G. W. F. Hegel, *Political Writings*, ed. Laurence Dickey and H. B. Nesbit, trans. H. B. Nesbit (Cambridge: Cambridge University Press, 1999), p. 79.

15 Eyal Weizman, *Hollow Land: Israel's Architecture of Occupation* (London: Verso, 2007), p. 247.

16 For an excellent example of an online journal article that fully exploits its multimedia capabilities and which works through the implications of aerial aesthetics and targeting, see Caren Kaplan's "Dead Reckoning: Aerial Perception and the Social Construction of Targets" in issue 4 of *Vectors*, available online at http://www.vectorsjournal.org.

17 See R. Bishop's "'The Vertical Order has Come to an End': The Insignia of the Military C3I and Urbanism in Global Networks," in Bishop, Phillips, and Yeo, *Beyond Description*, and Steve Graham's "Postmortem City" in *City*, vol. 8, no. 2 (2004), pp. 165–96 for a discussion of Le Corbusier's work on aerial aesthetics.

18 This can be seen, for instance, in the popular 1707 publication *Britain: Britannia Illustrata or Views of Several of the Queens Palaces also of the Principal Seats of the Nobility and Gentry of Great Britain*, with drawings and etchings by Johannes Kip and Leonard Knyff (London, 1707, published in the winter of 1708–9).

2 'But malice aforethought'

Cities and the natural history of hatred

Nigel Thrift

Introduction

> You may talk of the tyranny of Nero and Tiberius; but the real tyranny is the tyranny of your next-door neighbour. (Bagehot 1856, cited in Lane 2004: 15)

The idea of the city as doomed is one of the common tropes of urban representation, as Mike Davis (2002) has illustrated at length in one of his latest books.[1] For Davis, the Western city is rapidly coming unglued. It is a runaway train fuelled by equal parts hubris and fear. It is Roadrunner suspended over the abyss. In tapping in to this anxious tradition of writing on cities, Davis is hardly alone. For example, he cites approvingly that rather idiosyncratic Marxist, Ernst Bloch, in equally apocalyptic mode, arguing much earlier that, in contrast to the adaptive and improvisatory pre-capitalist city, the capitalist city is in a continual state of radical insecurity and dread. Transfixed by the idea of a totally safe and calculable environment, the capitalist city is fixed and unbending in the face of unexpected events: 'it has rooted itself in midair'. And so it is heading for a fall; 'where technology has achieved an apparent victory over the limits of nature . . . the coefficient of known and, more significantly, unknown danger has increased proportionately' (Bloch, 1929/1998: 307, 309).

Well maybe. I thought that I would begin this chapter by arguing against these increasingly common nightmare scenarios which seem to be so prevalent that they are now producing all kinds of echoes – such as the growing historical literature on metropolitan catastrophes.[2] I believe that on many dimensions the contemporary Western city is more robust than it has ever been and I will want to explain why (cf. Massard *et al.* 2002). But I am also sure that the inhabitants of Western cities often think the opposite and I will try to explain that too: my thesis will be that it is not only the images of war and disaster flooding in from the media that have generated a pervasive fear of catastrophe but also a more deep-seated sense of misanthropy that urban commentators have been loath to acknowledge, a sense of misanthropy that is too often treated as though it were a dirty secret.

This is not, I hasten to add, a Panglossian account. I do not think all is well in the urban world or that all will be well – of course, cities are and will no doubt continue to be vulnerable to all kinds of catastrophic events, from terrorist attacks to earthquakes to influenza epidemics. Rather, I want to provide a qualified account that by excavating the everyday life and varying time signatures of cities might lead the discussion of the future politics of cities in slightly different directions.

To this end, I will begin the chapter by noting that cities often bounce back from catastrophe remarkably quickly. I will argue that there are good reasons why that is, most particularly, the fact that Western cities are continuously modulated by repair and maintenance in ways that are so familiar that we tend to overlook them but which give these cities a good deal more resilience than Bloch, Davis and many others before and since have been willing to give them credit for.

Then, in the second part of the chapter, I want to take a more philosophical turn and start to address why urban inhabitants might have a sense of foreboding about cities. I am not sure that the evidence would suggest that cities are any more on a knife edge than they have ever been but a Cassandra tendency seems to infect many of the recent writings on cities. Why might this be? I want to suggest that this requires an analysis of the prevailing urban mood. In other words, I want to turn to a consideration of affect arising out of a series of papers I have published recently. In particular, I will consider the sheer incidence of misanthropy in cities and how it has been framed since industrialisation. My argument is that it is only by facing this misanthropy square on that we can start to understand kindness and compassion. I will want to argue that a certain amount of dislike of one's fellow citizens isinevitable, given the social-cum-biological-cum-technological make-up of human beings: the ubiquity of aggression is one of the by-products of living in cities.[3] But I also want to argue that part of the impetus for the increasing interest in the misanthropic side of cities that may not celebrate but certainly do not shy away from the darker side of human nature lies in the fact that modern urban spaces are increasingly seen as themselves implicated in human imperfectability in that rather more of their substance than was formerly acknowledged takes its cue from models of organisation that are founded on the systematic delivery of violence which are so engrained that we hardly notice their dictates, yet alone understand their origins. Certain kinds of violence have become engrained in our 'natures' by these models of organisation and our environment now simply confirms these truths.

Then, in the final part of the chapter, I want to argue that there is a nascent politics of foreboding centred around the idea of a politics of hope which involves engaging with the sentiment of compassion but is not thereby sentimental.

In other words, in this chapter I want to walk the line, veering between hope and then pessimism, and then hope again. To begin with I want to argue straightforwardly that, even though 'the myth of terrible urban vulnerability endures' (Konvitz 1990: 62), cities are much more robust entities than they are usually given credit for, continually being re-placed by activities of maintenance and repair.

But then I want to move on to argue, perversely some will say, for a more pessimistic view of the moral life of cities than is often put forward nowadays in that I do not believe that advances in material civilisation necessarily lead to moral progress. This is hardly a novel position. After all, it was forcefully put forward by Rousseau in his *First Discourse* (Rousseau and Gourevitch, 1997). But, even now, it is still an uncomfortable one, sometimes associated with fascism or various forms of mysticism, and most clearly articulated by an almost forgotten set of social theorists such as Gobineau, Le Bon, Sorel and Schmitt whose politics were not always attractive, to put it but mildly (Llobera 2003). However, of late, it is possible to argue that there has been a largely unacknowledged revival of this kind of thinking as a result of a number of developments, of which I will highlight just three. First, there has been a greater and greater interest shown in the biological constitution of human social orders. Although, arguably, a strain of eugenic thinking persists in modern societies (cf. Duster 1990), still it has become possible to talk about biology without being immediately accused of determinism and, in turn, to address issues such as violence and aggression and hatred as though they might have biological determinants without immediate censure. Second, there has been a renewed interest, in the guise of work on so-called agonistic politics, in forms of politics that are willing to tolerate a depiction of societies as not premised on the maintenance of shared orders but as, in large part, being the result of the carving out of very different worlds, worlds that cannot be expected to reach agreement and which may obdurately disagree because they do not even share shared premises about the world. Such work argues that politics is about disagreement as much as it is about consensus (cf. Rancière 1999; Mouffe 2002).[4] Third, there has been a general falling away of belief in the efficacy of large-scale projects of social change and their corresponding goals of forging a bourgeois or socialist heavenly kingdom, not just because they so often seem to crush difference but also because they so often seem to unleash mythopoetic forces that their own proponents do not seem to understand.[5]

Then, in conclusion, against this rather sombre background, I want to return to the later work of Ernst Bloch and argue for a politics of affective 'repair and maintenance' based around hope. This should not be interpreted as a call for blind optimism. Rather, it is an argument for a politics of disagreement that can still find a place for a sort of practical utopianism which cleaves to the idea that the 'the essence of the world is cheerful spirit and the urge to creative shaping' (Bloch 1959/1986: 16). Cities may have, as I will argue, a large reservoir of enmity but they also have a surplus of hope, an unconscious hunger for the future as well as the past.

In what ways vulnerable? The hum of maintenance and repair

In both old and more recent work, I have been trying to see the city as an object that has temporal extension into the future, rather than as a snapshot. It consists of a myriad of partially connected processes going forward at different rates and speeds (Amin and Thrift 2002). This vision has particular relevance in arguing about urban vulnerability. For it is often argued that cities are vulnerable and cannot survive the trauma of war and other dramatic events of destruction easily. This is an extreme judgement. To begin with, it tends to rely on thinking of cities as caught in the temporal aspic of the present, as if urban trauma consisted only of the act of destruction itself and its immediate aftermath. But there is another tradition of thinking about cities that thinks of them as existing over the longer term, for example by using devices such as building cycles with their various amplitudes, and would judge urban trauma using this longer-term perspective. This kind of work has fallen out of favour (see Parkes and Thrift 1980 for a review) but it has the useful by-product of conceptualising cities as having all kinds of periods of temporal return, many of which may extend over decades.[6] Then there is a simple empirical point. Cities generally tend to recover quite quickly from even the most damaging catastrophes. For example, back in the 1980s when I considered the history of large Vietnamese cities in the 1960s and 1970s (Thrift and Forbes 1985) and British cities in the Second World War (Thrift 1996), I was struck by the fact that their populations could survive repeated attacks quite well. Some decanting of population took place but many people soon returned. This resilience existed for all kinds of reasons, of course, not all of them good. For example, many people, and especially working-class people, had nowhere else to go. But there was one factor that was apparent at the time but whose wider significance I have only lately seen. Cities are based in large part on activities of repair and maintenance, the systematic re-placement of place, and this ability is still there in times of trouble to be adapted to the new circumstances. These activities provided a kind of glue, which hastened cities' recovery times, most especially because all kinds of processes are being intervened in, some of which are pretty easy to deal with quickly (e.g. broken power lines), others of which take far longer to mend (e.g. broken hearts). Cities, in other words, took hard knocks but with the aid of all these activities they could get up, dust themselves off and start all over again. This is a point I want to develop in more detail.

Repair and maintenance covers a whole host of activities and it has become, if anything, more prevalent since I was working on the impact of war on cities. To begin with, Western cities nowadays are populated by large national and international companies that specialise in activities as different as various kinds of cleaning, all forms of building maintenance, the constant fight to keep the urban fabric – from pavements and roads to lighting and power – going, emergency call-out to all manner of situations, the repair of all manner of electrical goods, roadside and collision repair of cars, and so on. These mundane activities, the quartermasters of urban culture as Loos (1898/1983) might have put it, may have been neglected by most urban commentators but it is possible to argue that they are vital, not least because of the large and systematised knowledge bases that underpin them which are currently seeing an unparalleled expansion. That expansion is taking place in three domains: new materials and techniques that are extending the service life of all the infrastructure that surrounds us, new means of presenting and commodifying this knowledge (e.g. there are now substantial degree programmes in topics such as logistics and facilities, maintenance and repair), and the fact that what counts as repair and maintenance is constantly extending into new fields [e.g. into the biological domain through activities as diverse as bioremediation (effectively, environmental repair) and the repair of DNA]. To give some sense of the current spread of activities, consider only the snapshot provided by Table 2.1. Then much of the general population is also

Table 2.1 A sample of facilities, maintenance and repair jobs

Aircraft electrician jobs

Aircraft maintenance supervisor jobs

Airframe and engine mechanic jobs

Assembly supervisor jobs

Concrete and terrazzo finisher jobs

Construction and building inspector jobs

Copy machine field service representative jobs

Dairy processing equipment repairer jobs

Electric home appliance and power tool repairer jobs

Electric meter installer and repairer jobs

Electric motor assembler jobs

Electrical powerline installer/repairer jobs

Electrical utility troubleshooter jobs

Elevator installer/repairer jobs

Estimating manager jobs

Facilities maintenance supervisor jobs

Facilities manager jobs

General labourer jobs

Groundskeeper jobs

Head of housekeeping jobs

Housekeeper jobs

Housekeeping supervisor jobs

Interior aircraft assembly manager jobs

Interior aircraft assembly supervisor jobs

Janitor jobs

Jig and fixture builder jobs

Lawn service manager jobs

Level I aircraft maintenance manager jobs

Level I aircraft painter jobs

Level I carpenter jobs

Level I electric/electronics technician jobs

Level I electrician jobs

Level I facilities maintenance manager jobs

Level I general maintenance worker jobs

Level I HVAC mechanic jobs

Level I operations research analyst jobs

Table 2.1 (continued)

Level I painter jobs

Level I plumber jobs

Level I rep., electro/mechanical equipment field service jobs

Level I rep., electronic equipment field service jobs

Level I rep., telecommunications equipment field service jobs

Level I spares coordinator jobs

Level II aircraft maintenance manager jobs

Level II aircraft painter jobs

Level II carpenter jobs

Level II electric/electronics technician jobs

Level II electrician jobs

Level II facilities maintenance manager jobs

Level II general maintenance worker jobs

Level II HVAC mechanic jobs

Level II operations research analyst jobs

Level II painter jobs

Level II plumber jobs

Level II rep., electro/mechanical equipment field service jobs

Level II rep., electronic equipment field service jobs

Level II rep., telecommunications equipment field service jobs

Level II spares coordinator jobs

Level III aircraft painter jobs

Level III carpenter jobs

Level III electric/electronics technician jobs

Level III electrician jobs

Level III general maintenance worker jobs

Level III HVAC mechanic jobs

Level III operations research analyst jobs

Level III painter jobs

Level III plumber jobs

Level III rep., electro/mechanical equipment field service jobs

Level III rep., electronic equipment field service jobs

Level III rep., telecommunications equipment field service jobs

Level III spares coordinator jobs

Level IV operations research analyst jobs

Level IV spares coordinator jobs

Level V operations research analyst jobs

Level V spares coordinator jobs

Maintenance supervisor jobs

Operations research analysis manager jobs

Operations research analysis supervisor jobs

Painter jobs

Parking lot attendant jobs

Security guard jobs

Senior airframe and engine mechanic jobs

Senior general labourer jobs

Senior groundskeeper jobs

Senior janitor jobs

Senior security guard jobs

Senior structural assembler jobs

Spares coordination manager jobs

Spares coordination supervisor jobs

Structural assembler jobs

Vehicle washer/equipment cleaner jobs

constantly involved in maintenance and repair. The growth of activities such as do-it-yourself indexes the way in which home maintenance and repair (including the maintenance of gardens, cars and the like) has itself produced a set of thriving commodity markets, made up of all kinds of electrical and other goods.[7] And, finally, these activities often involve a high degree of improvisation, even in their most systematised form. They involve solutions to very diverse situations that still resist standardisation, and so may often retain a good deal of often un- or under-appreciated skill and all kinds of 'underground knowledges'.[8]

What is interesting is that we have little idea if the increasing reach and complexity of activities like these has made cities more or less vulnerable to catastrophe. Some 'risk society' commentators might argue that their contribution is piffling compared with the new generation of global risks that are now emerging. But, equally, it would be possible to argue that cities are constantly adding new circuits of adaptability: the city is a knot of maintenance and repair activities that cannot easily be unravelled and which allow it to pick itself up and start again, so to speak, relatively easily. All we can say at the moment is that modern urban dwellers are surrounded by the hum of continuous repair and maintenance and that, furthermore, some of the quintessential everyday urban experiences are generated by them, from the noise of pneumatic drills boring in to roads to the knock or ring of a repairman come to mend a broken-down this or that.[9] The point becomes even more germane if the emergency services are added in, with their knowledge of clearing up little but sustained disasters such as accidents, fires and the like, all the way from the actual incident itself to the smooth running of the aftermath, which may involve all kinds of allied actors from builders to insurance assessors.[10] Again, the sight and sound of these services is a quintessential everyday urban experience.

Recently, this general hum of activity has been powered up by information technology. True, the speed and interconnectedness of information and communications technology may have produced new vulnerabilities but, generally speaking, information and communications technology has probably made cities more robust by adding more degrees of redundancy. Simple things such as risk analysis and other institutionalised forms of diligence, booking systems, etc. have made the business of maintenance and repair easier to carry out and, indeed, are beginning to automate at least some of this activity (as in, for example, the instance of machines that send messages that they are breaking down). More to the point, in situations of breakdown, whether epic or mundane, the humble mobile phone has extended the city's interactivity and adaptability in all kinds of ways and may well have been the most significant device to add to a city's overall resilience by adding an extra thread to the urban knot. In addition, all kinds of knowledges of maintenance and repair that are heavily dependent upon information and communications technologies are coming to the fore, all the way from logistics to disaster planning itself (which, in certain senses, is a branch of logistics).

I want to argue that this activity constitutes an urban technological unconscious that helps to keep cities as predictable objects in which things turn up as they are meant to, regularly and predictably (Thrift 2004a). Modern Western cities are in many ways mass engineerings of time and space and this engineering increasingly involves working with very small spaces (of the order of millimetres) and times (of the order of milliseconds). At this scale, this means working on the structure of anticipation, producing a comforting sense of regularity and a corresponding (and probably amplified historically) sense of annoyance when things do not play out exactly as it is intended that they should. In a sense, speed has produced a new landscape of anticipation. Some commentators see this landscape as a threat, likely to institute a new 'dromocracy'. I am more ambivalent. It seems to me that it offers possibilities too, and not least in providing rapid reaction to problems large and small. Indeed, as information technology systems come in that are based on continuous updating of information, some degree of capacity to track and trace and the ability to forecast forward in a very limited way (e.g. through profiling systems), so it seems to me that cities will add another landscape to their repertoire, one that works a few seconds or minutes or, in extreme cases, hours ahead of the present and which will add markedly to their resilience. Of course, there is a new repertoire of risk associated with this landscape of foresight but whether it is that much larger than many other developments remains to be seen. Computer systems are vulnerable to attack just like any other system but it is also important to remember the continuous amount of repair and maintenance that goes into these systems anyway and reactions to attacks by worms or viruses are rapidly being incorporated into this burgeoning structure.

Of course, there is a partial exception to this story of relative resilience: cities in the South. It could be argued that some of these cities are in a recurring state of emergency (Schneider and Susser 2003). They have not benefited from many recent developments in information technology or have even had much risk trans- ferred to them by the vagaries of uneven development but, whatever the cause, such cities have much less in the way of repair and maintenance infrastructure to begin with.[11] Writers such as Koolhaas (2003) have celebrated the informality of these cities and argued that they present a new model of flexibility: I doubt it! It seems more likely to me that these cities, through general lack of resources, are likely to have less maintenance and repair infrastructure and that they are forced to make up this deficit through even more acts of inspired improvisation and the widespread use of informal networks of help such as family and friends. Of course, in extremis, as in forced acts of 'de-modernisation' such as are found in Palestine, repair and maintenance infrastructures may start to break down completely [indeed it could be argued that one of the tactics of 'urbicide', to use Steve Graham's (2003) felicitous phrase, is to mount an assault on precisely these structures].

What cities of the South do illustrate is the importance of another kind of repair and maintenance to which I will return later in the chapter. That is what we might call the social repair occasioned by social networks of various kinds, kin and friendship networks that may offer a range of support. This is more, as far as I am concerned, than just so-called 'social capital'. It is practical political expression.

Dark feelings

So why, if the evidence for the increased vulnerability of cities is certainly ambiguous, and even at times downright tenuous, especially when compared with an everyday event such as, say, global traffic carnage (now standing at well over a million killed a year around the world), does a certain sense of defencelessness and foreboding persist in the populations of many Western cities? Why is fear of and for the future seemingly so widespread, to the point where the level of anxiety has touched off what Davis (2002) calls a whole urban 'fear economy' of surveillance and security? Why do so many seem to feel that their definition of the real is under threat, such that, for example, the normative relays between personal and collective ethics have become frayed and worn? To begin to understand this dynamic of unease, we need to stray on to the territory of affect and begin to think of cities as emotional knots.

I have been involved in investigations of urban affect or mood for a number of years now but can say that touching this sphere remains an elusive task, not least because so many definitions of affect circulate, each with their own problematisa- tions. For example, affect can be understood as a simple or complex biological drive, a pragmatic effect of the pre-cognitive or cognitive interactions of bodies, a set of capacities for affecting or being affected by, the communicative power of faciality, and so on (Thrift 2004b). In other words, affect is as much a nexus of a set of concerns –with what bodies can do, with the power of emotions, with the crossover between 'biology' and 'culture' – as it is a finished analytic.

But even given this diversity of focus, we can point to obvious causes of a sense of defencelessness and foreboding, none of which I would want to gainsay.

There is the evident peril of the current geopolitical conjuncture with all its pit-falls. More importantly, probably, there is the emotional aftermath of 9/11 and similar terrorist attacks. Images of these events have probably come to stand for something greater in many Western city dwellers' minds, not just the threat to life and limb but also the disruption of the pace and rhythm of everyday life, the sheer turn-up-again-ness of each urban moment and the quantum of hope that goes with it. Further, these images have been amplified by the media, which have a constitu-tive interest in presenting them as inherently magnified. Why? Because fear sells. There is a market in anxiety.[12] As Altheide (2002) shows in his seminal book on the subject, the overwhelming message of news reports is fear. Further, safety is increasingly promoted through association with fear. In other words,

> Fear has shifted from concerns with the physical world and the spiritual realm of salvation during the last four hundred years to the social realm of every-day life. It is other people but not just immigrants – the historical other that have troubled previous immigrants-now-solid-citizens; it is the 'other', that category of trouble that can unseat solid expectations and hopes for a future that can never be realized in what is perceived to be a constantly changing and out-of-control world. Fear rests on the borders between expectations and realizations, between hope and reality.   (Altheide 2002: 26)

But I want to go farther in to this sense of the future by considering the typical make-up of the 'unconscious' of the modern Western urban dweller. I shall argue that the current urban trauma is the particular expression of a more general set of affective potentials. But I shall not resort to Freudian explanations of this affective undertow. Rather, I will argue that the contemporary Western urban unconscious consists of sedimented cultural-cum-biological-cum technologi-cal (the clumsiness of these terms itself suggesting that they are unsatisfactory representations) shortcuts that produce particular kinds of interactional intel-ligence, stances towards how the world is negotiated. Human interactional intelligence is, so far as we know, predicated upon five qualities. First, it assumes sociality. As Levinson points out, human is biologically and socially predicated upon coordination of action with others: 'it is cooperative, mutual intersubjectiv-ity that is the computational task that we seem especially adapted to' (Levinson 1995: 253). So, for example, selfishness seems to be a secondary characteristic: 'people care both about other people, and about how social transactions occur – not just the outcomes' (Heinrich *et al.* 2004: 1). Second, and consequentially, human interaction recognises and privileges the special kind of intention with which a communicative act is produced. Third, human assumes the presence of tools that will be actively used and which are assumed to be active (indeed it is arguable that certain human bodily characteristics such as the hand and associ-ated parts of the brain have co-evolved with tool use). Fourth, human interaction utilises a massively extended affective palette that is learnt from birth (Gerhardt 2004). Fifth, human, because of these characteristics, tends to animistic thinking that humanises the environment and assumes that the environment interacts with it on similar terms, rather than as a series of partially disconnected and perceptually very different *umwelts*.

This interactional intelligence is perpetually criss-crossed by affect that acts both as a way of initiating action, a reading of the sense of aliveness of the situation, and as an intercorporeal transfer of that expectancy. Affect, in other words, acts as the corporeal sense of the communicative act. In the literature, some prominence has tended to be given to euphoric affects such as happiness, hope and joy. But there are a range of dysphoric affects that also repay attention which have also been studied, such as greed, cruelty and shame. I want to argue that interactional intelligence has therefore both a positive bias to sociality but also, in part precisely because of this, some misanthropic aspects.

One thing which is often neglected about affect is that it involves temporal extension. Perhaps because Freudian concepts of repression have circulated so widely, it is often thought that affect is solely concerned with projections of the past. But there is every reason to believe that affect is as concerned with projection or thrownness into the future, as a means of initiating action, as the power of intuition (Myers 2002), as a hunger for the future (as found in, for example, daydreams), as a set of fantasies (e.g. concerned with romantic love, which I will address again below) and as a general sense of physical motility (Balint 1959).

The rather long-winded preface to this section allows me to argue something about the nature of interactional intelligence that has often been neglected, namely that, although it has a social bias, there is another side to that bias. That is, that achieving sociality does not mean that everything has to be rosy: sociality is *not* the same as liking. In particular, it seems likely that from an early age interactional intelligence, at least in Western cultures, is also premised on exclusion and even aggression. Children tend to learn sociality and sharing, at least in part, through intimidation, victimisation, domination and sanction. In other words, the kind of empathy required by interactional intelligence does not preclude a good deal of general misanthropy. Though it hardly needs saying sociality does not have to be the same thing as liking others. It includes all kinds of acts of kindness and compassion, certainly, but equally there are all the signs of active dislike being actively pursued, not just or even primarily as outbreaks of violence (e.g. road rage or Saturday night fights) but more particularly as malign gossip, endless complaint, petty snobbery, personal deprecation, pointless authoritarianism, various forms of *schadenfreude* and all the other ritual pleasures of everyday life.[13]

None of this is to say that it is necessary to condone virulent forms of racism or nationalism or other forms of mass identification that often involve systematic exclusion and violence. It is to say, however, that we need to think more carefully about whether we really have it in us to just be unalloyedly nice to others at all times in every single place: most situations can and do bring forth both nice and nasty. Perhaps, in other words, we are unable to resist at least some of the forms of resentment and even cruelty that arise from the small battles of everyday life: recent work in the social psychology of childhood development, for example, shows how children gradually come to understand sharing and turn-taking but can also be 'happy victimisers' (Killen and Hart 1995). However, at some point, most (but by no means all) children link the two: the pain and loss of the victim begin to modify and reduce the victimiser's happiness. In other words, they begin to construct a practical *morality*.

Morality is not, of course, a purely cognitive process. It has strong affective components. It is quite clear that all kinds of situations are freighted with affective inputs and consequences that are central to their moral outcomes which come from affective histories that arise from complex histories of being victims and of victimisation that produce a sense of fairness and concern that will build into a consensus in some situations and not in others. How is it possible to apply insights like this to the affective fabric of cities? That is what I will now begin to attempt to elucidate.

The misanthropic city

Cities bring people and things together in manifold combinations. Indeed, that is probably the most basic definition of a city that is possible. But it is not the case that these combinations sit comfortably with one another. Indeed, they often sit very uncomfortably together. Many key urban experiences are the result of juxtapositions that are, in some sense, dysfunctional, that jar and scrape and rend. What do surveys show contemporary urban dwellers are most concerned by in cities? Why crime, noisy neighbours, a whole raft of intrusions by unwelcome others. There is, in other words, a misanthropic thread that runs through the modern city, a distrust and avoidance of precisely the others that many writers feel we ought to be welcoming in a world increasingly premised on the mixing that the city first brought into existence.

This is often framed in liberal accounts as a problem of alienation: the city produces solipsistic experiences that, in some sense, cut people off from each other and, presumably, from the natural condition of inter-relation they feel in smaller, rural communities.[14] But, as is now clear, I would want to argue for a different course, one in which misanthropy is a natural condition of cities, one that cannot be avoided and will not go away and which may even have been amplified by the modern mass media with their capacity to extend the reach of what counts. I want to argue that cities are full of impulses that are hostile and murderous and which cross the minds and bodies of even the most pacific and well-balanced citizenry. Perhaps, indeed, we need to face up to the fact that this underside of everyday hatred and enmity and malice and vengeance may be one of humanity's greatest pleasures, sieved through issues as diverse as identity (as in who belongs and who doesn't), sexuality (as in unfettered masculinity) and even the simple turn-taking of conversation (as in rude interruptions and the like). In other words, humanity may be inching towards perfectibility but, if that is indeed so, it is an even slower progress than we might have thought, worked through daily lacerations and mutilations of social relations. In turn, perhaps we cannot simply explain away this malign background but must learn to tolerate it, at a certain level at least, as a moral ambiguity that is part and parcel of how cities are experienced, an ambiguity that cannot be regulated out of existence.

However, I do not want to be misunderstood. This is not to express some cathartic horror of urban humanity in a long tradition that stretches back to at least Victorian times and no doubt before. It is rather an attempt to write back into social science accounts of the city a thread of understanding that has for too long been left to wither, a tradition that briefly flowered in the works of philosophers such as Schopenhauer and Stirner,[15] philosophical novelists such as Dostoyevsky, and social scientists and political theorists such as Le Bon, Sorel, Schmitt and others, but which has generally been left to novelists and poets to enquire into. This is surprising, not least because it could be argued that the foundation of social science itself rests on the response to various religious crises that prompted the production of increasingly secular and societal remedies for what had once been considered theological and metaphysical concerns: as Comte explained, 'theology's "treatment of moral problems [is] exceedingly imperfect" given its "inability . . . to deal with practical life"' (cited in Lane 2004: 5). Hence, his 'system of positive polity'.

What seems certain is that the actual expression of the misanthropy has been more or less excusable as an urban condition through the course of history. Thus, in eighteenth- and early-nineteenth-century England, misanthropy was understood as a problematic state but certainly not a state that was mad, iniquitous or perverse. For example, Hazlitt could argue that 'there is a secret affinity, a hankering after evil in the human mind [and] it takes a perverse, but a fortunate delight in mischief, since it is a never-failing source of satisfaction' (cited in Lane 2004: 9). But by the middle of the nineteenth century, such sentiments were fast becoming out of fashion in the face of a more pious stance to life that valued a controlled and benevolent heroism of the everyday and which increasingly regarded people-hating as a psychological affliction (often, indeed, caused by unrequited love) that must needs be be combated by social programmes and self-restraint, although in mid- and even late Victorian literature a series of radical or maudlin haters still continue to crop up as characters and attitudes, as instanced by authors such as Dickens, Brontë, Eliot, Browning, Hardy and Conrad. The turn against misanthropy may well have been hastened as well by other cultural shifts and, not least, the discovery of evolution and of animal passions that might seem all too natural if not shackled by reason.

In general, one might argue that this Victorian attitude to intolerance or even hatred of others as failed civility still inhabits Euro-American cities, leaving a large amount of *surplus emnity* as hard to express and likely to be interpreted as a sign of a subject not fully in control of their behaviour. Western cities are, indeed, chock full of institutions and mechanisms that are intended to channel and domesticate anger towards and hatred of others, all the way from institutions of socialisation such as schools through to all the paraphernalia of emotional control or appropriate expression that occur subsequently. But Western cities are also full of outbursts of violence and rancour, all the way from seemingly random outbursts of road rage through the drunken mayhem typical of, say, British cities on a Saturday night to the fury that can be generated by queue-jumping, all examples which suggest that a certain amount of hatred and rancour can still be generated in and by cities surprisingly easily. I would argue that the sense of defencelessness that is now being felt in large part is being channelled by and from this underside: it actually consists of the victimisations of childhood and the run of daily life more generally feeding back into the city's fabric as an undertow of spite. It is ourselves turning back on ourselves. It is the thin veneer of altruism at its thinnest.

But I want to go farther than this and suggest that this sense also arises from the fact that modern cities are criss-crossed by systems that channel and control anger and hatred in ways which are likely to produce random outbursts and occasional mayhem on a fairly regular basis amongst the citizenry that go beyond acts which are necessarily labelled as 'criminal'. I want to argue, in other words, that the potential for different combinations that are brought into existence by cities has, as an inevitable correlate, a dark side that we have too soon wanted to label as pathological. There are a number of sides to this problem. First, some of this dark side can be ascribed to biological pressures that we can only probably abate. Frankly, we cannot tell because we do not know what kind of animal we are and the range of territorial and other adaptations we can comfortably make. For example, it is by no means clear what the range of intuitive spatial behaviour of human beings can be (Levinson 2003). Second, many social structures themselves may generate enmity as they try to damp it down, a point close to Freud's (1930/2002) argument in *Civilization and its Discontents* that civilisation is a key cause of antagonism: 'society, in trying to protect us from what we want (ultimately, an end to internal tension), instills in subjectivity a profound malaise, while providing "an occasion for enmity"' (Lane 2004: 28).[16] Third, the issue becomes even more complex because some of our dark side comes from formally structured cultural behaviours that tap into these pressures and constraints and work with them to deliver anger and hatred in a structured and predictable way.[17] Engrained within cities are all kinds of imperatives towards enmity and rage that arise out of social institutions of feeling which are only just beginning to be understood.[18]

Let me take a particularly relevant example. That is the echoing presence of armed force and, in particular, militaristic organisation. I think it could be argued that military organisation has had rather more influence on cities than is conventionally allowed in most accounts. This is not just about the matter of the presence of armed forces, trained in ways of structuring violence that can have lasting impacts, though this presence can be extensive (see Woodward 2004). It is not just about a series of military innovations that have made their way into the everyday life of cities, such as logistics.[19] It is not even just about the construction of militarised bodies through the proliferation of disciplined routines that have at least some military forebears, such as boxing and martial arts, bodybuilding and even some of the forms of warrior charisma beloved of business (see Armitage 2003). And it is not, finally, just about the apparent ambition of so many forms of modern entertainment to recreate the heat of the battlefield by battering the senses into a non-representational sublimity (Ferguson 2004).

I want to suggest that military imperatives are much wider even than this and have led to the deployment of anger and hatred and resentment in cities on an even more systematic basis. In particular, I want to point to the way in which domesticity has been organised on military lines through the institution of the suburb and other normalising spaces to enforce a particular notion of domestic normalcy that at the same time very often leads to everyday violence. Here I want to draw on the provocative work of writers such as Lauren Berlant and Laura Kipnis to argue, provocatively I hope, that militarised imperatives are a part of the structure of the domestic system (and especially its spatial correlates) and produce and channel a surplus enmity that cannot easily be satisfied but tends to reveal itself in petty acts of cruelty, as well as actual violence.

Thus, the figures demonstrate that domesticity is associated not just with love and care but also with violence so widespread that it is difficult not to believe that it has a systematic nature based on 'happy victimisation'. For example, in the United Kingdom one in four women will be a victim of domestic violence in their lifetime and domestic violence accounts for more than a quarter of all violent crime (including over 150 murders each year). In the EU, one woman in five has been at least once in her life the victim of violence by her male partner and, as in the United Kingdom, a quarter of all violent crimes involve a man assaulting his wife or partner. And this is before we arrive at the figures for child abuse . . .

This system cannot be easily undone because, ironically, of the surplus of hope that also structures the system of domesticity in Euro-American societies in the shape of the notion and practices of romantic love. There is no doubt that romantic love has its positive tropisms. It clearly represents a kind of last and best hope in many people's lives, providing an emotional world to which they can escape or which they can use as a goal to escape to, an imagined future outside of the humdrum world. 'Romance is, quite obviously, a socially sanctioned zone for wishing and desiring, and a repository for excess' (Kipnis 2003: 43). Thus, as Kipnis (2003: 41–2) points out, adultery is very often a kind of affective escape attempt founded on the notion of an irresistible romantic love:

> Among adultery's risks is the plunge into a certain structure of feeling: the destabilizing prospect of deeply wanting something beyond what all conventional institutions of personal life mean for you to want. Yes, all these feelings may take place in the murk of an extended present tense, but nevertheless, adultery, like cultural revolution, always risks shaking up habitual character structures. It creates intense new object relations at the same time that it unravels married subjects from the welter of ideological, social, and juridical commandments that handcuff inner life to the interests of orderly reproduction. It can invent 'another attitude of the subject with respect to himself or herself'. In adultery, the most conventional people in the world suddenly experience emotional free fall: unbounded intimacy outside contracts, law, and property relations. Among adultery's risks would be living, even briefly, as if you had the conviction that discontent wasn't a natural condition, that as-yet-unknown forms of gratification and fulfilment were possible, that the world might transform itself – even momentarily – to allow space for new forms to come into being. Propelled into relations of non-identity with dominant social forms, you're suddenly out of alignment with the reality principle and the social administration of desire. A 'stray'.

But it is not difficult to argue that romantic love is also oppressive because it blots out so much of the affective else that may be less intense but socially more important, making everything else appear an insufficiency. Yet, in a striking parallel with misanthropy, anyone who declares themselves incapable of romantic love would be regarded by the majority of people as abnormal: 'all of us [are] allied in fearsome agreement that a mind somehow unsusceptible to love's new conditions is one requiring professional ministrations' (Kipnis 2003: 26). Thus, as Kipnis (2003: 3) puts it:

> It's a new form of mass conscription: meaning it's out of the question to be summoned by love, issued your marching orders, and then decline to pledge body and being to the cause. There's no way of being against love precisely because we moderns are constituted as beings yearning to be filled, craving connections, needing to adore and be adored, because love is vital plasma and everything else in the world just tap water. We prostrate ourselves at love's portals, anxious for entry, like social strivers waiting at the ropeline outside some exclusive club hoping to gain admission to its plushy chambers, thereby confirming our essential worth and making us interesting to ourselves.

Yet, at the same time, it would be difficult to deny that romantic love can also contain large amounts of care, compassion and intimacy and it is to values of attachment like these that I now want to turn, values that exist somewhere between the poles of romantic love and misanthropy but which aren't quite so demanding, perhaps so difficult to live up (or down) to.

The politics of urban trauma: from love to kindness

The notion of cities as potential nests of kindness has been at the root of the notion of social science since its inception. For example, Comte's *System of Positive Polity, . . . Instituting the Religion of Humanity* (Comte 1877) argued that 'in human nature, and therefore in the Positive system, Affection is the preponderating element'. Comte wanted to transform self-love into social love by promoting what he called, coining a new word, 'altruism'.[20] From there, it was but a short step to the notions of 'community' that have so entranced writers on cities who have been trying to increase the sum total of altruism in cities, from Park through Jacobs to Sennett.

I am perhaps less starry-eyed about the practice of altruism than these authors (though none of them could be counted as romantics). I have already rehearsed some of my reasons: for example, the prevalence of misanthropy and romantic love and the fact that we live in heavily militarised societies that are based in part around understanding cities as if they were armed camps – the model of armed force and the armed camp can be argued to be one of the organising principles of the modern city (Agamben 2001). But there are others too. For example, most subjects most of the time are clearly the receptacles of all kinds of contradictory desires; 'contradictory desires mark the intimacy of daily life: people want to be both overwhelmed and omnipotent, caring and aggressive, known and incognito' (Berlant 2004: 5). Then again, most subjects are more often than not ambivalent about the dilemmas that they face and often prefer that things should remain that way: they don't necessarily want them to become 'issues' that they have to explicitly address. As Berlant (2004: 6–7) puts it with regard to intimacy;

> When friends and lovers want to talk about 'the relationship'; when citizens feel that the nation's consented-to qualities are shifting away; when newsreaders or hosts of television shows bow out of their agreement to recast the world in comforting ways; when people of apparently different races and classes find themselves in slow, crowded elevators; or when students and analysands feel suddenly mistrustful of the contexts into which they have entered in order to change, but not traumatically, intimacy reveals itself as to be a relation associated with tacit fantasies, tacit rules and tacit obligations to remain unproblematic.

But I also believe that a politics of disagreement of the kind formulated by writers such as Rancière (1999) can take the practice of altruism under its wing and forge a critical politics of feeling that is inherently optimistic (Berlant 2004) but also realistic; that is, it does not demand too much – which is not, of course, the same as saying that it demands nothing at all! Thus, in what follows, I will want to argue that it is possible to think about a practical politics of the maintenance and repair of the city's structure of kindness. In turn, such a politics can begin to understand rather better what makes cities tick.

So far, we have mainly considered the temporal politics of foreboding, the sense that round the corner lies something rotten, something to be fearful of. But there is another kind of temporal politics that is also possible, a politics that amplifies the sense that around every corner is an opportunity – to open up and take hold of the future, to endow it with values like care and compassion, to value expectancy. I want to begin to open up this problem by returning to the work of Ernst Bloch.[21] For Bloch is probably best known not for his apocalyptic comments on cities but for his much later work on the politics of hope. Bloch was concerned with a temporal sense that he called 'hope'. For Bloch, 'hope' signed a kind of thirst or hunger for the future, a venturing beyond, a forward dreaming that mixes informed discontent with an ineluctable forward tendency: 'a heap of changing and mostly badly-ordered wishes' (Bloch 1959/1986: 50). What Bloch wanted to foreground was a politics of anticipation, a feeling of striving towards the future, an eager looking forward and reaching forth, a source of fresh strength, a production of the New, a dawning. And for Bloch, this fresh strength could be mapped: it would be found particularly amongst youth, in times on the point of changing, in moments of creative expression, and so on.

Using this framework amongst others, I want to turn to the embryonic politics of this chapter by considering some of the ways in which an *active*, so-called 'prosocial' everyday form of kindness might be installed in cities as a value that goes beyond 'simple' civility. This would not consist simply of the installation of good manners, as in certain middle-class mores, or of the inculcation of a kindness militant, as in certain religions, or the installation of a forced state project, as in the proposals to build up 'social capital' being proposed by many governments around the world currently. Rather, it would be a way of producing generosity in the body from the start by emphasising what Bloch calls 'productivity', the construction of a new horizon out of the subconscious, the conscious and the not-yet-conscious. Writing from another context, Diprose (2002) has called the ethical correlate of this kind of approach, which privileges emergence and becoming,[22] 'corporeal generosity', but I think that this phrase runs the risk of falling back into the domestic model of kindness that I am concerned to escape, a model that too often ignores the fact that force and violence permeate political life and, to an extent at least, defines politics as a domain and that means, to use a classi-cally Weberian insight, that nicely honed ethical actions do not necessarily lead to morally desirable consequences (Walker 2002). This is not, then, intended to be some starry-eyed account. I am quite clear that such a stance would not only be utopian in the worst sense but may also be trying to act against the basic features of interactional intelligence.

Of course, it would be possible to argue that certain kinds of generosity are being installed in cities continually in the many daily acts of everyday life. For example, a mother instructs her child not to pull another child's hair. Or someone helps a frail person to cross the road. But I want to go a little farther than this in that it seems to me that a kind city has to work on a number of dimensions, not all of which are conventionally 'human'.[23] Kindness has to be extended to other kinds of urban denizens, including animals. More to the point this kindness has to be built into the spaces of cities. Thus cities have to be designed as if things mat-tered, as if they could be kind too. Cities would then become copying machines in which a positive affective swirl confirmed its own presence.

So what kinds of relationships should be possible in cities, given that there is rather more misanthropy than commentators are willing to own up to, and equally rather too much romantic love?[24] I have tried to argue that too little has been made of kindness and compassion as a means of structuring cities in the race for a higher plane which just isn't there. In turn this suggests a twofold political task. On one side, we obviously need to continue to pursue a conventional macropolitics of urban care which draws on the deep wells of caring and compassion that currently typify many cities, the result of the often unsung work put in by the employees of various welfare systems and all manner of voluntary workers, and the strivings of an army of 'carers'. On the other side, we need an affirmative micropolitics of productivity that attempts to inject more kindness and compassion into everyday interaction, the arena on which I will concentrate (see Thrift 2004b). In other words, I want to think of kindness as a social and aesthetic technology of *belonging to a situation*, rather than as an organic emotion.

To illustrate the point, I want to return initially to the military. For what is clear is that the military demonstrates the way in which kindness and compassion is able to be systematically generated and amplified by war – but, generally speak-ing, in small combat groups only. In these groups, which usually consist of six to ten 'buddies', people routinely look out for each other, even die for each other, bound together by learned mechanical behaviour and tight social bonds that are able, at least to an extent, to banish fear (Ferguson 2004; Holmes 2003). Indeed, it has been argued, ironically, that these tight-knit groups are the bedrock of the deployment of successful armed force; their intense sociality acts as a structured means of producing death. Many other social orders have this same intensity but that intensity sometimes seems to summon up too much love/hate. Which is why, perhaps, lighter touch forms of sociality are now receiving so much attention, what one might call, following Latour (2004), 'gatherings'. These can be counted as attempts to privilege a little more expectation of *involvement* that do not, however, try to go over the affective top, to continue the military metaphor. These are attempts to foster the expectation of civility that do not try to set their hopes too high.

But how to assemble this lighter-touch urban politics of assembling intimacy, kindness and compassion, understood as social and aesthetic technologies of belonging? This is difficult. For a start, it can easily be confused with other agendas, for example in attempts around the world to build 'social capital' or simply to enforce civility, as in the UK's current war on anti-social behaviour.[25] Then, compared with other forms of politics, it can appear to be such a faint proposition that it may seem to be hardly worth pursuing. And finally, it operates in a domain of hope and expectation that is hard to see and whose results may be hard to discern until long after the event. It operates in the background – which is, of course, the point.

That said, I want to highlight four of these gatherings as an envoi, gatherings that are mobile, often ambiguous and which encompass a multivalent host of forms. In each case, as I have argued elsewhere, the gathering operates as much in the precognitive realm as in the cognitive, based around forms of expression that are not conventionally regarded as political but which may well conjure up all kinds of sometimes ill-formed hopes and wishes that can act to propel the future. This proto-political domain of added strength aforethought, of a politics of readiness, of what Lefebvre called *the politics of small achievements*, is now hoving into view as a much more explicit site of political effort than in the past, one which has much more time for affect as it is in this domain that so much affect is generated (see, for example, Connolly 2002; Thrift 2004b).

The first gathering concerns *the domain of politics itself*. In the past, politics has often been considered to be a case of building local coalitions that are able to assembled into ever larger movements which in time will become political forces in their own right. But I am struck by how many recent forms of politics do not necessarily have this goal in mind. They are determinedly local and have no necessary expectation of wider involvements. An example might be the growing number of urban environmental struggles based on fauna and flora that have usually been considered as mundane and/or disposable but for which people may have considerable affective bonds, or on leisure activities such as gardening which require considerable expressive capacities but, until recently, have been seen as without the right kind of cultural authenticity. Another example might be the choice of minor key targets for political action that are unexpected but have grip, such as garbage (Chakrabarty 2002) or even paving stones (Massey 2001). These are forms of politics that attempt to boost expressive capacities,

The second gathering is the city's light-touch, partially engaged, partially disengaged *modes of social interaction*. Long derided as the fount of blasé attitudes or cynicism or various other forms of alienation,[26] it might just be that they can be perceived as something quite different if they are understood as spaces of affective display and style in the manner recently argued by Charles Taylor, as a kind of continuously mobile sphere of public opinion expressed as much through mood as through any definite cognitive process:

> Spaces of this kind become more and more important in modern urban society where large numbers of people rub shoulders, unknown to each other, without dealings with each other, and yet affecting each other. As against the everyday rush to work in the Metro, where others can sink to the status of obstacles in my way, city life has developed other ways of being, as we each take our Sunday walk in the park or as we mingle at the summer street festival or in the stadiums before the playoff game. Here each individual or small group acts on their own, but with the awareness that their display says something to others, will be responded to by them, will help build a common mood or tone that will color everyone's actions.   (Taylor 2004: 168)

Taylor shows that these light-touch gatherings[27] are different from their nineteenth-century forebears in a number of ways. Most particularly, through the power of the modern media, they often rely on audiences dispersed beyond the space of the immediate event. But what seems clear is that these gatherings can constitute a binding affective force that, though 'not enframed by any deeply entrenched if common understanding of structure and counterstructure', can still be 'immensely riveting, but frequently also wild, up for grabs, capable of being taken over by a host of different moral vectors' (Taylor 2004: 170).

A third gathering is the institution of *friendship*. It seems to me that in the end it is the kind of lighter-touch social relationship signalled by the notion of 'friend' that probably has most to offer cities in making them resilient. Of course, the notion of 'friend' has changed historically over time (Bray 2004; Pahl 2000; Traub 2002; Vicinus 2004) from the remarkably intense relationships signalled by the term in the sixteenth and seventeenth centuries but I think that it is possible to suggest that the looser ties of friendship and conviviality, and the kind of stance implied by the term now, have had the most to offer in keeping cities resilient and caring. For, in the end, cities have survived trauma because they are concentrations of knowledges of routine as found in activities such as repair and maintenance, and the kind of energy and resourcefulness that has a large part of Bloch's quality of hope engrained within it, mediated by mundane but crucial social ties like friendship.

Friendship has three main things to recommend it. First, it is still widespread. For all the stories of the demise of sociality in alienated Western cities, the evidence suggests that friendship is still thriving, though inevitably mediated by all kinds of factors such as stage in life course (Pahl 2000). Then, the practice of friendship offers a model for intimacy and compassion that is achievable and which offers an automatic reaction to distress: a friend acts to help. It offers, in other words, a model of the future in which bad, even terrible, things may still happen but one in which 'my friends will still be there for me'. At its best, the help of friends is often given automatically as a subconscious attachment to a situation. Finally, it can be shown that these kinds of networks do work when catastrophe beckons. For example, in a recent brilliant book, Eric Klinenberg (2003) has looked at the way in which the populations of two relatively alike areas of Chicago reacted to the catastrophe of the week-long 1995 heatwave in which over 700 died. In one area, the death toll was low, in another it was high. The difference could be explained by a number of factors including poor or unresponsive public services but also, pivotally, by the actions of friendship networks. In one area, these were active and acted both as glue and as a means of social maintenance and repair. In the other area, no such networks existed and the area proved correspondingly brittle.

Again, it is important not to be starry-eyed. Friendship can involve all kinds of negative emotions and tensions. It may involve quite high degrees of competition. It does not necessarily do anything to lessen social divides.[28] But friendship can also form a kind of moral community, whose power should not be underestimated.

Then, as a final gathering, I want to point to the outpouring of various kinds of *practical affective politics*. I have reviewed these elsewhere (see Thrift 2004b), so I will only briefly reprise them here. What is important to note is the increasing range of performative methods that are now going to make up the practices of politics, many of which involve the explicit mobilisation of affect. These methods are often precisely involved in the stimulus of kindness and compassion and range from various kinds of work on the body (including manifold trainings, new means of showing awareness, various forms of pedagogic and cooperative psychology, and so on) to attempts to use urban space in ways that will produce new understandings of the moment (as in various kinds of performance art, psychogeography and other forms of spatial play). In every case, the intention is to engineer intention and increase capability by constructing automatic reactions to situations that can carry a little more potential, a little more 'lean-in', a little more commitment.

To summarise, in this chapter I have wanted to see cities as oceans of hurt resulting from the undertow of the small battles of everyday life but also as reservoirs of hope resulting from a generalised desire for a better future. My intention has been to consider the darker sides of cities by concentrating on the subject of misanthropy but equally to balance this picture up by injecting a wash of kindness. My intention has therefore been to approach, or more accurately sidle up to, the subject of moral progress but to discuss this issue in a much less grand way than is normally found in the literature.

In alighting on the difficulties of making moral progress I am not, of course, giving up all hope of such progress. Rather I have wanted to approach the subject by considering qualities such as kindness and compassion which are far from the unstinting love for others that is often envisaged as the ultimate measure of such progress. Put very simply, I want to conceive of kindness and compassion as elements of urban life we would want to nurture and encourage, against a background that often seems to militate against them. I want, in other words, to argue that in an agonistic city, where agreement is thin on the ground, a little more kindness may be what we should hope for and what we can get, whereas love is a bridge too far. Indeed, love may be part of the problem, insofar as it provides us with a vision of the world that we cannot possibly live up to.

As a parting thought, over the years, cities have been routinely lauded or deplored for the feelings they induce. Some cities have come to be regarded as generous or friendly. Others are regarded as hard-edged and hyper-competitive. Wouldn't it be interesting if, in the future, cities were increasingly pulled out of the mass on criteria such as some of the ones I have just mentioned? Cities would become known in new sensory registers, through haptic maps of affective localities (Bruno 2002), and not least as geographies of kindness and compassion, geographies that might leak out into the wider world.

Notes

1 As well as gleefully adding more such representations to the stock, I might add.
2 As in the recent conference on metropolitan catastrophes held at the Institute of Historical Research by the Centre for Metropolitan History, which featured a series of historians who were moving their attention from the battlefield to the city as battlefield.
3 This is, of course, a classical Freudian point, as is the point made later that destructiveness is very close to love. Freud's work acts, fittingly perhaps, as a perpetual undertow in this chapter.
4 Mouffe's work has, of course, been much influenced by Schmitt.
5 None of this, of course, is to suggest that no attempt should be made to rid the world of all manner of horrors: wars, genocides, tortures, famines and so forth. Rather, as will become clear, it may be better to attempt to institute lower-level forms of kindness, as a first step at least.
6 It also points to the fact, often forgotten, that *demolition* is as much a part of the history of cities as construction. But I know of remarkably little work on this aspect of cities, even after recent traumatic events, except that centred around sense of loss (e.g. of the byways of pre-boulevard Paris).
7 See, in particular, Gershuny (1978) on the self-service economy. I do not make much of it here but there is also an obvious connection to the second-hand market, which requires repair and maintenance as a matter of course.
8 For example, when broadband was first introduced, telecommunications engineers would tell each other of the different solutions and shortcuts they had discovered. Later, their telecommunications companies provided them with electronic bulletin boards so that this information could be more widely circulated.
9 Indeed, the standard devices of novels and films often include repair and maintenance workers as quintessential minor characters (Woloch 2003), iconic urban non-icons, from chimney sweeps to plumbers to car mechanics to window cleaners.
10 This is to ignore the plethora of major incident and disaster recovery plans that are periodically rehearsed.
11 Of course, this is a highly debatable statement. In many such cities, it may be that there is *more* repair and maintenance infrastructure oriented to the much greater problems of simply reproducing everyday life. I know of no evidence that would resolve this debate. I am indebted to Stuart Corbridge for this point.

12 Indeed, we might see the expectation of danger as constituting a kind of contract with the future (cf. Salecl 2004)

13 As Dalrymple (2004) points out, some of this may even be excusable, given how few people have any control over their lives. But certainly, once one starts looking, it is possible to see small acts of cruelty everywhere.

14 The fact that small rural communities are often shot through with feuds and vendettas is conveniently forgotten.

15 Thus, Schopenhauer argued in 'On Human Nature' that 'to the boundless egoism of our nature there is joined more or less in every human breast a fund of hatred, anger, envy, rancour and malice, accumulated like the venom in a serpent's tooth, and waiting only for an opportunity to vent itself', while Stirner wrote of 'surplus rage' and of the value of 'repelling the world' (cited in Lane 2004: 27).

16 And, it might be added, to Elias's argument in *The Civilizing Process*.

17 Notice here that I am not arguing for a reductionist notion of the biological that could simply read off behaviour rigidly from (say) genetic and/or evolutionary predispositions, as if there were a fixed relation of logical or empirical necessity (Oyama 2000).

18 There are obvious gender connotations in this paper which I am leaving to a later paper.

19 This military art began to migrate into civil society sometime in the nineteenth century but made more specific and extensive inroads after World War II when a whole series of logistical practices that had been invented in or just after that war became general means of planning and operationalising urban movement (Thrift 2004).

20 Comte coined the noun from the Italian *altrui* ('to or of others') and a phrase in French law, *le bien, le droit d'autrui* ('the well-being and right of the other').

21 I could no doubt have fixed on other authors than Bloch. For example, there is Levinas' extended commentary on war and peace in *Totality and Infinity*, and especially his explorations of exteriority and enjoyment that stress the constitutive role of the future (see Caygill 2002). But I prefer Bloch's more concrete approach.

22 Though I am aware that Diprose is intent on exposing a more general debt to life in a way that is reminiscent of both Bergson and Bloch.

23 I want to understand the city as an organisation that exceeds the human, conventionally defined, at every juncture. My sense of kindness therefore exceeds the human, in part because the human has become bogged down in precisely the kinds of stay-at-home ethics that I am most concerned to avoid. In particular, in what is by now a familiar move, I will be stressing the importance of 'thingness' as a determinant of human relationality.

24 Perhaps, indeed, the two are linked in much the same way as loneliness and communication.

25 Which, in a number of its emphases, seems to me to show just how misanthropy can bubble up as a formal government policy. Even as many indicators of such behaviour (e.g. vandalism) seem to be in decline, this policy is forging ahead.

26 Though it is important to point to the more positive contributions of Benjamin and Kracauer.

27 Though I do not go into it here, there is a whole literature on the profusion of 'familiar strangers' dating from the work of Milgram that shows up a similar kind of shadow presence.

28 Although this is often very difficult to know. For example, a recent UK survey showed that 94 per cent of white Britons said that most or all of their friends were of the same race, while 47 per cent of ethnic minority Britons said that white people form all or most of their friends; 54 per cent of white Britons did not have a single black or Asian person that they considered as a close friend while 46 per cent had at least one such friend (*The Guardian* 2004). But debate then raged about whether these results were actually a bad or a good indicator, given the overall ethnic make-up of the population and its spatial distribution.

References

Agamben, G. (2001) *Potentialities*, Stanford, CA: Stanford University Press.

Altheide, D. L. (2002) *Creating Fear. News and the Construction of Crisis*, New York: Aldine de Gruyter.

Amin, A. and Thrift, N. J. (2002) *Cities. Re-imagining Urban Theory*, Cambridge: Polity Press.

Armitage, J. (ed.) (2003) Special issue on 'Militarized Bodies', *Body and Society*, 9, 1–227.

Balint, M. (1959) *Thrills and Regressions*, London: Maresfield Press.

Berlant, L. (ed.) (2004) *Compassion. The Culture and Politics of an Emotion*, New York: Routledge.

Bloch, E. (1929/1998) 'The anxiety of the engineer', in *Literary Essays*, Stanford: Stanford University Press.

Bloch, E. (1959/1986) *The Principle of Hope* (three volumes), Oxford: Blackwell.

Bray, A. (2004) *The Friend*, Chicago: University of Chicago Press.

Bruno, G. (2002) *Atlas of Emotion. Journeys in Art, Architecture and Film*, London: Verso.

Caygill, H. (2002) *Levinas and the Political*, London: Routledge.

Chakrabarty, D. (2002) *Habitations of Modernity. Essays in the Wake of Subaltern Studies*, Chicago: University of Chicago Press.

Comte, A. (1877) *System of Positive Polity, Vol. 1*, London: Longmans, Green and Co.

Connolly, W. E. (2002) *Neuropolitics*, Minneapolis: University of Minnesota Press.

Dalrymple, T. (2004) 'Lynndie England was acting out the fantasies of frustrated people everywhere'. *The Times*, August 7, p. 24.

Davis, M. (2002) *Dead Cities and Other Tales*, New York: New Press.

Diprose, R. (2002) *Corporeal Generosity. On Giving with Nietzsche, Merleau-Ponty and Levinas*, Albany: State University Press of New York.

Duster, T. (1990) *Backdoor to Eugenics*, New York: Routledge.

Ferguson, H. (2004) 'The sublime and the subliminal: modern identities and the aesthetics of combat', *Theory, Culture and Society*, 21, 1–34.

Freud, S. (1930/2002) *Civilization and its Discontents*, London: Penguin.

Gerhardt, S. (2004) *Why Love Matters: How Affection Shapes a Baby's Brain*, Hove: Brunner-Routledge.

Gershuny, J. (1978) *After Industrial Society the Emerging Self-Serving Economy*, London: Macmillan.

Graham, S. (2003) 'Lessons in urbicide', *New Left Review*, 19, 63–77.

Heinrich, J., Boyd, R., Bowles, S., Camerer, C., Fehr, E. and Gintis, H. (eds) (2004) *Foundations of Human Sociality*, Oxford: Oxford University Press.

Holmes, R. (2003) *Acts of War*, London: Weidenfeld and Nicolson.

Killen, M. and Hart, D. (eds) (1995) *Morality in Everyday Life. Developmental Perspectives*, Cambridge: Cambridge University Press.

Kipnis, L. (2003) *Against Love. A Polemic*, New York: Pantheon.

Klinenberg, E. (2003) *Heat Wave. A Social Autopsy of Disaster in Chicago*, Chicago: University of Chicago Press.

Konvitz, J. (1990) 'Why cities don't die', *American Heritage of Invention and Technology*, Winter, 58–63.

Koolhaas, R. (2003) *Lagos: How it Works*, Harvard Project on the City, Baden: Lars Müller.

Lane, C. (2004) *Hatred and Civility: The Antisocial Life in Victorian England*, New York: Columbia University Press.

Latour, B. (2004) 'Why has critique run out of steam? From matters of fact to matters of concern', *Critical Inquiry*, 30, 225–48.

Levinson, S. C. (1995) 'Interactional biases in human thinking', in Goody, E. N. (ed) *Social Intelligence and Interaction*, Cambridge: Cambridge University Press.

Levinson, S. C. (2003) *Space in Language and Cognition: Explorations in Cognitive Diversity*, Cambridge: Cambridge University Press

Llobera, J. R. (2003) *The Making of Totalitarian Thought*, Oxford: Berg.

Loos, A. (1898/1983) 'Plumbers', in *Spoken into the Void. Collected Essays, 1897–1900*, Cambridge, MA: MIT Press.

Massard, C., Guilbaud, G., Platt, H. and Schott, D. (eds) (2002) *Cities and Catastrophes*, Frankfurt: Peter Lang.

Massey, D. (1991) 'A global sense of place', *Marxism Today*, June 24–29.

Mouffe, C. (2002) 'Which public sphere for a democratic society?', *Theoria*, June, pp. 55–65.

Myers, D.G. (2002) *Intuition. Its Powers and Perils*, New Haven, CT: Yale University Press.

Oyama, S. (2000) *Evolution's Eye. A Systems View of the Biology–Culture Divide*, Durham, NC: Duke University Press.

Pahl, R. (2000) *On Friendship*, Cambridge: Polity.

Parkes, D. N. and Thrift, N. J. (1980) *Times, Spaces and Places. A Chronogeographic Perspective*, Chichester: John Wiley.

Rancière, J. (1999) *Disagreement. Politics and Philosophy*, Minneapolis: University of Minnesota Press.

Rousseau, J. J. and Gourevitch, V. (1997) *'The Discourses' and Other Early Political Writings* (Cambridge Texts in the History of Political Thought), Cambridge: Cambridge University Press.

Salecl, R. (2004) *On Anxiety*, London: Routledge.

Schneider, J. and Susser, I. (eds) (2003) *Wounded Cities. Destruction and Reconstruction in a Globalized World*, Oxford: Berg.

Taylor, C. (2004) *Modern Social Imaginaries*, Durham, NC: Duke University Press.

The Guardian (2004) '90% of whites have few or no black friends', 19 July, p. 1.

Thrift, N. J. (1996) *Spatial Formations*, London: Sage.

Thrift, N. J. (2004a) 'Remembering the technological unconscious by foregrounding knowledges of position', *Environment and Planning D. Society and Space*, 22, 175–90.

Thrift, N. J. (2004b) 'Intensities of feeling: towards a spatial politics of affect', *Geografiska Annaler*, 86, 57–78.

Thrift, N. J. and Forbes, D. K. (1985) *The Price of War: Urbanisation in Vietnam 1954–1985*, London: George Allen and Unwin.

Traub, V. (2002) *The Renaissance of Lesbianism in Early Modern England*, Cambridge: Cambridge University Press.

Vicinus, M. (2004) *Intimate Friends: Women who Loved Women*, Chicago: University of Chicago Press.

Warner, M. (2002) *Publics and Counterpublics*, New York: Zone Books.

Woloch, A. (2003) *The One vs the Many. Minor Characters and the Space of the Protagonist in the Novel*, Princeton, NJ: Princeton University Press.

Woodward, R. (2004) *Military Geographies*, Oxford: Blackwell.

3   Targeting the imaginist city[1]

John Armitage

> Spectacular government, which now possesses all the means necessary to falsify the whole of production and perception, is the absolute master of memories just as it is the unfettered master of plans which will shape the most distant future. It reigns unchecked; *it executes its summary judgments*.
>
> (Debord 1998: 10)

The U.S. war on Iraq in March 2003 was a fast and enormously successful attack incorporating the utilization of a huge quantity of high-tech weaponry that led to the quick defeat of the despotic government of Saddam Hussein. The American armed forces' rapid victory in the Iraq war was due primarily to their "shock and awe" technological supremacy in weapons of intelligence and targeting, such as Unmanned Aerial Vehicles (UAVs) and Joint Surveillance and Target Radar Systems (JSTARs). Special Operations Forces (SOFs) and the Joint Operations Center (JOC) in Doha, Qatar, also performed essential functions in the U.S. military's conquest over the bewildered defenses prepared by Iraq's armed forces. The U.S. military's offensive on Baghdad, inclusive of "Thunder Runs" (tactical sorties through the center of the city), was then an extraordinary military and strategic accomplishment. But, as the Iraqi insurgents' strikes on the American armed forces and the newly U.S.-installed Iraqi government in Baghdad continue with assassinations and suicide bombers, it is difficult not to view the American armed forces' strategic achievement as resulting in spectacular political failure and the chaotic extrication of the U.S. military.

This chapter moves from a description of the U.S. war on Iraq in March 2003 to a speculative interpretation and analysis of the war through the prism of what I call the "new U.S. civilian–military elites'" war on Utopia today (Armitage 2004a: 68–82). Utopia is a real yet simultaneously imagined State that I consider to be ideal in the sense that it portrays an imaginary State representing a society without war. I examine the way that the new U.S. civilian–military elites' war on Utopia is, like the U.S. war on Iraq, an accelerated and extremely accomplished assault featuring the use of vast amounts of technologically advanced military hardware. I contend that if the elites' war on Utopia is not prevented, it will bring about the swift conquest of what might be called the Utopian regime of the global peace movement. Consequently, in the second section of this chapter, I focus on the Project for the New American Century's "Statement of Principles" (PNAC 1997), which summarizes PNAC's overt battle strategy concerning the targeting of what I call the "absolutely deterritorialized" (Deleuze and Guattari 1988: 55–6) "Imaginist City" of the global peace movement.

PNAC was founded in 1997 as a Republican Party/conservative-associated non-profit educational organization whose objective is to promote American global leadership. An initiative of the "New Citizenship Project," its chairman is William Kristol and its president is Gary Schmitt. PNAC is generally known for its "Statement of Principles," published on June 3, 1997, which declared that the then Democrat Clinton administration's foreign and defense policies were "adrift," almost "incoherent," while the Republican Party/U.S. conservatism was permeated with isolationist inclinations (PNAC 1997: 1). It is my contention that PNAC's "Statement of Principles," its "strategic vision of America's role in the world," is effectively an unabashed plan for "infinite global war" (Armitage 2004b: 360). PNAC's "Statement of Principles" is not merely a setting forth of the basic values of U.S. foreign policy and for the fixing of America's strategic goals but also a plan for the continual increase of the U.S. defense budget with the object of upholding American security and advancing U.S. interests across the world in the twenty-first century. PNAC's "Statement of Principles" is currently the official policy of the new U.S. civilian–military elite. And PNAC's strategy for infinite global war entails, among other things, the targeting of the Imaginist City of the global peace movement.

Yet the "Imaginist City" is not no-place but rather a real world city where global citizens resist permanent war and produce places of peace. I maintain that the new U.S. civilian–military elite, PNAC, and the elite "Republican Guards" (e.g. Richard Perle) are presently making a bold offensive on the Imaginist City. PNAC and the elite Republican Guards' high-speed triumph in their war on Utopia is dependent above all on their low-intensity yet no less overwhelming techno-logical pre-eminence as to weapons of intelligence and targeting such as UAVs and high- and low-tech surveillance systems. U.S. domestic Special Operations Units (SOUs), such as the Federal Bureau of Investigation (FBI) and Northcom, or Northern Command, the Pentagon's military command for the domestic United States, fulfill key tasks for the elites' victory over the confused defenses against the militarization of the United States or "everyday war" (Woods 1995: 47–53) organized by Utopia's unarmed forces. The new U.S. civilian–military elites' onslaught on the Imaginist City is increasingly conducted in terms of the "politics of noise," the impedance or barrier between the sending and receiving of technologically mediated political signals. I oppose the idea that Utopia's rebels, the global peace movement, should abandon its raids on the elite. All the same, I contest the cyberculture theorist and political activist Gray's (2005: 102–6) recent proposal that there is a certain "convergence" on epistemological and other (e.g. feminist) issues between elements of the global peace movement and the military elite. In my view, such a suggestion elides the distinction between the civilianiza-tion and the militarization of knowledge or what I label, after Virilio (1989), the "logistics of perception management." Gray's position demands that the global peace movement in effect be integrated into the military elites' media strategies for what I have identified as infinite global war.

Accordingly, this chapter journeys from my contentions regarding the elites' war on Utopia to a demonstration of their high-speed and increasingly success-ful assaults, taking in the exploitation of immense quantities of state-of-the-art weaponry and the elites' attempt to trigger the rapid subjugation of the global peace movement.

In the third and final substantive section, I illustrate how PNAC's "Statement of Principles" has activated a series of strikes on the Imaginist City. I also highlight how SOUs such as the New York Police Department (NYPD)/FBI Joint Terrorism Task Force and Northcom currently play important roles in the elites' war on con-temporary political activists. In particular, the new U.S. civilian–military elites' blitz on the Imaginist City during the anti-Iraq war demonstrations of 2002–3 was effected through the application of the politics of noise. I suggest why and how the global peace movement should not end its sorties on the military elite, but reject Gray's argument concerning the fusion of peace activism and military thinking. I achieve this by a critique of the logistics of perception management performed by the "information warriors" of the Rendon Group (Chatterjee 2004: 1–4) and of the idea that the global peace movement is obliged to conform to the media strategies of the military elite for infinite global war. But let us begin with the U.S. war on Iraq.

Targeting Baghdad

The strategic assumption powering the drastic and extremely successful Plan 1003 Victor was to make Baghdad the major target, with all other objectives taking second place (Cushman and Shanker 2003). The plan is well illustrated by the Third Infantry Division's audacious and accelerated push for Baghdad beginning on April 2, 2003, through the Karbala gap, a town on the periphery of Baghdad, which was within easy striking distance of Iraqi Republican Guard divisions. The plan entailed the Third attacking Karbala along with the 3/7 Cavalry, which commanded two Brigade Combat Teams or BCTs (self-sufficient close combat units incorporating Bradleys and Abrams tanks), with the intention of becoming the spearhead for the march on Baghdad. To fulfill the plan, the Third had to overcome a number of obstacles, including traversing hostile terrain, capturing dams, seizing bridges, and attacking Republican Guard units. It was a tough battle in marshy territory, yet the Third triumphed as Iraqi resistance collapsed, allowing the Division to conquer Saddam International Airport, the last major symbolic and military barrier standing before the Infantry as they stormed and encircled the administrative and political core of Baghdad on April 9. In other words, the Third Infantry Division facilitated the obliteration of the Iraqi power structure within a week.

Similarly, the goal of the First Marine Division was to be violent, in control, and to remain focused on Baghdad as the primary objective (Murray and Scales 2003: 219–22). Approaching the capital from the southeast, the First had to engage Republican Guard divisions while dealing with the fact that its supply line was overextended.

The Marines had no choice but to be inventive, launching armored reconnaissance patrols into the countryside in the hunt for *fedayeen* (irregular Saddam loyalists) and to prevent further ambushes by Iraqi troops along Highway 1. Setting up roadblocks in an attempt to control the movement of vehicles, the Division advanced to the south of Baghdad to secure the airbase at Hantush for use by C-130 support aircraft, which were supplying much-needed fuel to Cobra helicopters and so on. Like the Third Infantry Division, the First's goal was to remain in charge while keeping the *fedayeen* and Iraqi troops on the defensive as the Division continued its relentless drive to Baghdad.

Once in the capital, the Marines moved from zone to zone, improvising along the way. At this point in the war, the most important notion was that of exploiting the First's pace and military capability and connecting them to the Division's intelligence. When the critical question arose as to how to progress with the dangerous mission of capturing Baghdad, for example, several high-ranking officers expressed their concerns given the hazards of urban warfare. Yet, as Murray and Scales write, for Generals Tommy Franks and David McKiernan (overall commanders of U.S. military operations in Iraq), "the campaign thus far had consistently rewarded audacity." Indeed, Franks and McKiernan considered that "the Iraqis were incapable of dealing with an enemy who moved faster than their centralized regime could recognize or react" (Murray and Scales 2003: 208–9). Such confidence emerged from the sheer velocity of the firepower accessible to the First and other American divisions. Iraqi artillery systems that did manage to bombard the U.S. military had a brief existence as American forces were equipped with counter-battery radars that permitted the trajectory of artillery rounds to be tracked back to their source in real time. In fact, U.S. troops sometimes had artillery rounds en route to an Iraqi unit before that unit's first artillery rounds landed (Murray and Scales 2003: 263–4). Obviously, the First Marine Division attained the speed of its operations in Baghdad because of its knowledge of Iraqi forces. Nevertheless, it was the intelligence obtained from surveillance technologies that allowed the Marines to adapt their plans to unfolding conditions while simultaneously denying the Iraqis any knowledge of what was occurring on the ground or in the air.

Decisive for the swift conquest of the U.S. military in the Iraq war was its absolute technological pre-eminence in weapons of intelligence and targeting. UAVs took high-tech twenty-four-hour tactical intelligence to a new level, permitting U.S. commanders to benefit from unparalleled access to what the Iraqi military was doing on the ground and using images from at least ten different kinds of drones soaring over the battlefield. At the topmost end of the scale, the U.S. air forces' high-altitude RQ-4A Global Hawk can survey huge areas of terrain. At the bottom of the scale, the Marines' low-altitude Dragon Eye can be released speedily from a backpack for short distance surveys. Long-range medium-altitude UAVs, such as the Predator, in contrast, were employed to supply intelligence from more treacherous sites such as Baghdad. It was this multilayered coverage by UAVs that allowed the American armed forces to track Iraqi activities and comprehend their objectives. Even so, UAVs are not infallible. The Predator has a variety of problems linked to its inferior image quality, which arise from the fact that UAVs detect thermal energy sources rather than ambient light. Regardless, UAVs played a remarkable role in synchronizing U.S. military intelligence and operations in Iraq. Take the performance of the U.K.'s comparatively unrefined UAV, the Phoenix. When the momentum of the First Marine Division toward Baghdad began to drag the Marines away from the U.K.'s First Armored Division, the United Kingdom launched numerous Phoenixes simply to guarantee that the Iraqis were not moving to profit from the developing gap. Thus, a vital innovation during the Iraq war was the use of intelligent precision munitions and targeting. Furthermore, the Global Hawk offers pointers to what UAVs hold for the future of reconnaissance, especially when one of the main operational limits is the duration of the mission. For the longer an aircraft can remain aloft, the more intelligence it can gather; and it is precisely at this juncture that the Global Hawk stood out in the Iraq war. This is because other aircraft are restricted by what their human crews can bear, whereas a UAV such as the Global Hawk can take to the air for more than 24 hours before it needs refueling.

Yet it is not just a question of being able to *see* what one's opponents are doing. Rather, one must also be capable of *analyzing* the intelligence in advance to decide exactly what to strike. Consider the U.S. air force's JSTAR, the chief reconnaissance aircraft in the Iraq combat zone. This aircraft not only has a radar antenna that scans the terrain and permits its onboard controllers to target objects in motion at ground level over enormous distances; it is also able to sustain 24-hour coverage while transmitting intelligence to military ground positions. As a result, airborne commanders can warn ground troops of imminent attacks while simultaneously assigning aircraft to annihilate enemy forces. On March 25, 2003, flying into the heart of a sandstorm, one of the U.S. military's 14 JSTARs learned of a dense formation of Iraqi armored vehicles moving ahead to attack. Within moments, the JSTAR had conveyed the intelligence to ground positions that instantly discharged four global positioning system (GPS)-directed bombs which destroyed 30 vehicles and halted the formation (Murray and Scales 2003: 172).

U.S. SOFs also performed an essential function during the Iraq war. Even before the war commenced, SOFs were operating in Iraq's western deserts, where they blocked the possibility that Iraq might launch Scud missiles at Israel and cut supply lines to Syria. In the south, the SOFs played a key role in stopping the Iraqi military from devastating oilfields. SOFs have never been drawn on so comprehensively, proving adept at executing lethal small-unit actions while having an impact upon wider aspects of the war by diverting the Iraqi military and disrupting its communications. SOFs were also vital in the north where they were the contact with Kurdish *peshmerga* (the 60,000-strong militias of the Kurdish Democratic Party and the Party for a Unified Kurdistan) fighters. Here SOFs succeeded in assisting the Kurds to capture Kirkuk and Mosul, which confused the Iraqi military and prevented it from setting fire to the Kirkuk oilfields. Such missions brought into play all of the SOFs' abilities; they frequently utilized laser designators to organize combined aerial firepower at a distance. Still, a drawback of precision-guided weaponry is that to be of use it needs very specific intelligence. For this reason, SOFs had a tendency to function in regions that were on the point of attack and where they could attain and supply targeting intelligence to the artillery. Armed with a handful of Abrams tanks, truck-mounted weapons, GPS, and laser designators, SOFs were able to request precise artillery fire on the Iraqi military from AH-64 Apache attack helicopters and F-16 fighter planes. At the same time, Global Hawks and JSTARs prowled over the combat zone, showing U.S. commanders such as General Franks, based in Doha, Qatar, real-time images of Iraqi movements, targets, battleground conditions, and so-called "collateral damage."

At the core of "Operation Iraqi Freedom" was the top-secret JOC in Doha. A massive vault-like space, the JOC was where officers consulted with SOFs and other commanders in the field. Stuffed with laptop computers, email facilities, telephones, and huge flat plasma video screens, the JOC sped audio links and imagery of ships, troops, and targets from all across the Persian Gulf to the Pentagon and to the White House and back again. Without doubt, SOFs will perform a significant role in the future projection of U.S. military power while increasingly being incorporated into regular forces.

U.S. military casualties would indisputably have been larger and the move forward to Baghdad slower if the Iraqi armed forces had been in a serious position to wage a twenty-first-century war. However, the Gulf War of 1991 and the post-1991 U.S./U.K. no-fly zone over northern and southern Iraq both added significantly to the disintegration and growing incompetence of the Iraqi military. Even before the Iraq war, Iraq's armed forces were ill disciplined, disordered, badly taught, and weak. Most of the Iraqi military's equipment was obsolete. It is hardly surprising that Iraq's military commanders made no determined preparations to protect Baghdad. In a nutshell, Iraq's armed forces were unable to adjust to a battleground in which the U.S. military would move at near light speed with terrifying lethality before they could even *decide* to fire a shot. Saddam Hussein's 60,000-strong "elite" Republican Guard was confronted with the prospect of fighting a war against the American armed forces without maintained or up-to-date equipment, spare parts, or new information and communications technologies. Additionally, a large number of Republican Guard officers had been chosen for their allegiance to Saddam's regime rather than for their military expertise, or were on the brink of desertion.

The U.S. military's attack on Baghdad corroborated the worth and agility of Plan 1003 Victor. Following the crushing of four Republican Guard divisions encircling Baghdad, for example, the plan required Task Force 1–64 Armor to dispatch Thunder Runs through the heart of Baghdad before departing the capital and rejoining the Third Infantry Division at the recently renamed Baghdad International Airport. The initial Thunder Run, heralded by air strikes, took place on April 5, astonishing the Iraqi military and igniting an enormous battle before Task Force 1–64 Armor could return to the airport that afternoon. What was critical regarding the first Thunder Run was its demonstration effect. The American armed forces could now drive armored vehicles through Baghdad. Emboldened by the achievements of the original Thunder Run, a second was launched on April 6, with the aim of moving to and settling in the center of Baghdad. Again, a massive battle resulted and, as a result of the comparative success of the second Thunder Run, two more ultimately victorious Thunder Runs were instigated the same evening. The successful utilization of accomplishment and opportunity besides the occupation of central Baghdad by the U.S. military on the night of April 7 broke the Iraqi military's resistance.

The Thunder Runs were very much technologically mediated tactical clashes. Lt. Gen. William Wallace, for instance, viewed the Thunder Run assaults "live" on a Hunter reconnaissance UAV downlink transmitted direct into his in-theater command center, commenting afterward that the event was reminiscent of live-action TV imagery of bank robbery shootouts and car chases (Murray and Scales 2003: 210). Plan 1003 Victor thus provided the American armed forces with a target, Baghdad, and with new military tactics in the form of Thunder Runs that helped them to destroy the worn-out and disordered Iraqi military. But at the political level, Plan 1003 Victor has proved disastrous. For if at least one of the intentions of the U.S. military was to bring about human security and peace in Iraq then the present political conditions there are neither secure nor peaceful.

The elite war on Utopia

This section shifts from a literal account of the U.S. war on Iraq to a tentative explanation and examination of the Iraq war through the lens of the new U.S. civilian–military elites' war on Utopia. I describe the new U.S. civilian–military elite as that grouping in power which comprises the motivating force behind President George W. Bush's war on Iraq (Armitage 2004a: 77–8). Then-Vice-President Dick Cheney, Secretary of State Condoleezza Rice, and Defense Secretary Donald Rumsfeld were members of this new U.S. civilian–military elite. As noted, for the purposes of this chapter, I define Utopia as a very real yet simultaneously imagined State representing a society without war. Like the U.S. war on Iraq, then, the elites' war on Utopia is a fast and exceptionally successful offensive characterized by the deployment of enormous quantities of state-of-the-art weapons. I argue that if the new U.S. civilian–military elites' war on Utopia is not prohibited it will result in the speedy defeat of the global peace movement. Let me define what I mean by the global peace movement.

It is clear that, as long as there have been wars in the world, there have been movements for peace. The distinction between yesterday's peace movement and today's is that the peace movement is currently synchronized by new information and communications technologies in arguably a more effectual and novel manner, generating what Schell (2003: 1–3) calls "the other superpower" or the global peace movement. All kinds of individuals and groups from atheist pacifists and religious alliances, to the anti-Iraq war coordinators and activists of 2002–3, to anarchists and feminists, are a part of the global peace movement. Global citizens are thus organizing in innovative ways against neoliberalism or what Chomsky

(1999) terms the "new military humanism," involving themselves in affinity groups, social movements, and, increasingly, in networks. As Graeber (2002) notes, the Zapatista Army of National Liberation (EZLN) of Chiapas, Mexico, was an especially significant development, as its unstructured organizational configuration offers indigenous communities real control and advanced insight into that network of networks, the Internet.

Other important groups include anticorporate globalization protesters (e.g. at Seattle in 1999), San Francisco's Art and Revolution, the Landless Workers Movement in Brazil, the Narita protesters of Japan, London's Reclaim the Streets, and the Pink Block of Genoa. The global peace movement consists of a worldwide communal network of defiant voices. Because of new networked models of coordination, the global peace movement is currently equipped to marshal new information and communications technologies for its activities and for mobilizing support within the Imaginist City.

The Imaginist City? To begin with, I want to emphasize that my conception of the Imaginist City does *not* refer to an imaginary or an illusory city. Rather, it is a real if absolutely deterritorialized city in which global citizens cross a threshold where they can and do produce their own nonviolent places for peace activism in the age of infinite global war, a unified city where support for a radical yet peaceful state of mind prevails. Antiviolence protests, spiritual gatherings, and anarchist and feminist rallies are all districts of the Imaginist City, locations where peace advocates can experiment with techniques of gaining control over the means of war and redirecting them to peaceful ends. The 2002–3 anti-Iraq war protests brought these districts together, creating the first global Imaginist City for the global peace movement in the streets of the most important capitals of the world. The conclusion of the events of the global Imaginist City was the near-total refusal of the hypermodern values of infinite global war, coupled with a demand that the threat posed by Virilio's "military–scientific complex" (Armitage 2001: 168) yield to the civilianization of technoscience.

Action against the prolongation of infinite global war is consistent with the work of groupings such as Computer Professionals for Social Responsibility (CPSR) that developed out of organized opposition to the U.S. military's Strategic Defense Initiative or Star Wars. The global peace movement is then an association of practitioners and theorists that, within the limits of the Imaginist City, is an alliance of free-thinking rebels and experimental researchers into the civilianization of technoscience. Hence, the Imaginist City is not only a civilianized city built to offer refuge from the hypermodernized and evermore militarized contemporary city (Armitage and Roberts 2003: 87–104) but also a city erected to provide innovative possibilities for investigations into the end of war.

Yet the Imaginist City does have its outcasts. No longer, for example, will the global peace movement tolerate Marxist or other groupings that endeavor to take over the Imaginist City through front organizations, veiled political goals, and hierarchically focused attempts to construct the vanguard party along Leninist lines of democratic centralism. The global peace movement seeks to banish authoritarians from the Imaginist City with the object of preserving an amorphous mode of association whose political aspirations are open, nonhierarchical, and founded on a networked conception of democracy and citizenship. The residents of the Imaginist City are accordingly united by a sensation of incredulity with regard to the construction of increasingly militarized cities beyond their own metropolis. But they are also fused by a critical sense of how they might understand and transform such developments, glancing backwards, perhaps, to the pacifist Fellowship of Reconciliation in World War I, while looking forward to the next generation of networked models of organization and new information and communications technologies. The present-day perspective of the global peace movement is consequently that the advocates of infinite global war must discard their efforts to build more militarized cities and move toward extending the civilianized experimental municipality that is the Imaginist City.

Not surprisingly, PNAC, the architects of infinite global war, the new U.S. civilian–military elite, and the Republican Guard have every intention of constructing more and more militarized cities. The elite Republican Guard is that group which encompasses the outer edge of the new U.S. civilian–military elites' war on Utopia, a band that is made up of a few defense policy intellectuals and long-standing Iraq hawks (Purdum 2003). It incorporates people such as Richard Perle, previously a Reagan administration defense official who until recently supervised the Pentagon's consultative group, the Defense Policy Board. Another member is William Kristol, chairman of PNAC and former chief of staff to Vice-President Dan Quayle, who currently edits the conservative *Weekly Standard*. This group also includes a variety of Iraq specialists from the Clinton White House such as Kenneth M. Pollack, the author of *The Threatening Storm: The Case for Invading Iraq* (Pollack 2002). Finally, a key associate of the elite Republican Guard is Jeb Bush, U.S. President George W. Bush's brother, governor of Florida, and signatory, together with Cheney and Rumsfeld, and 21 others, including Francis Fukuyama, to PNAC's "Statement of Principles."

What makes the elite Republican Guard particularly important is that, in conjunction with the new U.S. civilian–military elite and PNAC, it is currently launching an aggressive onslaught on the Imaginist City. What is more, their war on Utopia is reliant on their low-intensity but overpowering technological ascendancy as regards weapons of intelligence and targeting such as UAVs and high- and low-tech surveillance systems. A number of federal agencies increasingly perceive a homeland security function for surveillance UAVs. Indeed, Sia (2002) has noted how the Department of Homeland Security, the Central Intelligence Agency (CIA), the U.S. Coast Guard and Border Patrol, the Transportation Department, the Energy Department, and the FBI are all pursuing strategies to exploit UAVs for aiding homeland security missions.

In addition, U.S. domestic SOUs, like the FBI and Northcom, are accomplishing crucial missions on behalf of the new U.S. civilian–military elite. For example, in May 2003, the new U.S. civilian–military elite sought to offer the CIA and the Pentagon extensive new powers to demand individual and financial records on U.S. citizens as part of foreign intelligence and terrorism operations (Lichtblau and Risen 2003). The request, which was defeated, would have permitted the CIA and the military to issue "national security letters" without prior court approval, requiring Internet providers, credit card corporations, libraries, and other organizations to supply data such as telephone records, bank transactions, and email logs. Likewise, in 2002, the Pentagon at last attained its goal of setting up a military command for the domestic United States (Dreyfus 2003). The basis for creating Northcom is to use the American armed forces to respond to a 9/11-style terrorist attack. The founding of Northcom is thus an acknowledgment by the new U.S. civilian–military elite that if it wishes to conduct infinite global war it follows that everything will have to be transformed within America. Of course the key change, if the new U.S. civilian–military elite is to crush the already inadequate ramparts arranged by Utopia's vulnerable troops, is the abandonment of the idea that the domestic United States is not a war zone.

The new U.S. civilian–military elites' saturation bombing of the Imaginist City, a kind of cybernetic Thunder Run, is frequently accomplished by its use of the politics of noise. But such salvos are not carried out using the politics of *semantic* noise or the impedance of political, linguistic, and visual codes and symbols. Rather, the new U.S. civilian–military elites' bombardment of the Imaginist City is generally achieved by the politics of *engineering* noise or the impedance of the political through the blocking of the physical and technological properties of the Internet in particular. For the blocking of the Internet leads to what might be termed an "informatics of confusion" whereby the multiplication of information blocks any rational understanding of events, as more information reduces and distorts any meaning occurring in the political communication processes of the Internet. This decrease and deformation of meaning is obviously not intended by the source, which in this case is the global peace movement. But the new U.S. civilian–military elites' assault on the Imaginist City is not only an achievement for the politics of engineering noise but also an extraordinary military and tactical feat. This is because the blocking of the Internet, the informatics of confusion, and the multiplication of information all negatively affect the reception of messages and impede their transparency.

Despite the problem of the politics of noise, I argue against the global peace movement discarding its strikes on military elites. On the other hand, my views on this issue are divergent from those of Gray (2005: 102–6), who claims that there is some genuine "convergence" on deep-seated epistemological, ontological, and ethical questions such as feminism between the global peace movement and the military elite. From my perspective, Gray's proposals ignore the logistics of perception management. Such an evasion causes difficulties because, in the age of infinite global war, it is cybernetic warfare that is paramount (Armitage 2001: 169). The arrival of cyberwar means that resistance against war can no longer be a resistance to militarism and weaponry as in the days of the pacifist Fellowship of Reconciliation. In our day resistance to war implies resistance to the cybernetic distortion of information. Hence, the global peace movement must include activists dedicated to frontline antiwar struggles. But it must also include activists devoted to the theoretical critique of the logistics of perception management, and of the relentless campaigns aimed at winning hearts and minds for cyberwar by means of the manipulation of the mass media. The global peace movement should not then just demonstrate in the streets. It must also learn somehow to protest against the logic of the society of the *"integrated spectacle"* (Debord 1998: 8), the logic of technologically enhanced information management capabilities, live videoconferences, and the never-ending transmission of the same messages over and over again by the mass media. If the global peace movement does not discover how to campaign against the logistics of perception management, it will rapidly find that it has been incorporated into the military elites' media planning for infinite global war.

Targeting the Imaginist City

My argument in this section moves from an exploratory account and investigation into the new U.S. civilian–military elites' war on Utopia, to a demonstration of the elites' accelerated and increasingly victorious assaults incorporating high-tech armaments in the endeavor to suppress the global peace movement. I first show how the new U.S. civilian–military elites' war on the Utopia of the global peace movement has, in company with PNAC's "Statement of Principles" and the elite Republican Guards' promotion of American global leadership, initiated a sequence of attacks on the Imaginist City.

The first strike on the Imaginist City took place directly after the elites' *coup d'état* or the "stolen election" of 2000 (Kellner 2001), when PNAC's and the Republican Guards' belligerent military and foreign policy was instigated by the new U.S. civilian–military elite. The second strike was not this triumvirate's declaration of infinite global war but, more importantly, its declaration of *pre-emptive* infinite global war. The official strategy of the new U.S. civilian–military elite declares that America now has the right to execute offensive military action against any country it deems a security threat because it has weapons of mass destruction. This policy is the practical implementation of the elites', PNAC's, and Republican Guards' yearning to "shape circumstances before crises emerge and meet threats before they become dire" (PNAC 1997: 1). The third strike is the new U.S. civilian–military elites', PNAC's, and Republican Guards' onslaught on the inhabitants of the Imaginist City, given that it is they, together with the residents of innumerable other cities, who are presently shouldering the $400 billion costs of such attacks. Increased expenditure on the "modernization" and deployment of the American armed forces in Iraq and Afghanistan is currently squeezing social, education, and health programs in the Imaginist and other cities and losing the United States countless former allies (*New York Times* 2003). The fourth and final strikes are the ongoing attacks that are taking place against those regimes, including Iraq, Afghanistan, and Utopia, that the elites, PNAC, and the Republican Guard judge to be antagonistic to American security and principles. Such principles are summarized in PNAC's "Statement of Principles" as unwavering support for everyday war, neoliberal global capitalism, and the notion of the United States as the world's only superpower.

The elites, PNAC, and the elite Republican Guard are also assailing the Imaginist City with speeding and apparently inconspicuous programmed weapons of intelligence and targeting such as the UAVs and surveillance systems deployed by U.S. federal agencies on the U.S.–Mexican border. What is significant about these developments is that it is not the U.S. military per se that is installing UAVs and surveillance systems but America's evermore privatized military–scientific complex operated by for-profit corporations (Singer 2003). Privatized UAVs are an ideal way for the elites to avoid the 1878 Posse Comitatus Act, which stipulates that the U.S. military cannot be used for domestic law enforcement. UAVs are then a perfect medium for the merger of the Border Patrol and the Department of Homeland Security and for the policing and acclimatization of the people of the Imaginist and other cities to permanent airborne surveillance as part of everyday war on the pretext of tracking illegal immigrants. After the CIA used a Predator equipped with Hellfire missiles to exterminate a few *suspected* terrorists in Yemen in 2002, the allure of UAVs has increased to mythological extent, particularly among UAV manufacturers such as General Atomics Aeronautical Systems, who want to market UAVs for commercial use. In June 2004, for example, the first UAVs, transmitting live pictures, were allocated to the Arizona Border Patrol in an unparalleled push to secure a 350-mile section of the U.S.–Mexican border that has grown to be one of the most common and deadliest passageways for illegal immigrants (Reuters 2004). But the influx of Arizona's UAVs has been criticized by the Mexican government's migrant welfare service Grupo Beta, over the border in Agua Prieta, as UAVs do not reduce but increase risk because they compel migrants to seek increasingly inaccessible places to cross so as to evade detection.

In the meantime, U.S. SOUs, such as the NYPD/FBI Joint Terrorism Task Force, are carrying out strategic missions in the elites' war on present-day political activists. In July 2004, for instance, the harassment of activists seeking to protest at the Democratic Party's National Convention (DNC) in Boston worsened according to Anarchist Black Cross (ABC) (2004). It appears that Boston police, together with police from New York City, commenced a campaign of *pre-emptive* action aimed at the suppression of free speech during the DNC. On July 8 the NYPD/FBI Joint Terrorism Task Force visited the residence of a New York City activist after acquiring his address from Boston police, which had compiled an inventory of "troublemakers" heading for the Boston DNC whom the Task Force intended to visit. In an effort to deter activists from engaging in political activity, organizing with others, or attending the DNC, the Task Force freely admitted that it had covertly observed the activist at home and investigated his medical and academic records and his previous history with the police. In brief, U.S. SOUs such as the NYPD/FBI Joint Terrorism Task Force are vigorously threatening, targeting, and harrying political activists in operations designed to generate fear in the community.

Northcom acts in a comparable manner to that of SOUs in that it operates to further undermine the Posse Comitatus Act. This process has been in train since at least the 1980s in America when internal duties were allocated to the armed forces as part of the disastrous "war on drugs." Now some want the Department of Defense (DoD) to be handed responsibility for supervising U.S. border crossings and defending the outskirts of strategic cities over and above being drawn into the

"War on Terrorism." However, departing from the custom of keeping the military out of police work is dangerous for democracy. Nor does such a policy make much sense as the military could perform a useful antiterror role only if al Qaeda were going to roll up for open combat, which seems unlikely. And so, like UAVs, Northcom is in the business of acclimatizing citizens to everyday war, to witnessing bands of soldiers on the streets, and to life in the post-democratic stratocracy that is present-day America.

Out of sight, Northcom has hundreds of individuals gathering domestic intelligence and receiving information from the police and the intelligence agencies. The justification for the second Cold War, like the first, when army intelligence units surveilled U.S. civilians, is naturally the communist/Islamist/terrorist (delete as appropriate) "threat." Accordingly, U.S. citizens must adapt to technologically advanced surveillance aircraft patrolling over their cities hunting terrorists. None of these events is liable to agonize the U.S. military. The unswerving DoD viewpoint on everyday war has been that the U.S. president has enough legal authority to make use of the military when he decides that doing so is apposite (Dreyfus 2003: 3). At present, there are practically no circumstances in the United States when its armed forces are constrained by the Posse Comitatus Act, given that the U.S. military already supplies ultramodern surveillance apparatus and helicopters to the police for suppressing demonstrations. The blurring of the boundary between civilian and military power is then already under way as Northcom starts to think through its interactions with the CIA and the FBI while significantly expanding the role of the U.S. military at home.

Moreover, the new U.S. civilian–military elites' blitzkrieg on the Imaginist City all through the anti-Iraq war rallies of 2002–3 was realized by means of the elites' exploitation of the politics of engineering noise regarding the blocking of the Internet or what Jodie Dean calls the strategy of "no response" (Dean 2005). When the new U.S. civilian–military elite made its argument over the heads of the population of the Imaginist City (over, that is, the critical standpoint of alternative or independent U.S. and non-U.S. media reports, commentaries, radio programs, magazines, e-lists, marches, protests, direct actions, and bloggers) for attacking Iraq, it obstructed the global peace movement's frequently Internet-based resistance to militarism, unilateralism, and the U.S.'s pre-emptive strategy of infinite global war. Certainly, the elites knew that peace messages were being disseminated on the Internet. But, following Dean, I want to argue that it sensed that the political and linguistic codes, images, and activities of the global peace movement, the political message of the global peace movement if you will, was not one that it was inclined to take delivery of. The political message of the global peace movement was endlessly circulated on the Internet and elsewhere but was also hindered by the material and technological properties of the medium. As Dean (2005: 52) puts it:

> Even when the White House acknowledged the worldwide demonstrations of February 15, 2003, Bush simply reiterated the fact that a message was out there, circulating – the protestors had the right to express their opinions.

He didn't actually respond to their message. He didn't treat the words and actions of the protesters as sending a message to him to which he was in some sense obligated to respond. Rather, he acknowledged that there existed views different from his own. There were his views and there were other views; all had the right to exist, to be expressed – but that in no way meant, or so Bush made it seem, that these views were involved with each other.

In a word, and despite the avalanche of anti-Iraq war commentary and information, the new U.S. civilian–military elite had no intention of engaging in a debate over the meaning and significance of the Iraq war, of engaging, that is, in a discussion about the politics of semantic noise with the people of the Imaginist City. Instead, in the run-up to the U.S. invasion of Iraq, they remained content to watch the antiwar message of the global peace movement evolve into the growing and continually circulating content of cyberspace. To speak of the politics of engineering noise in this instance, then, is to speak of a situation in which the official global strategy of the new U.S. civilian–military elite is pursued not by means of an engagement with its critics but by means of the encouragement of the never-ending flow of cybernetic content.

Unquestionably, even before the U.S. incursion into Iraq, the anti-Iraq war communiqués of the global peace movement were stymied by the informatics of confusion and by the sheer volume of anti-Iraq war announcements in media of various kinds, from websites and email lists to blogs and texts, which prevented reasoned comprehension of the impending war while reducing and warping the work of activists. There was no need for the new U.S. civilian–military elite to participate in a semantic debate with the residents of the Imaginist City; all it had to do was provide more and more institutional, bureaucratic, and legalistic contributions to the already congested political exchanges happening on the Internet. In brief, the political system of the new U.S. civilian–military elite functions almost entirely independent of, and in such a way as to block, the political system of the global peace movement. Clearly, the global peace movement did not anticipate the politics of incessantly circulating content and its attendant diminution and misrepresentation of meaning. This was a significant strategic achievement on the part of the new U.S. civilian–military elite. By hindering the Internet using the politics of circulating content, by using the informatics of confusion and the escalation of communication and information, the new U.S. civilian–military elite damaged the freedoms of speech and assembly, press coverage, publicity, transparency, accountability, and, crucially, the reception of the anti-Iraq war statements of the global peace movement in the public sphere and hampered their intelligibility.

Such events imply that as long as the global peace movement is preoccupied with the communicative interactions of the public sphere, with the politics of semantic noise as the circulation of content, it will never become "the other superpower" as it has increasingly little impact on official politics and policy. The elites are evermore skilled in the targeting of the Imaginist City, using the politics of circulation as content or what I have termed the politics of engineering noise.

Hence, the global peace movement must eschew the politics of the circulation of content and the informatics of confusion, wherein the escalation of hypermodern networks of global communications and information not only "relieves top-level actors (corporate, institutional and governmental) from the obligation to respond" (Dean 2005: 53) but also thwarts any comprehension of its messages. These reductions and perversions of meaning are also the lifeblood of "hypercapitalism," a form of capitalism dominated by "the speed at which processes of circulation and self-valorization occur, and the ephemeral nature of hypercapitalist commodities associated with its speed of light infrastructure of communications technologies" (Armitage and Graham 2001: 115).

Now, it is not my purpose to claim that resistance is futile. Rather, I contend that if the global peace movement does aspire to challenge the new U.S. civilian–military elites' offensive on the Imaginist City, then it ought to seek means by which it can circumvent the politics of engineering noise and the militarization of its own strategies. For this reason, in preference to becoming embroiled in the blocking of the Internet and the informatics of confusion, it is instructive to reconsider Schumacher's (1993) conception of "appropriate technologies." Without a doubt, the global peace movement would benefit if it rethought developments in the field of the politics of noise from the viewpoint of appropriate technologies. At least part of the answer to the global peace movement's problems should exemplify Schumacher's qualities of smallness and simplicity, along with nonviolence and the reduction of information excess. Appropriate technology should be applied to the politics of semantic and engineering noise. To create nonviolent situations that can match the countries dedicated to infinite global war, the appropriate technology of the global peace movement must be better than the pacifist varieties of yesteryear. But it should also be as uncomplicated and as inexpensive as the antiviolence of the past. Crucially, it must be autonomous of the hi-tech channels of communication controlled by the elite.

The aim, then, must be to create "freespaces" (Woods 1997: 16), spaces of political experimentation, meaningfully occupied, that disrupt the centralization of power and other deterministic and coercive schemes while encouraging self-organization and personal reinvention. Such freespaces ought to be constructed in abandoned spaces and occupied bases, anticipating new relationships in and beyond the Imaginist City. Hypercapitalism, the reigning economic order in those spaces that promote infinite global war, cannot accomplish this aim as it is already "socially overloaded" (Jeudy 1994) with information and currently disposing of everything but "immaterial," intellectual, and communicative labor (Hardt and Negri 2000: 29). Hypercapitalism is not then an appropriate model for freespaces, for the latter are anchored in a reduction of ineffective information and tangible and creative work. As a result, freespaces must be produced in the spaces where the population of the Imaginist City exists, and not in cyberspace into which they are inclined to virtually migrate or, more accurately, exile themselves from "the catastrophe of the real" (Baudrillard 1995: 28).

Likewise, freespaces should be accessible enough so that they can be created without a surplus of unproductive information or, insofar as it is feasible, introducing distorted information from those spaces committed to infinite global war. The creative techniques exercised ought to be straightforward in order to offset the call for convoluted information-related expertise not just in the creative process but also in matters of political organization, resources, funding, and in the dissemination of the idea of the global Imaginist City. Appropriate technologies are then critically concerned with reducing the dependence of the imagination of the global peace movement on universal technological and political complexity, on the politics of engineering noise, and most of all on the politics and processes of the machine. In other words, to overturn the harmful effects of the receipt of its emails and the blocking of their lucidity on the Internet, the global peace movement must request its own engineers to effect innovative and simple forms of political communication.

The tribulations of the politics of noise notwithstanding, I also want to demonstrate why and how the global peace movement ought not to halt its attacks on military elites or accept Gray's arguments concerning its future and resistance to war. Gray declares that to stop war the global peace movement must make elemental changes, such as merging its philosophy of nonviolence with that of what he calls "military practitioners." In fact, Gray, citing the Martial Ecologies conference of 2000 organized by Tel Aviv University and the Israeli Defense Forces (IDF), contends that "there is some real convergence on fundamental epistemological, ontological and ethical issues between parts of the peace movement and an interesting slice of the strategic studies community" (Gray 2005: 104). The significance of the conference for Gray is that several of the epistemologies and methodologies promoted by the "strategic studies community" are not unlike ones employed by the global peace movement, such as feminist epistemology. Additionally, Gray suggests that both feminists and "military practitioners" adopt epistemologies and methodologies that are crucially concerned with the question of embodiment, with the limitations and "situated" (Haraway 1991) characteristics of knowledge.

I argue against the global peace movement dropping its assault on military elites and therefore against any adjustments that will require combining its philosophy with that of "military practitioners." What Gray views as a genuine convergence on basic issues between the global peace movement and the "strategic studies community" at the Martial Studies conference was probably an IDF "reconnaissance battle" against the global peace movement. For, as Bauman (2002: 95) writes, in reconnaissance battles:

> units are not sent into action in order to capture enemy territory, but to explore the enemy's determination and endurance, the resources the enemy can command and the speed with which such resources may be brought to the battlefield. The units are ordered to lay bare the enemy's strong points and weaknesses and the shrewdness and miscalculations of the enemy commanders. Analyzing the course of the reconnaissance battle, staff officers hope to make intelligent guesses concerning the enemy's power of resistance and capacity for counterattack, and so suggest realistic war plans.

Equally, I dispute that the Martial Ecologies conference demonstrates that the epistemological and methodological perspectives of the "strategic studies community" are identical to those deployed by feminists in the global peace movement. As Höpfl has revealed, women are incorporated into the military body only on the epistemological condition that they are capable of demonstrating mastery by the acquisition of a metaphorical penis (Höpfl 2003). Female integration into the military body is actually attained by controlling women, and by positioning them not as bearers of knowledge but as either dolls or quasi-men.

Gray's perspective is also problematic because it disregards the logistics of perception management, which, in the era of infinite global war, the epoch of cyberwar, is critically concerned with the misrepresentation of information. The perception managers of the Rendon Group, for example, are effectively the sales force of infinite global war, as it is their mission not merely to justify cyberwar but also to develop "information as an element of power" (Chatterjee 2004: 1). I contend that the global peace movement must devote some attention to a theoretical critique of the logistics of perception management practiced by companies like the Rendon Group, which markets war strategies to countless government agencies and multinational corporations, political parties, and the military elite. Specializing in the invention and manipulation of war and media-related events, the Rendon Group is the industry leader in the field of tracking anti-U.S. foreign news reports for military elites and for planting misleading (read pro-U.S.) stories on the Internet, in print, and on TV. The real mission of the Rendon Group is to use military operations capabilities to market the rationale for cyberwar by way of the mass media. The declared ambition of the Rendon Group is to reduce the diversity of mass media messages while increasing the size of the "message population" to guarantee that "the message is received and not just sent" (Chatterjee 2004: 2). The global peace movement must work against the logic of the integrated spectacle and the logistics of perception management directed by such companies. Otherwise, the global peace movement will be incorporated into the media strategies of the military elite in their drive toward infinite global war.

Conclusion

The American armed forces' war on Iraq was an accelerated and virtually matchless offensive encompassing the application of massive amounts of technologically advanced military hardware, resulting in the rapid overthrow of Saddam Hussein's tyrannical government. In the first section of this chapter, I focused on the Pentagon's top-secret war plan, Plan 1003 Victor, in the targeting of Baghdad. The U.S. military's speedy triumph in the Iraq war was largely attributable to shock and awe, to its technological superiority in relation to weapons of intelligence and targeting such as UAVs and JSTARs. In addition, SOFs and the JOC in Doha fulfilled important tasks concerning the American armed forces' victory over the hopelessly inadequate protection organized by the Iraqi military. The U.S. military's final attack on Baghdad using Thunder Runs was a noteworthy strategic feat. However, the Iraqi insurgents' raids on the American armed forces and the recently U.S.-installed administration in Baghdad persist, as does the general belief that America's military escapade in Iraq will in the end generate an enormous political implosion and the frenzied departure of U.S. forces.

My account then shifted to an exploratory reading and examination of the Iraq war by way of the optic of the new U.S. civilian–military elites' war on Utopia. Like the U.S. war on Iraq, the new U.S. civilian–military elites' war on Utopia is a high-speed and exceptionally skillful offensive bringing forward immense quantities of hypermodern weaponry. If the elites' war on Utopia is not arrested, it will end in the early defeat of the global peace movement. PNAC's "Statement of Principles" can be shown to pertain to the targeting of the deterritorialized Imaginist City of the global peace movement. The new U.S. civilian–military elite, PNAC, and the elite Republican Guard are carrying out an audacious attack on the Imaginist City. This triumvirate's swift victory in their war on Utopia is principally contingent on low-intensity weapons of intelligence and targeting such as UAVs and high- and low-tech surveillance systems. US domestic SOUs such as the FBI and Northcom discharge strategic functions in the elites' everyday war on what Hart and Negri (2000: 60) describe as "the plural multitude of productive, creative subjectivities of globalization" presently discovering how to navigate the increasingly turbulent spaces of Utopia. The new U.S. civilian–military elites' targeting of the Imaginist City is realized more and more by their application of the politics of noise.

But it is neither my contention nor my purpose to advocate that the global peace movement should abandon its confrontations with the elite. My argument is that the global peace movement must question any synthesis of its epistemology with that of military elites. Such ideas obscure the difference between the civilianization and the increasing militarization of knowledge (Armitage 2005) or the logistics of perception management, and they encourage the incorporation of the global peace movement into the media strategies of the military elite for infinite global war.

The third section of this chapter demonstrated how accelerated offensives in the use of advanced military hardware are related to the effort to activate the defeat of the global peace movement. It showed how the military elites' series of strikes on the Imaginist and innumerable other cities embrace the exploitation of low-intensity weapons of intelligence and targeting such as the UAVs and surveillance systems deployed by the Arizona Border Patrol. It illustrated how SOUs such as the NYPD/FBI Joint Terrorism Task Force and Northcom are performing critical roles in the elites' war on hypermodern political activists. Further, I highlighted how the military bombardment of the Imaginist City through the anti-Iraq war demonstrations of 2002–3 was realized by way of the politics of noise. By means of the adoption of appropriate technologies, the global peace movement can maintain its forays into the territory of the military elite while refusing arguments involving the merger of peace activist and military thinking. The latter was in part by way of a critique of the logistics of perception management conducted by the Rendon Group.

In conclusion, Debord's "spectacular government" has all the means necessary to fabricate the productions and the perceptions of the global peace movement. It really is "the absolute master of memories" and of media strategies while it is also the unregulated master of the military elites' plans for infinite global war presently determining all our futures. To date, the military elites rule practically unimpeded. It is the mission of the global peace movement to ensure that their accelerated decisions are delayed and finally turned back.

Note

1 An earlier version of this paper was published in *Topia: Canadian Journal of Cultural Studies*, vol. 15 (Spring 2006), pp. 23–43.

References

Anarchist Black Cross (ABC) (2004) "Harassment of DNC protesters escalates," nettime, July 7: 1–6. Available at http://www.nettime-l@bbs.thing.net.

Armitage, J. (2001) "The Kosovo W@r did take place," in J. Armitage (ed.) *Virilio Live: Selected Interviews*. London: Sage.

Armitage, J. (2004a) "The totally mobilized hypermodern body," *Left Curve*, 28, 68–82.

Armitage, J. (2004b) "Beyond postmodernism? Paul Virilio's hypermodern cultural theory," in A. and M. Kroker (eds) *Life in the Wires: The CTHEORY Reader*, Victoria: CTheory Books.

Armitage, J. (2005) "Beyond hypermodern militarized knowledge factories," *The Review of Education, Pedagogy & Cultural Studies*, 27(3), 219–39.

Armitage, J. and Graham, P. (2001) "Dromoeconomics: towards a political economy of speed," *Parallax*, 18 (January/March), 111–23.

Armitage, J. and Roberts, J. (2003) "From the hypermodern city to the gray zone of total mobilization in the Philippines," in R. Bishop, J. Phillips and Y. W. Wei (eds) *Postcolonial Urbanism: Southeast Asian Cities and Global Processes*, New York: Routledge.

Baudrillard, J. (1995) *The Gulf War Did Not Take Place*, Sydney: Power Publications.

Bauman, Z. (2002) *Society under Siege*, Cambridge: Polity.

Chatterjee, P. (2004) "Information warriors," CorpWatch, August 4: 1–4. Available at http://www.corpwatch.org.

Chomsky, N. (1999) *The New Military Humanism: Lessons from Kosovo*, Monroe, ME: Common Courage Press.

Cushman, J.H. and Shanker, T. (2003) "Backup of war in Iraq provides model of new way of doing battle," *The New York Times*, April 10, pp. 1–5.

Dean, J. (2005) "Communicative capitalism: circulation and the foreclosure of politics," *Cultural Politics*, 1(1), 51–74.

Debord, G. (1998) *Comments on the Society of the Spectacle*, London: Verso.

Deleuze, G. and Guattari, F. (1988) *A Thousand Plateaus: Capitalism and Schizophrenia*, London: Athlone.

Dreyfus, R. (2003) "Bringing the war home," *The Nation*, May 26, pp. 1–4.

Graeber, D. (2002) "The new anarchists," *New Left Review*, 13 (January/February), 61–73.

Gray, C.H. (2005) "The future present of peace and resistance to war," in *Peace, War and Computers*. New York: Routledge.

Haraway, D. (1991) "Situated knowledges: the science question in feminism and the privilege of partial perspective," in *Simians, Cyborgs, and Women: the Reinvention of Nature*, New York: Routledge.

Hardt, M. and Negri, A. (2000) *Empire*, Cambridge, MA: Harvard University Press.

Höpfl, H. (2003) "Becoming a (virile) member: women and the military body," *Body and Society*, 9(4), 13–30.

Jeudy, H. (1994) *Social Overload*, New York: Autonomedia.

Kellner, D. (2001) *Grand Theft 2000: Media Spectacle and a Stolen Election*, Lanham, MD: Rowman and Littlefield.

Lichtblau, E. and Risen, J. (2003) "Broad domestic role asked for CIA and the Pentagon," *The New York Times*, May 2, pp. 1–2.

Murray, W. and Scales, R.H. (2003) *The Iraq War: A Military History*, Cambridge, MA: Harvard University Press.

PNAC (1997) "Statement of Principles," Available at http://www.newamericancentury.org/statementofprinciples.htm.

Pollack, K. (2002) *The Threatening Storm: The Case for Invading Iraq*, New York: Random House.

Purdum, T. (2003) "The brains behind Bush's war," *The New York Times*, February 1, pp. 1–3.

Reuters (2004) "Aerial drones assigned to Arizona Border Patrol," Reuters News, June 25, pp. 1–2. Available at http://www.reuters.com.

Schell, J. (2003) "The other superpower," *The Nation*, April 14, pp. 1–3.

Schumacher, E.F. (1993) *Small Is Beautiful: Study of Economics as If People Mattered*, London: Vintage.

Sia, R. (2002) "Agencies see Homeland Security role for surveillance drones," *Government Executive Magazine*, December 12, pp. 1–3.

Singer, P. (2003) *Corporate Warriors: The Rise of the Privatized Military Industry*, Ithaca, NY: Cornell University Press.

The New York Times (2003) "the defense budget spills forth," May 20, p. 1.

Virilio, P. (1989) *War and Cinema: The Logistics of Perception*, London: Verso.

Woods, L. (1995) "Everyday war," in P. Lang (ed.) *The Mortal City*, Princeton, NJ: Princeton Architectural Press.

Woods, L. (1997) *Radical Reconstruction*, Princeton, NJ: Princeton Architectural Press.

4   Thanato-tactics

Eyal Weizman

Throughout the years of the second intifada, a major Israeli effort was directed at the development of airborne assassinations and the specific technology related to it. From what was often described as a "rare and exceptional emergency method," it has become the Israeli Air Force's main form of attack in the Gaza Strip. According to Ephraim Segoli, a helicopter pilot and former commander of the air force base in Palmahim, located halfway between Tel Aviv and Gaza, from which most assassination raids have been launched and where now the largest fleets of remotely controlled killer drones are located, airborne "liquidations are the central component of Israeli Defense Forces (IDF) operations and the very essence of the 'war' it is waging." Segoli, speaking in May 2006, claimed, furthermore, that "the intention to 'perfect' these operations meant that Israel's security industries have . . . started concentrating [much of their efforts] on the development of systems that primarily serve this operational logic."[1]

According to data collected by the human rights organization B'Tselem, from the beginning of the intifada to February of 2008, 376 Palestinians were killed in targeted assassinations. Only 227 of those were the intended targets for assassination. The rest were Palestinians who happened to be in the wrong place at the wrong time. About fifty of those were children.[2] The assassinated included many of the political and military leadership of Hamas as well.

What follows deals with the methods – technological, operational, legal, and other – that form the basis of these operations and asks how they interact. How do these tactics of assassination intersect with political considerations and calculations? How does the Israeli government and military seek to justify these assassinations, legally, morally, and politically?

Beyond thinking of targeted assassination as a direct, pre-emptive response to terror, the aim here, an update and revision on my previous research on the subject,[3] is to show how Israeli security organizations conceived assassination as a central component in a political "project" and as an attempt to generate a degree of control over Palestinian politics and the population at large. It asks, following Achille Mbembe's essay "Necropolitics," "What is the relationship between politics and death" that these efforts form?[4] How, after the evacuation of the ground surface of Gaza, did bodies, rather than territories, or death, rather than space, turn into the raw material of Israeli sovereignty?

Targeting

Segoli explained that targeted assassinations are "a success story based upon a high degree of cooperation between the General Security Service (GSS) and the air force."[5] Above all, airborne targeted assassinations were fed by the information and organizational powers that the GSS developed under Avi Dichter, director of the GSS from 2000 to 2005, who gained considerable popularity with the public and with the prime minister, Ariel Sharon, as a result of their "success." The efficiency of the operations has relied on the close networking between the intelligence provided by the GSS, fast-tracked political decisions, and the strike capacity of the air force. The GSS drafts the death lists and recommends the time of the operation (once included, rarely has a name been removed from them alive); it provides the files on each person to be liquidated (including details of their involvement in the resistance and their prospective danger to Israel); a special ministerial committee gives its approval (the typical length of deliberation is fifteen minutes, and there are generally no objections); and the air force does the killing.[6]

Each targeted assassination is a large-scale operation that integrates hundreds of specialists from different military branches and security apparatuses. Beyond its reliance on background intelligence (much of it gathered in mass arrests and from Palestinians stopped at checkpoints), targeted assassination depends on sharing real-time information between various agents, commanders, operators, and different military planes and on their ability to act upon it. After a Palestinian is put on the death list, he is followed, sometimes for days, by a "swarm" of different kinds of unmanned aerial vehicles. Often, different swarms follow different people simultaneously in different areas of the Gaza Strip. In this way, the security services establish the targeted person's daily routines and habits and maintain continuous visual contact with him until his killing.[7] As well as being cheaper to operate, unmanned drones have the advantage over manned planes or helicopters because they can remain in the air around the clock, some for as long as thirty hours, and because their formations circulate in relatively small areas while providing a multiplicity of angles of vision. Moreover, drones are quiet and barely visible to the human eye. This is the reason that, beginning in 2004, the air force started to shoot its missiles from drones, rather than from its more visible battle helicopters. A swarm of various types of drones, each circulating at a different altitude, up to a height of 30,000 feet, is navigated by a GPS system and woven by radio communication into a single synergetic reconnaissance and killing instrument that conducts the entire assassination operation. Some drones are designed to view the terrain vertically in order to establish the digital coordinates of a targeted person, while others look diagonally in order to distinguish facial features or identify a vehicle's license plates. Some drones are designed to intercept radio signals and mobile phone transmissions, while others can carry and shoot missiles. With the development and proliferation of drone technology, "very few Israeli soldiers [are] in the airspace over Gaza," and "the air is mainly filled with Golems." It is "an army without soldiers."[8]

Airborne assassinations depend as well on other mechanisms within Israel's system of domination. Although targeted assassinations are explained as the alternative to collective punishment, to hardships imposed on the "uninvolved population," and to mass incarcerations, they are dependent on intelligence obtained in those mass incarcerations and interrogations. They rely, primarily in the West Bank, upon seducing Palestinians into collaboration in exchange for travel and work permits. The checkpoints themselves are part of Israel's "surveillance assemblages." In them, it is easy for the General Security Service to make contact with its informers without raising suspicions.

The clandestine Unit 504, jointly operated by military intelligence and the GSS, is responsible for the forced recruitment of Palestinians into collaboration. From one of its bases south of Haifa, where it also maintains Facility 1391, a Guantánamo Bay-style secret prison for "administrative detainees," Unit 504 trains groups of Palestinians to mark targets, plant and detonate bombs, or "shake the tree for the air force."[9] In previous years, members of this Palestinian military unit of the IDF would splash ultraviolet paint on the roof of a car to identify the target for a pilot to destroy.[10]

The missiles aim most often at a vehicle, but increasingly, and as Palestinians now often take the precaution to walk, also at pedestrians. Each assassination thus juxtaposes different spaces and domains: a control room in central Tel Aviv in which young soldiers navigate remotely piloted drones and missiles, as in a live computer game, into the narrow, dusty alleys of Gaza's refugee camps, where young Palestinians end their lives.

The IDF employs the sanitizing term "focused obstruction" or "focused pre-emption" (*SiKul memukad*) to describe these assassinations. Such rhetoric is repeated by most of the popular Israeli media, which conceals as far as possible the real impact of the killings, mostly avoiding mentioning the names of Palestinian civilians killed in Israeli attacks and the display of the corpses, blood, and body parts – the very images on which it lingers when covering the aftermath of a Palestinian terror attack. Indeed, the Israeli media's use of selective imagery allows it to project assassination not only as necessary, but also as ethical, rhetorically legalizing it by what Neve Gordon has called "the discursive production of a pseudo-judicial process."[11]

One of many counterpoints to these digitized visions of "precision" killing was provided by Aref Daraghmeh, a witness to an August 2002 targeted assassination in the village of Tubas in the West Bank, who has provided the following testimony for B'Tselem:

The helicopter . . . fired a third missile towards a silver Mitsubishi, which had four people in it. The missile hit the trunk and the car spun around its axis. I saw a man stepping out of the car and running away. He ran about 25 meters and then fell on the ground and died. The three other passengers remained inside. I saw an arm and an upper part of a skull flying out of the car. The car went up in flames and I could see three bodies burning inside it. Three minutes later, after the Israeli helicopters left, I went out to the street and began to shout. I saw people lying on the ground. Among them was six-year-old Bahira . . . She was dead . . . I also saw Bahira's cousin, Osama . . . I saw Osama's mother running towards Bahira, picking her up and heading towards the a-Shifa clinic, which is about 500 meters away. I went to the clinic and saw her screaming after seeing the body of her son, Osama.[12]

Operational planning

The operational aspect of airborne targeted assassinations relies on military developments that originated in Israel's war in Lebanon during the 1980s and 1990s. In February 1992, Hezbollah secretary-general Sheikh Abbas Mussawi was the first to be killed in an airborne assassination when a group of Israeli helicopters flying inland from the Mediterranean Sea attacked his convoy, killing him and his family. The first airborne targeted assassination in Palestinian areas took place on November 9, 2000, when an Israeli Apache helicopter pilot launched a U.S.-made Hellfire antitank missile at the car of a member of the Tanzim al-Fatah organization, Hussein Muhammad Abayit, in Beit-Sahur, near Bethlehem, killing him and two women, Rahmeh Shahin and 'Aziza Muhammed Danun, who happened to be walking by the car when it exploded in the middle of their street. The IDF's spokesperson announced that the killing was part of "a new state policy."[13] Since 2002, however, it has been Gaza that has become the world's largest laboratory for airborne assassinations.[14] The U.S. administration feebly protested Israeli assassinations, demanding through diplomatic channels that Israel merely "considers the results of its actions." Meanwhile, different branches of the U.S. security forces, themselves engaged in unacknowledged assassinations using unmanned drones, began to "examine Israeli Air Force's performances and results in order to draw lessons for its own wars."[15]

The planning and execution of these operations follows the principles of air force operational planning. The unit of "operational analysis" is part of the Israeli Air Force's "operational group" and is responsible, together with various intelligence agencies, for planning and optimizing bombing missions. There are three levels according to which bombing is planned: mechanical, systemic, and political.

At the mechanical level, planning is concerned with the matching of munitions with targets – calculating what size and what type of bomb is needed to destroy a particular target; what amount of explosives is needed to destroy a car, a building of a particular size, a tunnel, or a bunker. The mechanical level involves calculations by civil engineers and blast experts assessing the structure of the target and the quality of its construction. Military engineers then use a computer program to determine the munitions, attack angle, and time of day that will ensure the destruction of the target with the minimum use of munitions, destruction, and death to bystanders.

In the context of targeted assassinations, the mechanical level is concerned with the development of the warhead, the explosives used within it, and the accuracy of its delivery. Like the knife of the guillotine, the warhead and other innovations in the technologies of bombing aimed at making killing more efficient and "civilized" in fact enable its routine and frequent application. I will return to this point in a later part of the chapter. In this role – as the designer and employer of the knife of the guillotine – the unit of operational analysis has been criticized at least twice, once for the use of excessive force and once for excessive caution. The first case involved the decision, on July 23, 2002, to use a one-ton bomb to destroy a residential building in Gaza where the leader of Hamas' military wing, Salah Shehadeh, was spending the night, causing several buildings to collapse and killing Shehadeh and an additional fourteen Palestinian civilians, more than half of them children. In the second case, 2 years later, the operational analysis unit was criticized for allocating a quarter-ton bomb for the attack on a meeting of Hamas' leadership. The bomb failed to cause the collapse of the building, allowing the leaders to escape unharmed from the ground floor.

The second level of planning is the systemic. The function of the unit of operational analysis extends beyond the planning of physical destruction. It attempts to predict and map out the effect that the destruction of a particular target might have on the enemy's overall system of operation. Following the principles of "system analysis,"[16] the enemy is understood as an operational network of interacting elements. In air force targeting theories, cities, societies, and political regimes are vulnerable because of their reliance on networked infrastructures that sustain life. When translated to its war with the Palestinians, the killing of members of Palestinian organizations is similarly thought of in relation to a systemic logic. Unlike state militaries, much of whose power is grounded in physical infrastructure and equipment, in the case of the Palestinian resistance, the infrastructure of resistance is the people themselves.[17] The effectiveness of the Palestinian resistance is grounded in its people and in the efficiency of the relations between them: political and spiritual leaders, spokespersons, financiers, commanders, experienced fighters, bomb makers, and recruiters. The killing of a key individual is conceived in terms similar to the destruction of a command-and-control center or a strategic bridge. Both are intended to trigger a sequence of systemic "failures" that will disrupt the enemy's system, making it more vulnerable to further military action.[18] "Operational shock" is best achieved, according to the military and the GSS, when the rhythms of these operations is rapid and the enemy system is not given time to recover between attacks.[19]

The third level of planning is political. Aerial bombing has had a political dimension from the inception of air forces between World Wars I and II. In his 1921 *The Command of the Air*, the Italian Giulio Douhet recognized the effects of bombing on civilian and military morale. Air power could break a people's will by destroying a country's "vital centers," he argued. Douhet identified the six basic target types as industry, transport, infrastructure, communications, government, and "the will of the people." The first four are types of targets related to targeting military-systemic logic, while the last two could be attributed to political/psychological objectives. The political objective of targeting is to compel the enemy leadership to negotiate a surrender on the attacker's terms. Douhet was explicit about the fact that air war calls for the manipulation of civilian fear and suffering in order to achieve its political aims and that, according to these terms, an air war could be considered a terror war.[20] When considering the political rationality of targeting, the killing of the uninvolved civilians that the military calls "collateral damage" could no longer be simply considered as the by-product of the intention to hit military targets, but rather as the very aim of the bombing.

Often, the political logic of targeting is hidden behind military rhetoric that argues for the logic of bombing according to the first two levels of planning, the mechanical and systemic, which are considered legal according to international law. For example, in Israeli military announcements during the 2006 war between Israel and Hezbollah, Israeli targeting was explained according to a military logic: the destruction of airports, bridges, Hezbollah offices, launching sites, supply lines, infrastructure, and so on. It presented civilian casualties as the regrettable side effects of its attempts to hit military or dual-use targets. However, the destruction of homes and the killing and displacement of civilians was the main leverage of political pressure. This set of calculated acts has precedents in the logic of Israel's military interventions in Lebanon, which often aimed to manipulate differences and existing hostilities within Lebanon's complex social-political-ethnic fabric. The bombing in the 2006 war, according to Israeli speakers, aimed to turn the Lebanese populace against Hezbollah – a stratagem that was based on the assumption that a cold political calculus can triumph over vengeful rage in time of war. The creation of civilian casualties and their justification as "collateral damage" was part of an attempt to create a human catastrophe that could not be tolerated internationally and that would thus precipitate international intervention on Israel's terms. The bombing of Shiite towns and villages in the south was meant to force hundreds of thousands of civilians to flee northward toward Beirut. There, Israel hoped, their presence would put pressure on the government, who would in turn put pressure on the Hezbollah leadership to stop its military activities and disarm. Needless to say, these tactics led to crushing strategic failures. The refugees had neither the inclination nor the power to pressure the government in Lebanon or Hezbollah, and the bombings created nothing but public outrage and further support for Hezbollah.[21]

"Technology instead of occupation"

Perennial overoptimism regarding air power has led successive generations of airmen to believe that unprecedented technological developments would allow wars to be won from the air, with bombing to intimidate politicians into submission and native populations managed by air power. The role of this new technology was to reduce uncertainty and increase control. The fantasy of a cheap aerial occupation, or "aerially enforced colonization," is as old as air forces themselves. In the 1920s, Winston Churchill, as minister of war and air, was fascinated with what he perceived to be the economically efficient, quick, clean, mechanical, and impersonal alternatives that air power could provide to the otherwise onerous and expensive tasks of colonial control. Emboldened by a murderous aerial attack on a tribal leader in Somaliland in 1920 that put down a rebellion, he suggested that aircraft be further adapted to the tasks of policing the Empire. In 1922, Churchill persuaded the British government to invest in the air force and offered the Royal Air Force £6 million to take over control of the Mesopotamia (Iraq) operation from the army, which had cost £18 million thus far.[22] The policy, called "control without occupation," saw the RAF successfully replacing large and expensive army contingents. Sir Percy Cox, the high commissioner in Baghdad, reported that, by the end of 1922,

> on [at least] three occasions demonstrations by aircraft [have been sufficient to bring] tribal feuds to an end. On another occasion planes . . . dropped bombs on a sheik and his followers who refused to pay taxes, held up travellers and attacked a police station."[23]

Arthur "Bomber" Harris (so called after his infamous bombing campaigns on German working-class districts when commander of the RAF's bomber wing during World War II) reported after a mission in Iraq in 1924: "The Arab and Kurd now know what real bombing means, in casualties and damage. They know that within 45 minutes a full-sized village can be practically wiped out and a third of its inhabitants killed or injured."[24] The methods pioneered in Somaliland were also applied by the RAF against revolutionaries in Egypt, Darfur, India, Palestine (mainly during the 1936–9 Arab revolt),[25] and Afghanistan's Jalalabad and Kabul. Anticipating the logic of targeted assassinations, Harris later boasted that the Third Afghan War was won by a single strike on the king's palace.[26]

Similar belief in "aerially enforced occupation" allowed the Israeli Air Force to attempt to replace the network of lookout outposts woven through the topography of the terrain by translating categories of "depth," "stronghold," "high point," "closure," and "panorama" into "air defense in depth," "clear skies," "aerial reconnaissance," "aerially enforced closure," and "panoramic radar." With a "vacuum cleaner" approach to intelligence gathering, sensors aboard unmanned drones, aerial reconnaissance jets, attack helicopters, unmanned balloons, early-warning Hawkeye planes, and military satellites capture most signals out of Palestinian airspace. Since the beginning of the second intifada, the air force has put in hundreds of thousands of flight hours, harvesting a stream of information through its network of airborne reconnaissance platforms, information that was later put at the disposal of different intelligence agencies and command-and-control rooms.

Distinctions must be maintained, however, between the kind of operation that the IDF conducts in Gaza (ever more so after the "evacuation") and those in the West Bank. The degrees of violence that Israel employs in Gaza greatly exceed the levels of violence employed in the West Bank. These differences in military approach are shaped by differences in degrees of control over the territory and the population. In the West Bank, Israel has a massive civilian presence of about half a million settlers and soldiers and an extensive ground military presence, whereas even before the evacuation Gaza was always considered a territory that it is hard for ground troops to enter. Whereas Israeli soldiers have broken into all Palestinian cities, villages, and refugee camps in the West Bank again and again, they have done so much less often in the larger and more impoverished refugee camps of Gaza. The evacuation of Gaza sharpened this tendency, and the strip was thereafter controlled primarily from the air, but also from the territorial waters off its coastline and through border terminals along its fences.

In the West Bank, as its former chief commander, Yair Golan, mentioned in 2007, the military seeks to maintain a constant degree of "effective friction" for both operational and intelligence purposes, bringing the Palestinian civilian population into constant contact with Israeli soldiers and other security personnel.[27] The tactics of constant friction are maintained by the presence of settlements, roadblocks, checkpoints, and military offices for civilian administration. They control the population by constant harassment, as well as by modulating the flows of various kinds: people, goods, and services. Aerial assassinations in the West Bank have indeed ceased after Operation Defensive Shield on April 2002, when the IDF destroyed organized Palestinian police and military forces, as well as many government offices, and reinstated complete ground control over Palestinian population centers. Since the end of 2002, assassinations in the West Bank have been undertaken from the ground, many of them under the pretext of arrest operations. According to figures released by B'Tselem, between 2004 and May 2006, Israeli security forces killed 157 people during operations referred to as "arrest operations."[28] The most common justification for IDF killings conducted during ground raids in the West Bank is that the victim "violently attempted to resist arrest," but ground forces do not always allow militants to surrender and often try to steer them away from it.

The legal framework for targeted assassinations has developed in response to the pace of events. Immediately after the start of the second intifada, the head of the IDF's International Law Department, Colonel Daniel Reisner, stated that, because of the heightened level and frequency of Palestinian violence, Israel could start defining its military operations in the Occupied Territories as an "armed conflict short of war," which placed the intifada in the context of international law, rather than criminal law.[29] Such a definition implied that, for the purpose of their killing (but not their internment), members of militant Palestinian organizations could be seen as combatants and thus attacked at will, not only when in the process of a hostile action or while resisting arrest.[30] Given that, in international law, distinctions between "inside" and "outside" regulate the logic of security operations ("internal" operations are perceived as policing or security work; "external" ones as military) and that the definition of "inside" depends upon whether a state has "effective control" over the territory in question,[31] the evacuation of the Gaza Strip strengthened Israel's conviction that targeted assassinations are legal and has made their use more frequent. Politically, Israel expected that once it had evacuated the settlements and had retreated to the international border around Gaza, the international community would be more tolerant of these forms of military action.[32] This implies that the tactics of airborne assassinations have developed in response to the Israeli military ceding territorial control, or otherwise that the evacuation could be thought of as a means to facilitate the continuation of assassinations.

Indeed, the tactical precondition for Israel's policy of territorial withdrawal was that its security services be able to maintain domination of the evacuated areas by means other than territorial control. The members of an IDF think tank called the Alternative Team involved in rethinking Israeli security after the evacuation of Gaza admitted: "Whether or not we are physically present in the territories, we should still be able to demonstrate our ability to control and affect them."[33] The occupation that they conceived to follow the supposed end of the occupation – that is, the domination of Palestinians after the evacuation of the ground space of the Gaza Strip and parts of the West Bank is completed – was alternately referred to by these and other military planners as the "invisible occupation," the "airborne occupation," or "occupation in disappearance."[34]

The ability of the Israeli Air Force to maintain a constant "surveillance and strike" capability over Palestinian areas was one of the main reasons for the Sharon government's confidence in and popular support for unilateral ground withdrawals and for accordingly transforming the logic of occupation. Sharon's sacking of Chief of Staff Moshe Ya'alon and his replacement with the pilot and former air force commander Dan Halutz several months before the ground evacuation of Gaza testified to the perceived offset of military emphasis from the ground to the air and to the Israeli government's acceptance of Halutz's mantra "technology instead of occupation."[35] Halutz, as head of the air force, supervised almost 100 operations of targeted assassinations. Until the result of the 2006 war in Lebanon made him realize otherwise, he was known as the strongest proponent of the claim that air power can gradually replace many of the traditional functions of ground forces. In a lecture he delivered at the military's National Security College in 2001, he explained that "the capability of the air force today renders some traditional assumptions – that victory equals territory – anachronistic,"[36] and he even suggested that any subsequent war in Lebanon could be won from the air. "Why do you need to endanger infantry soldiers?" he asked. "I can resolve the entire Lebanon [situation] from the air in 3 to 5 days – a week, maximum."[37] The approach that Halutz promoted was drafted in a military publication that was handed out to members of the senior staff in April 2006, 2 months before the second Lebanon war, explaining that, in future conflicts, new military technology would allow for the transformation of warfare from conflicts based on manoeuvres to conflicts based on "standoff capacity, precise fire and the deadly effects of invisible forces, without the need to resort to occupation and with minimum friction with the enemy and the civilian population." The publication further emphasizes the importance of generating an "effect" on the enemy's leadership, either by searing their consciousness or by their "decapitation."[38]

Although previously the IDF would cordon off an area with fences and earth dikes and place checkpoints on the approach roads, the airborne occupation of Gaza enforces its closures by leafleting villages and refugee camps around the area to be shut off, declaring it off-limits and then targeting whoever tries to enter. In this manner, the evacuated settlements of the northern part of Gaza have remained under closure ever since the 2005 evacuation. Following the evacuation, a procedure, codenamed "A Knock on the Door," replaced military bulldozers with bomber jets for the purpose of demolishing houses. This new method involves an air force operator telephoning the house to be demolished, as happened at the a-Rahman family home in Jabalia refugee camp. On Thursday August 26, 2006, at 11:30.24 in the evening, someone called the telephone at the house of Abed a-Rahman in Jabalia, claiming to be from the IDF.

> The phone had been disconnected because the bill had not been paid to the Palestinian phone company, but was activated for the sake of this conversation. The wife of Abed a-Rahman, Um-Salem, answered the phone . . . [On the other side of the line, a voice] said "evacuate the house immediately and notify the neighbors." She asked "who is talking?" and was answered: the IDF. She asked again, but her interlocutor had hung up. Um-Salem tried to use the phone, but it was disconnected again . . . the entire family left the house without having the possibility to take anything with them. At 24:00, the house was bombed by military helicopters and was completely destroyed.[39]

This shows that the "evacuation" thus could not be thought of as an act of decolonization, but rather as the reorganization of state power and control and the enactment of a technocolonial rule.

The politics of killing

For targeted assassinations to assume the preeminence that they have among all other Israeli techniques of domination, they have had to rely upon not only the maturing of operational and technological developments, but also legal and popular support. When all these components were put in place, less than a year after the beginning of the intifada, and with successful assassinations carried out routinely since then, the appetite for assassinations has grown. A central factor helping maintain a high level of popular support for targeted assassinations was the daily terror alerts that the GSS under Avi Dichter routinely released. Their average during the height of the intifada, from 2001 to 2003, was between forty and fifty a day, and Israeli popular public support for targeted assassination, which seemed not only a response, but also a suitable revenge, stood at about 80 percent.[40] In government meetings called to authorize the attacks, Sharon's enthusiasm for successful attacks encouraged the GSS and the military to pursue such operations with greater vigor. Given the high level of Israeli public support for targeted assassinations, no government minister could afford to let slip his or her opposition to the policy or to the timing of a particular assassination as recommended by the GSS, less it be leaked to the media.

The partial relinquishment of control and the selective absence of government from these decisions brought about the growing autonomy of the security services, which started leading the pace of events. With targeted assassination, security operatives thus filled the political vacuum of the intifada years, dictating developments on the ground. From their own perspective, the GSS and the military believed that targeted assassinations provided the government with "military

solutions to situations that were thought of as militarily unsolvable." As the inti-
fadah wore on, an obsession with assassination gripped the entire Israeli security
system, so much so that in a 2002 meeting called to discuss the assassination of
several Palestinian leaders, a military officer suggested conducting one killing
every day as a matter of policy. The minister of defense thought it was "indeed
an idea," and Sharon seemed excited, but the GSS recommended that the idea be
dropped, because it was supposed to be for the GSS, not the military, to decide
where and when Palestinians should be killed. (At that point, in any case, killings
were already being carried out at an average rate of one every 5 days.)[41] The
military and the GSS, confident of their ability to hit anybody, anywhere, at any
time, started publishing in advance the names of those to be killed.[42] According
to a June 2003 statement by then chief of staff Yaalefalon, targeted assassinations
became the continuation of politics by other means. "Liquidations," he claimed,
"gave the political levels a tool to create a change of direction."[43]

The effects of targeted assassination on political developments were varied.
One of its effects was assuring that no diplomatic process "forced" on Israel could
occur. Whenever a political initiative, local or international, seemed to be emerging, threatening to return the parties to the negotiating table, an assassination
followed and derailed it. Until the opening of government and GSS archives, it
would be hard to establish this intention beyond a doubt, but the following examples demonstrate a clear pattern of action whose intention is the radicalization of
conflict when its level could be subdued. On July 31, 2001, the Israeli Air Force
bombed an apartment building in Nablus in which a Hamas office was located,
killing two Hamas leaders, Jamal Mansour and Jamal Salim, and two boys,
bringing to an end a nearly 2-month-long Hamas ceasefire. The January 2002
killing of Rahamzaad Karmi, a leader in Fatah's own militant group, al-Tanzim,
in the preparation of which the GSS has already invested millions of shekels,
was not prevented, although the killing was certain to bring about the collapse
of a ceasefire that started in December 2001 and to bury an American diplomatic initiative. The assassination led to the spate of Palestinian suicide attacks
of February and March 2002. On July 23, 2002, a day before al-Tanzim was to
announce a unilateral ceasefire, Salah Shehadeh was assassinated, foreclosing
this development. A year later, at the beginning of the summer of 2003, another
type of ceasefire, a *hudna*, or tactical truce, was declared, and another American
diplomatic initiative was launched. As it was being formulated, on June 10, 2003,
the military attempted to assassinate Abdul Aziz Rantisi, a political leader. A few
weeks later, Israeli security forces targeted al-Tanzim militant Mahmoud Shawer
in Qalqiliyah, derailing the initiative completely. On December 1, 2003, the same
day that the Geneva Initiative was launched, the IDF conducted a massive operation attempting to kill Sheikh Ibrahim Hamed, head of Hamas in Ramallah. In
June 2006, just as Mahmoud Abbas was about to declare a referendum vote on
a progressive political initiative of the "prisoners' document,"[44] Israel targeted
Jamal Abu Samhadana, the commander of the Popular Resistance Committees
in Gaza, and the idea for the referendum was cancelled.

From the very start of the intifada, Palestinian political leaders were targets of
assassinations. At the end of August 2003, government authorization was given to

kill the entire political leadership of Hamas in Gaza without further notice. A place on the assassination list was assured, according to Israeli speakers, to anyone who had crossed the threshold of being involved in planning terror attacks, but, in fact, the entire political wing of Hamas was placed on it, regardless of whether or not the target was directly involved in operational planning. The method was referred to as opening the "hunting season" – the first leader to reveal himself would be the first to be killed. The stated intention was to weaken Hamas, which led to armed resistance against Israeli settlers, civilians, and the military and reinforced Fatah's position in the Gaza Strip. The first one to be killed under these instructions was Ismail Abu Shanab, a relatively moderate political leader of Hamas who was targeted on August 21, 2003. On March 22, 2004, Israel assassinated the spiritual leader of Hamas, Sheikh Ahmed Yassin. A month later, on April 17, 2004, Yassin's successor, Abd al-Aziz Rantissi was killed. Dichter explained that the reason for these assassinations was to strengthen the position of Abbas and the moderates in the "Palestinian street." At the beginning of 2006, when the "moderates" were ousted by the newly elected Hamas government, Defense Minister Shaul Mofaz repeated the warning, promising that "no one will be immune," including the Palestinian prime minister, Ismail Haniyeh.[45] The logic behind these "decapitations" assumed that new leaders would not be as experienced as those killed and that the relative power of their organizations within the field of Palestinian politics would thus decline. "Killing," according to Shimon Naveh in a telephone interview, "injects energy into the enemy system, disrupting its institutional hierarchies." Although, as Naveh has said, "there can be no precise prediction of the outcome of these killings," the effect, according to the IDF, is a degree of institutional and political chaos that allows Israeli security forces to sit back and see "how the cards fall."

Not only assassination, but also its suspension, is being used as a weapon. Suspended credible threats of killing generate political effects regardless of the actual assassination taking place. The practical confirmation of this principle was paradoxically pronounced with its cancellation. In July 2007, as part of a package of gestures that the Israeli government "granted" to the Palestinian government of Mahmoud Abbas, Israel announced not only the release of Fatah prisoners (so that they fight Hamas in the West Bank), but pardons as well for other activists who were on its target list. The IDF and the GSS offered, under certain conditions that included travel restrictions, to remove from these lists a number of Fatah activists and announced that they would not further pursue attempts for their arrest or assassination. The enthusiastic acceptance by these wanted Palestinians of the conditions imposed by the Israeli security forces demonstrated the pressure that Palestinian militants felt being on Israel's death lists. At several other points during the intifada, Israel's suspension of targeted assassinations was itself used as an incentive to reach a ceasefire on Israel's term.

"Radical" Palestinian leaders could be assassinated to open the way for a more "pragmatic" politics. "Pragmatic" leaders could be assassinated in order to open the way for direct confrontation or to stave off a diplomatic initiative. Other assassinations could have been undertaken in order to "restore order," others still to "create chaos"; some assassinations would be undertaken simply because they could be undertaken and because no one happened to intervene to stop the assassination machine. Theorizing about the political effects of targeted assassinations has thus become almost an industry unto itself, heavily populated with intelligence analysts, game theorists, and other statistically oriented behavioral scientists –many of whom seem addicted to a jargon that is aimed at making unthinkable state behavior appear intelligent, responsible, rational, and inevitable.

A considerable part of Israel's security logic of assassination is grounded in the bias of Israel's intelligence agencies toward personality analysis. The Israeli sociologist Gil Eyal demonstrated that, following a long Orientalist tradition, the Israeli intelligence services have tended to seek motives for political developments, as well as for terror attacks, not in responses to a history of repression or in pursuit of rational political goals, but in the personal irrationalities, idiosyncrasies, and inconsistencies of Arab leaders.[46] When undertaken, political and economic analysis generally has provided no more than a context for the work of psychological profiling.[47] The natural consequence of this logic has been the belief that, in killing, Israel's security services remove not only a leader, but also the cause of a political or security problem. Understanding of the resistance to the occupation, in turn, has similarly been bound up with a focus on certain key figures, while the causes behind it have been ignored.

Although so much effort has been put into modeling enemy behavior, and the security services remain confident in their methods, years of targeted assassinations have not managed to limit violence, nor have they reduced Palestinian motivations for resistance, or strengthened President Mahmoud Abbas, or reinforced "the moderates in the Palestinian street." On the contrary, assassinations have fed the conflict by seeding terror, uncertainty, and rage and by promoting social chaos, creating further motivations for violent retaliations and dramatically increasing Palestinian popular support for acts of terror.

Assassinations thus have contributed to the actual emergence of the threat they were purportedly there to pre-empt. In this respect, Israel's security organizations have not "restored order," but have been acting instead as the agents of chaos. Israeli order is preserved by the systematic destruction of Palestinian order.

The power of targeted assassinations to affect politics has been most strongly felt within the Israeli political system itself. In the half year from the beginning of 2004, when the political debates regarding the evacuation of Gaza settlements began, to June 6, 2004, when the "disengagement plan" came to a vote and was authorized by the Israeli government, targeted assassinations were accelerated, leading to the death of thirty-three Palestinians. In anticipation of the evacuation operation itself, scheduled for August 2005, the level of assassinations increased again, with July 2005 being the bloodiest of that year. This bloodshed helped Sharon present himself as "tough on terror" while pursuing a policy that was understood in Israel as left leaning. In this manner, targeted assassinations and the supposed ability of the Israeli Air Force to maintain a constant "surveillance and strike" capability over Palestinian areas paradoxically increased the support for "territorial compromise" embodied in the ground evacuation of Gaza.

The "humanitarian" war

The policy of targeted assassination continuously interacted with domestic and international criticism of it to the effect of generating technological and procedural innovations that purportedly aimed at its self-moderation and at reducing the death of bystanders. The transformation in the procedures and technology of airborne assassinations accelerated after the protests that followed the death and destruction caused by the 2002 attack on Salah Shehade and increased significantly following the announced refusal of several Israeli Air Force Reserve pilots to take part in such missions if called to do so.[48] On the one hand, the security forces sought to improve legal arguments and moral justifications for the assassinations, and on the other, they sought to improve the precision of intelligence and attacks so that fewer bystanders would get hurt. The first approach was exemplified by an IDF invitation to Asa Kasher, a distinguished professor of philosophy at Tel Aviv University, to provide an ordered ethical defense for targeted assassinations. The resulting "principles of military ethics in fighting terror," developed with a team of officers of the IDF's College of National Defense, exemplified the intersection of military efficiency with ethical considerations. It emphasized the standard of self-defense and outlined the military's obligation to reduce the level of civilian casualties. Assassinations were argued for not as retribution for acts of terror already committed, but as responses to the *potential* of future threats. Unlike acts deemed illegal under criminal law, airborne executions should be considered legal (and moral) if responding not to what a person has done, but to what he may do. The document has been approved by the chief of staff and accepted as the basis for IDF standard ethical reference for these attacks.[49] Around the same time, the air force began to employ operatives whose task was to minimize "collateral deaths." Using cameras on auxiliary drones, they observed the surrounding context of an impending attack in order to judge the "safest" moment to launch missiles. These specialists have effectively become the "trigger" of the operation, deciding to what level of danger Palestinian bystanders can be acceptably subjected. As one of these operators explained to me, they see their work not as facilitating assassinations, but as saving lives, minimizing the slaughter that would undoubtedly have occurred were they not there to maintain vigilance.[50] I will later return to this line of justification.

Three years later, responding to the widespread condemnation of a March 2006 attack that killed a man and two children, the chief of the air force, Eliezer Shakedy, called a press conference at which he claimed that the air force makes "superhuman efforts in order to reduce the number of innocent civilian casualties in aerial strikes."[51] To prove his claims, he projected charts that numerically "demonstrated" how the air force had reduced the ratio between the victims of aerial raids that it defined as "combatants" and those victims it was willing to concede were "noncombatants" or "uninvolved civilians" – from the death of one "uninvolved person" for every target of assassination in 2002 to one civilian death for every twenty-five targets killed in 2005, he claimed.[52] Data collected by the Israeli human rights organization B'Tselem show that the military figures were skewed – largely because the military included within the definition of "combatants" any adult man who happened to be in the vicinity of the assassination,[53] but even according to their own and to Palestinian studies the number of "noncombatant" victims has radically decreased.

The change was due both to technological innovations in the warhead and the missile system and to a change in the command and regulation of these attacks. Most technological developments related to the *mechanical* level of the attacks – the design of the warhead. As part of its attempt to reduce unintended casualties, Israel's Armament Development Authority, Rafael, developed the Spike missile to replace the U.S.-made Hellfire – a laser-guided antitank missile – for the purpose of targeted assassinations. The Spike is itself a small, joystick-navigated "kamikaze" drone with an "optical HEAD."[54] Rafael also developed the Firefly, a missile with an even smaller warhead.[55] Clips from the "kamikaze" cameras on "smart missiles" and from other airborne sensors were routinely broadcast in the popular media to support IDF refutations of Palestinian accusations of indiscriminate killing and to focus political and public resolve for the further application of this tactic. The images and videos from these munitions are thus as much a media product as they are "operation footage."[56]

In the summer of 2006, a new type of explosive started to be used in missiles fired in targeted assassinations. That new munitions were used became apparent when doctors in Gaza hospitals started receiving Palestinian victims with horrifying burn wounds, amputations, and internal burns never seen before. A former Israeli Air Force officer and head of the IDF's weapons development program, Yitzhak Ben-Israel, explained that these new munitions – referred to as "focused lethality munitions" or "munitions of low collateral damage" – were designed to produce a blast more lethal but also of smaller radius than traditional explosives. "This technology allows [the military] to strike very small targets . . . without causing damage to bystanders or other persons." Medical and forensic research led an independent Italian investigative team to believe that these munitions were dense inert metal explosives, or DIMEs.[57]

At the end of November 2006, again in response to local and international protests regarding the killing of civilians, the Israeli government wanted to demonstrate that it was acting to regulate targeted assassinations further. It established a "legal committee" to rule on the assassination of individuals, with the assassination of senior political leaders subjected to the opinion of the attorney general. A few weeks later, on December 14, 2006, in response to petitions by the Public Committee against Torture in Israel and the Palestinian Society for the Protection of Human Rights and the Environment (known by its Arabic acronym, LAW), the Israeli High Court of Justice issued a ruling in which other regulatory directives were outlined: assassinations could take place only when there is "well-founded, strong and persuasive information as to the identity [of the person assassinated] and his activity"; if they could help curtail terror attacks; if other, more moderate uses of force, such as arrest, cannot take place without gravely endangering the lives of soldiers; and if the assassination does not lead to "disproportionate collateral harm to innocent civilians."[58]

Whether or not these measures have reduced and will reduce the deaths of bystanders in targeted assassinations, a critical perspective cannot allow this possible outcome to exonerate the act. Instead, it must contend with the *nature* of the claims that these and other military developments in the technology, techniques, and proficiency of targeted assassination will eventually bring about fewer unintended deaths. Otherwise, one would have to accept the Israeli terms of a necroeconomy in which a "lesser evil" or "lesser evils," represented by a lower body count, should be measured against an imaginary or real, present or future "greater evil" in the form of more suffering and death on both sides.[59]

The problem of the "lesser evil" presents itself as the necessity for a choice of action in situations where the available options seem to be limited. The condition by which choice presents itself affirms an economic model embedded at the heart of ethics according to which various forms of suffering can be calculated (as if they were algorithms in mathematical minimum problems), evaluated, and acted upon. The articulation of the dilemma of the "lesser evil" has its origin in the classical philosophy of ethics and in theology and has been invoked in a staggeringly diverse set of contexts—from individual situational ethics through political choices to international relations. Significantly, it has recently been prominently invoked in the context of attempts to govern the economics of violence in the context of the "war on terror" and to moderate the power of brutal regimes, but also in maneuvering through the paradoxes and complicities of human rights and humanitarian aid.

In relation to the "global war on terror," the terms of this argument were recently articulated by the human rights scholar and now deputy leader of the Liberal Party of Canada, Michael Ignatieff. Ignatieff claims that, in the "war on terror," democratic societies may need to establish state mechanisms that would regulate the breach of some rights and allow their security services to engage in other covert and unsavory state actions – in his eyes, a "lesser evil" – in order to fend off or to minimize potential "greater evils" such as terror attacks.[60] Ignatieff is even willing to consider Israeli targeted assassinations under conditions similar to those articulated by the Israeli High Court of Justice as "qualifying within the effective moral-political framework of the lesser evil."[61] For Alan Dershowitz, one of the most vocal apologists for Israel in the United States, "targeted assassination [is] the polar opposite of collective punishment" and is therefore not only legal, but, under the conditions stated above, also ethical.[62]

In the terms of this necroeconomy, targeted assassinations are to be understood as the "lesser evil" alternative to possible greater evils that could occur to Israelis, but that could occur as well to the Palestinians themselves. Israel, which undertakes these operations, would like Palestinians to understand that, beyond protecting its own population, the use of targeted assassinations helps it restrain more brutal measures that would affect the entire Palestinian population, with targeted assassinations killing only – or mostly – those "guilty." According to former chief of staff Yaalefalon, "focused obstructions are important because they [communicate to the Palestinians that we] make a distinction between the general public and the instigator of terror."[63] As I mentioned above, however, the intelligence necessary for targeted assassinations relies on "collective measures" such as mass arrests and the checkpoint/terminal system.

However, as Adi Ophir has suggested, this conception of the "lesser evil" is problematic even according to the terms of its own proposed economy. The economy of violence assumes the possibility of a lesser means and the risk of more violence, but questions of violence are forever unpredictable. The supposed "lesser evil" may always be more violent than the violence it opposes, and there can be no end to the challenges that stem from the impossibility of calculation. A less brutal measure is also a measure that may easily be naturalized, accepted, and tolerated.[64] When exceptional means are normalized, they can be more frequently applied. Elevating targeted assassinations into a legally and morally acceptable practice makes them part of the state's legal options, part of a list of counter-terrorism techniques, with all sense of horror lost. Because they help normalize low-intensity conflict, the overall duration of this conflict can be extended, and, finally, more "lesser evils" can be committed, with the result that the greater evil is reached cumulatively. "Lesser evils" can thus bring about greater evils, even according to the very economy they invoke.

However, because "lesser evil" arguments measure and compromise only Palestinian life and rights for the sake of Israeli security, which stands as a nonnegotiable or measured value, they cannot be understood as properly moral arguments and should simply be understood according to the Israeli utilitarian logic of warfare, its efficiency, and the way it is mediated locally and internation-ally. Cases of colonial powers seeking to justify themselves with the rhetoric of improvement, civility, and reform are almost the constant of colonial history.

An analogous phenomenon that can help clarify the paradox of the "lesser evil" can be observed in the IDF's use of rubber-coated steel munitions. Soldiers believe that "rubber bullets" are nonlethal munitions and that their use demon-strates restraint in situations that are not life-threatening. But this perception leads to their more frequent and indiscriminate use, causing death and permanent injury to many Palestinian demonstrators, mainly children.[65] Similarly, the purported military ability to perform "controlled," "elegant," "pinhead accurate," and "discriminate" killing can bring about more destruction and death than "tradi-tional" strategies do, because these methods, combined with the manipulative and euphoric rhetoric used to promulgate them, induce decision makers to authorize their frequent and extended use. The illusion of precision, here part of a rhetoric of restraint, gives the military–political apparatus the necessary justification to use explosives in civilian environments where they could not be used without injuring or killing civilians. The lower the threshold of violence that a certain means is believed to possess, the more frequent its application tends to become.

The "lesser evil" approach that has sought to moderate Israel's war on the Palestinians and to normalize Israeli control led the IDF to inaugurate, in the middle of 2003, the program Another Life, whose aim was to "minimize the damage to the Palestinian life fabric in order to avoid the humanitarian crisis that will necessitate the IDF to completely take over the provision of food and services to the Palestinian population."[66] This program has turned "humanitarianism" into a strategic category in Israeli military operations and has influenced the design of its various instruments of control. Indeed, "humanitarian" has become the most common buzzword in various matters of occupation design, with the designation of "humanitarian gates," "humanitarian terminals," "humanitarian technology," and "humanitarian awareness," as well as – according to a procedure already put in effect since the beginning of the intifada – a "humanitarian officer" (usually a middle-aged reserve soldier) employed in checkpoints to smooth the process of passage and to mediate between the needs of Palestinians and the orders of soldiers.

The paradox of the lesser evil further affects most practitioners who operate the various systems in the ecology of the occupation: the army commander who, according to international law, is responsible for the territories under his domination and who attempts to administer Palestinian life (and death) in an enlightened manner; the security agents who introduce new spatiotechnological means of domination (arguing for them as more humane) and who generate new types of powers; the Palestinian civilian who is the subject of this regime, sometimes assisted by human rights organizations and lawyers, lodging petitions challenging the legality of those means and powers; the human rights lawyer and campaigner who represents the struggle for human rights and civil liberties in those territories, but who affirms the logic of the system; the humanitarian agent providing life-sustaining substances and medical help and who thus sustains the occupation; the Palestinian administrator, the politicians, the intellectuals – and so on.

In regard to the latter, Israel's system of domination has learned to use the work of Palestinian, international, and Israeli organizations to fill the void left by a dysfunctional Palestinian Authority and to manage life in the Occupied Palestinian Territories. In spite of the fundamental moral differences between these groups, the logic of the lesser evil allows for moments of cooperation between organizations whose stated aims are widely different. Indeed, the urgent and important criticism that peace organizations often level at the IDF to the effect that it is dehumanizing its enemies masks another, more dangerous process by which the military incorporates into its operations the logic of, and even seeks to cooperate directly with, the very humanitarian and human rights organizations that oppose it. Israeli theorist Ariella Azoulay has claimed that, although it has brought the Occupied Territories to the verge of hunger, the Israeli government tries to control the flow of traffic, money, and aid in such a way as to prevent the situation reaching a point of total collapse because of the international intervention, possibly under a UN mandate, that might follow.[67]

It is in this "pragmatic" approach that the principle of the "lesser evil" justifies and naturalizes crimes and other forms of injustice and masks political responsibilities. By accepting the necessity to choose the "lesser evil," oppositional and advocacy groups accept the validity of the systems that have imposed these choices, blocking possible ways to struggle against and refute the logic and validity of the governmental rationality that grounds them. Writing about the collaboration and cooperation of ordinary Germans with the Nazi regime, mainly by those employed in the civil service (but also by the Jewish councils set up by the Nazis), Hannah Arendt explained that the argument for the "lesser evil" had become one of the most important "mechanisms built into the machinery of terror and crimes." She explained that "acceptance of lesser evils [has been] consciously used in conditioning the government officials as well as the population at large to the acceptance of evil as such," to the degree that "those who choose the lesser evil forget very quickly that they chose evil." She further claimed that, even for the practical consequences, it is always better if enough people refuse to partici-pate in criminal state behavior, rather than engage in moderating it.[68]

Against all those who stayed in Germany to make things better from within, against all acts of collaboration, especially those undertaken for the sake of the moderation of harm, against the argument that the "lesser evil" of collaboration with brutal regimes is acceptable if it might prevent or divert greater evils, she called for individual disobedience and collective disorder. Participation, she insisted, communicated consent; moreover, it handed support to the oppressor. When nothing else was possible, to do nothing was the last effective form of resistance, and the practical consequences of refusal were nearly always better if enough people refused. In her essay "The Eggs Speak Up," a sarcastic refer-ence to Stalin's dictum that "you can't make an omelet without breaking a few eggs," Arendt pleaded for "a radical negation of the whole concept of lesser evil in politics."[69]

The moral principle of the "lesser evil" could be discerned in the legal category of "proportionality" employed by the High Court of Justice when it was called to rule on matters relating to "security" and "human rights" considerations in the context of the occupation. According to the principle of "proportionality," the state must weigh its alternative security measures in a way that balances security needs against the livelihood of the Palestinian inhabitants. Because of the constant international criticism of the occupation, it is always in the interest of the state to moderate its violence and take into account the "humanitarian issues" arising from occupation, thereby deflecting attention from the fundamental illegitimacy of the entire project. Although it often has seemed as if the Israeli High Court of Justice has adopted a profoundly adversarial position toward the government, by moderating the attitudes of the military and "balancing" rights against security, the court has effectively taken part in the very logic by which the occupation works.[70]

Furthermore, when, in the aftermath of the court's rulings, the military itself began using the vocabulary of international law, principles such as "proportional-ity" started to become compatible with military goals such as "efficiency," helping make military action more economical. In this sense, the "lesser evil" argument relates to the discursive nature of warfare and especially to the discursive nature of low-intensity war.

Military threats can function only if gaps are maintained between the *possible* destruction that an army can inflict in the application of its full destructive capac-ity and the *actual* destruction that it does inflict. Restraint is what allows for the possibility of further escalation.[71] A degree of restraint is thus part of the logic of almost every conventional military operation: however bad military attacks may appear to be, they could always get worse. At the moment when this gap between the possible and the actual application of force closes, war is no longer a language, and violence is stripped of semiotics and simply aims to make the enemy disappear as a subject.[72]

The promoters of the instruments, techniques, and rhetoric supporting such "lesser evils" believe that, by developing and perfecting them, they actually exercise a restraining effect on the government and on the rest of the security forces, which would otherwise succeed in pushing for the further radicalization of violence, and that targeted assassinations are the more moderate alternative to the devastating capacity for destruction that the military actually possesses and would unleash in the form of a full-scale invasion or the renewal of territorial occupation, should the enemy exceed an "acceptable" level of violence or breach some unspoken agreement in the violent discourse of attacks and retaliations. Confirming this logic, only a few weeks before the June 2006 invasion of Gaza, air force chief Shakedy, arguing for targeted assassinations, explained that "the only alternative to aerial attacks is a ground operation and the reoccupation" and that targeted assassination "is the most precise tool we have."[73]

The reoccupation of Gaza starting in June 2006 and the Lebanon war of July–August 2006 demonstrated that more destructive alternatives are always possible, especially when the "unwritten rules" of low-intensity conflict are perceived to have been broken. From the June 28 kidnapping of an Israeli soldier in Gaza until December 2006, over 500 Palestinians were killed, including eighty-eight minors, and more than 2,700 injured.[74] In total, $46 million worth of infrastructure, including a power plant, and 270 private houses and residences, was destroyed. This should be understood as an eruption of violence meant to sustain the threat of greater measures. In terms of their justification, targeted assassinations thus exist at the middle of the spectrum between war and peace.

Naturally, I am not suggesting that "greater evils" should be preferred to lesser ones or that wars should be more brutal. Rather, I am suggesting that we question the very terms of the economy of evils, the system that has presented to us its choice as inevitable.

The dilemma, if we are still to think in its terms, should thus be not only about which of the bad options to choose, but also whether to choose at all and thus accept the very terms of the question. When asked to choose between the two horns of an angry bull, Robert Pirsig suggested alternatives: one can "refuse to enter the arena," "throw sand in the bull's eyes," or even "sing the bull to sleep."[75] The positioning of the lesser-evil dilemma is integral to political militarism – a culture that sees violence as a permanent rule of history and thus military contingencies as the principal alternative available to politicians. Israeli militarism accordingly always has sought military solutions to political problems.[76]

Locked within the limits defined by the degrees of violence, Israel continually forecloses the exploration of other avenues for negotiations and participation in a genuine political process. In an interview at the beginning of 2006, Chief of Staff Dan Halutz expressed this view when he stated that "the Intifada is part of an un-resolvable . . . permanent conflict between Jews and Palestinians that started in 1929." The military, according to Halutz, must therefore gear itself to operate within an environment saturated with conflict and in a future of permanent violence. With this, he echoed an often-recurring claim within Israeli security discourse, as when, in June 1977, Foreign Minister Moshe Dayan explained that the presumption that Israel's conflict with the Palestinians could be "solved" was fundamentally flawed. "The question was not, 'What is the solution?' but 'How do we live without a solution?'"[76] The "lesser evil" approach thus relates to Israeli unilateralism, to the perception that there is no partner, and to the idea of infinite conflict. Territorial ground occupation is thus projected as a "necessary evil" in the West Bank and assassinations as a "necessary evil" in Gaza. In the absence of both options – a political solution, on the one hand, and the possibility of a decisive military outcome, on the other – the Israeli military thus merely "manages the conflict." The ideology of the lesser evil, the lesser-evil occupation, has thus replaced the political horizon and a quest for justice. At the beginning of 2006, Halutz still thought that the precision methods of the Israeli Air Force would help keep the conflict "on a flame low enough for Israeli society to be able to live and to prosper within it."[77] This projection of endless war accordingly in all likelihood will fulfill itself.

Notes

1 Interview with Ephraim Segoli, Tel Aviv, May 22, 2006.
2 B'Tselem, the Israeli Information Center for Human Rights in the Occupied Territories, "Statistics: Fatalities," available online at http://www.btselem.org/English/Statistics/Casualties.asp (last accessed May 10, 2008).
3 See Chapter 9 in Eyal Weizman, *Hollow Land: Israel's Architecture of Occupation* (London: Verso, 2007).
4 In "Necropolitics," Achille Mbembe follows Michel Foucault to argue that sovereignty is located not only within the institutions of the geographically defined nation-state or, as postmodern thinkers suggest, within the operational networks of supranational institutions, but also in the capacity of power to make decisions regarding life and death. According to Foucault, the other side of the politics that engages with the management of life (bio-politics) is the administration of death (thanato-politics). See Michel Foucault, *Society Must Be Defended: Lectures at the College De France, 1975–1976*, ed. Mauro Bertani, Alessandro Fontana, and François Ewald, trans. David Macey (New York: Picador, 2003), p. 25, and Achille Mbembe, "Necropolitics," *Public Culture*, vol. 15, no. 1 (Winter 2003), pp. 11–40.
5 Interview with Ephraim Segoli, Tel Aviv, May 22, 2006.
6 See Raviv Druker and Ofer Shelah, *Boomerang* (Jerusalem: Keter Press, 2005), pp. 161–216 [in Hebrew] .
7 Aharon Yoffe, "Focus Preemption, Chances and Dangers," *Nativ*, vol. 109, no. 2 (March 2006) [in Hebrew]. See also Yedidia Yaalefari and Haim Assa, *Diffused Warfare: War in the 21st Century* (Tel Aviv: Miskal – Yediot Aharonot Books and Chemed Books, 2005), p. 37 [in Hebrew]. The book is the summary of positions developed within the so-called "Alternative Team" and under the influence of the Operational Theory Research Institute (OTRI). Yedidya Yaalefari, the former commander of the Israeli Navy, and Haim Asa, a former member of a comparable Israeli Air Force think tank, directed the team. Affiliated with it were air force pilot Dror Ben David, Brigadier-General Gadi Eisenkott, and Brigadier-General Aviv Kochavi. General Benni Gantz was assigned to implement this study within the Israeli Defense Forces. The Alternative Team was operating in cooperation with the U.S. Transformation Group under the U.S. secretary of defense, Donald Rumsfeld. In 2006, the Israeli chief of staff, Dan Halutz,

dismantled the Alternative Team. There were also a large number of parallel and smaller teams with similar aims, such as the Military Research Centre for the Study of the Tactical Environment, directed by Gabrial Siboni. On the latter, see Gabrial Siboni, "The Importance of Activity," *Bamahane* ("In the Camp"), the IDF's official journal, December 31, 2004, pp. 14–18 [in Hebrew].

8 Interview with Brigadier-General (ret.) Shimon Naveh, former director of the OTRI in the IDF. All of the following quotes from Naveh are based on interviews conducted on September 15, 2005 (by telephone), March 7, 2006 (by telephone), and April 11, 2006 and May 22–23, 2006 (at an Israeli Army Intelligence military base in Glilot, near Tel Aviv). All transcripts and translations to English of the interviews were sent to Naveh for confirmation of their content. All future references to the interview refer to those above unless mentioned otherwise.

9 Interview with former member of Unit 504, May 2006, who preferred to remain anonymous.

10 Robert Fisk, "Death by Remote Control as Hit Squads Return," *The Independent*, May 13, 2001.

11 Neve Gordon, "Rationalizing Extra-Judicial Executions: The Israeli Press and the Legitimization of Abuse," *International Journal of Human Rights*, vol. 8, no. 3 (Autumn 2004), pp. 305–24, p. 305. In 2005 *Ha'aretz*, Israel's liberal daily, started to publish, as a matter of policy, the names of Palestinians killed by Israel in all its military operations.

12 B'Tselem, "IDF Helicopter Missile-Fire Kills Four Palestinian Civilians and Wounds Dozens," August 2002, available online at http://www.btselem.org/English/Testimonies/20020831_Tubas_Killing_Witness_Aref_Daraghmeh.asp (last accessed September 6, 2008).

13 Orna Ben-Naftali and Keren Michaeli, "'We Must Not Make a Scarecrow of the Law': A Legal Analysis of the Israeli Policy of Targeted Killings," *Cornell International Law Journal*, vol. 36, no. 2 (Spring 2004), pp. 233–92, p. 234, n. 22.

14 See Naomi Klein, "Laboratory for a Fortressed World," *The Nation*, July 2, 2007: "Another star of the Paris Air Show will be Israeli defense giant Elbit, which plans to showcase its Hermes 450 and 900 unmanned air vehicles. As recently as May, according to press reports, Israel used the drones on bombing missions in Gaza. Once tested in the territories, they are exported abroad: The Hermes has already been used at the Arizona-Mexico border."

15 In November 2002, a car travelling in a remote part of Yemen was destroyed by a missile fired from an unmanned Predator drone, killing six suspected members of al Qaeda. Although the U.S. administration did not publicly acknowledge responsibility for the attack, officials let it be known that the CIA had carried it out. The June 2006 killing of Abu Musab al-Zarqawi and the January 2006 attempt to kill Ayman al-Zawahiri were undertaken from the air. Previous strikes killed Mohammed Atef, al Qaeda's military chief, and Hamza Rabia, a senior operative in Pakistan. Currently, the U.S. military plans to double the number of Predator and Global Hawk drones used for surveillance and targeting. See Anthony Dworkin, "The Yemen Strike: The War on Terrorism Goes Global," Crimes of War Project, November 14, 2002, available online at http://www.crimesofwar.org/onnews/news-yemen.html (last accessed September 6, 2008); Chris Downes, "'Targeted Killing' in an Age of Terror: The Legality of the Yemen Strike," *Journal of Conflict and Security Law*, vol. 9, no. 2 (2004), pp. 277–9.

16 Ludwig von Bertalanffy defines a system as a complex of interacting elements. Thus, a system's problems, according to Bertalanffy, are problems of the inter-relations of a great number of variables that occur in the field of politics, economics, industry, commerce, and military conduct. See Ludwig von Bertalanffy, *General System Theory: Foundations, Development, Applications* (New York: George Braziller, 1976). In military discourse, systems analysis originated after the end of World War II and was instrumental in the conception in 1982 of the U.S. military doctrine of "Airland Battle," which emphasized targeting an enemy at its systematic bottlenecks – bridges,

headquarters, and supply lines – in the attempt to throw an enemy's system of operation off balance. It was conceived to check Soviet invasion in Central Europe and was first applied in the Gulf War of 1991. The advance of this line of thinking led to the development of the Network-centric Warfare Doctrine in the context of the Revolution in Military Affairs (RMA) after the end of the Cold War. (In fact, what the military refers to as "networks" – implying the nonhierarchical cooperation of dispersed parts – should technically be referred to as "systems," which are distributed structures with a centralized command.) In the context of the IDF, systems analysis is used in both the air and ground forces. One of the main promoters of systems theory and analysis is Shimon Naveh (see note 8).

17 The idea of people as infrastructure was developed in another context – that of African cities. See AbdouMaliq Simone, "People as Infrastructure: Intersecting Fragments in Johannesburg," *Public Culture*, vol. 3 (Fall 2004), pp. 407–29.
18 This logic was reflected in a March 2006 presentation to U.S. security personnel at the Washington, D.C. Brookings Institution by Avi Dichter, the former chief of Israel's General Security Service. Dichter, the driving force behind the tactical success and frequent application of targeted assassinations, observed that "by eliminating . . . generators of terror through arrests (the preferred method) or by targeted killings (if absolutely necessary), a state can greatly disrupt the operations of terrorist organizations." See Avi Dichter and Daniel Byman, "Israel's Lessons for Fighting Terrorists and their Implications for the United States," Analysis Paper Number 8 (Washington, D.C.: Saban Centre for Middle East Policy at the Brookings Institute, March 2006).
19 Interview with Brigadier General (ret.) Shimon Naveh.
20 Giulio Douhet, *Command of the Air* (1921; London: Ayer Publishing, 1942). The full text is available online at http://www.airforcehistory.hq.af.mil/Publications/fulltext/command_of_the_air.pdf (last accessed September 6, 2008).
21 However, an important distinction must still be maintained. The military approaches that the IDF employed in Lebanon are strategically distinct from those employed in the Occupied Palestinian Territories. According to the political scientist James Ron, in Lebanon, Israel employed degrees of violence that greatly exceeded those employed in the Occupied Territories, and, consequently, casualty figures in Lebanon were much higher than those in the West Bank and Gaza. Ron explains that these differences in military approach are shaped by differences in degrees of control over territory and population. In the Occupied Territories, enclosed within Israeli-controlled territory, Israel still bears some responsibility for the welfare of the populations, whereas in Lebanon – which is completely beyond the state's frontier – the civilian population could be attacked with ferocity without economic and other repercussions to Israel. James Ron, *Frontiers and Ghettos: State Violence in Serbia and Israel* (Berkeley: University of California Press, 2003).
22 Sven Lindqvist, *A History of Bombing*, trans. Linda Haverty Rugg (New York: New Press, 2000), entry 101.
23 Philip Anthony Towle, *Pilots and Rebels: The Use of Aircraft in Unconventional Warfare, 1918–1988* (London: Brassey's, Defence Publishers, 1989), p. 17; David Willard Parsons, "British Air Control: A Model for the Application of Air Power in Low-Intensity Conflict?" *Airpower Journal* (Summer 1994), available online at http://www.airpower.maxwell.af.mil/airchronicles/apj/apj94/parsons.html (last accessed September 7, 2008).
24 Quoted in Lt. Colonel David J. Dean, USAF, "Air Power in Small Wars: The British Air Control Experience," *Air University Review*, vol. 34, no. 5 (July–August 1983): http://www.airpower.au.af.mil/airchronicles/aureview/1983/jul-aug/dean.html.
25 Dean, "Air Power in Small Wars." David Omissi, *Air Power and Colonial Control: The Royal Air Force 1919–1939* (Manchester: Manchester University Press, 1990). David MacIsaac, "Voices from the Central Blue, The Air Power Theorists," in Peter Paret, ed., *Makers of Modern Strategy, From Machiavelli to the Nuclear Age* (Oxford: Oxford University Press, 1986), pp. 624–47, especially p. 633.

26 Lindqvist, *A History of Bombing*, entry 102.
27 Brigadir General Yair Golan, in a discussion with the research group for the study of the catastrophization in the Occupied Territories at the Van Leer Jerusalem Institute, April 20, 2007.
28 Ronen Shnayderman, "Take No Prisoners: The Fatal Shooting of Palestinians by Israeli Security Forces during 'Arrest Operations,'" B'Tselem, May 2005, trans. Shaul Vardi, available online at http://www.btselem.org/Download/200505_Take_No_Prisoners_ Eng.pdf (last accessed September 7, 2008). See also AL-HAQ, "Indiscriminate and Excessive Use of Force: Four Palestinians Killed During Arrest Raid, May 24, 2006," available online at http://asp.alhaq.org.
29 David Kretzmer, "Targeted Killing of Suspected Terrorists: Extra-Judicial Executions or Legitimate Means of Defense?" *European Journal of International Law*, vol. 16, no. 2 (2005), pp. 171–212, pp. 196, 207.
30 Press briefing by Colonel Daniel Reisner, director of the International Law Department of the IDF Legal Division, Israeli Ministry of Foreign Affairs, November 15, 2000, available online at http://www.mfa.gov.il/MFA/MFAArchive/2000_2009/2000/11/ Press%20Briefing%20by%20Colonel%20Daniel%20Reisner-%20Head%20of (last accessed September 7, 2008).
31 The Israeli legal scholar Eyal Benvenisti claimed that the proper measure to judge whether Israel continues to be bound by the obligations of an occupying power is the facts on the ground: "If there were areas under Palestinian control, they were not subject to Israeli occupation." See Eyal Benvenisti, "Israel and the Palestinians: What Laws Were Broken," Crimes of War Project, available online at http://www.crimesofwar. org/expert/me-intro.html (last accessed September 7, 2008). Charles Shamas, a Ramallah-based legal expert, joined others in claiming that, as Israel still exercises effective control over movement between localities, over the supply of goods, and over access to natural resources, it has in effect authority over the enactment of Palestinian legislation and therefore continues to be bound by the duties of an occupying power. Compare, as well, Baruch Kimmerling's notion of "system of control" in "Boundaries and Frontiers of the Israeli Control System," in Baruch Kimmerling, ed., *The Israeli State and Society: Boundaries and Frontiers* (Albany: State University of New York Press, 1989), pp. 265–84.
32 Indeed, since the evacuation of Gaza, the IDF became even more willing to employ violence against the Palestinians. In 2006 alone, Israeli forces killed 405 Palestinians in Gaza, half of them civilians, including eighty-eight minors. During the same year, Israel killed twenty-two Palestinians in targeted assassinations. Following a certain decline in 2007 (293 Palestinians killed in Gaza, approximately one-third of them civilians) the level of violence peaked again at the beginning of 2008: according to B'Tselem, in only one week, from February 27 to the afternoon of March 3, 106 Palestinians were killed in the Gaza Strip, at least fifty-four of whom were civilians. In June 2006, Israel bombed the electric grid in Gaza, cutting off 700,000 people from electricity, and has repeatedly restricted electricity and fuel supplies to Gaza ever since. For data on causalities see, respectively, B'Tselem, "683 People Killed in the Conflict in 2006," available online at http://www.btselem.org/english/press_releases/20061228. asp; B'Tselem, "Human Rights in the Occupied Territories, 2007 Annual Report," available online at http://www.btselem.org/Download/200712_Annual_Report_eng. pdf; and B'Tselem, "Contrary to Israel's Chief of Staff, at least Half of Those Killed in Gaza Did Not Take Part in the Fighting," press release, March 3, 2008, available online at http://www.btselem.org/english/Press_Releases/20080303.asp (all last accessed September 7, 2008).
33 Yaalefari and Assa, *Diffused Warfare*, pp. 9–13.
34 The last of the terms was coined in a joint program between the former commander of a fighter squadron, Dror Ben David, and researchers at the Operational Theory Research Institute.

88   *Eyal Weizman*

35 Halutz constantly defended the technology behind his airborne assassinations, even when it regularly has taken the lives of many bystanders. When asked for his reaction to the death of many civilians in an operation of targeted assassination, he famously retorted, "If you want to know what I feel when I release a bomb, I will tell you: I feel a light bump to the plane as a result of the bomb's release. A second later, it's gone, and that's all. That is what I feel." See Vered Levy-Barzilai, "Halutz: The High and the Mighty," *Ha'aretz Magazine*, August 21, 2002.
36 Israel Harel, "The IDF Protects Itself," *Ha'aretz*, August 29, 2006.
37 Amir Rapaport, "Dan Halutz is a Bluff, Interview with Shimon Naveh," *Ma'ariv*, Yom Kippur Supplement, October 1, 2006.
38 Ofer Shelah and Yoav Limor, *Captives of Lebanon* (Tel Aviv: Miskal – Yedioth Aharonoth Books and Chemed Books, 2007), p. 199.
39 Darryl Li, "Gaza Consultancy – Research Findings, 20–27 August 2006," draft submitted to B'Tselem, September 10, 2006. Testimony number 3287. Unpublished.
40 A *Ma'ariv* Gallup Poll of August 10, 2001 revealed that 76 percent of the public polled supported assassinations. In later years, and in particular as a result of the killing of many bystanders, public support dropped considerably. In June 2003, at the start of the campaign to assassinate the leadership of Hamas, an opinion poll by the daily newspaper *Yedioth Ahronoth* found that 58 percent of Israelis polled said that the military should at least temporarily discontinue targeted killings. After the "disengagement" from Gaza and a quite persistent rocket shelling on neighboring Israeli towns and villages, support for assassination grew again. On January 6, 2003 *Ha'aretz* estimated this support to be more than 80 percent. See Druker and Shelah, *Boomerang*, p. 216.
41 Ibid., p. 161.
42 "The IDF Published a List of Seven 'Assassination Candidates,'" *Ha'aretz*, July 6, 2001.
43 Yaalefari and Assa, *Diffused Warfare*, p. 147; Druker and Shelah, *Boomerang*, p. 162 and n. 96.
44 Officially called the National Conciliation Document of the Palestinian Prisoners, "the prisoners' document" was written by Palestinian prisoners in Israeli jails. In it, representatives of Fatah, Hamas, Islamic Jihad, the Popular Front for the Liberation of Palestine (PFLP), and the Democratic Front for the Liberation of Palestine (DFLP) tried to articulate policy positions that would reconcile the various factions.
45 Quoted in Amos Harel and Arnon Regular, "IAF Probe: Civilians Spotted Too Late to Divert Missiles in Gaza Strike," *Ha'aretz*, March 7, 2006. See also Soha Abdelaty, "Intifada Timeline, September 30–October 6, 2004," Al-Ahram Weekly Online, available at http://weekly.ahram.org.eg/2004/710/fo5.htm (last accessed September 7, 2008) and Vincent Cannistraro, "Assassination Is Wrong – and Dumb," *The Washington Post*, August 30, 2001.
46 For many years, Yassir Arafat remained at the top of Israel's most wanted list. The *dibbuk* haunting Israeli security services, Arafat's "irrational character" was blamed for almost every political stalemate or outbreak of violence. Chief of Military Intelligence Amos Gilead, who developed a personal obsession with him, described Arafat thus: "Mentally, Arafat feels at his best, when he is surrounded by a reality of flames, fire, suffering and blood." Only an explicit promise extracted from Sharon by George W. Bush prevented the IDF from doing what it really wanted to do and assassinating Arafat himself. Gil Eyal, *The Disenchantment of the Orient: Expertise in Arab Affairs and the Israeli State* (Palo Alto, CA: Stanford University Press, 2006), p. 290, nn. 93, 189.
47 Eyal, *Disenchantment of the Orient*, p. 183.
48 Chris McGreal, "We're Air Force Pilots, Not Mafia. We Don't Take Revenge," *The Guardian*, December 3, 2003.
49 The principles of the military ethics of fighting terror were developed by a team of the Israeli Defense Force College of National Defense, headed by Major General Amos Yadlin, then commander of the college. The team included other officers with

experience in such military activities, as well as experts in international law and ethics. The final document, produced by Yadlin and Asa Kasher, was presented to the IDF chief of staff and to generals involved in fighting terror. The document was approved, and, besides being used in different stages of the education of officers, is currently being used for the preparation of proposed explanatory guidelines for a variety of specific situations and operations. Asa Kasher and Amos Yadlin, "The Military Ethics of Fighting Terror: An Israeli Perspective," *Journal of Military Ethics*, vol. 4 (2005), pp. 3–32. See also Asa Kasher and Amos Yadlin, "Assassination and Preventive Killing," *SAIS Review*, vol. 25, no. 1 (2005), pp. 41–57.

50 Interview with an Israeli Air Force operator of unmanned drones, April 2005. The operator's name cannot be revealed.
51 Harel and Regular, "IAF Probe."
52 Further data published in *Ha'aretz* states that, between 2002 and 2003, 50 percent of people killed were uninvolved civilians, that in 2005 the number dropped to 3.5 percent, that in 2006, when attacks accelerated after the abduction of an Israeli soldier, it was 10 percent, and that in 2007 it dropped again to its lowest level, between 2 and 3 percent. Amos Harel, "Precise Military," *Ha'aretz*, December 30, 2008.
53 Amos Harel, "Military Mishaps/Nothing 'Surgical' about IAF Attacks," *Haaretz*, 22 June, 2006 (http://www.haaretz.com/print-edition/news/military-mishaps-nothing-sur-gical-about-iaf-attacks-1.191120). The B'Tselem figures are available online at http://www.btselem.org/English/Statistics/Casualties.asp (last accessed September 7, 2008).
54 David A. Fulghum and Robert Wall, "Israel Starts Reexamining Military Missions and Technology," *Aviation Week*, August 20, 2006.
55 Laura Blumenfeld, "In Israel, a Divisive Struggle over Targeted Killing," *The Washington Post*, August 27, 2006.
56 Indeed, during the 1991 Gulf War, the public was fed images of "kamikaze bombs" as proof of the technological superiority and surgical skills of the U.S. military. Harun Farocki, "War From a Distance," lecture delivered at the Academy of Fine Arts, Vienna, January 13, 2005.
57 Quoted in Meron Rapoport, "Italian TV: Israel Used New Weapon Prototype in Gaza Strip," *Ha'aretz*, October 12, 2006. These weapons are made of a carbon-fiber casing filled with tungsten powder – a metal capable of conducting very high temperatures. Upon detonation, the tungsten particles are propelled outward in a relatively small (about 4 meters) but very deadly cloud, causing severe burns, amputated limbs, and internal burns. See Air Force Research Laboratory 2005 accomplishment, available online at http://www.afrl.af.mil/accomprpt/may05/accompmay05.asp.
58 HCJ 769/02, The Public Committee against Torture in Israel *v.* The Government of Israel. Previous petitions to the High Court of Justice against targeted assassinations (e.g. HCJ 5872/2002, M. K. Muhammed Barake *v.* Prime Minister and Minister of Defense) were dismissed.
59 "Evil" in this context is best understood, following Adi Ophir, as a category displaced from the realm of the divine or diabolical and relocated in a social order in which suffering and pain could have been, but were not, prevented. See Adi Ophir, *The Order of Evils: Toward an Ontology of Morals*, trans. Rela Mazali and Havi Carel (New York: Zone Books, 2005). "Evils can only be justified by appealing to more grave hypothetical evils that could have been caused if the prevention or disengagement actions would have taken place" (section 7.100, p. 339). "The justification displaces the discussion from one order of exchange, in which the one harmed tries to create a link between damage or suffering and compensation, to another order of exchange, in which the defendant tries to create a link between evils that occurred to possible evils that might have occurred" (section 3.432, p. 152).
60 Michael Ignatieff, *The Lesser Evil: Political Ethics in an Age of Terror* (Princeton, NJ: Princeton University Press, 2004).

61 These conditions are "applied to the smallest number of people, used as a last resort, and kept under the adversarial scrutiny of an open democratic system." Furthermore, "assassination can be justified only if . . . less violent alternatives, like arrest and capture, endanger . . . personnel or civilians . . . [and] where all reasonable precautions are taken to minimize collateral damage and civilian harm." Ibid., pp. 8, 129–33.

62 Alan M. Dershowitz, *The Case for Israel* (Hoboken, NJ: John Wiley, 2003), p. 173.

63 Quoted in Amos Harel and Avi Isacharoff, *The Seventh War* (Tel Aviv: Miskal – Yedioth Aharonoth Books and Chemed Books, 2004), p. 343.

64 Ophir, *The Order of Evils*, section 7.100, p. 339; sections 7.2 and 7.3, pp. 327–9. See also, for example, section 7.335, p. 375.

65 Iris Giller, "A Death Foretold: Firing of 'Rubber' Bullets to Disperse Demonstrations in the Occupied Territories," trans. Zvi Schulman, B'Tselem, November 1998, available online at http://www.btselem.org/Download/199812_Death_Foretold_Eng.rtf (last accessed September 7, 2008).

66 Harel and Isacharoff, *The Seventh War*, p. 343.

67 Ariella Azoulay, "Hunger in Palestine: The Event That Never Was," in Anselm Franke, Rafi Segal, and Eyal Weizman, eds., *Territories, Islands, Camps and Other States of Utopia* (Cologne: Walter Koening, 2003), pp. 154–7. According to the chief of military intelligence, Amos Gilead, "hunger is when people walk around with a swollen belly, collapse and die. There is no hunger in Palestinian territories." Druker and Shelah, *Boomerang*, p. 329. Since Hamas was elected to power in January 2006, Israel has used the weapon of economic strangulation as a means of political pressure, withholding all Palestinian tax monies – about $60 million a month – that it is legally obligated to transfer to the Palestinian Authority. Israel has also mobilized the international community to suspend aid until Hamas recognizes "Israel's right to exist" and enters into a political process. However, the international boycott of Gaza residents to pressure the Hamas government has been counterproductive, with both Israel and donor countries desperately seeking a way out. The poverty created in Gaza is more threatening.

68 Hannah Arendt, *Responsibility and Judgment* (New York: Schocken Books, 2005), p. 36.

69 Hannah Arendt, "The Eggs Speak Up" (1950), in Jerome Kohn, ed., *Essays in Understanding, 1930–1954: Formation, Exile, and Totalitarianism* (New York: Schocken, 2005), pp. 270–84, especially p. 271. Arendt claims that Stalin's "only original contribution" to socialism was to transform the breaking of eggs from a tragic necessity into a revolutionary virtue.

70 David Kennedy, *The Dark Side of Virtue: Reassessing International Humanitarianism* (Princeton, NJ: Princeton University Press, 2004), pp. 235–323. See, in particular, the chapter "Humanitarianism and Force," especially p. 295. See also discussion of this issue and of Kennedy's ideas in articles by his former student, Aeyal M. Gross: "The Construction of a Wall between The Hague and Jerusalem: The Enforcement and Limits of Humanitarian Law and the Structure of Occupation," *Leiden Journal of International Law*, vol. 19 (2006), pp. 393–440 and "Human Proportions: Are Human Rights the Emperor's New Clothes of the International Law of Occupation?" *European Journal of International Law*, vol. 18, no. 1 (2007), pp. 1–35.

71 See Ariella Azoulay and Adi Ophir, "The Order of Violence," in Adi Ophir, Michal Givoni, and Sari Hanafi, eds., *The Power of Inclusive Exclusion: Anatomy of Israeli Rule in the Occupied Territories* (New York: Zone, 2009), pp. 99–141..

72 Beyond their meaning in the total mobilization of society, "total wars" – marking the other limit of the conceptual spectrum – are wars that no longer allow any communication to take place. Colonial wars have often been total wars, because the "natives" were not perceived to share the same "humanity" as the colonizers and thus could not be considered a party capable of rational behavior and discourse. Terror is "total," as well, because, most often, it places no legal or moral limits on violence and makes no distinction between innocence and guilt. Moreover, it acts to attack the very possibility of discourse. Degrees and distinctions are precisely what make war less than total.

73 Quoted in Harel, "Nothing 'Surgical.'"
74 B'Tselem, "683 People Killed in the Conflict in 2006."
75 Robert M. Pirsig, *Zen and the Art of Motorcycle Maintenance* (New York: William Morrow, 1984), pp. 206–7.
76 On Israeli militarism, see Uri Ben-Eliezer, "Post-Modern Armies and the Question of Peace and War: The Israeli Defense Forces in the 'New Times,'" *International Journal of Middle East Studies*, vol. 36 (2004), p. 50. See also Uri Ben-Eliezer, *The Making of Israeli Militarism* (Bloomington: Indiana University Press, 1998), pp. 1–18; Baruch Kimmerling, *The Invention and Decline of Israeliness: Society, Culture, and the Military* (Berkeley: University of California Press, 2001), p. 209; and Michael Mann, "The Roots and Contradictions of Modern Militarism," *New Left Review*, vol. 162 (March–April 1987), pp. 35–50.
77 Dayan's quote is from "Sharon's Enduring Agenda: Consolidate Territorial Control, Manage the Conflict," Report on Israeli Settlement in the Occupied Territories 14, no. 1 (January–February 2004), available online at http://www.fmep.org/reports/archive/vol.–14/no.–1/PDF.
78 Amir Oren, "The Tenth Round," *Ha'aretz* weekend supplement, January 14, 2006.

5 Theme park archipelago[1]

Convergences of war, simulation and entertainment in urban targeting

Stephen Graham

Introduction

A hidden archipelago of between 80 and 100 mini cities is rapidly being constructed across the world. Rising far from the world's main metropolitan corridors, in obscure edge-of-city and rural locations, these new 'cities' are set deep within military bases and training grounds. The vast majority are located in the United States, presenting jarring contrasts with the strip-mall suburbia that surrounds them. Others are rising out of the deserts of Kuwait and Israel, the downs of Southern England, the plains of Germany and the islands of Singapore.

Some such cities are replete with lines of drying washing, continuous loop-tapes playing calls to prayer, wandering donkeys, Arabic graffiti, even ersatz 'minarets' and 'mosques'. Others have 'slum' or 'favela' districts and underground sewers with built-in olfactory machines that can create the simulated smell of rotting corpses or untreated sewage on demand. Still others are populated occasionally by itinerant populations of Arab-Americans, bused in to wander about and role-play in Arab dress.

Beyond these temporary inhabitants, few, beyond military personnel, ever see or enter these new urban complexes. Unnoticed by urban design, architecture, and planning communities, and invisible on maps, these sites constitute a kind of shadow world urban system. As a global system of military urban simulations, they lurk in the interstices between the planet's rapidly growing metropolitan areas.

Practised destruction

Rather than being monuments to construction, dynamism and growth, these cities are violent theme parks for practising urban destruction, erasure and colonial violence targeting real, far-off cities. These sites are being constructed by US military specialists, with the help of military corporations, theme park designers, Hollywood experts, universities and video game specialists. They are simulations of the burgeoning Arab and Third World cities that are deemed the *de facto* zones of current and future warfare for Western forces. It is in such complexes that Western and Israeli military forces learn to take on what Mike Davis has called our 'planet of slums' (Davis 2006). They are small capsules of space designed to mimic in some way what US military theorist, Richard Norton (2004), has pejoratively labeled the 'feral' cities that Western military planners deem to be the strategic environments dominating contemporary geopolitics.

Along with a wide range of simulated Western cities developed as sites within which to practise police and military responses to terror attacks, civil unrest or infrastructural collapse, these sites provide a global architectural simulation, a shadow archipelago of 'cities' that mimic the urbanisation of real wars and conflicts around the world. As Bryan Finoki argues, these sites 'tackle calamity in an amusement park of unrest, insurgency and its abatement, architectures both elaborate and artful, designed solely for the purposes of being conquered and reconquered' (Bryan Finoki, independent researcher, 2009, personal communication).

After centuries when Western military doctrine preached an obsessive avoidance of urban combat, or the need to simply try and erase cities that did get in the way, the catastrophe on the streets of Iraq is helping to force the challenges of counter-insurgency or 'asymmetric warfare' within large, global south cities to the heart of Western military doctrine for the first time. US military doctrine increasingly stresses the challenge of controlling the micro-geographies of slums, favelas, industrial districts and casbahs, as well as the globe-spanning power of new network, stealth and surveillance technologies (Davis 2005).

Phil Misselwitz and Eyal Weizman emphasise that Israeli and Western military doctrine now stresses the need not just to enter and try to control large urban areas (Misselwitz and Weizman 2003); also important here is the challenge to physically reorganise colonised city spaces so that high-tech weapons and surveillance systems can work to the occupiers' advantage. Weizman (2005: 74) calls this 'design by destruction'. As he puts it, 'contemporary urban warfare plays itself out within a constructed, real or imaginary architecture, and through the destruction, construction, reorganisation, and subversion of space' (Weizman 2005: 74)."

Thus, as in Iraq, districts and neighbourhoods can be turned into camps through checkpoints, razor wire and the enforced use of biometric identity cards. Areas deemed to be so dense and complex that they harbour resistance and shelter insurgents from the gaze of drones, satellites and aerial targeting can be physically bulldozed, as in Jenin in 2002 (Graham 2003). And the infrastructural systems that sustain life in all cities can be either totally destroyed – as in the urbicidal assaults on the infrastructure of Iraq in 1991, Lebanon in 2006, and Gaza between 2006 and 2009 – or manipulated to try and coerce resistant populations, fighters and political leadership, through the forced immiserisation of enduring a non-infrastructural urban life in a modern city (Graham 2005).

To support these forced restructurings of urban space, an extending body of theory and doctrine is being built up. Weizman (2005: 74) has shown how Israeli military theorists of the urbanisation of war are even using the post-structuralist insights of critical theorists such as Deleuze and Guatarri to try and find ways of 'walking through walls' to penetrate the refugee camps and dense casbahs of Gaza and Nablus.

Amongst US military thinkers, meanwhile, there is a powerful sense that the rapid urbanisation of Middle Eastern and Arab countries radically undermines the high-tech advantages that US forces have so expensively built up since the start of the Cold War. This is widely assumed to directly support the decisions by various non-state adversaries of the United States to shelter within the three-dimensional entanglements of expanding urban areas. 'The long term trend in open-area combat', writes the rabidly hawkish U.S. 'urban warfare' commentator, Ralph Peters (2006: 7), 'is toward overhead dominance by US forces'. As a result, he suggests that 'battlefield awareness [for US forces] may prove so complete' that the United States' 'enemies will be forced into cities and other complex terrain, such as industrial developments and inter-city sprawl'.

In keeping with this post-Cold War mutation of Western military doctrine into the planned remodelling of cities by force, the sole purpose of simulated urban warfare training cities is to allow US, Western and Israeli forces to hone their skills in designed urban destruction and incarceration. Following extensive training in these sites, Western and Israeli military units deploy to the real cities of Iraq, Palestine, Lebanon or elsewhere to undertake what, in military parlance, are termed 'Military Operations on Urban Terrain' (or simply 'MOUT' for short).

Like the rest of the world, then, military training sites are rapidly being urbanised. Colonel Thomas Hammes (1999), writing in the US *Marine Corps Gazette* in 1999, was one of many defence planners arguing at that period that a wide range of new mock cities were needed because US military training sites were out of phase with 'the urban sprawl that dominates critical areas of the world today'. He reflects further that US forces know that 'we will fight mostly in urban areas'. 'Yet, we conduct the vast majority of our training in rural areas – the hills of Camp Pendleton, the deserts of Twenty Nine Palms, the woods of Camp Lejeune, the jungles of Okinawa, Japan.'

The US military's response has been dramatic. Between 2005 and 2010, the US Army alone was planning to build a chain of sixty-one urban warfare training 'cities' across the world (McDonald 2006). Although some of these are little more than air-portable sets of containers, designed to provide basic urban warfare training when deployed around the world, others are complex spaces mimicking whole city districts or sets of villages, as well as surrounding countryside, infrastructure, even airports. Leading examples of the more complex sites include Fort Carson, Colorado (which by 2006 had three different mock 'Iraqi villages'), the national 'Joint Readiness Training Center' at Fort Polk, Louisiana, 29 Palms in California, Fort Benning, Georgia, and Fort Richardson, Alaska.

Urban warfare training 'cities' are stark embodiments of the imaginative and real urban geographies that lie at the heart of the global 'war on terror'. Powerful materialisations of what Derek Gregory (2004) has called our colonial present, they need to be understood as part of a much wider effort at physically and electronically simulating Arab or global south cities for tightly-linked imperatives of war, profit and entertainment.

Such complexes thus take their place within a wide constellation of simulated Arab cities and urban landscapes, which draw on similar Orientalist traditions. These are emerging within video games, virtual reality military simulations, films, newspaper graphics and novels. Together, these contribute to one massive discursive trick: to construct Arab and Third World cities as stylised, purely physical and labyrinthine worlds which are somehow both intrinsically terroristic and largely devoid of the civil society that characterises normal urban life. The result is that Arab cities emerge here as little more than receiving points for US military ordinance and colonial military incursions – whether real or fantastical.

Where the cultures and sociologies of Arab cities have been considered in urban warfare simulations – as has started to be necessary since the military take-over of Iraq's cities turned to the challenges of occupation – Orientalist cliché, or high-tech dehumanisation, have been the norm (Gregory 2004: 229–30). When simulated Arab cities emerge with a population at all, it has been provided in person by role-players in *keffiyehs* muttering Orientalist clichés. Or it has simply been generated by computer software as electronically imagined 'crowds' populating electronic simulations of Arab cities under simulated US or Israeli attack. Either way, this constellation of urban simulacra thereby do the important geo-political work of continually reducing the complex social and cultural worlds of Arab or global south urbanism to the city as mere target, or 'battlespace', to be assaulted in a purported campaign against 'terror', or for 'freedom'.

The construction by militaries of physical simulations of places to be targeted and destroyed is not new of course. Nor is the close relationship between play, toys and war, or the mobilisation of Hollywood special effects for a war effort. In the Cold War, for example, atomic and thermonuclear bombs were regularly exploded near simulated suburban homes, complete with white picket fences and nuclear families of mannequins placed around the table having mock meals (McEnaney 2000). Earlier, during World War II, the Dugway Proving Grounds in Utah saw the construction of a village of extremely accurate Berlin tenements along with a cluster of Japanese wood and rice-paper houses (Davis 2002: 65–84).

The former were designed by modernist luminary Eric Mendelsohn, freshly exiled from Germany. The latter were created by Antonin Raymond, a US architect with Japanese experience, who scoured the United States for authentic types of Russian spruce wood to use in the construction. These buildings were then repeatedly burnt by the US Chemical Warfare Corps who used the new techniques of operations research to tailor the composition and design of incendiary bombs to the task of comprehensively razing Japanese and German cities. To ensure accuracy, real German furniture was placed within the tenements and the buildings were watered to mimic the temperate climes of Berlin.

'Planet of slums' simulacra

The global complex of urban warfare training cities involves a different relationship to political violence from the atom-bombed suburban homes or fire-bombed tenements and rice-paper structures of the twentieth century. For here, the simulation is not designed to sustain attempts at outright urban annihilation through total war. Rather, its purpose is to hone skills of occupation, counter-insurgency warfare and urban remodelling via expeditionary, colonial war.

A bizarre, reverse urban beauty contest emerges here. As a mirror image to the more familiar global place marketing contests through which real cities parade themselves through gentrification, cultural planning and boosterism, here the marks of success are decay and an architecture of collapse. Colonel James Cashwell, a US squadron commander, reported recently, after an exercise in an urban warfare training city within George Air Force Base in California, that 'the advantage of the base is that it is ugly, torn up, all the windows are broken [and trees] have fallen down in the street. It's perfect for the replication of a war-torn city' (Wilson 2003).

Ted Leza, who runs the US Baumholder urban warfare training site in Germany, meanwhile reflects that soldiers using the site have repeatedly asked for it to be populated by a veritable menagerie of dead and live animals to help simulate life in Iraqi cities. Thus, along with realistic Baghdad-style orange and white taxis, the simulated taxi stand and the market, the operators of the site are 'trying to get that for them. I don't know if we'll get a camel. Maybe a donkey, goats . . . stuff like that' (cited in Boyd 2006).

Urban warfare training sites also integrate multi-sensory systems for projecting war-like special effects into the ersatz buildings, streets and structures. 'We have a wide variety of special effects smells we can do', admits Manuel Chaves, who runs the special effects suite built into the urban warfare site at Fort Wainwright, Alaska. 'For instance: coffee, apple pie, dead bodies, burning rubber, diesel fumes. I can do nine different buildings, nine different smells. Generally, if it's a burning building, we put something really nasty in there like burning bodies' (cited in Associated Press 2002).

A rather different complex, built with unintended irony from 23,000 discarded cluster bomb containers discarded during the Vietnam War, is emerging at Yodaville in the Arizona desert. This site, which opened in 1998, is the first simulated global south city created specifically for live, urban bombing and close sir support training (Shaffer 1999). The complex apparently has '178 buildings, 131 personnel targets, 31 vehicle targets and is equipped with streetlights' (Usry n.d.). A RAND report states that the US military's first urban bombing training site looks, from the ground, 'like stacks of shot-up shipping containers' (Glenn *et al.* 2006). From the viewpoint of the fighter pilots who continually target it with cluster and 'precision' munitions, however, it is 'convincingly urban' (ibid.). Mark Shaffer (1999), reporter with the *Arizona Republic*, notes that the 'town', which has 167 buildings and encompasses 'a large shanty town', has a 'decidedly Third World' feel. 'A mock soccer field is painted green on the edge of town. Streets are narrow. There's a large shantytown. And talk about ambience. The seeringly hot desert teems with sidewinders and an occasional scrub creosote bush or cactus' (ibid.).

Apparently, local right-wing militia groups – never slow to jump to conspiratorial conclusions – are convinced that the Yoda complex is being used to train US and UN forces at the behest of a putative 'New World Order'. Seven miles from the border with Mexico, bombing runs are stopped at least twice weekly so that immigrants, newly arrived across the border, can be removed from the site, before the ordinance once again rains in. There is evidence that this does not always do the job, however. 'Madzukes' – presumably a US Marine – asks in the discussion of a Marine military video on Youtube if 'any border jumpers ran out of Yodaville after a rocket shoot this time?' (see http://www.youtube.com/watch?v=mgt8L_RxgZQ).

'This is our playground'

> it is here, in this parallel world, that the occupation of the Palestinian territories is played out by generations of Israeli soldiers, over and over again.
> (Broomberg and Chanarin 2007: 12)

Undoubtedly the most ambitious and controversial mock 'Arab' city so far constructed is not a US facility at all. Ostensibly, it is an Israeli one: the 'Baladia' facility at Israel's Ze'elim base in the Negev desert. However, given that the site has been paid for by US military aid, has been built between 2005 and 2006 by the US Army Corps of Engineers and is used by US Marines, perhaps 'US–Israeli' would be a more accurate description.

Costing $40 million and covering 7.4 square miles, Baladia has 472 complete concrete structures and 4 miles of roads; it is the first urban warfare mock city that begins to mimic the scale of real urban areas. This scale allows it to be flexibly rearranged in order to provide a purported simulation of any specific city within which the IDF or other forces are planning to launch operations. Baladia can thus be easily reconfigured into renditions of 'Gaza', 'Lebanon', the 'West Bank' or 'Syria'. 'This is our playground to practice for anything we need', reported Lt. Col. Arik Moreh, the base's second in command (Heller 2007). In June 2007, military journalist, Barbara Opall-Rome, reported that:

> Lebanon and Syria [were] the highest-priority threat theaters, and creative engineering [was] required to transform the area into what IDF officers here call Hezbollahland. During a late-May visit, IDF planners were busy transforming large portions of Baladia City into Bint Jbeil, a Hezbollah stronghold from which extremist Shiite forces extracted a heavy price on IDF ground troops in last summer's Lebanon War.   (Opall-Rome 2007)

The Baladia complex has been explicitly built to generalise the purported military lessons of Israel's regular incursions into Palestinian cities and refugee camps since 2002 to the whole of Israel's armed forces (as well as friendly militaries). The complex simulates a complete Palestinian town. The 'town' is split into four 'quarters' and is wired up with surveillance equipment to monitor the 'combat'. Most notable at Baladia are a range of mechanical cut-out bearded caricatures of Arab men that are programmed to pop-up in windows and street corners during live-fire exercises.

Baladia has simulated apartment buildings, a market place, a mosque and a concrete 'casbah'. It's 'cemetery . . . doubles as a soccer field, depending on operational scenario'; its 'nature reserve' hides Hezbollah-style rocket launchers

(Opall-Rome 2007). 'Charred automobiles and burned tires litter the roadways' (Opall-Rome 2007); streets are filled with mock booby traps. As well as a 'complex surveillance system to track soldiers' performance, an elaborate audio system . . . replicate[s] helicopters, mortar rounds, muezzin prayer calls, and about 20 other distinct sounds' (Ward 2007: 16).

As in US complexes, 'hundreds of soldiers, most of them 19- and 20-year-old women, graduates of Arabic language and cultural programs, [operate as] play-acting civilians and enemy fighters' (Ward 2007). Baladia even has ready-made 'worm-holes', the openings in the walls of buildings that Israeli soldiers use to routinely blast their way through Palestinian cities and refugee camps to avoid the perceived vulnerabilities of the street.

In 2006, Adam Broomberg and Oliver Chanarin, two Israeli photographers, succeeded in making a detailed study of Baladia (which they referred to by it's other name, 'Chicago'). Their research about the complex concludes that it 'was not based on a specific town but is a generic "Arab" place, designed by the soldiers themselves, building on their intimate experience of the minutiae of Arab cities' (Ward 2007: 16). Great attention has been paid to detail. 'Graffiti has been applied to the walls with obscure declarations in Arabic: "I love you Ruby" and "Red ash, hot as blood" (Broomberg and Chanarin 2007: 12).

Baladia embodies strange contortions of simulation and denial. As Broomberg and Chanarin (2007: 12) suggest,

> this convention of using the name "Arab", rather than Palestinian, effectively obscures identity, and in this sense Chicago as a ghost-town evidences the thread of denial that runs through much of Israeli discourse about relations with Palestine towns like Ramallah and Nablus.

Following their visit to the complex to complete their photography, Broomberg and Chanarin (2007: 15) spoke about its deeply unnerving qualities. 'It is difficult to pinpoint what it is about the place that is so disturbing', they said. 'Perhaps it's the combination of the vicariousness and the violence. It's as if the soldiers have entered the enemy's private domain while he's sleeping or out for lunch . . . It's a menacing intrusion into the intimate'.

War ghost towns

Despite their recent proliferation, senior Pentagon officials are convinced that current urban warfare training sites are completely inadequate to train US forces to counter future urban insurgencies in fast-growing megacities. To explore future options, in 2006 the US Congress commissioned the RAND national military think tank to produce a 400-page report on future provision of urban warfare facilities (Glenn *et al.* 2006).

The report starts with the premise that 'US armed forces have thus far been unable to adequately reproduce the challenges their soldiers, sailors, marines and airmen meet in the towns and cities of Iraq and Afghanistan' (ibid.: 63) Initially, the RAND researchers evaluate the potential of the various existing urban warfare training sites for offering the architectural and infrastructural features deemed to be most challenging in undertaking military operations within large, global south cities. Those with 'clutter/debris/filth', 'slums/shanty towns/walled compounds', 'subterranean complexes' and simulated 'government, hospital/prison/asylum structures', such as the Marines' 29 Palms facility in California, score highest (ibid.: 61).

To address the need for more realistic physical simulations of whole cities and city districts, the RAND team recommend the construction of four new urban warfare cities with more than 300 structures each, located in the Kentucky/North Carolina/Georgia area, at the existing Fort Polk base, at Fort Hood in Texas, and in the US Southwest. They also explore the possibility of appropriating entire 'ghosts towns' within the continental United States that have been catastrophically deindustrialised and largely abandoned. The report states that 'the use of abandoned towns [for urban warfare training] has moved beyond the concept phase into what might be considered the early test and development phase' (Glenn *et al.* 2006: 63).

Attention here is focusing on the virtually abandoned copper-mining town of Playas, in the southwest corner of New Mexico. This town has already been used for the training of anti-suicide bomb squads for the US Department of Homeland Security. 'Over the course of time, towns and cities eventually die', writes Steve Rowell (n.d.) of the Center for Land Use Interpretation in Culver City, California.

> Despite this and despite the receding U.S. economy, the industries of defense and disaster preparedness are flourishing, reversing this trend in some of the most remote areas of the nation. The war on terror is redefining the American pastoral in an unexpected way. (ibid.)

In the case of Playas, its new role is 'as a generic American suburb under simulated attack', and, in future, as a simulated Arab city within which to hone skills of expeditionary war (ibid.).

The entire town of Playas is rented for this purpose from the New Mexico Institute of Mining and Technology, who bought it explicitly for use as an urban warfare training site. However, live-fire exercises will probably not be possible in Playas 'since the owners of the town would consider the structural repair costs prohibitive' (Glenn *et al.* 2006: 63).

RAND's report considers that Playas would be improved as a training site if its structures were rebuilt along Arab lines. It suggests that 'the architecture of the abandoned town [should be] modified to include walled compounds of the type that US troops in Iraq and Afghanistan must at times isolate and clear' (Glenn *et al.* 2006: 63).

Despite being portrayed as a 'ghost town', a few remaining residents cling on in Playas. They largely make their living as extras in urban war and terrorist exercises; their down-at-heel town essentially makes its living being repeatedly assaulted and targeted by military power. Residents are apparently grateful for this new economic niche. 'We're glad things are going on down here', Linda McCarty, a Playas resident, remarked to *USA Today*. 'Until New Mexico Tech took over', and the town was given over to urban warfare training, 'it was really sad' (quoted in Hall 2005). The population of Playas is now around twenty-five families; most adults work for the training program as role players in the various scenarios portrayed in the exercises.

A network of existing 'low population' towns in North Dakota is also being considered for such a role. RAND also recommend use of a range of abandoned public infrastructures for urban war training across the United States. Included here are ships (as 'reasonable facsimile of subterranean environments' such as urban subways), abandoned factories, office complexes and strip malls, abandoned schools and hospitals or disused entertainment complexes (Glenn *et al.* 2006: 67). They note that some such facilities have already being taken over, or new simulations constructed, for rich consumers seeking the thrills of 'urban warfare' whilst staying at nearby luxury resorts.

The potential for real US metropolitan areas to act as urban warfare training grounds is also not ignored by RAND. They recommend a new range of urban warfare exercises, modelled on the Urban Warrior and Project Metropolis exercises, in which Marines 'invaded' Little Rock, Arkansas, Chicago, Illinois, Oakland, California, and Charleston, South Carolina, between 1999 and 2002 (Book 2002). In 1999, in a precursor to the treatment of Fallujah 5 years later, the Urban Warrior exercise in Oakland even involved the biometric scanning of 'resistance fighters' (Lettice 2004).

Such exercises will be even more necessary in the future, RAND argue, because 'no purpose-built urban training site and no simulation for many years to come will be able to present the heterogeneity and complexity of a modern megalopolis' (Glenn *et al.* 2006: 83). Such exercises centre on learning to disable the electrical, communications, transport and water infrastructures of a real city. The Oakland experience in March 1999, for example, involved major amphibious and airborne landings, staged to generate recruitment interest, as well as exercises in abandoned hospitals and sewer networks.

Destruction diorama

Although physical urban simulations for urban warfare training draw heavily on the expertise of Hollywood and theme park designers, a widening range of electronic ones link intimately into the booming video games and electronic simulations industries. Increasingly, such physical and electronic simulations of Arab cities are being produced together. The theory here, according to Scott Malo and Christopher Stapleton of the Media Convergence Laboratory at the University of Central Florida, is that 'the theme park technology of today adds the thrilling nature of full body stimulation and activity. So what if theme parks and video game combined their strengths?' (Malo and Stapleton 2004)

One such project, known as the 'Urban Terrain Module', is based at Fort Sill, Oklahoma. It blurs the latest electronic simulation technologies seamlessly into physically staged dioramas of devastated 'Arab' urban environments. This one-house space, embedded in a large media studio, is:

> decorated in a decidedly Middle-Eastern manner. A picture hangs on the wall, the smashed remnants of a small vase lie on a small circular table near the kitchen area. Like a Broadway show, walls and other set pieces can be swapped out as the training merits. (Associated Press 2004)

Built with the help of Hollywood stagecraft professionals, this site can project electronically simulated 'virtual humans', with suitably swarthy 'Arab' features, who are programmed to 'populate' the electronic screen spaces between the physical, ruined diorama. The electronic screens can conjure up apparently life-like Arabs as targets for the US military personnel who are 'embedded' within the module for their training session.

As well as all the now-familiar stage-set paraphernalia of simulated explosions, smoke and a computerised, desert landscape, the project's designers argue that the electronic simulations at Fort Sill are so convincing that the borders between the virtualised and the physical elements are increasingly indistinguishable to US soldiers undertaking training there. One promotional brochure at a major military simulation conference recently gushed that such artificial intelligence packages 'allows trainers to manipulate character responses on the fly, changing crowds into violent mobs with a keystroke' (Loredo 2004).

Fort Sill's operators imagine that, in the near future, the simulation will be modified to project real satellite and digital mapping data from Iraq, or other urban warfare locations, so that, as project director Colonel Gary Kinne puts it, 'individuals could train on the actual terrain that they would occupy someday – maybe in a future theatre of war' (quoted in Loredo 2004). Simulated smells, such as those used in physical urban war facilities, are also envisaged.

Here, digitised human targets blur with the tricks of Hollywood 'war-wound artists' to provide extra realism for such hybrid simulations. A similar facility, embedded inside San Diego's only television and movie studio at Stu Segall Productions, even employs amputee Marines returning from Iraq. 'They would go out on patrol with their squad' through the hybrid physical and virtual spaces of the simulated Iraqi city, reports Stu Segall, owner of the studio. 'A bomb would explode, and we'd pretend they lost a leg' (quoted in Loredo 2004).

The US Marines, meanwhile, are developing a 32,000-square-foot disused tomato factory in Penleton, California, into what they call their 'Infantry Immersion Trainer'. This 'augmented reality' of a 'hybrid' complex attempts a complete simulation of an entire Iraqi city block. 'Hardly a detail is overlooked among the props, modeled with Hollywood set-design techniques', writes *Wired* magazine.

> Laundry hangs on the clotheslines. A grill sits against a wall. Propane tanks are placed here and there amid the musky scent of unpaved streets and alleys. Perched in the rafters are projectors that cast life-size images of civilians and

insurgents on wall after wall in the building. Live actors and pyrotechnics round out the integration of sight, sound and smell.   (Shachtman 2008)

Jakarta, 2015

Much larger simulations of developing world megacities are also providing the sites for the main war-gaming activities through which US forces are imagining full-scale counter-insurgency warfare in the future. In the most important electronically simulated urban wargame – named 'Urban Resolve 2015' – a huge swathe of 8 square miles of Jakarta, in Indonesia, has been accurately digitised and 'geo-specifically' simulated in three dimensions. This has been done down to the interior of the (1.6 million) buildings, and also involves 109,000 mobile 'vehicles' and 'civilians', as well as the subterranean infrastructures. A virtual 'Baghdad' has been similarly rendered. Both cities have been conjured up within arrays of supercomputers as, in the words of James Winnefeled, director of the US Joint Forces Command's Joint Experimentation Directorate, future 'toxic environments for extremist ideologies' necessitating massive US military response (cited in Dawson 2007: 170).

The initiative has been used as the basis for a series of massive military simulations, involving over 1,500 participants, and using some of the US military's most sophisticated supercomputers across nineteen separate military bases, between 2003 and 2008. These projected the cities as the sites of massive urban wars involving US forces in 2015, complete with a range of envisaged new US sensors, surveillance systems and weapons geared specifically towards warfare unveiling the 'fog of war' in such a massive megacity. Opposition forces, who were programmed to fight autonomously within the virtualised megacity, were equipped with technologies imagined to be available on the open market in 2015 (including robotic vehicles).

As part of its mandate to 'replicate real-world geography, structures and culturally relevant population behaviors' (Axtell 2006), Urban Resolve even simulated the daily rhythms of the virtualised 'Jakarta' or 'Baghdad'. 'Roads [were] quiet at night, but during weekday rush hours they [became] clogged with traffic'. Virtualised 'people [went] to work, [took] lunch breaks and visit[ed] restaurants, banks and churches' – apparently unaware that they inhabited a major war zone. And 'traffic and civilian presence increase[d] around mosques at the appropriate times for daily prayers' (Wielhouwer 2005).

Players in Urban Resolve 2015 projected their imaginations of future war into a completely virtualised rendition of Jakarta or Baghdad. The city was pure battlespace; a receiving space for future ordinance. Bryan Axtell, a military PR spokesman, reported from one part of the exercise in October, 2006. Watching the 'players', he noted how 'Targeting crosshairs float across alleys and rooftops while one hand delicately nudges the ergonomic control sporting weapons toggles, and the other dances across the top of a box full of backlit red buttons and more joystick controls' (Axtell 2006).

Importantly, Urban Resolve was a major space through which the US military's efforts to develop future high-tech weapons geared towards urban insurgencies have been trialled within virtual renditions of future wars. In October 2006, for example, the armed drones 'flying' above Jakarta were equipped with imaginary versions of the 'directed-energy' or laser weapons that are being developed by the military's research and development outfits. The findings of Urban Resolve were apparently of such significance that they 'led to overhauling the entire U.S. Defense Department master plan' for future urban warfare (Lawlor 2007).

Nevertheless, all the state-of-the-art high-tech does not prevent Urban Resolve from having what Ashley Dawson calls 'a curiously hermetic feel to it' (Dawson 2007: 170). Most of the participants he observed sitting at the supercomputer terminals were 'balding white men with handlebar moustaches, the same blend of superannuated spooks and worn-out Special Forces hot-shots who have been running the real occupation of Iraq to such disastrous effect since 2003' (ibid.). Behind all, Dawson diagnoses a 'blinkered disavowal of the fact that it is the US occupation itself that is creating a toxic environment in Baghdad' (ibid.).

An army of gamers – 1

Today's troops received their basic training as children.   (Hamilton 2003)

Citizens. Countries. Video Games. The US Army keeps them all free.
    (US Army advertising slogan for it's video game, *America's Army, 2003)*

The simulation of Arab cities as receiving spaces for US military firepower goes well beyond the confines of the military. As the military blur with entertainment industries, so the electronic simulations of Arab cities used to train US soldiers are also used as the basis for successful commercial video games. Most notably here, *America's Army* and the US Marines' equivalent, *Full Spectrum Warrior*, have been developed by their respective forces, in partnership with entertainment industries, using urban training simulations as a basis (see http://www.americasarmy.com and www.fullspectrumwarrior.com, respectively).

The main purpose of these games is public relations: they are a powerful and extremely cost-effective means of recruitment. 'Because the Pentagon spends around $15,000 on average wooing each recruit, the game needs only to result in 300 enlistments per year to recoup costs' (Stahl 2006: 123). Forty per cent of those who join the Army have previously played the game (ibid.). The game also provides the basis for a sophisticated surveillance system through which Army recruitment efforts are directed and targeted. In the marketing speak of its military developers, *America's Army* is designed to reach the substantial overlap in 'population between the gaming population & the army's target recruiting segments'. It 'addresses tech-savvy audiences and afford the army a unique, strategic communication advantage' (cited in Lenoir n.d.).

Most startling of all, the game is designed as a recruitment device to exploit the fact that 'veteran [video] gamers exhibit higher performance in certain military skills requiring high visual attention'. In other words, as we shall see, the US military considers the playing of video games to be a form of preparatory military training (ibid.). Moreover, there is no attempt to disguise this fact. An article in

Defense Horizons magazine, for example, argues that 'video games made better soldiers and sailors faster, safer and cheaper' (Herz and Macedonia 2002). Former US Army psychologist, Lieutenant Colonel David Grossman, has spoken about how the use of video games and similar electronic training simulations helps to indoctrinate soldiers to kill more readily in real combat. The absence of 'blood, gore and emotions' from such games, he writes, helps in the 'teaching [of] children to associate pleasure with human death and suffering. We are rewarding them for killing people. And we are teaching them to like it' (cited in Leonard 2004).

America's Army, as Roger Stahl puts it, is 'a monumental step into twenty-first-century military-consumer culture' (Stahl 2006: 122). By 2008, the game had been downloaded over 38 million times; 8 million were registered users (Land 2007). The 'mission' of the game, writes Steve O'Hagan, 'is to slaughter evildoers, with something about "liberty" [. . .] going on in the back ground [. . .]. These games may be ultra-realistic down to the caliber of the weapons, but when bullets hit flesh people just crumple serenely into a heap. No blood. No exit wounds. No screams' (Hagan 2004). Roger Stahl (2006: 130) notes that, 'sometimes a mist of blood escapes an invisible wound, but the victims neither flail nor cry. Bodies tend to disappear as if raptured up to heaven'.

The lobby group, Empowered Muslim Youth, also argues that the careful targeting of children and young people through these games amounts to a form of cultural brain washing. 'These visual games are a perfect opportunity to psychologically prepare and even mentally train children to fight in battle', they argue. 'There is no doubt that this [is a] well-thought tactic, issued by high-ranking government officials' (Axe 2008).

Both *America's Army* and *Full Spectrum Warrior* – which were amongst the world's most popular video game franchises of 2008 – 'propel the player into the world of the gaming industry's latest fetish: modern urban warfare' (DelPiano 2004). Both centre overwhelmingly on the military challenges allegedly involved in occupying and pacifying stylised, Orientalised, Arab cities. They also force players to undertake basic training in an electronic simulation of one of the US military's largest physical urban warfare training sites at Mount McKenna. Andrew Deck argues that the proliferation of urban warfare games based on actual, ongoing US military interventions in Arab cities works to 'call forth a cult of ultra-patriotic xenophobes whose greatest joy is to destroy, regardless of how racist, imperialistic, and flimsy the rationale' for the simulated battle (Deck 2004).

Games like *America's Army* and *Full Spectrum Warrior* work powerfully to construct the US soldier as a hyper-masculine agent of (just and honorable) violence just as they construct the stylised, Arab Other as a loose and unspecified existential threat to vague ideas of 'freedom' or 'America'. These two, of course, are rendered inseparable: 'in articulating the other the Army concomitantly constitutes itself' (Kumar 2004). The depiction of this vague, threatening and patently evil racialised Other further reinforces imaginary geographies equating Arab cities with 'terrorism' and the need for 'pacification' or 'cleansing' via US military invasion and occupation. More than further blurring the already fuzzy boundaries separating war from entertainment, it demonstrates that the US entertainment industry 'has assumed a posture of cooperation towards a culture of permanent war' (Deck 2004).

Complex and self-reinforcing connections between war and entertainment emerge here that deepen the long-established role of toys and films as outlets for militaristic propaganda. On the one hand, it has been estimated that around 90 per cent of the 75,000 men and women who join the US Army each year are 'casual' gamers; 30 per cent consider themselves 'hard-core' gamers. Immersive video games within which players endlessly practice counter-insurgency warfare within stylised Arab cities work here as a powerful recruitment, training and public relations device (Lenoir n.d.).

Within urban warfare video games it is striking that Arab cities are, once again, represented merely as 'collections of objects not congeries of people' (Gregory 2004: 201). When people *are* represented, almost without exception, they are rendered as the shadowy, subhuman, racialised Arab figure of some absolutely external 'terrorist' – figures to be annihilated repeatedly in sanitised 'action' as entertainment, or military training, or a blurred version of both. *America's Army*, for example, simulates 'counter terror' warfare in densely packed Arab cities in a fictional country of 'Zekistan'. Almost every building is dark, shadowy, burning, and rendered in stylised Islamic architecture.

Here, then, once again, the only role for Arab cities is as environments for military engagement. The militarisation of the everyday sites, artefacts and spaces of the simulated city is total. 'Cars are used as bombs, bystanders become victims [although they die without spilling blood], houses become headquarters, apartments become lookout points, and anything to be strewn in the street becomes suitable cover' (DelPiano 2004). Indeed, there is some evidence that the actual physical geographies of Arab cities are being digitised to provide the three-dimensional 'battlespace' for each game. One games developer, Forterra Systems, which also develops training games for the US military, boasts that 'we've [digitally] built a portion of the downtown area of a large Middle Eastern capital city where we have a significant presence today' (Deck 2004).

Disappearing death

Just as the main commercial video game and electronic entertainment corporations actively seek to build physical and material versions of their products in the form of theme parks and shopping malls, so the US military has sought to cash in on the astonishing popularity of its own video games to extend its recruitment push. One result is the 'Virtual Army Experience' – a massive 20,000-square-foot touring roadshow that pitched up at airshows, rodeos, car races, car shows and other 'patriotic' events. This allows potential recruits to experience a propagandised version of the Army for 20 minutes. 'Only Soldiers know how it feels to fight in a combat zone, but civilians now have an opportunity to get a virtual taste of the action', gushed the Army News Service on the initiative's launch in February 2007 (Hayner 2007).

'Guests' of the 'experience' are given fake army dog tags, extensively interviewed and then briefed on their 'mission', which is to drive a convoy or heavily armed Humvee vehicles into an 'Arab' city and extract a purported terrorist leader. Given the nature of war in Iraq, it is quite apt, of course, that participants *drive* their mock-up vehicles over and through the simulated and stylised Arab city, before entering their own cars and SUVs to drive home.

The six simulated vehicles are surrounded by virtual renditions of the town drawn from the America's Army game; participants use their weapons and, as in a shoot-'em-up game, their targets die when hit. As with the game itself, of course, 'when the bad guys die, they fall bloodlessly and disappear. They keep coming – standing atop silos, pouring from buildings' (Six Flags Blog n.d.). One gun-ho video gamer, recalling his 'experience' of the simulation at the 2007 DigitalLife Expo, recounts that:

> The action started out a bit slow with a civilian or two running by to go hide inside their home before being blasted with a stray bullet. As our Humvees began to roll forward, we were presented with varying degrees of enemies that would either pop out around corners, run out into the street, or rest atop a placement on top of a building. The actual shooting experience was fairly solid. There was a small amount of kickback with the weapon and because it was the real thing, the weight of the gun took its toll over the course of our time inside the truck.   (GGL Wire 2007)

After the 'mission', a 'debriefing' is dispensed and participants are then interviewed as to their interest in an Army career:

> The 'debriefing' consisted of a short recruitment video and the highest-scoring participant receiving an action figure of Sgt. Tommy Rieman, one of four real soldiers in the America's Army Real Heroes program and upon which a line of action figures are being based.   (Green 2007)

The whole process is carefully organised with a view to building up profiles of possible recruits that can be followed up later. The consumer surveillance company Fish Technologies was tasked with collecting data profiles of participants as they were processed through the site, which could later be used to support Army recruitment efforts.

Even US military veterans have expressed revulsion at this latest virtualisation of military killing. The Missouri group, Democracy for Missouri, who have picketed the display, for example, recall the experience. 'This obscene display has folks lining up to play virtual war complete with surround video and realistic explosion sounds', they write. 'The screams of women and children were not a part of the "Experience"'   (Democracy for Missouri n.d.).

The ultimate gated communities

> The excesses of American culture are strikingly evident in the way that the U.S. military builds its outposts. The defense of the United States has led to

the massive imposition of tract homes and strip malls on the world – creating mini-Americas that inhibit cultural understanding between U.S. troops and our allies abroad.   (Gillem 2007).

Just as mock and stylised 'Arab' cities dot the heartlands of the United States, so, in a striking parallel, simulated and stylised US cities now pepper the fringes of Empire. As architecture professor Mark Gillem (2007) has shown, the 700 or so foreign US military bases, located within 140 of the world's 195 countries, which anchor the imperial and geographic power of the nation, increasingly resemble carefully designed capsules of prototypical US suburbia, implanted into foreign nations.

Replete with their golf courses, strip malls and 'drive-thru' fast-food franchises, their manicured lawns and their perfect simulations of US schools, fire stations, split-level ranches, hotels, bars, parking lots and cinemas, all is set within the sprawl of extremely low-density US-style suburbs. The architecture and design of US bases reflect the strict application of US norms of urban design. This allows America's service personnel, wherever they are posted around the world, to 'arrive in the same familiar vision of "home"' (ibid.: 73).

Allowing US service personnel and their families to inhabit a complete simulacrum of US suburbia, whilst absorbing vast tranches of foreign land, US bases thus allow military residents to almost completely disengage from the world beyond the gate. Gillem argues that the new imperial land-use model sustaining the proliferation of US bases around the world is one of 'avoidance' (ibid.: 263). This amounts to relocating military bases to 'isolated but well-appointed compounds designed to prevent contact with the residents' (ibid.: 74). 'The US government has dispersed its soldiers across the globe to protect the flow of empire' (ibid.: 74):

> [US service personnel] are living a diaspora experience and are trying to define themselves with reference to their distant homeland, a common feature of diaspora communities. They have multiple homes, but they are trying to reconcile difference through design. Wherever these soldiers go, they are homeward bound – bound to the same sprawling subdivisions, franchised restaurants, and vacuous shopping malls.

Gillem's work illustrates that perhaps it is time to consider the vast, globally stretched archipelago of US military camps and bases to be the ultimate transnational array of gated communities. The 'community' web page for 'Joint Task Force Guantanamo' – where 7,000 military personnel organise the war on terror's most notorious torture camp – actually promotes the complex by arguing that 'sun, sand and a close knit community make the naval station one of the finest "gated communities" in the Caribbean' (see http://www.jtfgtmo.southcom.mil/community.html). Meanwhile, Lieutenant Colonel Goyette (2007) of Holloman Air Force Base in New Mexico admits that her relatives, who had recently visited the base, had gushed that:

there [are] people who pay good money to live in a gated community as nice as this one. You have a free fitness center with an amazing amount of fitness opportunities, reduced cost medical and dental care, good schools within walking distance from your house, movies for a dollar, reduced golf fees, reduced grocery costs and you get to watch really cool planes all day long.

'Isn't that an interesting way to look at how we live?', she argued:

My husband and I really appreciate the feeling of security we get living on base. While I still watch my kids when they play in the front yard, I know I don't have to worry about drive-by shootings or drug sales on the sidewalk. I don't have to worry about gang bangers living next to me, bringing dangerous traffic to the neighbourhood.

However, rather than rendering the rest of the domestic city as a feared and residualised space, these bases are geographical capsules that turn their back on the lands and peoples they are (putatively) defending. Here we confront sites that render the world beyond the walls as alien Other in the most extreme way. This is done beyond the obvious military–civilian contrast and also works linguistically, culturally, ethnically and in terms of architecture and landscape design. Of course, this comparison does have its limits. The gates, walls and fences, too, are obviously rather more heavily militarised than those around the average US gated community. Design protocols also have to deal with the need for setbacks and blast zones designed to inhibit truck and car bombs from causing damage to important facilities. And, of course, not many suburban gated communities house squadrons of tanks or stealth fighters, or are protected by batteries of Patriot missiles – at least not yet.

The most extraordinary example of these strange shadows of the mock Arab cities within the US heartland are the $2.5 billion 'tourist and development' plans, announced by the US Army in May 2008, to turn Baghdad's infamous Green Zone into the 'Tigris Woods Golf and Country Club'. Cordoned off from the turmoil of Iraq beyond the walls the *Guardian*'s Michael Howard (2008), having analysed the plans, asks us to:

Picture, if you will, a tree-lined plaza in Baghdad's International Village, flanked by fashion boutiques, swanky cafes, and shiny glass office towers. Nearby a golf course nestles agreeably, where a chip over the water to the final green is but a prelude to cocktails in the club house and a soothing massage in a luxury hotel, which would not look out of place in Sydney harbour. Then, as twilight falls, a pre-prandial stroll, perhaps, amid the cool of the Tigris Riverfront Park, where the peace is broken only by the soulful cries of egrets fishing. Improbable though it all may seem, this is how some imaginative types in the US military are envisaging the future of Baghdad's Green Zone, the much-pummelled redoubt of the Iraqi capital where a bunker shot has until now had very different connotations.

Toys of war

> Recording-launching. Seeing-aiming-firing. A realtime flow aligns with,
> contains, produces a target . . . A target-object to be seen, saved, destroyed. A
> projectile sent to seal the deal. A radically new perspective-as-control tech-
> nology. A perspective that obliterates all perspectives.   (Crandall 2002)

Military simulations also now take their place within the proliferating spectacles
and themed fantasy landscapes, peppered with digital screens and digitally 'augmented architecture', that now dominate urban consumption and tourism in the
US (and elsewhere).

In 2006, at Fort Belvoir, Virginia, for example, the US Army considered a
proposal from a private developer to complement a major new military museum
at the site with a 125-acre, $300 million military theme park and simulation centre
along with a massive hotel complex. According to the *Washington Post*, the proposal promised that visitors would be able to 'command the latest M-1 tank [or]
feel the rush of a paratrooper's free-fall, fly a Cobra gunship' (CNN.com 2006).

The developer, Orlando-based Universal City Property Management, argued
that the complex would put visitors 'in an interactive world where [they'd] feel
firsthand what it's like to defend American freedom'. Visitors would be able to
'live the greatest battles of all time in a multi-sensory 4-D presentation' (cited in
USA Today 2006). However, the proposal generated criticism that it would 'make
a mockery of the Army experience' and was quickly withdrawn. The Army is now
seeking another 'visitor destination concept' to go with its main museum that will
be built on the site (ibid.).

With experience within such simulators becoming more and more indistinguishable from that of the 'pilots' or armed drones used in the CIA's frequent
assassination raids in the Middle East and Pakistan, a further and troubling blurring of metropolitan heartland and colonial frontier emerges. For these pilots are
actually located in anonymous container-like trailer housing virtual reality 'caves'
at Nellis Air Force Base on the edge of that icon of urban simulation – Las Vegas.

Here the ubiquity of virtual simulations and games merges seamlessly and
disturbingly into the video game-like reality of the very real weaponry and killing. *Wired* magazine, talking to one Predator pilot, Private Joe Clark, points out
that he has, in a sense, 'been prepping for the job since he was a kid: He plays
videogames. A lot of videogames. Back in the barracks he spends downtime with
an Xbox and a PlayStation' (quoted in Shachtman 2005). After his training, 'when
he first slid behind the controls of a Shadow [Unmanned aerial Vehicle] UAV, the
point and click operation turned out to work much the same way. "You watch the
screen. You tell it to roll left, it rolls left. It's pretty simple," Clark says' (cited in
Shachtman 2005).

Indeed, such crossovers are intensifying further. The newest Predator control
systems from the arms maker, Raytheon, deliberately use the 'same HOTAS
[hands on stick and throttle] system on a . . . video game'. Raytheon's UAV
designer argues that 'There's no point in re-inventing the wheel. The current generation of pilots was raised on the [Sony] Playstation, so we created an interface

that they will immediately understand' (Richfield 2006). Added to this, many of the latest video games actually depict the very same armed UAVs as those used in assassination raids by US forces.

The fact that the training simulators for armed drones 'are said to be so realistic that it would be difficult to distinguish, without previous knowledge, between them and the actual ground stations' adds a further layer to the blurring of simulation and reality (Technology.com n.d.). These simulators, 'running 1 terabyte of memory, replicate actual terrain and actual locations of the world, such as Afghanistan and Iraq' (ibid.).

Another UAV controller, interviewed by Robert Kaplan (2006), pointed out the extreme geographical juxtapositions involved in 'piloting' armed drones on the other side of the planet from a metal box on the edge of Las Vegas. 'Inside that trailer is Iraq; inside the other, Afghanistan', he explained, enthusing that 'If you want to pull the trigger and take out bad guys, you fly a Predator'. In perhaps the ultimate juxtaposition of domestic suburbia and the distant projection of colonial violence, strikingly, as another 'pilot' admits, 'at the end of the work day, you walk back into the rest of life in America' (quoted in Newman 2003).

Here the main issue confronting military personnel is the extreme contrast between the hyper-real killing-at-a-distance within the trailers and the searingly familiar world of urban America that lies outside the door. 'Inside the trailers, crews don't get even the sensation of flying that one gets in a flight simulator', writes Kaplan (2006):

> The real tension for these pilots comes from the clash with everything outside the trailers. Beyond Nellis is the banal world of spouses, kids, homework, and soccer games not to mention the absurdity of a city where even the gas stations have slot machines. Simply entering or leaving one of the trailers is tremendously disorienting.

But the blurring of weaponry and toys – which have, of course, always been closely associated – is accelerating even further. For as well as directly shaping the output of toys, films and video games to encourage children to be potential recruits, the US military's weapons are now reciprocating these links by imitating toys and video games. Some US military equipment, as we have seen with the Predator, now has control consoles that directly mimic those of Playstation 2s.

The 'Dragon Runner' urban surveillance robot, which has now been deployed in the Marines, is another example. 'The toy-like Dragon Runner', writes Nick Turse (2003), 'is guided by a six-button keypad, modeled after Sony's PlayStation 2 videogame controller'. Major Greg Heines, of the Marine's Warfighting Laboratory, stresses that the design was chosen because 'that's what these 18-, 19-year-old Marines have been playing with pretty much all of their lives, [so they] will pick up [how to drive the Dragon Runner] in a few minutes' (quoted ibid.). In March 2000 the emergence of Playstations as weapons controls actually had an unforeseen effect: they were classified by the Japanese government as a 'general purpose product related to conventional weapons', a change that considerably reduced export levels and led to a global shortage of the consoles (Stahl 2006: 112).

Sim cities

Tied intimately into entertainment industries, this collection of simulations produces the mock streets, immersive cities and entire digital cityscapes of America's others as the key landscapes for perpetual violence, permanent war and militarised entertainment. But these, as always in the history of colonialist warfare, actually say more about the preoccupations and assumptions of urban life in colonial heartlands – in this case the United States – than about the realities of their current colonial target: Arab urbanism.

The military 'simulacral collective' speaks volumes about the fragmenting landscapes and radicalised politics of US cities in the neoconservative era. This is particularly so as US law enforcement becomes increasingly militarised, and the US Army and Marines become more involved in 'urban military operations' centred on US cities. A key legitimisation here is the latest US military doctrine that sees all cities as key nodes within an all-encompassing global 'battlespace' within which a wide spectrum of 'asymmetric' conflicts need to be confronted, with no conventional military 'front' and 'back' regions. Such doctrine increasingly undermines long-standing military distinctions between the 'inside' and the 'outside' zones of colonial military power and security policy.

Along with the boom in 'homeland security' since 9/11, this means that the military simulacral collective now centres as much on simulating Los Angeles as on Baghdad, on imagining major military operations to 'take back' US cities from civil uprisings or social protests as much as projecting forces to occupy Arab urban regions. The Los Angeles riots of 1992 appear on US military Powerpoints about 'lessons learned' as often as Mogadishu, Baghdad, Jenin or Grozny.

Meanwhile, in the United States, simulated Arab cities are being joined by dozens of physical simulations of US city districts in which law enforcement and National Guard personnel practise operations against civil unrest, terrorist attack and natural disaster. 'Another architecture is rising in the expanding landscape of preparedness', writes the programme notes for the Center for Land Use Interpretation's 'Emergency State' programme. 'Condensed simulacra of our existing urban environments are forming within our communities, where the first responders to emergencies, on a small or large scale, practice their craft of dealing with disaster' and 'the police contend with civil decay, robberies, hostage situations, looting, riots, and snipers' (CLUI n.d.). As part of the drive for 'preparedness', simulations and exercises of major civil disturbances and terror attacks are now regularly held in Western cities, which link closely to those sustaining military incursions aboard. The Urban Resolve exercise, for example, which is mainly centred on Jakarta and Baghdad, also has a component centred on the US naval base city of Newport, Virginia. Echoing the olfactory simulations used in mock urban warfare cities, the Israeli military have even perfected a scent resembling rotting bodies to add a sense of realism to their homeland defence simulations.

Military simulations are helping to produce US cities in another, more direct way. For generating them now takes up large swathes of the US economy, especially in high-tech metropolitan areas. Many of the much-vaunted high-tech suburban 'hotspots' that house what Richard Florida (2003) has called the US 'creative class' – places such as the Washington Beltway, North Carolina Research Triangle, Florida's 'High-Tech' Corridor or San Diego's High-Tech Cluster – are actually heavily sustained by producing symbolic violence against Arab, as well as US central, cities.

As well as being the foundaries of the security state, and the sites of the most militarised and corporatised research universities, these locations are the places where the vastly profitable and rapidly growing convergence between electronic games and military simulation is being forged. Orlando's 100 large military simulator firms, for example, generate around 17,000 jobs and are starting to overshadow even Disney as local economic drivers. Behind the blank facades and manicured lawns, thousands of software engineers and games profession-als project their Orientalised electronic imaginaries onto the world through the increasingly seamless complex of military, entertainment, media and academic industries.

The importance of military simulation industries is not lost on those tasked with developing cities' local economies. The municipality of Suffolk, Virginia, for example, now proudly boats that a 'world-class cluster of "Modeling and Simulation" enterprises has taken root around the U.S. Joint Forces Command and an Old Dominion University research center' (Suffolk News-Herald 2005). To support further growth in these sectors, local governments and economic develop-ment partnerships are directly working to support the Joint Forces Command who 'asked how the state of Virginia could better support JFCOM and its mission'. This economic convergence will gain support from the Virginia Modeling and Simulation Initiative (VIMSIM), which will be geared to 'stimulate develop-ment of a unique high-tech industry with multi-billion dollar revenue potential'. Already, Lockheed Martin has opened a major simulation complex there. 'As a growing high technology hub with proximity to major defense, homeland security and other important customer installations', the CEO, Vance Coffman, pointed out in 2003, 'Suffolk is the ideal location for our new center' (ibid.).

Self-fulfilling worlds

All efforts to render politics aesthetic culminate in one thing – war.
(Benjamin 1999: 241)

Since 9/11, simulations (war games, training exercises, scenario planning, and modeling) and dissimulations (propaganda, disinformation, infowar, deceit, and lies) were producing a hall of mirrors, reducing the 'truth' about the 'Global War on Terror' to an infinite regression of representations that defied authentication.   (Der Derian 2004)

The complex constellation of simulations of Arab and global south cities discussed here works most powerfully as a collective. Their various physical, electronic and blended physical-electronic manifestations operate together, as do all simulacra, by collapsing the real with artifice to the extent that any simple boundary between the two effectively disappears (Baudrillard 1994).

More properly, as Jean Baudrillard famously stressed, it is best to consider the above simulations, not as 'copies' of the 'real' world, but as hyper-real constructions – simulations of things that don't exist – through which war and violence are constructed, legitimised and performed. 'Simulation is no longer that of a territory, a referential being, or a substance', he writes. 'It is the generation by models of a real without origins or reality: a hyperreal' (ibid.: 166).

The point, then, is not that these simulations are less 'real' than the things they purportedly represent. Rather, they provide spaces through which the violence of the 'war on terror' can be generated and performed, which gain their very power from their radical disassociation from any meaningful connection with the real places (or, less commonly, people) that they are said to represent. In the process, these simulacra 'participate in the construction of a discourse of security which is self-fulfilling' (Kumar 2004: 8).

Because the worlds of threat and risk are projected through this collective of simulations, state violence and colonial war is necessary, just and honorable. In turn, more simulations are required to improve the effectiveness of such violence, to tempt and train more recruits, to deal with the psychological devastation once they return home, and so on. It follows that the notion of 'security', at least as constructed through the military simulacral collective, is actually possible only through permanent war. 'War makes security possible by creating that which is to be protected and what makes war possible: . . . The mechanization of soldiers, the obscuring of the enemy and the sanitisation of violence' (ibid.).

The mediatisation of contemporary war is such that the 'fighting' of wars takes place as much in TV lounges, in multiplexes and on Youtube or Playstation screens as in the real streets and alleys of 'combat zone' cities. In such a context, it is crucial that the military simulacral collective permeates through a whole host of media simultaneously as always-vague distinctions between civil and military media and technology blur completely away. Previously considered largely distinct, multiple media domains are currently fusing and interpenetrating within and through the simulacral collective. This is happening in ways that are confusing, disturbing and extremely fast moving. 'We see', writes Roger Stahl (2006: 123):

> that various genres once thought to be discrete are forging new and strange alliances. Wartime news looks like a video game; video games restage the news. Official military training simulators cross over into the commercial entertainment markets; commercial video games are made useful for military training exercises. Advertisements sell video games with patriotic rhetorics; video games are mobilized to advertise patriotism. The business of play works closely with the military to replicate the tools of state violence; the business of state violence in turn capitalizes on playtime for institutional ends.

An army of gamers – 2

In addition, as we have seen, video game technologies are progressively merging with weapons technologies. Experiences of controlling and using real weapons are in some cases blurring so completely with the military simulators of such weapons, as well the use of video games offering other simulations of the use of such weapons, that users are beginning to struggle to define which realm they inhabit at any time.

Projecting current trends, Brian Finoki, author of the superb subtopia blog (see http://subtopia.blogspot.com/), speculates about a near-future in which 'video games become the ultimate interface for conducting real life warfare' as 'virtual reality simulators used in video gaming converge completely with those used is military training and exercises' (Finoki 2006). Finoki takes the video game-like existence of the Las Vegas Predator 'pilots', with their Playstation-style controls, as his starting point. 'Could gamers', he asks:

> become decorated war heroes by virtue of their eye-and-hand coordination skills, which would eventually dominate the triggers of network-centric remote controlled warfare? Taking this notion to the extreme, could casual assemblages of home bodies on couches strewn across America become the new command posts for an intercontinental sprawl of robotic warfare? Good old American homes could 'adopt a war bot' abroad, while little Johnny controls it with his new joystick that he's gotten for Christmas. These kids would pass back and forth game pads while taking turns hitting simulated bunkers on their little screens that set off real-world explosions on bunkers the other side of the world, under siege from a brackish platoon of swarming militarized war bots; is this where we're headed?   (Finoki 2006)

War re-enchanted: the end of death

The military simulacral collective is the main product of what James Der Derian (2001) has called the 'military–industrial–media–entertainment network'. As a complex, this is dedicated to 'the disappearance of the body, the aestheticization of violence, the sanitization of war' (Gregory 2008: 19). This 'exorcism of harm from war' (Kumar 2004: 8) operates because the whole spectrum of simulations – from those used for actual killing through those used for training to those used for entertainment – are all based on their own variation of the axiom of what Der Derian (2001) calls 'Virtuous War'. This involves what he calls 'the technical capability and the ethical imperative to threaten, and if needed, actualize violence from a distance, with no or minimal casualties' (to the 'home side' that is) (ibid.).

We might add to this that the threatened or actualised violence tends to operate through the complex of simulacra discussed above: video gamers as well as Predator drone pilots use virtually identical technologies of control and electronic visualisation to dispatch violence at a distance. Increasingly, the only difference is that the latter may actually be killing someone, rather than watching a ghostly set of pixels that magically disappear when hit.

The result, as Derek Gregory (2008: 17) argues, is that, paradoxically, an enterprise expressly devoted to killing magically proceeds without death'. The complex of simulations depicted here thus play a massive – perhaps dominant role – in what has been termed the 'contemporary re-enchantment with war' (Coker 2004). This is especially seductive as, on the one hand, they manage to 'reintroduce corporeality to war – cyber-cities are re-peopled, Virtual Humans made to breathe', whilst, on the other, 'snuff[ing] out' all hints of the realities of mortality (Gregory 2008: 17).

Such a process of death-denial moves even further beyond the marshalling of physical, electronic of blended simulations of purportedly Arab cities in training sites, video games, movies or recruitment fairs. Through what are euphemistically called 'perception management operations' (Gough 2003), it extends, too, to the banning of images of dead service personnel's coffins and the careful construction of Hollywood-esque news propaganda for supine mainstream media as part of its doctrine of managing an often compliant media through 'information operations'. It is now clear that the Pentagon carefully fakes material for its orchestrated news 'splashes' using techniques of physical and electronic simulation. Such actions are deemed to be merely another element in the apparently infinite spectrum of 'information' or 'psychological operations' necessary to sustain the United States's 'full spectrum' or 'information dominance' in a highly mediatised and globalised world (see Crotts and Metcalfe 2006).

In early 2002, for example, the Bush administration considered establishing an Office for Strategic Influence that would deliberately plant news items with media organizations through outside concerns that might not have obvious ties to the Pentagon. The stage-managed 'rescue' of Jessica Lynch is the most well-known example here.

Such media simulations are combined with the violent targeting of media channels that do show images of the war dead to the world. In April 2003, US aircraft, for example, bombed Al-Jazeera's Baghdad office, killing one of its journalists; this happened 5 months after destroying the network's Kabul office with a missile (Deans 2003). 'With high technology involving satellite and lap-top "cross-hair" accuracy and awareness of Al-Jazeera location for over two years, we were meant to believe that the T.V. station, lying in a residential neighbourhood with three satellite dishes on its roof – was an accident' (Metcalfe n.d.). Tony Blair and George Bush even seriously considered bombing Al-Jazeera's headquarters, in Qatar (Regan 2005).

'Virtual citizen-soldiers'

The radical denial of the social and cultural worlds, and lived urbanism, of the cities targeted by the military simulacral complex is the key to the encircling militarism in the current period. US nationalism and militarism thus increasingly rest not just on an extending and integrating army of immersive and physical simulations of war. They also rely on an extending archipelago of ersatz urban environments – physical, electronic and hybrid – within which the calls to colonial and Orientalised violence can be enacted and repeated whilst at the same time being continually distanced from the real bodies, and places, destroyed by such violence. For the one thing that binds the complex archipelago of simulation addressed in this chapter is the distancing and denial of the death and destruction sustained by the blurring of symbolic and actual violence that these simulations perpetuate.

The military simulacral collective, in particular, works by naturalising Arab and global south cities as little but physical battlespace, populated, when peopled at all, by lurking, dehumanised and radicalised 'terrorists', to be assaulted and erased by violent Western or Israeli interventions, for the good of 'freedom'. It does this to the three closely linked imperatives: of profit, commodified entertainment and the culture of permanent war. For all of these benefit hugely from the seductive militaristic gloss and relentless, repetitive sanitisation at play.

As well as producing endless fields of repetitive, symbolic, sanitised and preparatory violence, the military simulacral collective forces its participants – whether in physical wargames, military electronic simulations or video games – to conform to the rituals of urban combat through narrowing down the possibilities of action to one only: aggressive and hyper-masculine military assault. Soldiers thus consume the various simulacra and use them to base their real treatments of the spaces and inhabitants of the global south cities that they patrol, assault and occupy. They inhabit the stylised and Orientalised worlds of US military video games whilst on leisure time in the encampments of Baghdad. And they even confront their post-war psychological traumas by re-immersing themselves within more electronic, urban simulacral, as the all-too-real streets of Iraq's cities recede into troubled sites of memory.

A major concern here is that a lifetime of being conditioned to wage war against virtual enemies in pixellated 'Arab cities' will starkly influence the behaviour once they are recruited and deployed as soldiers. Thus, 'once in the field . . . these soldiers may become "charged" in the same way stimulated by the games and with lethal results, thanks to the "disconnect" between 3-D flesh and blood and 2-D pixel people' (Seal 2003). Here, the concern is that the 'play' or war merges with actual US military killing into a singular, cinematic landscape – all performed under the sonic assault of thrash-metal.

Citizens, meanwhile, become what Roger Stahl (2006: 123) calls 'virtual citizen-soldiers' in a boundless, networked culture of permanent war where everything transmogrifies into 'battlespace'. Their very childhood experiences of militarised play increasingly blur seamlessly into the actions of contemporary war as weaponry and toys fuse. This is accompanied by a deepening process of militarisation marked by the 'recoding of the social field with military values and ideals' (ibid.).

As a result, in line with the wider themes addressed in this book, these constellations of new media and simulations operate to 're-map traditional lines between battlefield and home front' (ibid.: 130). The most disturbing part of this process is the way it forecloses the very possibilities of democratic engagement. 'The conditions for this deliberation', communications theorist Roger Stahl (ibid.: 125) argues, 'depend on a clear demarcation between the political role of the citizen and the apolitical role of the soldier. While the citizen's role is to deliberate, the soldier's role is to take orders'.

If 'citizens-soldiers' are habituating to personally participating in a culture of permanent war against a virtualised and Orientalised Other, questions of why this violence is necessary will recede further and further from the cultural landscape. 'The virtual citizen-soldier's integration into a sanitized fantasy of war is a seduction whose pleasures are felt at the expense of the capacity for critical engagement in matters of military might' (ibid.).

Note

1 This chapter is a revised version of a chapter in the book Graham, S. (2010) *Cities under Siege: The New Military Urbanism*, Verso: London.

References

Associated Press (2002) 'Urban combat training center will be Army's largest', Citizen Review Online, December. Available at http://www.citizenreviewonline.org/Dec_2002/urban.htm.

Associated Press (2004) 'Army unveils new, ultra-real simulation', MSNBC.com, December 20. Available at http://www.citizenreviewonline.org/Dec_2002/urban.htm.

Axe, D. (2008) 'America's army game = brainwashing?', *Wired*, January 29. Available at http://blog.wired.com/defense/2008/01/army-game-worri.html.

Axtell, B. (2006) 'Urban warfare experiment draws many players', USJFCOM Public Affairs, October 24. Available at http://www.jfcom.mil/newslink/storyarchive/2006/pa102406.html.

Baudrillard, J. (1994) *Simulacra and Simulation*, Ann Arbor: University of Michigan Press.

Benjamin, W. (1999) 'The work of art in the age of mechanical reproduction', in H. Arendt (ed.) *Illuminations*, trans. Harry Zohn, New York: Schocken, pp. 217–52.

Book, E. (2002) 'Project metropolis brings urban wards to U.S. cities', *National Defense Magazine*, April. Available at http://www.nationaldefensemagazine.org/issues/2002/Apr/Project_Metropolis.htm.

0Training site replicates Iraqi village', Stars and Stripes.Com, July 26 Available at http://www.military.com/features/0,15240,107000,00.html.

Broomberg, A. and Chanarin, O. (2007) *Chicago*, London: SteidlMack.

CLUI (n.d.) 'Exhibition review: emergency state: first responders and emergency training architecture'. Available at http://www.clui.org/clui_4_1/pro_pro/exhibits/emergency.html.

CNN.com (2006) 'C'mon kids, let's go to Army world!', August 8. Available at http://www.cnn.com/2006/US/08/08/military.theme.park.ap/index.html.

Coker, C. (2004) *The Future of War: The Re-Enchantment of War in the Twenty-First Century*, Oxford: Blackwell.

Crandall, J. (2002) 'Fingering the trigger', Nettime, April 2. Available at http://www.nettime.org/Lists-Archives/nettime-l-0204/msg00007.html.

Crotts, D. and Metcalfe, J. (2006) 'Operational Implications of Public Affairs – Factors, Functions, and Challenges of the Information Battlefield', USA Iosphere, Winter 2006. Available at http://www.au.af.mil/info-ops/iosphere/iosphere_win06_crotts.pdf.

Davis, M. (2002) *Dead Cities, and Other Tales, New York*: New Press, pp 65–84.

Davis, M. (2005) 'The urbanization of Empire: megacities and the laws of chaos', *Social Text, 22(4), 9–15.*

Davis, M. (2006) *Planet of Slums*, London: Verso.

Dawson, A. (2007) 'Combat in hell: cities as the Achilles' heel of U.S. imperial hegemony', *Social Text*, 25(2), 169–80

Deans, J. (2003)' Al-Jazeera cameraman killed in US raid', *The Guardian*, April 8 2003. Available at http://www.guardian.co.uk/media/2003/apr/08/iraq.iraqandthemedia.

Deck, A. (2004) 'Demilitarizing the playground', No Quarter. Available at http://artcon-text.net/crit/essays/noQuarter/.

DelPiano, S. (2004) 'Review of Full Spectrum Warrior', Games First. Available at http://www.gamesfirst.com/reviews/07.10.04/FullSpectrumRev/fullspectrumreview.htm.

Democracy for Missouri (n.d.) 'Democracy for Missouri confronts the "Virtual Army Experience" at Recruitment . . . er . . . Memorial . . . Day'. Available at http://democracyformissouri.org/d/node/1159.

Der Derian, J. (2001) *Virtuous War: Mapping the Military–Industrial–Media–Entertainment Complex*, Boulder, CO: Westview.

Der Derian, J. (2004) 'Conference Brief for Dis/Simulations of War and Peace Symposium'. Available at http://www.watsoninstitute.org/infopeace/dissim/.

Finoki, R. (2006) 'War room', Subtopia blog, May 20. Available at http://subtopia.blogspot.com/2006/05/war-room_20.html

Florida, R. (2003) *The Rise of the Creative Class*, New York: Basic Books.

GGL Wire (2007) 'DigitalLife 2007: the Virtual Army Experience', August 12. Available at http://wire.ggl.com/2007/09/29/digitallife-2007-the-virtual-army-experience/.

Gillem, M. (2007) *America Town: Building the Outposts of Empire*, Minneapolis: University of Minnesota Press.

Glenn, R., Jacobs, J., Nichiporuk, B., Paul, C., Raymond, B., Steeb, R. and Thie, H. (2006) 'Preparing for the Proven Inevitable: An Urban Operations Training Strategy for America's Joint Force', report prepared for the US Secretary of Defense. Santa Monica, CA: RAND National Defense Research Institute.

Gough, S. (2003) 'The Evolution of Strategic Influence', paper for the U.S. Army War College, Carlisle Barracks, Pennsylvania. Available at http://fas.org/irp/eprint/gough.pdf.

Goyette, C. (2007) 'Perspective: Holloman Air Force Base or gated community?', Holloman US Air Force Base, March 22. Available at http://www.holloman.af.mil/news/story_print.asp?id=123045873.

Graham, S. (2003) 'Lessons in urbicide', *New Left Review, 19(January–February), 63–78.*

Graham, S. (2005) 'Switching cities off: US air power and urban infrastructure', *City, 9(2), 170–91.*

Green, W. (2007) 'The Virtual Army Experience', Crave.CNET, October 1. Available at http://crave.cnet.com/8301-1_105–9788521–1.html.

Gregory, D. (2004) *The Colonial Present, Oxford*: Blackwell.

Gregory, D. (2008) 'The rush to the intimate: counterinsurgency and the cultural turn in late modern war', *Radical Philosophy*, 150(July/August), 8–23.

Hall, M. (2005) 'War on terror takes over a thankful town', USAToday.Com, March 13. Available at http://www.usatoday.com/news/nation/2005–03–13-smalltown-terror-drills_x.htm.

Hamilton, W. (2003) 'Toymakers study troops, and vice versa', *The New York Times*, March 30, 2003. Available at http://query.nytimes.com/gst/fullpage.html?res=9C05E5D81639F933A05750C0A9659C8B63&sec=&spon=&pagewanted=print.

Hammes, T. (1999) 'Time to get serious about urban warfare training', *Marine Corps Gazette*, April. Available at http://www.jfsc.ndu.edu/library/publications/bibliography/urban_warfare.asp.

Hayner, H. (2007) 'Virtual experience lets civilians act as soldiers', *US Army News*, February 27. Available at http://www.army.mil/-news/2007/02/27/2005-virtual-experience-lets-civilians-act-as-soldiers/.

Heller, A. (2007) 'Israeli army using mock city to train', *Washington Post*, January 23. Available at http://www.washingtonpost.com/wp-dyn/content/article/2007/01/23/AR2007012300203_pf.html.

Herz, J. and Macedonia, M. (2002) 'Computer games and the military: two views', *Defense Horizons*, April. Available at http://www.ndu.edu.

Howard, M. (2008) 'Luxury hotels and golf: welcome to the Green Zone', *The Guardian*, 6 May 2008. Available at http://www.guardian.co.uk/world/2008/may/06/iraq.

Kaplan, R. (2006) 'Hunting the Taliban In Las Vegas', *Atlantic Monthly*, August 4.

Kumar, A. (2004) 'America's Army Game and the Production of War', YCISS Working Paper Number 27, March. Available at http://www.yorku.ca/yciss/publications/documents/WP27-Kumar.pdf.

Land, S. (2007) Best practices for software engineering: using IEEE Software and System Engineering Standards to support America's Army: Special Forces (Overmatch). Available at http://www.dau.mil/regions/South/4thAnnual/Land.pdf.

Lawlor, M. (2007) 'Military changes tactical thinking', *Signal Magazine*, October. Available at http://www.afcea.org/signal/articles/templates/signal_article_template.asp?articleid=1403&zoneid.

Lenoir, T. (n.d.) 'Taming a Disruptive Technology: America's Army, and the Military-Entertainment Complex', undated presentation, Stanford University. Available at http://www.almaden.ibm.com/coevolution/pdf/spohrer.pdf.

Leonard, D. (2004) 'Unsettling the military entertainment complex: video games and a pedagogy of peace', *Studies in Media & Information Literacy Education*, 4(4). Available at http://utpjournals.metapress.com/content/v82m304n44j9/?p=7a01628ef784443989da98ae9c269b66&pi=11.

Lettice, J. (2004) 'Marine Corps deploys Fallujah biometric ID scheme', *The Register*, 12 September. Available at http://www.theregister.co.uk/2004/12/09/fallujah_biometric_id/.

Loredo, H. (2004) 'Hollywood magic prepares Marines for combat', Marines.Com, July. Available at http://www.marforres.usmc.mil/Archive/2004.08/mout.html.

McDonald, G. (2006) 'Bullets in the bricks; urban operations training', T2Net, 23 August. Available at http://www.t2net.org/briefs/news/Bullets_in_the_bricks.pdf.

McEnaney, L. (2000) *Civil Defense Begins at Home, Princeton*, NJ: Princeton University Press.

Malo, S. and Stapleton, C. (2004) 'Going Beyond Reality: Creating Extreme Multimodal Mixed Reality for Training Simulation', paper given at the Interservice/Industry Training, Simulation and Education Conference (I/ITSEC).

Metcalfe, J. (n.d.) 'The hype dimension'. Available at http://www.cassiopaea.org/cass/hype_dimension.htm.

Misselwitz, P. and Weizman, E. (2003) 'Military operations as urban planning', in A. Franke (ed.) *Territories, Berlin*: KW Institute for Contemporary Art, pp. 272–5.

Newman, R. (2003) 'The joystick war', *U.S. News, 19 May. Available at* http://www.usnews.com.

Norton, R. (2004) 'Feral cities', *Naval War College Review*, 56(4), 97–106.

O'Hagan, S. (2004) 'Recruitment hard drive', *Guardian Guide, June 19–25, pp. 12–13*.

Opall-Rome, B. (2007) 'Marines to train at new Israeli combat center', *Marines Corps Times*, June 25. Available at http://www.marinecorpstimes.com/news/2007/06/marine_israel_combattraining_070624/.

Peters, R. (2006) 'Our soldiers, their cities', *Parameters, Spring, 1–7.·*

Regan, T. (2005) 'British paper: Bush wanted to bomb Al Jazeera', *Christian Science Monitor*, November 23. Available at http://www.csmonitor.com/2005/1123/dailyUp-date.html.

Richfield, P. (2006) 'New "cockpit" for Predator?', *C4isr Journal*, October 31, 2006. Available at http://www.c4isrjournal.com/story.php?F=2323780.

Rowell, S. (n.d.) 'Playas, New Mexico: A Modern Ghost Town Braces for the Future', Center for Land Use Interpretation. Available at http://www.clui.org/clui_4_1/lotl/v28/i.html.

Seal, C. (2003) 'Was the excessive violence of US Troops in Iraq fuelled by military-funded computer games?', Baltimore Indymedia. Available at http://baltimore.indyme-dia.org/newswire/.

Shachtman, N. (2005) 'Attack of the drones', *Wired*, Issue 13.06. Available at http://www.wired.com/wired/archive/13.06/drones.html.

Shachtman, N. (2008) 'Tomato factory becomes Marines' high-tech trainer', *Wired*, January 17. Available at http://blog.wired.com/defense/2008/01/holograms-train.html.

Shaffer, M. (1999) 'Yodaville exists for bombing runs – Arizona's newest town inviting target', *Arizona Republic*, August 23. Available at http://www.geocities.com/Pentagon/6453/yodavillea.html.

Six Flags Blog (n.d.) 'At Six Flags, the war is a virtual reality experience', April 12. Available at http://www.military-quotes.com/forum/six-flags-war-virtual-reality-t59498.html.

Stahl, R. (2006) 'Have you played the war on terror?', *Critical Studies in Media Communication*, 23(2), 112–30.

Suffolk News-Herald (2005) 'SimCity will be huge', May 10. Available at http://www.hamptonroadsmedia.com/.

Technology.Com (n.d.) 'Learning to fly . . . UAVs'. Available at http://www.military-training-technology.com/print_article.cfm?DocID=1256.

Turse, N. (2003) 'Bringing the war home: the new military-industrial-entertainment complex at war and play', Tom Dispatch, October 17. Available at http://www.common-dreams.org/views03/1017-09.htm.

USA Today (2006) 'Army shoots down proposal for military theme park in Va.', 8 August. Available at http://www.usatoday.com/travel/news/2006-08-08-military-theme-park_x.htm.

Usry, F. (n.d.) 'The urban target complex (UTC) – "Yodaville"'. Available at http://www.geocities.com/Pentagon/6453/utc.html.

Ward, J. (2007) 'Embattled urban terrain', *Engineering in Europe: US Army Corps of Engineers*, 3 (summer), 16–19.

Weizman, E. (2005) 'Lethal theory', *LOG Magazine, April, 74.*

Wielhouwer, P. (2005) 'Preparing for future joint urban operations: the role of simulation and the Urban Resolve experiment', *Small Wars Journal, July. Available at http://www.smallwarsjournal.com/documents/swjmag/v2/wielhouwer.htm*

Wilson, J. (2003) 'Army expands home-based MOUT training', Military Training Technology, March. Available at http://www.military-training-technology.com/article.cfm?DocID=361.

6 Rescripting visions

Towards a 'subaltern' architecture

Pal Ahluwalia

> in the face of modernity one does not turn inward, one does not retreat; one moves sideways, one moves forward. All this is creative adaptation. Non-Western people, the latecomers to modernity, have been engaged in these maneuvers now for nearly a century. (Goankar 1999: 17)

> Exile is predicated on the existence of, love for, and bound with, one's native place; what is true of all exile is not that home and love of home are lost, but that loss is inherent in the very existence of both. (Said 1984: 171)

The most pressing issues of our time – poverty, hunger, unemployment, disease (AIDS in particular), the possibility of nuclear war, the movement of refugees, the debt crisis and environmental degradation – in a single swoop have been displaced by the threat of terrorism. The utter centrality of terrorism has meant that priorities have shifted and a 'new' politics has emerged based on the belief that imminent terror acts are inevitable. Terrorism now overrides history, politics, law, economics and common sense. It cannot be easily defined or challenged but it has come to have an amorphous capacity whose ramifications are being felt everywhere but especially in cities around the world.

From the colonial wars that were fought to bring civilisation to 'pre-modern' peoples to the liberation struggles that were central to the decolonisation process to the current war against the 'axis of evil', political violence has often been seen as a progressive historical force. Indeed, it was Hegel who observed that man was willing to die for a cause of greater value to him than life itself. As Mahmood Mamdani points out, 'what horrifies our modern sensibility is violence that appears senseless, that cannot be justified by progress' (Mamdani 2004: 4).

Habermas and Derrida reflected on the post-9/11 world with the former raising the possibility of a new cosmopolitan order as the most urgent challenge in the wake of the twin tower attacks in New York and the attack on the Pentagon in Washington, D.C. The idea of cosmopolitanism was advocated by Kant and based on the notion of creating a world community in which violations of rights in one part of the world would be felt everywhere. It was only when this happened, Kant argued, that we would be able to realise that 'we are continually advancing towards a perpetual peace'. For Kant, this entailed a sense of hospitality that would replace enmity among nations. Hospitality, he argued, 'means the right of a stranger not to be treated with hostility when he arrives on someone else's territory' (Kant 1970: 105).

It is nationalism that Habermas singles out as the epicentre of contemporary terrorist discourses. The holy warriors of today are those who were disenchanted with secular nationalistic authoritarian regimes such as those of Iran Iraq, Saudi Arabia and Pakistan. It is this that makes religion 'more subjectively convincing' (Borradori 2003: 56). The effects of this are, of course, most clearly manifested in the notion of the city as target.

In 1996 Derrida was invited to address the International Parliament of Writers in Strasbourg on the question of the cosmopolitan rights of asylum seekers, refugees and migrants. In that address, titled 'On Cosmopolitanism', Derrida questions whether it is possible to make a distinction between two forms of the metropolis – the City and the State. Derrida argues that at the very moment that the 'end of the city' is being proclaimed, 'how can we still dream of a novel status for the city, and thus for the "cities of refuge", through a *renewal* of international law?' (Derrida 2003: 3). Derrida is picking up here on the constitution of the Parliament of Writers that has been advocating the need for cities of refuge. The task of establishing such cities is no less than to 'reorient the politics of the state'. He calls for a transformation and reform of the very way in which the city belongs to the state and is 'still dominated by the inviolable rule of state sovereignty' (p. 4). Derrida argues that the focus on the city is a result of the failure of the state to 'create a new image of the city' (p. 6). In the following pages it is precisely such a rescripted vision of subaltern architecture that is explored.

During the latter part of 1994 and early 1995, in the aftermath of the Rwandan genocide, whilst conducting research in the refugee camps surrounding Goma, in the then Zaire, I often had the opportunity to visit Kibumba camp, which had an estimated population of over 300,000. It was located about 27 kilometres away from the town of Goma. The camp had no amenities, with even water being trucked in by various aid agencies from the lake around which the town of Goma was situated. Refugees at Kibumba endured some of the harshest conditions that humans anywhere could possibly face. And yet, I was particularly struck by survival strategies that were a characteristic feature of the camp. I discovered very quickly that the refugee camp was a complex site (Ahluwalia 1997). Giorgio Agamben (1998) offers an interesting way of thinking about what constitutes modern bare life and its relationship to sovereign power. The 'mode of conceiving of bare life/ sovereignty comes with its varied instantiation – in "the camp", refugees, *zones d'attentes*, and others – added to the rendering of one of them, "the camp" as paradigm' (Fitzpatrick 2001: 11–12). For Agamben, the Holocaust camp was not a site of exception but rather paradigmatic. The refugee camp challenges the very conception of the historical essence of national identity as being embedded within a particular place – a sovereign territorial space.

Kibumba was like a small city-state that had been uprooted and transplanted into another sovereign state – a state within a state. Amid the blue sea of refugee tents, made of blue plastic sheeting provided by the United Nations High Commissioner for Refugees (UNHCR), as well as the haze of smoke from the burning charcoal, was the remarkable manner in which the camp was divided into sections that corresponded to areas in Rwanda from where the refugees had fled. No doubt, this allowed the Hutu paramilitaries to police the camps and control the refugees through fear and terror. The camps were signposted with names painted on anything that could be found and displayed. The street names in the various parts of the camp were divided and sub-divided with precisely the same names that were used at 'home'. As Lisa Malkki in her study of the Burundi refugees in Tanzania points out:

> The precisely planned ordering of space . . . in any refugee camp – was an intriguing issue, not only in terms of the rationalization of that ordering, but in terms of the socio-political effects that different kinds of spatial regimes might be expected to produce. The creation of disciplinary spaces for the purpose, not only of containing, but also of normalizing people has been explored by Foucault . . . and others. In a refugee camp where people are contained for one overarching reason, their statelessness, the compartmentalization and regulation of space comes to have heightened practical and political significance. (Malkki 1995: 137)

And yet, what struck one in Kibumba was the spontaneity with which the camp itself had been constructed, the haphazard manner in which people marked out space that would become 'home' for as long as the camp existed. If a rationalisation and ordering of space came about, it was certainly not planned. The compartmentalisation and regulation came about well after the refugees arrived in the thousands, often after having walked for days. They simply claimed whatever area they could demarcate for themselves. Whenever I visited Kibumba, I was struck by how many people were on the move. They were walking either to work the farms of the local Zairians or to areas that they had cultivated wherever they could. In the evenings, after what had been clearly a long and arduous day, one would see literally thousands of people walking to the camp with bunches of plantains (the basic staple) on their heads as payment for working the fields. Many Hutu refugees had established vegetable gardens in the surrounding area of the camp, growing mostly products like lettuce and tomatoes that they could sell to the vast community of mostly European aid workers who were temporarily living in the town of Goma. The refugee camp itself had quickly been transformed with its own rhythm, its own temporality that was a characteristic feature of its inhabitants.

At the entrance to Kibumba camp was a bustling market surrounded by makeshift eating and drinking places with blaring music. Here, one could literally buy anything from food, to sex, to electronic goods, to spare parts, even cars and trucks. The market, it appeared, never shut down and was the hub of the refugee camp where everyone seemed to converge. The market embodied that very notion of spontaneity, chaos and indeterminacy around which the camp was constructed. It was here that refugees engaged with the world, it was here that they came to fetch the trucked-in water in their jerrycans. It was in the market that the refugees engaged with the world.

What is remarkable about Kibumba was that it came to represent that which its architects had never envisioned, 'the most central place from which to imagine a "pure" Hutu national identity' (Malkki 1995: 3). It was not surprising that the Tutsi-led Rwandan government invaded the camp a couple of years later to ensure that its security was not threatened by this most intense site of Hutu nationalism. Nevertheless, the camp was emblematic of forms of national identity, where space, place and habitation were brought together. It was an artificial, indeterminate and spontaneous site that was shaped by the conditions that the refugees endured and the political machinations that meant that they were removed as far as possible from the township. As such, the camp becomes critical to an exploration of the manner in which space itself is re-scripted. What I am interested in is to see how space is taken and made into a 'place', how it is named so as to make it a part of the everyday, how it is given meaning within a particular culture, and the manner in which place is made 'habitable' – that is, how it becomes 'home'.

The market in Kibumba is central to this process of re-scripting. The centrality of the market to the practice of everyday life and the manner in which the market as a site was re-appropriated and liberated were constitutive of the way that Africans engage with the world. The Kibumba market was an important site in which people interacted as they did in Rwanda. Its recreation and reformulation within the refugee camp made that very space into something akin to a place that was central to the process of imagining 'home', the very site through which an intense Hutu nationalism developed and a particular form of national identity was expressed. But let me turn to examine why the African market, the Asian bazaar, the Arab medina play such a crucial role in the lives of post-colonial subjects and why these sites were denigrated within European discourse.

The bazaar

Markets in South Asia have been recognised as important sites of exchange where peoples from different classes converge to conduct business, share news and information as well as to engage in various social, cultural, religious and political practices (Yang 1998: 1–2). What is particularly significant about markets is that they are 'microcosms containing a representative array of the elements comprising a regional environment. Markets provide a compressed display of an area's economy, technology, and society – in brief, of the local way of life' (Eder 1976: 76). Anand Yang, however, points out that, in order to view the market as the site of exchange relations that elucidates the 'local way of life', one has to challenge the exoticised 'Oriental market' that is so much a part of the Western imagination (Yang 1998: 2).

It is Edward Said who pointed out vividly the power of such an imaginative geography which legitimates a vocabulary, a representative discourse peculiar to the understanding of the Orient that becomes *the* way in which the Orient is known. Orientalism thus becomes a form of 'radical realism' by which an aspect of the Orient is fixed with a word or phrase 'which then is considered either to have acquired, or more simply be, reality' (Said 1978: 72). This can be seen clearly in the way the Oriental bazaar is deeply embedded in the Western imagination. In

Colonising Egypt, Timothy Mitchell writes about an Egyptian delegation on their way to the Eighth International Congress of Orientalists held in Stockholm in 1899. On their way to Sweden, the Egyptians stopped over in Paris and visited the World Exhibition where they were most disturbed to witness the Egyptian exhibit that was built by the French:

> The Egyptian exhibit had also been made carefully chaotic. In contrast to the geometric lines of the rest of the exhibition, the imitation street was laid out in the haphazard manner of the bazaar. The way was crowded with shops and stalls, where Frenchmen dressed as Orientals sold perfumes, pastries, and tarbrushes. To complete the effect of the bazaar, the French organisers had imported from Cairo fifty Egyptian donkeys. (Mitchell 1988: 1)

What was remarkable about these exhibitions was that they 'became so accurate and so extensive, no one ever realised that the "real world" they promised was not there' (Mitchell 1988: 10). No one, that is, except for the visiting Egyptians. In the age of colonialism, such was the confidence that the colonial world itself could be known simply through exhibition.

Although the Oriental bazaar or market occupies an important place in the Western imagination, in 'reality' it has been overlooked primarily because of the focus on caste and village that were deemed to be the major sites through which, for example, the 'real India' could be known.[1] For the colonial state, the village became the core site of the Indian social, economic and political body because 'of its primary interests in maintaining law and order and in extracting taxes from the subject population' (Yang 1998: 8). The privileging of the village not only served the colonial state's revenue collection strategy but also reinforced colonial ideology with the village representing tradition and backwardness, thereby legitimating the Raj's rule that was founded on the superiority of European modernity.

The African market

In Africa, much as in South Asia, the market has received little scholarly attention. Here, the village and the 'tribe' became the focus of attention for much the same reasons. The obsession with 'tribes' was part of the divide and rule strategy of the colonial powers. The village was the most important organising unit for revenue collection as well as the site of a cheap labour reservoir. Usually through deploying coercive methods such as the Hut and Poll Tax, the subject population of the village were forced to work on plantations or for the state in order to meet their taxation obligations (Leys 1975). As in India, the village represented tradition that was equated with backwardness and reinforced both colonial ideology as well as notions of the civilising mission.

The African market was known to be a site of great activity, a hub of trade, a space in which there was a considerable flow of goods, people and information. From at least the time of the trans-Atlantic slave trade, slaves often began their horrific journeys to the 'new world' from the market. The slave trade, conducted in the market itself, implicitly evoked the notion of equality between sellers and buyers. The imposition of colonialism proper marked by territorial occupation, however, meant that any vestiges of equality had to be removed. The African market had to be denigrated. The traditional African market was represented as a site of tradition, backwardness, the very repository of primitiveness – in contrast to the perception of European shopping areas and trading places. The situation was analogous to the compartmentalisation of the Manichaean colonial world that Frantz Fanon so vividly captured:

> The zone where the natives live is not complementary to the zone inhabited by the settlers . . . The settlers town is a strongly built town, all made of stone and steel . . . a well-fed town, an easy-going town; its belly is always full of good things. The settlers town is a town of white people, of foreigners.
>
> The town belonging to the colonized people, or at least the native town, the Negro village, the medina, the reservation, is a place of ill fame, peopled by men of evil repute . . . It is a world without spaciousness . . . a hungry town starved of bread, of meat, of shoes, of coal, of light . . . a town of niggers and dirty Arabs.   (Fanon 1967: 39)

Architecture and civilisation

It is this colonial Manichaeism, that particular desire of denigrating the other, that was also at the heart of colonial architecture. Stephen Cairns outlines the debate sparked by Charles Batteux during the eighteenth century in which architecture's place within the hierarchy of fine arts was accorded a low status on the grounds that it was not an art form purely for pleasure but was essentially a mechanical art. In his defence of architecture, A. C. Quatremère de Quincy, a prominent theorist of French art and architecture, sets out to illustrate the centrality of architecture to aesthetics. However, what I am interested in here is that the defence was built upon a process of 'othering' because he was determined to illustrate that architecture was not simply about the 'art of building' – such a definition would be far too general and encompass virtually all of humanity. As he put it:

> The art of building is found even among the savage people; the art of architecture, on the contrary, can only be the fruit of societies that have been most perfected by civilization, by all moral causes and with the collaboration of all the other arts.
>
> Architecture only takes on the form of an art, amongst those peoples where it is found, when they have already attained a certain degree of culture, of opulence and of luxury. It is at this point, then, that men – retreating more and more from rural life and work and settling in cities – sought to replace the pleasures of nature, of which they had lost sight, with the enjoyment of the arts, imitators of these pleasures.   (cited in Cairns 1998: 217)

So in such a formulation, it is only the 'civilised', the 'cultured' as opposed to the 'primitive', 'the natives' who are able to claim architecture as a form of aesthetic production as opposed to those who are capable of producing only a mere building – albeit 'the primitive hut' – that were so important to the very notions of the origins of architecture. At the beginning of the nineteenth century, Lewis Morgan reiterated the notion that architecture was linked inextricably to civilisation when he argued that 'house architecture, which connects itself with the form of family and the plan of domestic life, affords a tolerable complete illustration of progress from savagery to civilisation' (Morgan 1978, cited in Demissie 2004: 435).

The market as an alternative lens

The bazaar, the market, the medina, crowded, chaotic, haphazard, not conforming to clear geometric lines, challenging to the European imagination, offers a different perspective and a different understanding of the relationship between space, place and habitation. It is in this context that the market as an alternative lens is important precisely because it forces us to challenge our imaginative geography. As Yang argues: 'Both as an analytical unit and at a metaphoric level, bazaars speak the language of exchange and negotiation, of movement and flow, or circulation and redistribution – in short, of extra community or supra community connections and institutions' (Yang 1998: 17).

The centrality of the market in West Africa to the 'local way of life' is best captured by Manthia Diawara. The West African markets of which Diawara speaks are at once unique to that region whilst also representing the way in which the African market that had been denigrated by the colonial state is restored all over sub-Saharan Africa as an important site of resistance. In addition, it is one of the most important sites from which Africa engages with globalisation, largely through consumption. The re-emergence of the market is linked inextricably to the recognition that the state is unable to perform its role, resulting in what Colin Leys has labelled the 'African Tragedy' (Leys 1994).[2]

The state in Africa, by subscribing to the very notion of development, has succumbed to the notion of the superiority of European modernity, progress and rationality. Furthermore, it has internalised the stereotypical views of the backwardness and primitivity of the African market. This has meant that the African state and global institutions have not been attuned to the complexities of the African market. They are not able to understand the dynamic of an alternative modernity that has been developing and is an integral part of this newly liberated and reclaimed space.

The marketplaces of West Africa, which have a long history, including the trade in slaves, are linked to globalisation and are the venues of international consumption. They are sites of resistance to the World Bank's conception of globalisation as espoused under the terms of structural adjustment programmes (Ahluwalia 2001). The African markets are seen as obstacles to modernisation because they 'challenge the World Bank and other global institutions that consider the nation-states the only legitimate structure with which to conduct business in Africa' (Diawara 1998: 116). Moreover, the markets are seen as parasitic with corrupt traders selling smuggled goods and not providing much-needed taxation to the state.

This existence of a secondary or parallel economy is rooted deeply in the market system. It is in this market that Africans from diverse backgrounds are able to meet and assert their 'local way of life'. Rather than resisting globalisation, these marketplaces are constantly appropriating and transforming globalisation and in the process ensuring that consumers have choice and availability of goods at affordable prices. This is made possible through illegal practices such as corruption and smuggling. Market corruption is different from state corruption, which is largely the result of the interaction between the elites and donors. 'Market corruption . . . benefits the masses by increasing the variety of goods in the marketplace, lowering prices, and making consumption possible' (Diawara 1998: 123). It is consumption and the desire for commodities that makes globalisation a dynamic reality for sub-Saharan Africa.[3] As Diawara points out: 'Markets, aside from being the best reflection of West African societies, are the place where Africa meets Europe, Asia, and America; as they say in West Africa, "Visit the market and see the world" ' (Diawara 1998: 122).

The bazaar, medina and market are key sites from which post-colonial subjects engage with the world. These sites are generally the hub and serve as the nerve centre of a community. They are sites from which we can conceptualise alternative modernities.

Alternative modernity

Michael Hanchard suggests the conception of Afro-modernity as a means of understanding modernity as well as modern subjectivity for people of African descent. Afro-modernity, he suggests:

> consists of the selective incorporation of technologies, discourses, and institutions of the modern West . . . It is no mere mimicry of Western modernity but an innovation upon its precepts, forces, and features. Its contours have arisen from the encounters between people of African descent and Western colonialism not only on the African continent but also in the New World, Asia, and ultimately Europe itself.   (Hanchard 1999: 247)

African modernity is intertwined with the very history of colonialism. Since then, the complicity between modern knowledges and modern regimes of power has meant that African subjects have been represented as mere consumers of universal modernity. As Partha Chaterjee has pointed out, it is because of this that 'we have tried for over a hundred years, to take our eyes away from this chimera of universal modernity and clear up a space where we might become the creators of our own modernity' (Chatterjee 1997: 14). It is in the African market that we can see an alternative modernity, a modernity that is not simply a mimicry of some universal modernity but a modernity with its own peculiarities. In the age of globalisation, in the post-colony, it is a modernity fuelled by consumption made possible by the market.

In any number of African cities from Cape Town, Dakar, Kampala, Kinshasha, Johannesburg to Nairobi, it is evident that there is a rage for modernity. These decaying post-colonial cities are, as Alessandro Triluzi describes them, under-pinned by street buzz. Not only is this street buzz the new centre for politics, it is also a product of the chaos of everyday life marked by small traders and peddlers engaged in different ways in the practice of urban survival (Triluzi 1996: 79). Nowhere is this rage captured better than in the markets that aim to lure potential customers with the latest modern commodity, fashion or fad. As Dilip Goankar points out:

> Those who submit to that rage for modernity are not naive; they are not unaware of its Western origins, its colonial designs, its capitalist logic and its global reach. In haphazardly naming everything modern, they are exercising one of the few privileges that accrue to the latecomer: license to play with form and refigure function according to the exigencies of the situation.
> (Goankar 1999: 17)

However, as Albert Paolini has pointed out, 'modernity is consumed, not merely as some fetishized commodity but as an appropriated, hybridized feature of everyday life. It thus becomes as much part of the local and particular as the traditional and "indigenous"' (Paolini 1999: 169). The significance of the market as an alternative lens from which to glean the local way of life is that it demon-strates that the appropriation of the modern does not simply entail concession to the global or a loss of agency. It is important, then, to examine the relationship between the market as a site, and the transformation of a space into a place. Indeed, markets are often referred to as marketplaces, signifying their transformation and importance to local communities and the practice of everyday life.

Space, place and habitation

What was significant about the camp and the market in Kibumba was the manner in which what was elsewhere, what was in Rwanda, was being recreated precisely in the same way as a 'foreign' space is inhabited and made part of the everyday. The circumstances and conditions that the Hutu refugees had to encounter were very different from those of the colonisers. Nevertheless, there is some congruity in the manner in which a particular space that one is not familiar with is recreated through a process of naming it, of giving it some meaning within local culture. It is this process of naming which entails the establishment of at least an imagi-nary, if not an actual, boundary that is an important way of gaining power over a space. To recreate a market in a refugee camp, that captures something of what was at 'home', in another country, is a form of re-scripting something that no longer exists. It is a particular form of remembering and memorialisation that has a profoundly spatial dimension. The attempt to remember and to replicate that space is a form of mimicry. In his essay, 'Of Mimicry and Man', Homi Bhabha (1994) illustrates the manner in which mimicry became an important strategy of colonial power and knowledge. But for Bhabha, mimicry is not a simple aping of the imperial master. Rather, it characterises the ambivalent relationship between both the coloniser and the colonised. This is necessarily so, because when the imperial master encourages its colonial subject to 'mimic', the resultant product is never exactly the same. As Bhabha points out, 'mimicry represents an *ironic compromise*' which entails that 'colonial mimicry is the desire for a reformed recognizable Other, *as a subject of a difference that is almost the same, but not quite*' (Bhabha 1994: 86). Mimicry for the colonised is about becoming like the coloniser whilst remaining different. But mimicry has a menacing side – it has the potential to become mockery and parody. As Bhabha notes, 'mimicry is at once resemblance and menace' (p. 86). A particularly good illustration of different forms of mimicry is the following description by Ackbar Abbas who argues that:

> the nature of Hong Kong as a place has gone through a series of mutations and reinventions, as it moved from local manufacture to global finance. On the one hand, we find its increasing inscription in a global economy; on the other, the residues of a colonial history and a special relation to China; the overlapping and non-synchronised histories producing an always unfamiliar sense of place. (Abbas 1998: 185)

The control of space and its occupation have been crucial to processes of imperialism. The physical occupation of colonies, usually under the pretext that the land was unoccupied, *terra nullius*, and the control of space were central to British imperialism. Furthermore, it relied on architectural symbolism 'of residences to provide the visual confirmation of imperial solidity, stability and even majesty' (Ashcroft 2001: 124). But perhaps even more symbolic was the power accorded by the map. The map was perhaps one of the most powerful symbols of the control of space and through naming or renaming places it was the ultimate capacity of control and power. Architecture and mapping provided British colonialism with 'a two-pronged grip on the spatial reality of colonial societies' (p. 124). It is not surprising, then, that the legend on all maps of India have the following inscription: 'The Government of India states that "the external boundaries of India are neither correct nor authenticated"' (as cited in Young 2003: 59).

Most cultural historians and literary scholars, Edward Said argued, failed to note the geographical notation, the theoretical mapping and charting of territory in Western fiction, historical writing and philosophical discourse. This notation is particularly pertinent to the assertion of cultural dominance:

> There is first the authority of the European observer – traveller, merchant, scholar, historian, novelist. Then there is the hierarchy of spaces by which the metropolitan centre and, gradually, the metropolitan economy are seen as dependent upon an overseas system of territorial control, economic exploitation, and a socio-cultural vision; without these stability and prosperity at "home" . . . would not be possible. (Said 1993: 69)

This reliance upon the colonised territories cannot be overemphasised. Underlying social and cultural 'spaces' are 'territories, lands, geographical domains, the actual geographical underpinnings' of the imperial contest, for geographical possession of land is what empire is all about. 'Imperialism and the culture associated with it affirm both the primacy of geography and an ideology about control of territory' (p. 93).

In all the instances of the appearance of the empire in cultural products such as novels:

> the facts of empire are associated with sustained possession, with far-flung and sometimes unknown spaces, with eccentric or unacceptable human beings, with fortune-enhancing or fantasized activities like emigration, money-making, and sexual adventure. (p. 75)

The perspective of the inhabitants of those far-flung places, indeed the people themselves, exist only (when they are not actively debased as 'primitives' or 'cannibals') as shadowy absences at the edges of the European consciousness. As Bill Ashcroft points out:

> The Eurocentric control of space, through its occularcentrism, its cartography its development of perspective, it modes of surveillance, and above all through its language, has been the most difficult form of cultural control faced by post-colonial societies. Resistance to dominant assumptions about spatial location and the identity of place has occurred most generally in the way in which such space has been inhabited. (Ashcroft 2001: 15)

In short, the power of language, the process of naming and giving it presence on a map, was to turn space into place. However, what remains central is the question of belonging. The question of belonging, as the refugee camp has demonstrated, is rather complex and is not simply reliant upon a spatial location or territoriality. So immediately the notion of place is disrupted. It is dynamic and not simply a cultural memory that can be obliterated by colonial practices. Place is like culture, it continually forms and reforms and is linked inextricably with the culture and identity of those that are located there. But '[a]bove all place is a result of habitation, a consequence of the ways in which people inhabit space' (Ashcroft 2001: 156).

How we inhabit place, then, can be seen as a strategy that deals with the manner in which Western representations universalise place. By this, I mean that it suggests a way of being in a place, a way that not only defines place but one that also allows its very transformation. It has great potential because it ultimately means that colonialism or even globalisation cannot exercise its coercive power over it. As bell hooks points out: 'Home is that place which enables and promotes varied and ever changing perspectives, a place where one discovers new ways of seeing reality, frontiers or difference' (hooks 1991: 148).

Conclusion

The refugee camp and the market at Kibumba, indeed the Asian bazaar, the African market, the Arab medina, sites denigrated by colonialism, are important registers through which to understand the cultural exchanges that are so vital to the practice of everyday life. The market, for so long forgotten, is being reclaimed, liberated, and is fast emerging as the new site of the symbolic production of the post-colony. It is here that post-colonial subjects brutalised by the new colonial administrators – the World Bank and the IMF, through structural adjustment programmes – are able to engage with the world. It is market consumption which evokes both wonder and resonance that links perhaps the most marginalised constituency to the processes of contemporary globalisation as they navigate their own modernity.

In his *Critique of Pure Reason*, Immanuel Kant writes about 'the architectonic of reason': '[b]y an architectonic I understand the art of constructing systems. As systematic unity is what first raises ordinary knowledge to the rank of science, that is, makes a system out of a mere aggregate of knowledge' (Kant 1933: 653).

The significance of this architectural metaphor is one that is often repeated to capture the overall structure of a particular text. For example, in Homi Bhabha's construction of the 'Third Space' the architectural metaphor is not one that is suggestive of the structure of a particular space but rather his conception is aimed precisely at displacing and transforming the metaphor. Hence, the 'Third Space' is a hybrid space, an interstitial space, an in-between space that knowingly challenges the idea of a determinate dwelling which appears to be important to the architectural metaphor. For Bhabha:

> architecture is a paradigmatic image of theory, and is an image of what postcolonial criticism must resist . . . the language metaphor activates a temporality which undermines the authority of architecture's spatiality, and in doing so opens up the possibility of imagining less architectural kinds of theory.
> (Cairns 1998: 219)

The bazaar, the medina, the market are sites that challenge our imaginative geography, their chaotic, haphazard and indeterminant nature force us to come to grips with a different kind of architecture – an architecture that we might well conceptualise as 'subaltern'.

Notes

1 The term 'bazaar' has Persian origins. It refers 'to market or marketplace, generally a permanent market or street of shops' (Yule and Burnell 1968 [1903]: 75–6).
2 It is important to note that Claude Ake has argued that the assumption that there has been a failure of development is misleading. For Ake, the real problem is that development has never been on the agenda (see Ake 1996).
3 Such a reading of corruption is, of course, significantly different from Samuel Huntington's (1968) 'Modernization and Corruption'. Patrick Chabal and Jean-Pascol Daloz argue that 'corruption is in reality a complex of behavioural patterns which are the key ingredients of the continent's modernity' (Chabal and Daloz 1999: 101).

References

Abbas, A. (1998) 'Building, dwelling, drifting: migrancy and the limits of architecture. Building Hong Kong: from migrancy to disappearance', *Postcolonial Studies*, 1(2), 185–99.

Agamben, G. (1998) *Homo Sacer: Sovereign Power and Bare Life*, trans. D. Heller-Roazen, Stanford, CA: Stanford University Press.

Ahluwalia, P. (1997) 'The Rwandan genocide: exile and nationalism reconsidered', *Social Identities*, 3(3), 499–518.

Ahluwalia, P. (2001) *Politics and Post-colonial Theory: African Inflections*, London: Routledge.

Ake, C. (1996) *Democracy and Development in Africa*, Virginia: Donnelly and Sons.

Ashcroft, B. (2001) *Post-Colonial Transformation*, London: Routledge.

Bhabha, H. (1994) *The Location of Culture*, London: Routledge.

Borradori (2003) *Philosophy in a Time of Terror: Dialogues with Jurgen Habermas and Jacques Derrida*, Chicago: University of Chicago Press.

Cairns, S. (1998) 'Postcolonial architectonics', *Postcolonial Studies*, 1(2), 211–35.

Chabal, P. and Daloz, J.-P. (1999) *Africa Works: Disorder as Political Instrument*, Oxford: James Currey.

Chatterjee, P. (1997) 'Our Modernity', SEPHIS/CODESRIA Lectures, Dakar: Codesria.

Demissie, F. (2004) 'Editorial note', *Social Identities*, 10(4), 435–8.

Derrida, J. (2003) *On Cosmopolitanism and Forgiveness*, London: Routledge.

Diawara, M. (1998) 'Toward a regional imaginary in Africa', in F. Jameson and M. Miyoshi (eds) *The Cultures of Globalization*, Durham, NC: Duke University Press.

Eder, H. (1976) 'Markets as mirrors', in S. Cook and M. Diskin (eds) *Markets in Oaxaca*, Austin: University of Texas Press.

Fanon, F. (1967) *The Wretched of the Earth*, Harmondsworth: Penguin.

Fitzpatrick, P. (2001) *Bare Sovereignty: Homo Sacer and the Insistence of Law*, Baltimore: Johns Hopkins University Press.

Goankar, D. (1999) 'Alternative modernities', *Public Culture*, 11(1), 1–18.

Hanchard, M. (1999) 'Afro-modernity: temporality, politics, and the African diaspora', *Public Culture*, 11(1), 245–68.

hooks, b. (1991) *Yearning: Race, Gender and Cultural Policy*, London: Routledge.

Huntington, S. (1968) *Modernisation and Corruption*, New Haven: Yale University Press.

Kant, I. (1933) *Critique of Pure Reason*, New York: St. Martin's Press.

Kant, I. (1970) 'Toward perpetual peace: a philosophical sketch', in H. Reiss (ed.) *Kant's Political Writings*, Cambridge: Cambridge University Press.

Leys, C. (1975) *Underdevelopment in Kenya: The Political Economy of Neo-colonialism 1944–1971*, Berkeley: University of California Press.

Leys, C. (1994) 'Confronting the African tragedy', *New Left Review*, 204, 33–47.

Malkki, L. (1995) *Purity and Exile: Violence, Memory, and National Cosmology among Hutu Refugees in Tanzania*, Chicago: University of Chicago Press.

Mamdani, M. (2004) *Good Muslim, Bad Muslim: America, the Cold War, and the Roots Terror*, New York: Pantheon.

Mitchell, T. (1988) *Colonising Egypt*, Cambridge: Cambridge University Press.

Paolini, A. (1999) *Navigating Modernity: Postcolonialism, Identity and International Relations*, Boulder, CO: Lynne Rienner.

Said, E. (1978) *Orientalism*, New York: Vintage Books.

Said, E. (1984) *Reflections on Exile*, London: Granta.

Said, E. (1993) *Culture and Imperialism*, London: Chatto and Windus.

Triulzi, A. (1996) 'African cities, historical memory and street buzz', in I. Chambers and L. Curti (eds) *The Post-Colonial Question: Common Skies, Divided Horizon*, London: Routledge.

Yang, A. (1998) *Bazaar India: Markets, Society, and the Colonial State in Gangetic Bihar*, Berkeley: University of California Press.

Young (2003) *Postcolonialism: A Very Short Introduction*, Oxford: Oxford University Press.

Yule, H. and Burnell, A. C. (1968 [1903]) *Hobson-Jobson: A Glossary Of Coloquial Anglo-Indian Words and Phrases*, New Delhi: Munshiram Manoharlal.

7 The city as target – retargeting the city

French intellectuals and city spaces

Verena Andermatt Conley

Several years ago, the media circulated news online that terrorists were targeting the world's cities and that urban guerrilla warfare would be the way of the future. This predicament seems to have been borne out with the events of September 11, 2001 when a small band of terrorists killed nearly 3,000 civilians in New York City and transformed lower Manhattan into a zone of death and devastation. Other attacks on civilians in cities have since followed, from London (2005) to Mumbai (2008) and Moscow (2011), not to mention those in Iraq, Pakistan, and elsewhere. Terrorists have always had a preference for cities and civilians, from the Algerian war of independence when more bipartisan terrorist acts were aimed against urban colonial landmarks in Algiers to recent attacks in cities all over the world – from Baghdad to Tel Aviv, from Madrid to London and Bogota. The image of the city as a safe area governed by its citizens and protected by the police – an image that, in reality, may never have existed – has given way to another: the city and its inhabitants as the target of terrorists. Although terrorist attacks are the most spectacular, over the last two centuries many critics have denounced other forms of targeting. The city was said to be targeted by the state and its administrators, more recently by the military and, with the advent of economic globalism, by transnational companies and the media.

Two preliminary questions arise: what do we mean by "city" and how do we define "target." "The city" is not an empty term. In the West, when we speak of "the city," we still tend to refer to modern, European, "walking" cities that have evolved since Greek and Roman times, and that, having been built in slow time and extensive space, bear a specific history and geography.[1] Next to this classic model, there are other, more postmodern cities, such as those recently built from grids applied to the desert in the Western United States; Asian cities such as Singapore, composed of high rises and shopping facilities built over fishing villages and sites of colonial plantations;[2] African cities where sizable populations live in makeshift accommodations next to skyscrapers.[3] The word "target" too has, in English at least, a double valence. The city can become a site of destruction. Although the two tendencies are often difficult to distinguish, the city can also become the site – or target – for reconstruction, however ambiguous the latter term may be.[4]

Part I: targeting the city

In the pages to follow I will investigate how the Western city-as-target functions in this double orientation specifically through recent works of French intellectuals. I will argue that, even in a climate of destruction, it is important to think simultaneously of the city's reconstruction. Already in the nineteenth century, numerous writers and officials decried the loss of the old pre-revolutionary city with its insalubrious housing and tortuous streets that Haussmann had targeted.[5] The baron's strategic construction project was decried by many for relocating the city's inhabitants who were sheltered in tightly knit communities and eliminating street life and cafés. Over the last hundred years, with two world wars and technological innovations, the widespread feeling of loss both of the city and of citizenship has been intensified manifold. During the decades following May 1968, many French intellectuals wrote about the targeting of city spaces in the context of Michel Foucault's disciplinary society. The city as concept was administered by the state and its representatives in order to control and direct its inhabitants. By disciplining them mentally and physically, administrators and educators, thanks to their affiliation with institutions, would produce obedient subjects. Both Henri Lefebvre and Michel de Certeau argued that those in power – especially those belonging to the state apparatus – control the city and immobilize its inhabitants. Abstract or geometric spaces and concepts replace existential or anthropological spaces characterized by myths and legends that had defined the inhabited world. Signs replace lived space. The philosopher and the historian urged people to reappropriate the city by way of spatial practices. Although Lefebvre celebrated urbanization that did away with essences and oppressive traditions, he also deplored the decline of the political city. He called on citizens to reclaim the city through the streets that he felt to be the popular medium of political activity.[6] He emphasized lived experience and the importance for citizens to reappropriate the body in a city whose existence he saw threatened not only by the state but also increasingly by consumer capitalism. Certeau noted how, in their everyday lives, people subvert administrative powers through playful tricks. People conceive spatial practices that enable them to reappropriate the city privately. Publicly, for Certeau, power always reconstitutes itself.

Evolution in technology and capitalism lead to the weakening of the state and the seeming reemergence of the city. However, urban spaces are transformed. When consumerism is put in place, symbolic places in the home and in the city are lost. In the dramatic words of Jean Baudrillard, the vital links between map and territory, essential to space as it is lived, are cut. Instead of being tied to place by lineage or bloodline, people access it with a code. They are manipulated by signs and subjected to structural laws of value. On the one hand, people are free to invent their own spaces. On the other, the rupture between word and referent contributes further to the loss of existential territories.

In less extreme terms, Marc Augé declares that, with ongoing gentrification spurred on by economic globalism and finance capitalism, the city is emptied of its inhabitants who now live outside the older urban centers. Erstwhile symbolic places lose their function to become museums (Le Louvre and Notre Dame are monuments given to the paying guests of Paris). The city becomes an attraction for tourists. Images take over and control human experience. A sense of derealization is accompanied by a proliferation of new spaces under the impact of transportation and tele-transmissions. In the new "non-places" that work with digital access cards, symbolic orders and kinship structures that might have governed human societies for centuries are no longer valid. Symbolic relations have been weakened and disrupted by these new places but, claims Augé, they do not simply disappear. People shuttle back and forth between the two; as new hybrids, they even belong to both. Over time, non-places proliferate and become the measure of the economically targeted city. Non-places are not part of the social fabric and belong especially to the elite. The more anthropological, popular places are those where the general population mill about. Most of these writers discussed in the paragraphs above continue to see the state as targeting the city and its inhabitants. They also sense that a shift occurs that leads to the waning of the state and the reemergence of a city devoid of its politics and in which citizens may have lost their active status.

This shift from a disciplinary society to what Gilles Deleuze, in the wake of William Burroughs, calls "societies of control," takes a tragic turn in the writings of Paul Virilio who sees these changes as related not only to economic, but also to military operations. The critic informs his readers how cities as *polis* were enclosed by walls. Citizens who were also part of the military took as their duty to protect the general population. During World War II, when planes began to fly over the protective walls along the Atlantic shores and drop bombs in the cities behind the fortified lines, the relations between the military and civilians changed forever. Cities and their inhabitants are henceforth doubly targeted. On the one hand, war is waged against civilians in what has become an "open city." On the other, under the impact of means of transportation and later of teletechnologies, the postwar city becomes increasingly "overexposed."[7] Architecture and solid infrastructure lose their importance. Images and screens transform the old-style built city into a precarious and even fragile entity. Citizens are invisibly targeted by those in power. They are immobilized in front of television sets and computer screens, or they are shuttled around to and from work in cars or by mass transportation. As subjects they lose their right to be, and as citizens their power to act. They are forced to move and denied the right to dwell. Virilio sees these conditions as spelling the demise of the erstwhile political city, which is transformed into a mere urban effect but without the positive spin that Lefebvre put on it. Individuals engage in vain in ecological struggles to reclaim their right to a habitable territory. City dwellers lose their rights as citizens in an era that, paradoxically, emphasizes the importance of human rights. They are bombarded with propaganda – in the form of images and clichés – and are prevented from taking part in shaping the world in either a physical or a mental way. Virilio detects a shift from the military–industrial complex in the Cold War period that he called "pure war" to the military–informational complex with its "infowar."[8]

Virilio reenters the current debate about the city and its inhabitants by way of citizenship and democracy to point to their collective demise. Following a standard critical line that dates back to his earlier writings, Virilio argues in *City of Panic* that the city has taken on renewed importance with the waning of the nation-state as a result of economic globalization and electronic technologies.[9] However, today's city as metropolis or urban concentration is far from the *polis* with its active citizens. While urbanization continues to destroy popular Parisian neighborhoods with their secret mental networks and popular city life, terrorism spreads fear across the city of New York. Jumping from the French city where he lives to New York that he imagines, Virilio extrapolates ideas of a quasi-universal city. After the aeropolitics of World War II, the city has become the target of terrorists and, worse, of an even more insidious infowar. Reiterating his belief that technologies are invasive and that they contribute to the loss of the animal, social, and territorial bodies, he condemns the ubiquitous use of numerical images and digital technologies that eradicate history and geography in favor of an eternal present.[10] Digital technologies replace language with numbers, and as a result reality is lost.

The consequences for the city, the citizen, and democracy, Virilio claims, are disastrous. Not only is there no more opposition between city and country but the globe turns into a sprawling urban concentration without center or periphery. Under the impact of globalization made possible by an accelerated passage of information, the imperative of speed dramatically alters the way that humans experience space and time. During the Cold War, Virilio wrote about the "insécurité" of a territory that always risks being lost in a war that has become increasingly aimed at civilians. The result is double when, with the advent of the "infowar," the city is being targeted anew. First, it leads to further erosion of political *democracy*, which has been entirely transformed into one of *emotion*[11] Second, the open city of World War II becomes a *panic city*, where, according to the etymology of the word "panic," people's minds are disquieted so much that they are prevented from thinking and live in constant fear.[12] Panic has been enhanced by recent – as well as the threat of future – attacks of global terrorism. Citizens are kept in check by a military and political theater that plays with their emotions and hides the true facts, to begin with the one that this form of terrorism is endemic to a global world.

In addition to the standardization of production already discussed by Baudrillard, democracy becomes a casualty of "infowar," based on the synchronization of emotions. The latter are far from the Deleuzian "affects" that deal with new sensations, the altering of states, and new ways of connecting with the world so as to enhance – or diminish – humans' possibilities to act. Emotions are produced through the administration of fear and panic. Citizens rely on opinions and polls rather than on critical thinking and active participation. Parodying the Bush administration's well-known mantra about the threat of weapons of mass destruction in Iraq, Virilio claims in *City of Panic* that today's war is waged with "weapons of mass communication" (p. 43). He notes a crisis of the political in an era of mass communication. A collective emotion produces mass individualism. This individualism is but an illusion. In war – military or economic – it is the quicker and more resourceful person who wins. Winning is not linked as much to physical strength as to faster technologies. Advanced technological war is based on strategic deployment of images. When the mirror of the real has been broken, Virilio notes, demarcations between truth and falsehood erode, and so do just and unjust, real and virtual. The loss of territory through interactivity that leaves a mere urban effect now enables those in power to manipulate citizens' emotions for their own benefit.

The demise of democracy is closely related to that of the city. Virilio claims that the city is the major "catastrophe" of "progress" in the twentieth century. No longer a geopolitical capital of nations, it has become a *metacity* that does not take place. As the subtitle of *City of Panic* indicates, in an era dominated by the speed of light, "elsewhere begins here," *"ailleurs commence ici."*[13] Virilio now sees the necessity to wage a double civil war against terrorists of uncertain origin and the media in collusion with the present "military–informational complex." The information war is based on the illusion of a liberation of the multitude.[14] People feel that they are "liberated" from local constraints. They are no longer tied to a specific place but live in virtual space. They are not part of a nation but of a vague metropolis. The loss of limits is presented by the media as people's salvation when, in fact, it spells their doom. Citizens are excluded in a world that is foreclosed. With the disappearance of geopolitics, humans have no relation to the world. As citizens, they are excluded from active politics. In a global world that has become a kind of huge metacity, with no center or periphery, there remains only endless circulation in ever-changing networks. By exploiting terrorism, the government and the military by way of the media appeal to emotions and even help produce panic at the very same time that the city is held in check by an anti-panic army. When people are "liberated" from the real and gain access to the virtual, they become the easy targets of whoever wants to manipulate them to gain power. Somewhat out of context, Virilio quotes the actress Susan Sarandon who states: "Since September 11, all our emotions and our fears have been taken hostage."[15] The actress denounces the actions of the American government and the media. Virilio decontextualizes, even universalizes, her remarks. This kind of appropriation and easy generalization can be used as a transition toward raising some questions. If Virilio is one of many thinkers in post-68 France who declare that cities are targeted, he is the most apocalyptic. For him, there is little, if any, space for reconstruction. More than terrorists, a generalized "infowar" eradicates geophysical space, geopolitics, and spells the demise of the city. Is the city really the total catastrophe that Virilio makes it out to be?

No one will deny Virilio's perspicacity when he shows how changes brought about by globalization seem to erase the boundaries of nation-states and replace them with a generalized *metacity*. Virilio pushes to their limit many of the ill-understood consequences of globalization such as the omnipresence of images that, for him, are always manipulative. Continuing in his melancholic vein, he declares that the world is lost and humans are excluded from active participation in the city. However, as it becomes evident in his appropriation of Susan Sarandon's remark, Virilio too tends to liberate himself from the place in which he speaks. He engages in a meta-discourse in a global, networked world that, as he himself argues, disallows such a practice in a world where there is no outside. The critic's voice is just one of many circulating in the network. Although, most likely, we live in a state of transition from the nation-state to something else, from the old city to new configurations of the city, we may wonder if Virilio does not mistake a tendency for the truth. It is important to realize that city spaces have been – and are being – transformed and that they have even become, in his words, "critical," that is, the object of critical attention as a result of perceived shifts. Rather than demonizing and bemoaning the loss of the animal, social, and territorial body under the onslaught of technologies, could we not ask ourselves how the contemporary metropolis is, or can be, retargeted from today's conditions? Without denying Virilio's compelling and much-needed criticism of media, are images only manipulative? Is panic really all that remains of the city? Are all citizens permanently under the sway of emotions? Let us rephrase his criticism through recourse to another chiasmus – a figure dear to Virilio – and shift the emphasis from the city as target to ways of retargeting the city.[16]

Virilio sees Paris, one of his prime examples of a metropolis, as a long traveling shot, a continuous, moving *plan-séquence*. The choice of example is revealing. Traveling shots tend to be linear. They go from beginning to end. They might show us what Serge Daney calls "the world as bad cinema."[17] Yet we can also see the city as a multiplicity of images, or a *cascade of images*, as Bruno Latour has it.[18] It is only once they are arrested and framed that images accede to meaning. "*Paris n'est pas tout*," "Paris is not all Paris," writes Virilio,[19] and we readily agree. We could add too that neither is New York. Paris and New York are perhaps not as much "panic cities" as cities that emerge, always temporarily, at the intersection of many discourses – artistic, philosophical, sociological, economic, political – among which we find those of the media. At different times, certain discourses may take on more importance than others. For the last decade, economics and the media seem to have preponderant roles. In the current climate, it can be asked how is it possible for the critic to speak of the city in ways other than those of doom?

Part II: retargeting the city

Although one cannot disagree with Virilio that global cities bring with them new problems and injustices, they are also productive of new mobilities and sensibilities. Over time most Western cities that Virilio and other French intellectuals discuss have turned out to be quite resilient. European cities have been mending themselves after various military and terrorist attacks. Some will even argue, albeit perversely, that city dwellers derive a certain pleasure and excitement from new dangers lurking in the city. New York managed to cope after the destruction of the World Trade Towers, as did London and Mumbai after terror attacks in those cities. With the advent of globalization, many appear to have undergone renewal and have even acquired a new cultural diversity and glamor. Bloggers and political conspirators exploit computers to sway opinions and spread panic. Terrorists appropriate them for their use. Yet computers also help administrators run today's large urban agglomerations that may be much too vast for older forms of democracy based on more direct contact and participation. As Bruno Latour has shown, computers enable humans to see what is otherwise invisible. There are no more panoramas, only dioramas that offer ephemeral totalizations that make possible the functioning of the city that is far from a traveling shot. It consists of a multiplicity of images and transformations that, far from simply eradicating the map, link it to a territory. Not only is Paris not all of one piece, computers help solve problems and make the city habitable. They are necessary to run the city, from predicting the weather to assigning classrooms to directing traffic. Humans move in different, at times overlapping, networks that make up the contemporary metropolis. It is impossible to totalize this city. Humans neither have emancipated themselves from the concrete and are living entirely in the virtual, nor are they immobilized by an evermore perfected military-informational system. Instead of trying to recover an existing real behind appearances the way that Virilio would have it, we can say that the real is but a construction, a fiction of sorts. We do not have to separate lived experience from abstract space or to recover a lost totality that would be hidden under today's multiple possibilities of existence. Even if it has undergone dramatic changes and social and political problems abound, a city like Paris is nonetheless functioning, even with a substantial increase in demographic size. Latour reinflects the old French proverb, *se porter comme le Pont-Neuf*, to be like the Pont-Neuf, a metaphor referring to someone who is close to death.[20] He changes the meaning to designate a city that is – like the old bridge that is in constant repair – in constant metamorphosis. Even when the military, administrators, or even terrorists target them, cities are not only dying, they also regenerate themselves.

To make today's metropolis habitable would be impossible without the increasing mediation of machines, such as computers. Inhabitants move along many different networks that have no outside. The problem consists in believing that an all-powerful double click of the mouse would arrest and control life in the city. Nothing can be controlled top down. Cities are made of "cascades" of images. It is only once an image is framed, or a sentence repeated, that *clichés* begin to appear. Eventually, the latter put in place scenarios of emotion and panic. Of importance is the realization that the city, especially in so-called hot societies that undergo rapid change, consists of a multiplicity of images and words and a choice of existences. Explicitly critical of Baudrillard, Latour declares that, even if some people sitting at computer terminals may appear to control the city, these totalizations are always in the plural: "All totalizations are in the plural and ephemeral, images or sentences are part of a performance that constantly composes and recomposes the social."[21] The city emerges at the intersection of many lines and it is flat. Though he repeatedly alludes to it, Latour downplays the fact that economic and media discourses currently push others aside. He dwells on the pragmatic functioning of the city and social process that cannot be totalized.

If the city is composed of new "centers," the latter are in constant transformation. Lines detach themselves at the fringes of urban territories, they might even break off, bifurcate, and lead to new compositions altogether. New affects can lead to a transformation of perceptions and new concepts. Virtuals are actualized.

The city in its widest sense enables more connections and produces more sociality. The problem is that, even if we think that everything is linked by networks, the city nonetheless produces new centers and exclusions such as the *banlieues* in Paris. Violence, produced by exclusion, is worked out in the city. The tension that for Foucault, Lefebvre, and others had functioned along the division between state and society is now seen between the state and the city or the social. For Deleuze, John Rajchman writes, "what is 'outside' the state is not a nice 'civil society,' but rather a social with all sorts of *fuites*, minorities, becomings that escape states or that they must try to 'capture.'"[22] These becomings can be positive or negative. Some "negative" becomings could be terrorism that military forces try to capture while anti-panic forces control the population. Virilio showed how, by means of an ongoing infowar, the military–informational complex tries to capture the population. Yet can the population be captured or do new multitudes continue to rise that are not under strategic control?

In *A Thousand Plateaus* Deleuze and Guattari (1988) saw a "becoming minoritarian" taking place in a post-68 world. They argued that the intolerable of World War II and of colonization led to a generalized becoming minoritarian in the second half of the twentieth century. For them, the changed postwar city sees a proliferation of new texts and images, from poststructural theory to New Wave and Third World cinema up to the events of May 1968. Yet if cities make possible new connections or the formation of new affective circuits, if they enable new multitudes to rise and produce new pressure points and social energies, the new society of control under the spell of money and the media at the same time tends to reduce the number of possibilities. Images, discourses that were productive in the postwar years, lose their force. A decade later, "The Post-scriptum to the Societies of Control," Deleuze is less enthusiastic about becomings and minorities. He writes that:

> speech and communication have been corrupted. They're thoroughly permeated by money – and not by accident but by their very nature. We've got to hijack speech. To create has always differed from communicating. The key thing may be to create *vacuoles* of non-communication, circuit breakers, so we can elude control.[23]

When money corrupts the world, fewer virtuals can be actualized.[24] What new thoughts, what new images are possible that would lead to other sensibilities or forms of intelligence and reorient the city targeted by money and propaganda? Some of the media have reinforced clichéd thinking by appealing to emotions and by creating panic. A real interruption equated with a "hijacking of speech" will be necessary to open new spaces. The problems of today's global cities are clearly no longer the same as those of the former disciplinary societies from which humans tried to escape by transgressing an order imposed by the state and its institutions. Today's control is more insidious because it is flexible and smooth. People are immobilized by clichéd images that, as Virilio showed, are no longer representations of spaces but simple presentations in time. How can people still *create* "vacuoles" or open small spaces? When, in order to survive and "succeed," they are instructed to acquire the necessary skills, invention and creation become more difficult. A kind of global cognitive Darwinism is set in place that works independently of cultures and places.[25] Terrorists targeting cities may even be a symptom. They may point to their own exclusion from modernization with both its glamour and its vicissitudes. They may also signal pressure points, or what Etienne Balibar calls the *blind spots*, in a dominant Western order.[26]

The old-style city has been replaced by a general urbanness of the world in which there are, however, continued urgent needs to open new spaces, make connections, produce new ways of becoming and new networks of sociability. The intolerable continues to exist in the glamorized Western global city whose shame is the *banlieues*. This shame exists even more in many parts of the Third World that have become a generalized *banlieue* or zone. Virilio wants to see the new social order as a pyramid while Latour would argue that it is connected by networks or threads linked by ongoing transformations. In today's context, we will ask whether new social groups, new multitudes can rise and produce change in view of not only the size of the media machine but also the magnitude of political, economic, and ecological problems as a result of increased demographic pressures? Should these multitudes with their new forms of subjectivation be recognized and institutionalized by rights and by citizenship?

This is the position of Etienne Balibar who argues that Deleuze is too romantic. He criticizes what he calls Deleuze's *hyperspace* for being anarchic, open to all kinds of politics in today's global urban context. With a nod to Deleuze, Balibar declares that the social is based on conventions. It is, however, composed of ever-changing force fields. In today's context, given the magnitude of problems – from demographic pressures to those of an all-encompassing propaganda – while the world is in becoming, change must be instituted by rights and citizenship. Humans have to appeal to existing institutions and transform them from within. Multitudes without rights cannot create public spaces.[27] New ways of feeling, perceiving, and thinking make possible the opening of new spaces. New ways of thinking, however, have to be given the *droit de cité*, the right to dwell in the city.[28] In French, Balibar reminds us, one can play on the city as *la ville*, but also as *la cité*, both an architectural space and a ethical space where inhabitants practice their rights. To have this right (*avoir droit de cité*) means to be able to practice one's citizenship; to have access to a space from which one can speak. To retarget today's targeted *megacité*, intellectuals and artists have to reintroduce other, or rephrase existing, ideas. To have a *droit de cité* is to be a citizen who has the right to dwell, to move, and to speak in a public place. Balibar notes the common etymology of city, citizen, civilization, and civility. Civility has been decried as echoing the colonizers' "art of civilizing." Today, the dichotomy, civilization and barbarity, is also circulating without a center or a periphery. Civility emphasizes ways of being civil, of exchanging, negotiating, or of being sociable with a twist. A city of panic and emotion has to be retargeted to give its inhabitants access not only to their desire but also, simultaneously, to citizenship and rights.

To retarget the city, as Deleuze put it, one would have to "hijack speech."[29]

The political strategies implemented by way of media coverage after the events of September 11 prompted Susan Sarandon to declare that people's emotions had been taken hostage. A violent appropriation of people's affect and speech can be countered only by another violent capture that Balibar, in turn, calls civil disobedience. The shame of the *banlieue* cannot be solely left up to television and politicians. It has to be rearticulated by speaking for, but also by letting others speak and by speaking with others in a participatory manner. Citizenship, as Balibar argues, has to be granted regardless of nationality. The city is not a self-contained, fixed entity. It is defined by ongoing participation and is in constant flux. Since 9/11 and with the resurgence of terrorism, the *banlieue* is also said to hide terrorists. It is of importance not to fall into the trap of a propaganda that makes of each inhabitant of the *banlieue* a potential terrorist. One can begin by situating terrorism and by following its genealogy – or threads – instead of fetishizing the term and masking not only the fact that, as Virilio puts it well, it is endemic – and has been for some time – but also the fact that it is being used in a war of propaganda that promotes color-coded fear and panic as theater.

In a world where the passage of information accelerates, intellectuals or critics are no longer oracles prophesying the future. Each speaks from the present, as one voice among many. They do not reveal a hidden truth but through their pronouncements, in participation, translation, and negotiation with others, they help invent new spaces. Becomings have to be accompanied by the institution of rights. Negotiations can go through existing institutions and alter them in the process. Each context is local and immediately global. Critics have to translate affects into words and concepts. It is not as much a question of interpreting an object – such as the targeted city – as of continually inventing new spaces that will always be both real and fictional. Real places do not simply disappear in a computerized, digitalized world.

Despite the magnitude of problems facing cities, they continue to function. In the words of the Iranian film-maker Abbas Kiraostami, famous for his filming of roads as an intertwining of lines: "and life goes on."[30] The important question is about the quality of life. Not only terrorism but also political and economic propaganda by way of the media target cities. One can say that every context produces new social energies and mobilities. Yet to escape the present predicament actively, citizens have to construct and reconstruct the city outside of political clichés and fetish terms that foreclose democracy by appealing to emotions and spreading panic. Susan Sarandon's critical remark shows that not everyone is made hostage. Cities emerge at the intersection of many different networks, images, ongoing negotiations, and translations. The critic's task is to continue to retarget today's targeted city, each according to her or his conventions or historical and geographical context. Recent efforts at retargeting the city have shifted to focus on a new "eco-urbanism" that would develop truly at the scale of today's cities.[31] This eco-urbanism wants to retarget the city by being more socially inclusive *and* sensitive to the environment. It would be less ideologically driven than some earlier efforts combating technological violence. Ecological urbanism is an expression that follows Guattari who, over 20 years ago, argued for a new ethics and aesthetics of the urban. In addition to the forms of violence discussed in this paper, it also pays attention to another, less spectacular form, that of the sheer number of people exploiting increasingly limited resources. It retargets the city by opening ecological spaces at the mental, social, *and* natural level. "If you believe in the world," writes Deleuze, "you precipitate events, however inconspicuous, that elude control, you engender new space-times, however small their surface or volume!"[32] By believing in the world and the city, by appealing to the strength of others' discourses, critics can help retarget the city and help increase its inhabitants' possibilities for action and reconstruction.

Notes

1 Edward Soja discusses this point in a comparison of Los Angeles and Amsterdam in *Third Space* (New York: Blackwell, 1996), pp. 280–320.
2 Rem Koolhaas, *The Harvard Design School Guide to Shopping* (Köln: Taschen, 2001). See also Rem Koolhaas, "Pearl River Delta," in Catherine David, ed., *Politics and Poetics* (Kassel: Cantz, 1996), pp. 557–92.
3 Okwui Enwezor, ed., *Under Siege: Four African Cities* (Kassel: Cantz, 2002).
4 Cities are also vulnerable to natural catastrophes whose effects, because of demographics, are much more powerful.
5 Jules Ferry, *Les Comptes Fantastiques d'Haussmann* (Paris: edn Guy Durier 1868), p. 10.
6 In their recent edited book, *Space, Differerence and Everyday Life: Reading Henri Lefebvre* (New York: Routledge, 2008), Kanishka Goonewardena, Stefan Kipfer, Richard Milgrom, and Christian Schmid claim that the way to read Lefebvre today is less in relation to space than to a reappropriation of the city and especially the street, by the excluded parts of the population.
7 Paul Virilio, *L'espace critique* (Paris: Christian Bourgois, 1984).
8 Paul Virilio, *The Information Bomb*, trans. Chris Turner (New York: Verso, 2000).
9 Paul Virilio, *City of Panic*, trans. Julie Rose (Oxford: Berg, 2005).
10 Paul Virilio and Philippe Petit, *Politics of the Very Worst*, trans. Michael Cavaliere (New York: Semiotext(e), 1999).
11 Similarly, in a recent interview with Patrick Crogan, Bernard Stiegler criticizes what he calls the power of "psycho-technologies" [*Cultural Politics*, vol. 6, no. 2 (2010), p. 159].
12 *Littré*: "*Panique*" (*Terreur panice*, 1534; latin, *Panicus*; *de Pan, dieu qui passait pour troubler, effrayer les esprits*) (Pan, a god who was said to unsettle and scare people's minds, our translation). The definition in the *OED* is more violent. Panic is said to come from the Greek God of nature to whom woodland noises were attributed and whose appearance or unseen presence was held to induce terror.
13 Virilio, *City of Panic*, p. 90.
14 Virilio, *City of Panic*, p. 111. By contrast, American sociologists such as Dalton Conley in *Elsewhere, U. S. A.* (New York: Pantheon, 2009), simply show how communication through teletechnologies transforms and informs the social.
15 Virilio's use of "multitude" has a derogatory ring. It differs from Michael Hardt and Toni Negri's "multitude" as a spontaneous, often subversive, grouping. Michael Hardt and Toni Negri, *Empire* (Cambridge,MA: Harvard University Press, 2000); Michael Hardt and Toni Negri, *Multitude* (New York: Penguin, 2004).
16 Virilio ends *Ville panique* with a palindrome. Arguing for the desertification of the world, he shows that the palindrome of desert, tresed, can be read in French as "le trait cède" (the trait gives in), that is, the horizon, so important since the Quattrocento as the vanishing point and perspective, disappears. Contrary to Deleuze and Guattari or

Bruno Latour, who want to abolish perspective, he deplores that humans are left in a world without directions.

17 Virilio, *City of Panic*, p. 4.
18 John Rajchman, *The Deleuze Connections* (Cambridge, MIT, 2002), p. 136.
19 Bruno Latour and Emilie Hermant, *Paris, ville invisible* (Paris: La Découverte, 1998).
20 Latour and Hermant, *Paris, ville invisible*, p. 145.
21 Latour and Hermant, *Paris, ville invisible*, pp. 132–3.
22 Rajchman, *The Deleuze Connections*, pp. 102–3.
23 Gilles Deleuze, *Negotiations*, trans. Martin Joughin (New York: Columbia University Press, 1995), p. 175.
24 This danger is less obvious to Guattari who in *Three Ecologies* (London: Athlone, 1989), one of his last texts, continues to write about emergence and the actualization of virtuals.
25 Rajchman, *The Deleuze Connections*, pp. 137–8.
26 Etienne Balibar, *L'Europe, L'Amérique, La guerre* (Paris: La Découverte, 2003), pp. 168–70.
27 This, for Balibar, is the case of the *altermondialistes* who create their own forum in Porto Alegre, Brazil. Their *folkloric happenings*, Balibar argues, have no real effect on the world.
28 Etienne Balibar, *Droit de cité* (Paris: Editions de l'Aube, 1998).
29 Michel de Certeau makes this observation about May 1968 in *The Capture of Speech*, trans. Tom Conley (Minneapolis: University of Minnesota Press, 1997).
30 Abbas Kiarostami, *And Life Goes On* (DVD, Pandora Film, 1991).
31 Jeb Brugman, *Welcome to the Urban Revolution: How Cities Are Changing the World* (New York: Bloomsbury Press, 2009).
32 Deleuze, *Negotiations*, p. 176.

Bibliography

Armitage, J. (ed.) (2011). *Virilio Now*, London: Polity Press.
Augé, M. (1995). *Non-Places*, trans. John Howe, New York: Verso.
Augé, M. (1996). "Paris and the ethnography of the contemporary world," in M. Sheringham (ed.) *Parisian Fields*, London: Reaktion Books.
Balibar, E. (1998). *Droit de cite*, Paris: Editions de l'Aube.
Balibar, E. (2003). *L'Europe, l'Amérique, la guerre*, Paris: La Découverte.
Brugmann, J. (2009). *Welcome to the Urban Revolution: How Cities Are Changing the World*, New York: Bloomsbury Press.
de Certeau, M. (1984). *The Practice of Everyday Life*, trans. S. Rendall, Berkeley: University of California Press.
de Certeau, M. (1997). *The Capture of Speech*, trans. Tom Conley, Minneapolis: University of Minnesota Press.
Conley, D. (2009). *Elsewhere, U.S.A*, New York: Pantheon.
Deleuze, G. (1995). *Negotiations*, trans. M. Joughin, New York: Columbia University Press.
Deleuze, G. and F. Guattari (1988). *A Thousand Plateaus*, trans. B. Massumi, Minneapolis: University of Minnesota Press.
Enwezor, O. (ed.) (2002). *Under Siege: Four African Cities*, Kassel: Cantz.
Ferry, J. (1868). *Les Comptes fantastique d'Haussmann*, Paris: Guy Durier.
Goonewardena, K., S. Kiepfer, R. Milgrom, and C. Schmid (eds.) (2007). *Space, Difference, Everyday Life: Reading Henri Lefebvre*, New York: Routledge.

Koolhaas, R. (1996). "Pearl River Delta," in C. David and J.-F. Chevrier (eds.) *Politics and Poetics*, Documenta X. Kassel: Cantz.

Koolhaas, R. (2001). *The Harvard Design School Guide To Shopping*, Köln: Taschen.

Latour, B. and E. Hermant (1998). *Paris, Ville invisible*, Paris: La Découverte.

Lefebvre, H. (2003). *The Urban Revolution*, trans. R. Bonono, Minneapolis: University of Minnesota Press.

Mostafavi, M. and G. Doherty (2010). *Ecological Urbanism*, Baden, Switzerland: Lars Müller.

Rajchman, J. (2002). *The Deleuze Connections*, Cambridge: MIT.

Soja, E. (1996). *Third Space*, New York: Blackwell.

Stiegler, B. with P. Cogan (2010). "Knowledge, care and trans-individuation: an interview," *Cultural Politics*, 6(2), 157–69.

Virilio, P. (1984). *L'espace critique*, Paris: Bourgois.

Virilio, P. (2000a). *The Information Bomb*, trans. C. Turner, New York: Verso.

Virilio, P. (2000b). *Strategy of Deception*, trans. C. Turner, New York: Verso.

Virilio, P. (2005). *City of Panic*, trans. J. Rose, Oxford: Berg.

Virilio, P. and P. Petit. (1999). *The Politics of the Very Worst*, trans. M. Cavaliere, New York: Semiotext(e).

8 Tokyo
Water, earthquake, and island universe

Suzuki Hiroyuki

Redevelopment drives in Tokyo have often been conducted in response to destruction from war or disasters. The creation of Ginza "Bricktown," the first urban development project of the Meiji era (1868–1912), followed a major fire, while Tokyo's two biggest urban transformations since then came in the wake of the devastating 1923 earthquake and the destruction of World War II. Aside from these reconstruction efforts, urban renewal in Tokyo has amounted to little more than consuming the legacy of earlier times by converting properties from old to new uses. Following the 1868 Meiji Restoration, when the shogunate and the system of domains was abolished and Edo renamed Tokyo, many of the residences that the *daimyo* (domain lords) had established in the shogun's capital were confiscated by the Meiji government, which put the land to new uses. The estates of the Owari and Mito *daimyo*, which were especially large, became military facilities, and that of the Kaga *daimyo* was converted into a university campus. Edo Castle, which had served as the shogun's seat, became the Imperial Palace.

When Tokyo prepared to host the Olympics in 1964, the authorities again resorted to using up some of the city's Edo inheritance, namely its many natural and artificial waterways, which were exploited as routes for a new network of expressways. Thus it came to pass that the historic bridge of Nihonbashi, marking the starting point of the storied Tokaido highway that linked Edo to the old imperial capital of Kyoto, ended up in the shadow of an elevated motorway. Another example of land-use conversion from the same period was the construction of the indoor arena housing the Olympic swimming pool in Yoyogi on land that before World War II had been used by the imperial military, and after the war had served as the Washington Heights district of US military residences. Nearly 60 years after the destruction wrought by World War II and nearly 40 years after the Olympics, is there any land left in Tokyo that is still suitable for conversion? The redevelopment drives that have transformed Tokyo repeatedly in the past have always had access to ample supplies of land. After World War II, for example, not only districts devastated by firebombing but also many former military bases were available for civilian construction. Public housing projects such as the ones at Toyama Heights and in Akabane are examples of former military sites that were converted into residential districts. In the first decade of the twenty-first century Tokyo entered a redevelopment boom, and projects centering on super-high-rise office buildings went up all over the city. In one year alone, the Marunouchi Building in front of Tokyo Station was completely rebuilt as a skyscraper; a cluster of high-rises known as Shiodome Shiosite transformed the Shiodome district; the area around the south exit of Shinagawa Station was redeveloped; and in the Roppongi area the Izumi Garden development was completed adjacent to the Ark Hills complex, and the new Roppongi Hills complex established itself as a major Tokyo landmark. These are just some of the better-known examples. Numerous other corners of Tokyo have also been redeveloped, including part of the Harumi Itchome district; the Mitsui Honkan building and the former site of the Tokyu Department Store in Nihonbashi; Meiji Seimei Kan (head office of Meiji Life Insurance Co.), the Nihon Kogyo Club (Industry Club of Japan) building, and the former Japanese National Railways headquarters site in Marunouchi; and the areas around Akihabara and Iidabashi Stations. Slightly earlier projects included the Atago Green Hills development in the area between Kamiyacho and Onarimon Stations and the construction of Sanno Park Tower and Prudential Tower near Tameike Station. The completion of so many skyscrapers in such a short space of time has made Tokyo a city replete with state-of-the-art office space.

The offices of companies and other organizations are highly mobile, and tenants of office buildings have no hesitation in relocating when a place that is a bit cheaper or one that is better equipped becomes available. So the glut of new office space is not only causing rents to collapse but also causing a chain reaction of relocations as tenants of existing buildings move to offices in newer buildings vacated by tenants moving to even more recently completed edifices. In the case of the greater Tokyo region, the mass availability of new office space in central locations is also disrupting the secondary urban centers located at a radius of about 30 kilometers from central Tokyo. In places such as Makuhari to the east, Omiya, Kawagoe, and Hachioji to the north and west, and Yokohama to the south, development has been driven by the goal of making the greater Tokyo region a ring-shaped megalopolis. But with the center of the capital being the focus of such a sustained bout of large-scale redevelopment, the resulting new complexes are sucking up not only central Tokyo tenants but also some that would otherwise occupy offices in these secondary centers.

An especially large amount of new office space became available rather suddenly in 2003, and the effects of this supply surge are commonly referred to as the "2003 problem." I frequently hear references to this phenomenon in conversations with people involved in the real estate and construction businesses. They talk of the fact that tenants are now able to find better and cheaper offices every time they relocate, of the plummeting cost of building leases, especially for older edifices, of soaring vacancy rates, and of the growing number of large new office blocks that are having trouble finding tenants. Statistics tell the same story. According to a report from the Ministry of Land, Infrastructure, and Transport, the vacancy rate for large buildings in the five central wards of Tokyo, including Chiyoda, Chuo, and Minato, was 6.9 percent in fiscal 2002 (April 2002–March 2003), compared with a mere 0.8 percent in fiscal 2000, and the vacancy rate for all twenty-three wards rose to 6.1 percent. The report expresses concern that some older buildings with empty offices may not be able to fill their vacancies. Even state-of-the-art skyscrapers are having to fight each other tooth and nail for tenants. With so many vacancies, an urban legend has arisen that one of the new high-rises is actually haunted. The urban renewal policy currently being pursued is one of the main planks of the current administration's program and started life as an emergency economic stimulus measure. In the Edo period (1603–1868) there was a traditional antirecession policy known as *otasuke fushin* (helping-hand construction work) by which village heads and other notables would help to combat unemployment in lean economic times by commissioning construction work, such as the rebuilding of their houses. I used to think that the government's urban renewal policy was simply a modern-day form of *otasuke fushin*, but there appears to be more to it than that. The fact that it carries the label "urban renewal" gives it a purpose that goes beyond economic stimulus. In the case of the recent redevelopment rush, that objective is to make Japanese cities more internationally competitive. The government also hopes that this renewal will improve the urban environment, both in cities and in surrounding areas, and enable cities' cultural and tourist resources to be exploited more effectively. There is no clear way of measuring a city's international competitiveness, but if we look, for example, at the global rankings for hosting of international conferences we find that Tokyo ranks far below Seoul and even slightly below Beijing.

Tokyo is notoriously expensive, and it is sorely lacking in attractions for people to enjoy outside of work. For this reason, people who come to Tokyo from overseas, whether to attend a conference, do business, or study, inevitably keep their stays as short as possible. Many factors need to be considered if the city is to be made more internationally competitive and more attractive to visitors. This is the purpose of efforts to improve the urban environment in and around Tokyo and exploit the city's cultural and tourist resources more effectively. The recent skyscraper-centered redevelopment projects fall into three general categories. The first is the conversion of large swathes of real estate, notably land formerly owned by the Japanese National Railways. The projects in Shiodome, Shinagawa, and Akihabara fall into this category. The second is the redevelopment of mature business districts, such as Marunouchi and Nihonbashi. The third is the amalgamation of one substantial piece of property with a number of adjoining plots of land in order to form a zone suitable for a large-scale redevelopment. Atago Green Hills, Izumi Garden, and Roppongi Hills are examples of this type of project.

The projects of the first type are largely the outcome of policies pursued by the administration of Prime Minister Nakasone Yasuhiro (1982–7), namely the privatization of the national railways and the tapping of private-sector dynamism. Basically what has made these projects possible is the selling off of public-sector urban assets to private-sector developers. Unfortunately, however, these first-type projects have generally made little positive contribution to the urban environment. They tend to be lacking in both green spaces and cultural character. The only positive cultural contribution so far is the restoration of the old Shinbashi Station in the Shiodome district, but even here it is hard to escape the feeling that the restored building has been grudgingly squeezed in between the newly built high-rises. None of the other first-type redevelopments offers anything that might attract visitors from among the general public. It is hard to escape the conclusion that these projects achieve little more than making Tokyo more overcrowded and more "functional."

The second and third types of redevelopment project, by contrast, do appear to be succeeding to a certain extent in creating new cultural and other public assets. The redevelopment of the area around Tokyo Station offers some good examples. This project involves the central business districts of Otemachi, Marunouchi, and Yurakucho, Dai-Maru-Yu for short, an area that is home to a number of important cultural assets. These include Tokyo Station itself, Meiji Seimei Kan, and the Nihon Kogyo Club building. Under the redevelopment plans currently being implemented, the Meiji Seimei Kan, head office of Meiji Life Insurance Co., will be completely preserved; the part of Tokyo Station that was destroyed by fire in World War II will be restored, refurbished, and put to new use; and the Nihon Kogyo Club building, home of the Industry Club of Japan, has been partly preserved and partly restored. The project is thus creating a renewed business hub for Tokyo while maintaining the historical heritage of the area. Another example is the redevelopment of the Mitsui Honkan building in Nihonbashi, where work has begun on construction of a high-rise as part of a project in which the original structure will be completely preserved. Redevelopment projects of the second type can thus be said to culturally enrich their areas by preserving historic buildings. The Japanese garden in the Roppongi Hills complex restores the image of the garden kept by the Mori family (lords of the Choshu domain) in the Edo period, while the Izumi Garden complex incorporates the garden of the former Tokyo mansion of the Sumitomo family, a great merchant house, which is said to have involved work by the renowned garden designer Ogawa Jihei (1860–1933). These examples reflect a desire on the part of developers to culturally enrich the areas in which they are working by retaining historical gardens as green spaces that are open to the public.

As in the above examples, some of the redevelopment projects of the second and third types are noteworthy for contributing to urban renewal while carrying the torch for Tokyo's heritage. It is not a simple matter, however, to judge whether these projects deserve our unreserved approbation and whether their consequences will truly be favorable. They are just beginning to reveal how the wave of high-rise development is likely to reshape Tokyo's urban environment, both for better and for worse, in the years to come.

I do not intend to be overly critical of the trends that are changing the face of Tokyo as a modern city. As far as possible, I would like to focus on discerning the possibilities these changes offer. Nevertheless, in the transformation Tokyo is currently experiencing I detect a perhaps overly Japanese kind of urbanism. I have noted that many of the current development projects involving the construction of clusters of office buildings include efforts to retain the heritage of the sites on which they are built. Through my involvement in a number of these projects I have encountered first-hand some of the real problems faced by cities. These experiences have taught me that fashioning a pleasant urban environment takes more than the redevelopment of a particular building or plot of land. This goal can be achieved only when the area surrounding a particular project is also comprehensively redeveloped.

In the case of the Marunouchi Building across from Tokyo Station, it would have been difficult to formulate a preservation-and-development project encompassing the surrounding area, because the building takes up a whole block in its own right. Those in charge of the project decided instead to completely rebuild the structure. But developers were able to partially preserve the original Nihon Kogyo Club building while putting up a new thirty-story building behind it on the same block. Similar approaches, combining high-rises with historic older buildings in blockwide redevelopment projects, enabled the preservation of the Mitsui Honkan and Meiji Seimei Kan buildings in their entirety. Adopting a different approach, the developers of Izumi Garden and Roppongi Hills succeeded in incorporating open spaces into these massive complexes by building them from scratch. Yet in Shinagawa and Shiodome, even though the developers had the advantage of access to large plots of land previously used by the national railways, the resulting redevelopment projects lack an overall cultural dimension. Inasmuch as these two projects had their origins in the sale of land to help cover the massive liabilities left over when the Japan National Railway was privatized, it may be that the developers were reluctant to include in their plans any elements that would not generate profits. But it is deeply regrettable that these plots of land, which in their previous incarnations were of great public benefit, have been redeveloped with little regard for cultural enrichment.

Although some of the recent redevelopment projects have more of a cultural hue than others, each of the resulting zones constitutes, I believe, an "island universe" in the heart of Tokyo, a high-rise oasis floating in the chaos of the city. People flock to these oases seeking rest and relaxation. It is with the idea of finding a new oasis in the urban desert that so many visitors have converged on such recently completed projects as the Marunouchi Building, Shiodome Shiosite, and Roppongi Hills.

Omote-Sando is a little different but an interesting area. This area used to be a typical residential district on the outskirts of pre-war Tokyo. The area was developed in the process of the creation of Meiji Shrine, which commemorates the late Emperor Meiji. The main street was laid out to approach the shrine. Alongside the street, residences of rich families and idealistic public housing called the Dojunkai Apartment Houses were built. Recently, the area became one of the most fashionable in Tokyo, because of the attractiveness of an exceptionally well-planted main street. Many shops, restaurants, and boutiques accumulated here. At the same time, many talented architects are asked to design shops here. Now the Omote-Sando area is a showcase of contemporary architectural design.

Here we encounter the urban context of Tokyo. Architects can design their buildings on their own sites, but they cannot choose their neighbors on the site next door. Each building stands alone along the main street of Omote-Sando just like on a website in a network. We realize the character of Tokyo again. It's already a kind of three-dimensional cyber city. Some of these oases also involve lateral extension and links between projects. The Dai-Maru-Yu district redevelopment project, for example, encompasses Marunouchi, including both sides of Tokyo Station, and the neighboring Otemachi and Yurakucho districts. The skyscraper-dominated complexes of Ark Hills, Izumi Garden, Shiroyama Hills, and Roppongi Hills, meanwhile, form a semi-contiguous area. The redevelopment project in the section of Nihonbashi around the Mitsui Honkan building is reportedly part of a broader concept for redevelopment extending into the neighboring Yaesu district. And the development on the south side of Shinagawa Station is very close to Goten'yama Hills and the Tennozu Isle district.

Will these island universes extend and link up to transform Tokyo into a Western-style high-rise city? I consider that unlikely to happen. Japan's capital will probably continue to be a city of islands, a model unto itself.

Tokyo is certainly different from New York. I have heard that film-makers often shoot scenes in Toronto for movies set in New York. There are all kinds of hurdles to filming on the streets of New York, and Toronto is regarded as a good alternative for action scenes and the like. Seen from ground level, Toronto's orderly grid of streets and rows of skyscrapers give the city a very New York-like aspect. This rectangular layout makes for a cityscape utterly unlike Tokyo's hodgepodge of island universes in a sea of relatively low-rise edifices. Tokyo also differs decisively from cities like Paris that feature straight avenues radiating from central points. It is likely that the transformation of Japan's capital into a city of skyscrapers will continue to take place on a piecemeal basis. This model of urban development is at the heart of Tokyo's identity. After the great earthquake in 1923, former red brick buildings in Tokyo were replaced by reinforced concrete ones. Earthquake-resistant design was in fashion then. In Japan, earthquakes are an important factor not to be overlooked. After World War II, many buildings were constructed in a short time. Those buildings are functional but neither strong nor durable. Now, after the Kobe earthquake of 1995, ugly additions to increase seismic reinforcement are in fashion. Typically, one of the most recent buildings on the campus of the University of Tokyo shows off its anti-seismic reinforcement in an aggressively anti-aesthetic fashion. The leading role played by major real estate firms and other private-sector actors has been one of the major factors in Tokyo's development as a city of island universes. The government's current urban renewal policy is concerned principally with facilitating high-quality private-sector development by, for example, simplifying and accelerating planning and other procedures in order to minimize delays in the implementation of development projects. Private-sector developers naturally focus their efforts on what they consider to be strategically valuable areas. This results in the formation of development pockets. The government's efforts to encourage what are called "private finance initiatives" are another element in its policy of promoting private-sector-driven urban renewal. Previously the common approach to tapping private-sector funds for public projects was through the creation of joint public–private ventures – what are commonly called "third-sector" enterprises in Japan. Often the top posts in these ventures went to bureaucrats. In Private Finance Initiative (PFI) development projects, by contrast, the leadership of the private sector is more clearly defined. This is the approach now being used, for example, in the project to redevelop the Toranomon district, centering on plans for the buildings housing two central government organs, and also in the project to redevelop lodgings for members of the National Diet. Advancing urban renewal through PFIs is likely to lead to the formation of new pockets of development, with the result that Tokyo will be further transformed into a city of skyscraper-dominated islands.

This raises two questions. First, what should be the role of the public sector when urban redevelopment is increasingly driven by the private sector? Second, in the island universe model of redevelopment, from what will the redeveloped "islands" derive their identity?

The basic role of the public sector is to provide infrastructure. Specifically, it should put in place and improve such facilities as roads, water supply and sewerage systems, energy and information infrastructure, and open spaces. A city cannot function without these basics. Each pocket of redevelopment provides oasis-like facilities for rest and relaxation, and public works must be targeted at providing support for these oases. It is no exaggeration to say that Tokyo's future depends on whether or not the public sector is successful in fulfilling this role.

On the question of how island universes can establish identities, I have already noted that the identities of districts transformed in the recent wave of redevelopment can be divided into two basic types. The first derives from the expression of a district's heritage, principally through the preservation of historic buildings. The former Shinbashi Station, Tokyo Station, Nihon Kogyo Club building, Mitsui Honkan, and Meiji Seimei Kan, for example, are central to the identities of their respective districts. The second type of identity derives from areas of greenery, such as historical gardens. Examples of these are the Mori garden in Roppongi Hills and the Sumitomo garden in the Izumi Garden project. These redevelopment pockets with heritage may be considered districts with a distinct identity. Heritage is culture; and unless redevelopment projects incorporate culture, they will merely create greater crowding by increasing the number of high-rise buildings.

Compared with the heritage contained in each island, the shapes of skyscrapers, however distinctive, do not impart a particularly strong sense of identity. Although the new Marunouchi Building has attracted great attention, few people can instantly recall how it is shaped. The same goes for the new Dentsu headquarters building in Shiodome, despite its unusual contours. Although Ishiyama Osamu, an architect and a professor at Waseda University, has compared the high-rise in the middle of Roppongi Hills to a giant plastic bottle, I have great difficulty picturing the outline of this building in my head. Redevelopment zones derive their identity and attractiveness from their cultural significance, which is rooted in the history contained in these places and expressed through their redevelopment.

What is happening, essentially, is that the creation of islands of redevelopment is transforming Tokyo from an advanced uni-functional city into a multifunctional cultural metropolis. Central Tokyo – in many ways the face of Japan – has until now been dominated by the headquarters of large corporations and been a place largely for elite white-collar workers. Yet it offered few options for people who had worked late in the city's office blocks and wanted to grab something to eat before heading home. Based on the idea that economic activity is something that happens during the day, this economic city offered little in the way of night-time relaxation.

Under globalization, however, businesses now operate twenty-four hours a day, and even economic cities cannot afford to take a break. This may explain why Tokyo's new development islands have so many restaurants and shops. If this were the only change, it would mean little more than that an advanced economic city had become even more advanced. I believe, however, that it is by incorporating historical culture that the new developments are finding their identity. I would like to think that this is what lies behind the popularity of the newly redeveloped island universes.

9 Vast clearings

Emergency, technology, and American de-urbanization, 1930–45

Gregory Clancey

The house as emergency response

> The Federal government's concern for housing developed through a series of emergencies . . . but piecemeal emergency measures have not solved the problem.
> (Catherine Bauer, 1951)[1]

The automobile's role in American urban change is obvious and well studied. Ford's Model T emerged as a mechanical bull in the china shop of the early twentieth-century pedestrian and street-car city, a rampage that never really abated. There were less direct ways in which the mass-production automobile destabilized American cityscapes, however, which have gone largely unremarked. Beginning in the late 1920s, as the automobile became a metaphor for the dwelling, and the assembly line for the building process, increasing numbers of people began to imagine *the house* (a new keyword of that era) as a mass-producable commodity abstracted from community and even space. This was not a fantasy sprung from the mind of Le Corbusier. New Deal housing policies were actually crafted amid widespread and serious discussion of *the house of tomorrow* as a secret economic weapon, and one that would not necessarily be deployed by government. At the very moment when American cities were plunged into new categories of crisis by the failure of industrial capitalism, the machine-made house promised to set things right as the successor industry to automobiles; the next new technology for cities to absorb, if they could. Here is another, less-explored origin point for the post-war hollowing out of American civic life.

The large-scale deconstruction of American cities that began with the New Deal (and gathered speed with its Fair Deal extension under Truman) is most often portrayed as a well-meaning but ultimately misguided welfare policy for the poor, coupled with a far more successful extension of welfare and infrastructure to a newly mobilized middle class. Another way to approach it, I'll argue, is as a strategic targeting of cities, under the guise of *emergency*, by groups previously external to the practices of city-building, and intent on using urban concentrations to leverage other goals. These "external groups" include not only the vastly expanded federal bureaucracy, but also mass-production industries, universities, and coalitions of reformers and design professionals, most of whom already lived in the suburbs. Beginning in the early years of the Depression (or *the Emergency*, as it was just as frequently called by contemporaries), *the house* far more than *the city* drew these disparate groups around itself and provided a common language – a pidgin – as well as an object-world and set of vaguely convergent goals.

The house and *housing* as American utterances of power date to the 1930s, a full decade after they had entered the political language of Europe. Only with the seeming collapse of capitalism did they begin to appear in state pronouncements, professionalizing projects, business plans, and research agendas, and become key-words in political, journalistic, and advertising accounts of the future. As *factors* and *processes*, inscribed with the charisma of technology, science, and econom-ics, they were constructed against the local, casual, unquantifiable, and feminine – against *houses* and *homes*. General and specific enough – as in *the house of x* and *the x house* – to signify a range of sometimes conflicting schemes, they both marked and generated instability in the most mythically stabilizing of artefacts or spaces. *The house/housing* was arguably the central American imagineering project, discursively and technically, of the period between *the automobile* and *total war* with multiple links to both.

Many American cities in the period before the 1930s commonly styled themselves *cities of homes, home-towns,* or *the home of x* (e.g. the Red Sox, or the American automobile industry). This *homeyness* of course belied (and per-haps resulted from) a ferocious urban mobility sustained by the boom and bust rhythms, and resulting requirements for labor mobility, of advanced industrial capitalism. Whether or not Americans yearned for permanent homes, statistics tell us that most urban residents were simply passing through; that American cities were spaces of transit as much as places of work and rest. *The house* of the 1930s captured this essential mobility of American urban life even while promising to stabilize it in a new but vaguely drawn system of emergency space.

That space was not the street-car and pedestrian city of the 1920s. Nor was it clear at the time that it would become the post-war commuter suburb. The *emergency housing space* of the 1930s was a formative zone of clearance: a vast, evacuated, and repopulated space most often presented as drenched in sunlight and full of new freedoms and securities. It was a zone where high technology would be given full, unhindered play, and hopefully create something healthier and cleaner, but above all brand new. It was not considered absolutely necessary that *the city* survive this spatial displacement.

The 1930s language of *the house* and *housing* was not so much urban as national. Its links to the city were tenuous, and often purposely confrontational. The city and its *home-builders* had, in the language of *housers* (another new term of the 1930s), failed not urban residents but *the American people*. The national – even trans-nationally *human* – desire at the heart of urban in-migration had, according to the contemporary critique, been left unfulfilled if not betrayed. Roosevelt found "one third of a nation ill-housed," a problem that demanded a national rather than a specifically urban response.[2] Indeed the city, so widely celebrated in the 1920s jazz age, was thoroughly pathologized in the home-spun economic emergency that followed. And the most pathological thing about it, in many writings of the period, was the rotten state of its micro-unit, *the house*.

The house as industrial target

> Unless drastic measures are taken to save it, the whole capitalist system throughout the civilized world will be wrecked within a year.
>
> (Bank of England governor Montagu Norman, 1931)[3]

The onset of emergency in 1929–32 focused the attention of both the federal government and private industry on *the house* as simultaneously a problem, potential solution, and new site of political and economic brinksmanship. Because the housing industry had collapsed even before Black Friday – housing starts declining steadily from over 900,000 in 1925 to less than 100,000 in 1933 – certain industrialists and engineers enframed it as a leading cause for the Depression itself. House-making, they argued, was a wooden cog slowing the gears of modern production, or to use Thomas Hughes' image a *reverse salient* in the moving front of mechanization and business consolidation.[4] Targeting the house also helped answer the common and danger-filled charge that the emergency was caused by over-production in the mass-production industries (whose proponents were called "over-production terrorizers" by industrialist and mass-production housing advocate Albert Bemis). The key to solving the business crisis, for textile magnate Bemis, General Electric's Owen D. Young, General Motor's Charles Kettering, and others who put themselves on record, was finding an expanded array of products for America's super-heated assembly lines to make. With mortgage foreclosures accelerating and building trades prostrate, *housing* was an attractive idea for a dangerous moment.[5]

Hoover himself was the first to recognize the possibilities in this argument, convening a "President's Conference on Home Building and Home Ownership" in 1931, which brought together over 500 delegates in twenty-five separate committees, overseen by six correlating committees, and engaging an audience of 3,700 registered participants. This conference was the real cradle of the house-provision culture that would grow exponentially in the Roosevelt administration. An innovation of Hoover's conference was to decontextualize *the house* from *the city*. The largest social grouping considered was *the community* but more often just *the house* itself was under discursive design. The emphasis on science (Secretary of Commerce Lamont advised "the application of the microscope" to the housing problem) set a tone for reductionism, but the new turn toward technology advanced it further. The house was no longer to just be *improved* by experts, as in the Progressive-era discourse of home economics and domestic science, but *produced* by business with government cooperation.[6]

In his own remarks to the conference Hoover consistently avoided the word *city* in describing the location of the house-product. He criticized the "helter-skelter building of homes adjacent to our cities" while speaking more positively of "the problem of creating real and systematic home areas adjacent to industry." The president's spatial vagaries seemed sometimes to anticipate the future explosion of suburbs, as in "the automobile has made such communities [*which* or *where* he doesn't say] far more practical than ever before." Housing, he offered, was the "greatest field for absorption of our surplus national energy" and called for "some radical new departure" in economics and design. *Urban* energies were not immediately enlisted, however: the nation's mayors were conspicuously absent from Hoover's conference.[7]

The conference's most radical proposals came from its Committee on Technological Developments, one of six correlating committees, none of which had the word *city* in their titles. Its members were certain that "houses can be thoroughly worked out in the laboratory" and "machines can be developed to perform most of the [building] operations." They were even open to dramatic changes in form. "These new houses . . . will appear queer to most of us at first," the committee warned, but "as we become accustomed to them we gradually will realize that they are beautiful because they are logical." Signing their names to this vision were two high-level Commerce Department officials, the deans of two engineering colleges, two female professors of home economics, and, most tellingly, the research directors of both General Motors and General Electric. The few architects also attending the conference had been segregated in a separate subcommittee on design, where they had nothing to say about mass production despite Le Corbusier and Gropius. The Technological Committee was aware of "efforts made in Europe, particularly Germany and Russia," which were "interesting and suggestive." It believed, however, that "a very different solution" had to be engineered for the American workman, who wanted "an individual home with a garage for his automobile."[8]

The "queer" dwellings that the Committee on Technological Development had in mind may have been the designs of Gropius and other Europeans modernists, such as those at the mid-1920s Weisenhof Seidlung in Stuttgart. They could also have been thinking, however, of Buckminster Fuller's Dymaxion House of 1927. A highly publicized utopian object that made the automobile analogy most explicit, Fuller's house was "demountable" (capable of being rendered mobile) and technologically self-sufficient (not needful of connection to city utilities). Its physical location, like that of an automobile, was thus ambiguous and unsettling, an object existing more in national than in urban space (particularly the space of newspapers, magazines, and newsreels). Fuller's house was intended to be a prototype for serial line production, but it took the economic emergency to interest those with actual access to assembly lines, such as Bemis, Young, and Kettering, in the possibilities of re-tooling for house production.[9]

The *repro-shelter* project: General Houses and Houses, Inc.

> What other industry pays its labor to think rather than act mechanically?
> (John Burchard, Director of the Bemis Foundation, MIT, on the
> deficiencies of the American house-building industry, 1939)[10]

As automobile consumption wound down and skyscraper building simply stopped, the metal-based fabrication industries began to consider how the residential districts of cities (not just their cores) might be *pre-fabricated*, a new and entirely

American term of the early 1930s. The addition of the prefix to the 1920s term *fabrication* (used to describe the preparation of steel frames for skyscraper and bridge construction) emphasized that assembly would take place in factories *prior to* the delivery of the house or its components to the building site. The *building site* would be made to disappear as a site of production (including perhaps urban production) and become a less complicated and more vaguely located space of consumption. Prefabrication (or as Buckminster Fuller called it, *repro-shelter*) was the incipient re-tooling of factory-based assembly lines to produce and con-tinually re-produce the cities around themselves; the ultimate "technological fix" to a problem created by these same industries in the form of the automobile.

"The manufacturer", noted the editor of the *Architectural Forum* in 1932, "now finds in housing the potential market for unheard of quantities of his materi-als."[11] But although American houses consumed massive amounts of lumber and brick, they used little or no steel, aluminum, rubber, baked enamel, or engineering talent. This was the heart of *the housing problem* for many American industrialists and engineers. With traditional markets for mass-production goods drying up, the *housing market* became a battleground between those industries that traditionally supplied construction materials – lumber, ceramics, copper wiring, etc. – and the steel-based mass-production and fabrication newcomers. "The steel industry sees housing as a tonnage-builder" noted a 1936 article in the *Real Estate Record*, and "the highly-mechanized industries see building (housing in particular) as an outlet for excess production."[12]

In the waning months of the Hoover administration (1932–3), highly capital-ized firms with names like General Houses, American Homes, National Houses, and Houses, Inc. entered the business world on a wave of expensively purchased national publicity. Houses, Inc. was a patent-pooling syndicate organized by General Electric, the Celotex Corporation, American Radiator, the Container Corporation of America, Pittsburgh Glass, the Pullman Car and Manufacturing Company, and more than a dozen other corporations with newly instituted pro-grams of *housing research*. American House's engineers and laboratory facilities were on loan from General Electric, and Houses, Inc. employed the son of GE's president, Gerard Swope. Republic Steel, the Aluminum Corporation of America, and eventually U.S. Steel would make similar investments in prefabrication companies. The houses these firms began to produce around 1932 were radically unlike those made by local builders. They had steel frames covered largely with metal and ceramic fittings, and eschewed most of the other materials common in American house-building, particularly lumber and masonry. Moreover, their appearance was strikingly *modernistic*, with flat roofs, strip windows, and smooth white exterior walls. American Houses' products were delivered "complete" in a single truck emblazoned with the slogan "This truck contains one American Home." They were advertised as *moto-homes*.[13]

Although it seemed to most observers that prefabrication had merely "caught fire" with the public by 1932, the enthusiasm was largely fueled by a public rela-tions campaign centered in the *Time–Life–Fortune* conglomerate (which also owned the *Architectural Forum*). The editors of *Fortune* published a series of major articles in 1932 (ghostwritten by Pulitzer prize-winning author Archibald McLeish) that skillfully and at length laid out the case for prefabrication, and ended with an endorsement of General Houses ("The General Motors of the New Industry of Shelter").[14] MacLeish pathologized the American city as a product of collusion between archaic building trades unions, gangsters, and corrupt politicians. His text even includes a photograph of a union-connected gangster lying dead in the streets of Chicago. Because political machines had failed to produce adequate home life, suggests MacLeish, momentum was now passing to the machines of industry. Industrial efforts were presented as already far advanced, and potentially radical: "Shrouded in secrecy have been the plans of the AO Smith Corp., the world's largest manufacturer of automobile frames, to apply to housing their famous mass-production techniques."[15] The house that would roll from this and other factories would be "nearly self-sufficient, and as nearly free from the political nuisances of city water and city sewage and city electricity and city light as may be. And its adoption might well expedite the urban decentralization."[16]

Although housing would turn out to be an extremely difficult market for mass-production industries to crack (most of these ventures failed to turn a profit until the economic emergency became a war emergency), *Fortune* and *Life* would remain strong advocates of corporate-produced prefabricated housing into the late 1940s.

Despite initial business setbacks, the change from Hoover's New Era to Roosevelt's New Deal only furthered the momentum of the prefabrication idea. The new administration's interest in *public housing* appeared to some observers to be "competing" with private house production, but it was in fact complementary. By 1933–4 it was apparent to General Houses and other mass-production firms that a host of unforeseen difficulties lay in their way, from local building codes, to the non-cooperation of building trades unions, to the resistance of local real estate interests and home-loan banks, to the need for basic research programs in materials and production methods to reduce the costs of transport and erection. The automobile analogy had revealed its shortcomings; it was not as simple to feed mass-production houses into the city as it had been to feed cars. The gates to the city might still be opened, however, with the help of the national government.[17]

Prefabrication had strong advocates in nearly every New Deal agency related to housing, from the Public Works Administration (PWA), to the U.S. Housing Authority (USHA), the Federal Housing Administration (FHA), the Tennessee Valley Authority (TVA) (which created its own trailer-like prefabricated dwelling), the Farm Resettlement Administration (FSA), and even the Justice Department, where Attorney General Thurmon Arnold attempted to prosecute the building trades unions (considered fierce opponents of prefabrication) for the crime of Luddism, using anti-trust and "restraint of trade" legislation. Although some private-sector prefabrication advocates were worried that the center of the program was passing from themselves to the state, the state actually did its best to clear away obstacles to a national housing market, one that almost everyone believed would eventually coalesce under big-business control. The Roosevelt administration was more than willing to sacrifice the conservative (and generally

Republican-voting) building trades unions of the American Federation of Labor (AFofL) in order to deliver house production to the Congress of Industrial Organizations (CIO) and United Automobile Workers (UAW), industrial unions headquartered in assembly-line manufacturing.[18]

The federal government and the mass-production industries, working sometimes separately and sometimes hand in glove, were attempting to fashion a new housing product somewhere between themselves, in an abstract space whose contours or location were, until the late 1940s, never entirely clear. But the new concentration of capital, engineering, design professionalism, journalism, and federal support was clearly set against the dispersed, the locally based, and the small: from city savings banks, to building trades unions, to existing real estate interests and urban politicians, who together constituted the normative system of American city-building.

The house as R&D bandwagon

> There is no doubt that we [architects] can get into this picture . . . Housing is a public issue, nobody has a patent on it. It is yours if you want it . . . How can we become a factor in the housing movement?
>
> (Alfred Kastner, Chairman, Housing Committee of the Washington, D.C. chapter of the AIA, 1938)[19]

> At the moment, it seems a fair question whether the controlling influence may not rest with the pioneers in new methods of production, to whom the architect will be a servant rather than a master.
>
> (Albert Bemis, industrialist and engineer, 1936)[20]

Once government, the mass-production industries, and consortiums of private development capital had signaled a convergent interest in *the house*, professional groups with previously little experience in urban housing began jumping on the prefabrication bandwagon. American architects actually had little to do with "the broad masses" prior to the 1930s (except when designing train stations or office buildings), but they now saw prefabrication as a way of penetrating a design market that had long denied their entry. Even during the 1920s building boom, American architects had designed less than 5 percent of American houses. Wrote the editor of the *Architectural Forum* in 1932:

> The search for the way out [of the emergency], by this process of elimination, has led to the large and practically untouched field of providing living quarters for the mass of the population . . . circumstances seem to be conspiring to make possible the dreams of the city planner – architect.[21]

The possibility inherent in mass-production housing was the principal reason for American architects' discovery, in the early to mid-1930s, of European theorists such as Gropius, Corbusier, and Meis van der Rohe, whom they had long ignored or viewed as impossibly *long-haired*, to use a term recurrent in professional journals of the period to describe eccentric theorists. Gropius was brought to Harvard in 1935 largely on the strength of his prototypes for machine-made housing, and his known interest in working with engineers and industrial corporations on the problems of mass production.

The housing project also caught the attention of American social scientists. To University of Minnesota sociologist A. Stephen Stephan, public housing projects were "made to order test tubes," and *decanting* renters from slums to new apartments "would be like transferring a population mass from Test Tube 1 of Liquid A to Test Tube 2 of Liquid B and finding out what happens." In promoting housing research, Stephan pointed out that social scientists "have suffered from a lack of large-scale experimental set-ups to match the everyday resources of their brothers in the laboratory." In fact, the University of Minnesota sociology department would take the lead in producing highly abstract social science research products around the urban exodus in Minneapolis/St. Paul.[22]

A score of American universities opened institutes and laboratories in the early to mid-1930s dedicated to making *the house* a research object. At Purdue University and the University of Illinois (Urbana), small "test neighborhoods" of new houses were established where everything from technics to design to the psychology of the inhabitants (mostly professors, graduate students, and their families) were systematically studied. MIT sponsored the Bemis Foundation, a prefabrication clearing house funded by alumnus Albert Bemis, which coordinated inter-departmental research and sponsored national housing conferences. At the Foundation's inaugural "Homes of Tomorrow" conference in 1937, dean of engineering and MIT vice-president Vannever Bush spoke on "The Scientific Approach to our Housing Problem," attempting to translate the standard American discourse on slum reform into the language of cost–benefit analysis:

> as the standard (of housing) is raised, the cost to society of the presence of marginal areas, due to health and social hazards, decreases. The total cost to society is the sum of these, and the sum of these two curves is undoubtedly the saddle-shaped figure which is so thoroughly familiar to engineers. Once such a curve is before us, it is financially justifiable to set the minimum standard at the base of that saddle, and it is not justifiable from a financial standpoint to set it above or below that point.

In straining to create a pidgin between the previously distinct cultures of housing reform and engineering, Bush was attempting to influence what he saw as New Deal attempts to wrest the lucrative housing market from private industry. His speech ended with an attack on "the growing tendency, born of loose and emotional thinking" to assume that only "an extension of government" could solve social problems. That was properly the job of engineers and private capital. Bush himself would be instrumental in solving the social problems of research scientists, ironically by orchestrating huge extensions of federal funding for university laboratories during and after World War II. In 1937, however, MIT research labs were actually focused on *the house* as the coming technology.[23]

A New Deal for poor neighborhoods: clearance as urban technology

The pace of industrial advance can be speeded up by planned elimination of obsolete forms.   (K. Lonberg-Holm and C. Theodore Larson, 1938)[24]

Another field for enterprise which should be studied is slum clearance.
(K. K. Stowell, 1932)[25]

Franklin Roosevelt's New Deal housing policies remain so iconic that their darkest manifestation – large and unprecedented urban clearances resulting in the displacement of tens of thousands of renters and poor home-owners – is normally mentioned only in passing by historians of the Depression. In fact, the clearance of *slums* and *blighted areas* was a much more important part of the New Deal, in terms of money, strategic planning, and energy, than was the construction of new housing, although both projects were intimately linked. Slum clearance was "the more dramatic and popular" of the two practices, even in the words of a retrospective PWA publication.[26]

There is also little recognition in the secondary literature that the people *decanted* from condemned neighborhoods, to use the term of art from that period, were not necessarily re-housed with government help. In contrast to policy in Britain of the same period, the United States and its local housing authorities gave no guarantee to tenants of condemned buildings that they would be accommodated in replacement projects. A neighborhood could be condemned, its tenants evicted, its buildings demolished, and a new development eventually constructed and occupied on the site with little concern for the fate of the original inhabitants. In keeping with the *national* rhetoric of the program, and the new market language surrounding housing, the government made its re-housing promises to *the poor* (a statistical category determined by personal income) rather than to specific, nameable individuals or families, even those subjected to eviction. British housing reformer Sir Raymond Unwin expressed surprise at the brutality of this process, which was referred to as *clearing from ground*.[27]

Like mass housing, urban clearance had first been suggested by Hoover, whose Emergency Relief and Reconstruction Act of 1932 targeted, among other projects, "the reconstruction of slum areas." The first large clearance project approved by the resulting Reconstruction Finance Corporation (RFC) made space for the Knickerbocker Village development in lower Manhattan. Thousands of residents from the Lower East Side were evicted to build new housing at rents none of them could afford. The "stock of people" whom Knickerboker's private but government-subsidized developers "targeted from the beginning," according to the *Architectural Forum*, were "the swarms of middle-waged city, state, and federal employees who crowd down into lower Manhattan each day." Developer Fred French told the journal that "the 3,000 people who were living there before we began demolition have benefited indirectly" from his project, however, "because they have been forced to scatter about." Eviction would often be portrayed as just such a productive mobilization; a rational geographic sorting out by function and income. "Most of these people," said French, "did not really need to live on Manhattan Island."[28]

Clearance became a sustained federal project under the Emergency Administration of Public Works (more commonly known as the Public Works Administration or PWA) in 1933. The PWA was created by the Industrial Recovery Act whose stated purpose was to "increase employment quickly." It also provided, however, for "aiding in the redistribution of the overbalance of population in industrial centers."[29] Largely because demolition was labor intensive, quickly organized, and required so little skill (and because the "attack on slums" proved popular with the middle class) it became a more important PWA activity than the construction of new housing. But the urban clearance campaign was also tied into the logic – and conducted against the backdrop – of continuing efforts to foster factory housing. Proponents of prefabrication believed that "liquidating" the existing housing stock, in the words of one theorist, was essential to preventing "obsolete" houses from competing in price with new ones. The Committee on Large-Scale Operations of the President's Conference of 1931 had proclaimed that "the houses of the country constitute our largest mass of obsolete and discredited equipment," unlike "motor cars, radios" etc. that were periodically discarded.[30] Significant investments would not be made by capitalists in factory housing, according to a Russell Sage Foundation report of 1939, "until they are confident that city government will continue to condemn and turn over to them . . . a succession of large plots."[31] Clearance was thus seen by many as a production-oriented task that only government could perform, and the easiest (the most politically popular) place to begin was in the much-derided *slums*.

An influential advocate of linking clearance to mass production was architect-planner Henry Wright, principal adviser to Robert Kohn, the first director of the PWA. "I have coupled the fate of 'scientific machine production' in building with the program of slum clearance and low cost urban housing," wrote Wright in 1934, "rather than with its more popular aspects of demountable houses for the suburbanite." Like many housing reformers in the 1930s, Wright was not certain exactly which landscapes – urban or suburban – prefabrication would first transform. Factory-based systems might well find their easiest market in the clearance zones of inner cities. Wrote Wright:

> Its anybody's guess whether we are about to so completely decentralize as to leave our older cities with their antiquated housing equipment to rot in their tracks, or whether business necessity is going to stage a big comeback in the rehabilitation of our blighted cities. While I am traditionally on the side of the decentralizers, I am not sure that there may be strong points in favor of saving the credit of our good old cities however much they deserve to be numbered among the forgotten and deserted of the earth.

The repro-shelter industry had seemed imminent in 1932, he noted, but "then faded out like a meteor" because of land-related, legal, and research difficulties, many related to suburban sites. Prefabrication was still the solution "for the great over-equipped automotive industry," but government needed to help, and that project could start in urban areas. "I'm heart and soul for low dwellings and not for tenements of 4 or 5 stories," he wrote, and "I'm not an advocate of the modern versus traditional in construction." But Americans "need to break down our sentimental attitude toward home ownership" and producing urban rental property for the poor could be an opening wedge. Wright would "give them [urban dwellers] unlimited sunlight and freedom." And how could they refuse? As the least-loved, and hence most vulnerable spots in the urban fabric, poor and minority neighborhoods would be the first to go.[32]

In 1934, PWA administrator Harold Ickes personally started demolition of two *slum areas* in Atlanta by pressing a detonator and blowing up what appears in photographs to be detached single-family houses. One *Architectural Forum* photograph shows a cottage in the process of exploding, its chimney toppling into its roof. This is one among very few images to appear in this or any other journal of the period of the mechanics of urban clearance. The following page of the same article featured a more common portrayal of urban roll-back: an aerial photograph of a densely-populated 160-acre area of Chicago – a patchwork of row-houses and small stores – marked out for the same treatment.[33]

Accounts of large-scale clearance from this period are, to modern sensibilities, surprisingly celebratory and generally bereft of any mention of the hardships, fate, or even the identities of the displaced. There is typically an emphasis on quantity – calculated either in acreage or persons or both – and sometimes, as with the Atlanta photographs, on the peculiar satisfactions of physical destruction ("Ickes blows slums of Atlanta sky-high" read the caption). David Ostreicher, Director of Demolition for the New York Housing Authority, proudly reported that in only two and a half years (1934–6) he had razed buildings "with a combined frontage of 6.8 miles":

> Visualize if you can, tearing down the entire building frontage on the west side of Fifth Avenue in Manhattan from Washington Square at 4th Street up to 142nd Street . . . and you will get a fair picture of the work accomplished. Thus a little over seven miles of slums covering a ground area of 2,700,000 square feet, about 61 acres of land, containing some 7,900 dwellings arranged to house approximately 35,500 humans, were literally wiped from the face of the earth.

A follow-up survey in late 1936, he reports, indicated that, although ten of the cleared lots had been converted to playgrounds, eighty were being "temporarily" used for "auto parking, auto repairs, lunch wagons, material and junk yards." Only six had been built on and the vast majority (900 lots) remained vacant. This was considered not a defeat but a victory, as the undeveloped lots had actually increased in value. Providing cleared and vacant land had become part of normal government business, or of government service to the embryonic mass-housing business. No government agency or report traced the fate or location of Ostreicher's "35,000 humans."[34]

The Wagner–Steagall Act of 1937, considered the cornerstone of New Deal housing legislation, greatly extended the practice of clearance by requiring that one *slum unit* be eliminated for every unit of public housing erected. This satisfied real estate interests by guaranteeing no net increase in the American housing stock, thus keeping rent and vacancy levels uniform. It also produced a vastly greater number of urban clearance sites that, it was hoped, would encourage the industrial market for urban house-building. Yet over the long run (at least to the end of the Truman administration) the amount of affordable housing demolished would exceed the amount built.

Most inner-city public housing was in fact constructed using existing low-tech systems of brick-laying, wooden partition-building, and even plastering (to accommodate still-powerful local building trades unions and keep costs to a minimum). Most housing advocates fully expected, however, that the "bricks and morter" projects they were constructing in the clearance zones were destined to be succeeded by prefabricated or mass-production ones, and their faith in the process of *product development* and a *mass market*, again based on the example of the automobile, may help to explain the general casualness, if not carelessness, about the immediate effects of clearance. The short-term goal was to mobilize (people), clear (space), and design (prototypes) for a formative system of industrial production, which *in the long term* was expected to positively transform American cities. Prefabrication would provide better housing for everyone *given space to develop*. When it didn't, at least through the later 1930s, the solution was to give it even more space.

Widening the clearance zone: from slums to "blighted areas"

> We saw (in Detroit) our first "blighted area". That is one of the things in which Americans specialize. They do not specialize in slums.
>
> (Sir Ernest Simon, Ministry of Public Works and Planning (UK), describing a fact-finding trip to the U.S. in 1944)[35]

The United States in the early twentieth century had inherited from Victorian Britain an elaborate language of urban containment, targeting, and excision whose central concept was the *slum* and whose ultimate goal was *clearance*. The responsibility for *slum clearance* was, in Anglo-American practice from the late nineteenth century onward, located in urban Health Departments and Sanitary Commissions (and sometimes, as in Philadelphia, the Fire Department), thus amalgamating the spatial practice of de-housing with that of disease and disaster control.

Appeals to the affluent to support slum clearance projects had long been made in the language of self-interest: "The homes of the rich," suggested American Progressive-era housing reformer Lawrence Veiller, "are not exempt from the dangers of the typhoid fly." Although slum clearance was far more widespread in Britain than in pre-emergency America (because of the greater political power of local real estate interests in the United States), poor neighborhoods in the latter were capable of even more grotesque caricature in reformist accounts, because the population they housed was largely "foreign." Veiller targeted, for instance,

> those foreign colonies which we have allowed to spring up in the various sections of our cities, "empires within an empire", segregated from American institutions, isolated communities, feeling but slightly the touch of democracy – "social Saharas" as they have been aptly called.[36]

Although this medicalizing and exoticizing language never disappeared from housing reform, it proved limiting to a subsequent generation with expanded ambitions for urban clearance. The 1930s required a more bloodless economic, social, and technological sanction for demolition, because the areas now to be cleared extended so far beyond the traditional *slum*. Disease, for all its flexibility, could not be stretched to cover this expanded range of targets, particularly as epidemics themselves receded from the American imagination after the Great Influenza of 1918 had run it course. Moreover, restrictions on immigration were firmly in place by the 1930s, making the specter of foreign "empires within an empire" less convincing as a lever of public policy or action.

Most critical literature on early twentieth-century urban planning focuses on its invention of *the zone* and the process of *zoning* – the mapping of an abstract functionalism on formerly lively urban neighborhoods. A relatively overlooked but no less important mapping object, invented in the same period, was *the blighted area*. Whereas the term *slum* had an almost olfactual sense of putridness and decay, *blight* was a term borrowed from agriculture, and simply described the condition of crop failure. Evoking withered stalks of corn resulting from bad weather or an attack of pests (as in the contemporary "Dust Bowl" of Oklahoma) it was sufficiently natural, and neutral, to describe areas of cities that had ceased to provide a bumper crop of tax revenues.

The naming of *urban blight* was a movement outward from the bounded *sore center* of the slum to a more spacious though no less apocalyptic landscape that covered cities more generally. It was expansive in the sense of having familiar resonance in a still largely agricultural country; the rural areas around big cities occasionally suffered a malady of identical description. To housing official Coleman Woodbury, the blighted area was "analogous to a swampy or an arid agricultural section [where] improvement cannot be carried out until some way is found of applying it on a large scale." *Disease* might be contained and tumors removed (by experts or professionals) but *blight* simply settled, and required concerted, large-scale, and above all cooperative reclamation efforts. "One owner," wrote Woodbury, "cannot successfully drain or irrigate his land."[37]

Urban blight was semantically related to the earlier, Progressive-era term *housing famine*, whose carnality was compatible with the language regime of epidemic. *Famine* was dropped from the vocabulary of housing reformers after the 1920s, however, and *blight* became the term of choice in the emergency era, because it could more effectively link Progressive-era housing reform with the more powerful New Deal arenas of economics and planning. Crop failure (in the sense of commodity shortage or loss of revenue) appealed as a crisis to the economy-minded more than did starvation, a state in which people cease to be consumers and thus drop out of econometric sight into the laps of charities. The housing problem had for too long been "confused with the problem of slums and their removal," wrote Miles Colean of the FHA. "The housing problem," he stated, was actually "a problem of industrial organization and efficiency."[38]

In emergency-era America, of course, *blight* in its economic sense had absolutely broken out. *Blighted areas* could be increasingly framed as synonymous with American cities generally. A series of maps showing Cleveland in the period 1910–40, published in 1944, illustrated *blight* as a creeping blackness that had grown to engulf two-thirds of the city. "This is typical of what has happened to most American cities," read the caption. The same report noticed nascent rehabilitation in such neighborhoods as Beacon Hill in Boston and Georgetown in Washington, D.C., but called it "a scattered process" that "has had a negligible influence on the neighborhood in general." Once afflicted, it seemed, everything would have to go.[39]

The central piece of emergency-era literature on blight was Mabel Walkers' *Urban Blight and Slums* of 1938, commissioned by the Harvard School of City Government. Subtitling her study "Economic and Legal Factors in their Origin, Reclamation, and Prevention," Walker subjects the whole corpus of Progressive-era slum-related language to bureaucratic makeover. An area may still be blighted, she concludes, simply because "its characteristics are changing and its future is indefinite." Among the factors making the blighted area "a liability rather than an asset" are the "mixed character and uses of the buildings" or when "the majority of buildings . . . are old." The malady could cover a zone "even though the housing in it may be relatively good." Economic development in the blighted zone has been "retarded as compared with the development in the larger area," although how large an area or what sort of development she doesn't say. Blighted zones were above all "interstitial areas" where the uses of land "are in a state of constant flux."[40]

Despite the studied neutrality of Walker's prose, violence sometimes breaks out. A chronology of slums in Chicago begins with an area "raided and burned down by Mayor Wentworth" in 1858. In her chapter entitled "Siphoning off Slum Populations," Walker quotes various city housing authorities who report home-wrecking on a scale that might have shocked even Chicago's pyrotechnic mayor. The Philadelphia Housing Authority notes, for example, that an area equivalent to eighteen and a half normal city blocks had been demolished in 1934, "more than in any other year during the last two decades." Over the last 12 years "accommodations have been destroyed for a population of 71,910," but "an even larger program of demolition must take place" before the areas concerned "can show any marked improvement."[41]

Fabricating new identities in the clearance zone

> *Racial Invasion*: A "racial invasion" [occurs when] new races move into an area where blight has begun. They add then the factor of inharmonious society. The situation has developed in Chicago where a negro invasion followed

> a business invasion and caused a blighted area on the south side of the city.
> (Johnson O'Conner, 1937)[42]

Eleanor Manning O'Conner, one of the first women to graduate with an architecture degree from MIT, worked extensively in the 1930s to turn *housing estate management* into a new profession for women. O'Conner was chairperson of the Housing Committee of the Massachusetts Civic League, and, like many American architects and planners of her generation, traveled to Europe in the 1930s to see English and German housing experiments at close hand. O'Conner once advised women architects that the two keys to success in their profession were to become "tremendously interested in one thing" and to "get word conscious" by building their technical vocabularies. For O'Conner and many other women architects that "one thing" was clearly housing. In a 1943 article on "House Management: A New Career," O'Conner wrote that "mass production of housing should open doors for new careers for women" because housing might be framed as a women's issue. That indeed seemed to be happening at the moment O'Conner wrote. The chairperson of the Boston Regional Housing Authority in the 1940s was a woman, and O'Conner herself was an officer of the New England Regional Council of the National Association of Housing Officials.[43]

O'Conner's "word consciousness" led her to collaborate with her husband, the psychometrician Johnson O'Connor, on an odd sort of dictionary named the *Johnson O'Conner English Vocabulary Builder*, which was first published by his starkly titled Human Engineering Laboratory of Boston in 1937. Manning contributed architectural and planning terms to her husband's book in the form of a typewritten manuscript preserved amidst her personal papers, a dictionary-within-a-dictionary that creates a "social" vocabulary over the bloodless economic framework of Mabel Walker's "blighted area." This last phrase becomes in Manning's manuscript a *socially blighted area* or SBA, a zone "where the people are no longer harmonious, where misfits have crept in, and where the original dwellers have moved out." This resulted in *social depletion*, or SD, which took place "when lower-grade people have gone in and the original inhabitants have left." She pinpoints the West and South Ends of Boston as SD zones. The opposite of SD was SC, or *social conservation*, in which the neighborhood preserves its better elements and polices its boundaries against outsiders. *Segregation* in her dictionary was not social isolation imposed by one group on another, but *the setting apart by itself of a group*. This normative state of affairs was upset by the *racial invasion*, which in O'Conner's novel interpretation was triggered by changes in business use. Thus could a blighted neighborhood be defined by inharmony "of use," "of architecture," or "as a result of invasion by inharmonious people," all of which seem, in her account, to be different sides of the same problem.[44]

It is difficult to determine from O'Conner's vocabulary builder just where she located herself on the political spectrum. Her draft also defines such words as *soviet* ("a council of representation based on labor organizations"), *privileged class* (those "exempt from danger, from blame"), and *intellectual groups* (those who exercise "the power and faculty of knowing, as opposed to feeling"). On the other hand, this daughter of an Irish-American building contractor includes within her vocabulary *good form* and *savoir faire*. And mixed among all of her social/spatial definitions are many dozens of architectural terms, including such archaicisms as *crenellated parapet*.[45]

As in Walker's book (which was published the same year), O'Conner's *blighted area* extends the zone of potential clearance considerably beyond the *slum* to any area where *invasion* might take place or *inharmony* might break out. It makes demolition a pre-emptive strike, re-constructing the city as a series of firebreaks between areas singled out for *social conservation*. Public housing for O'Conner is a sort of institutional cachement where racial invasions can be channeled and tamed.

The charge that New Deal public housing represented communism/socialism, so famously made by Republican opponents, has tended to deflect the interest of historians from conservative housing reformers such as O'Conner. O'Conner, writing for the Civic League in 1940, speaks of housing as "the first step" to "keep[ing] our country safe from those who would foist discontent," and thus an "important part of our defence program."[46] Likewise, C. W. Ferrier, technical director of the National Housing Agency (NHA), wrote that "lowered morale offers a fertile ground for the implanting of ideologies foreign to the general pattern of our democratic heritage."[47] The Massachusetts Civic League, in addition to O'Conner's committee on housing, had committees on "the cause and cure of crime," "the police," and "public health."[48] Civic involvement for the Civic League was not social revolution, but a reaction against all manner of urban degeneration.

What *was* revolutionary about O'Conner's agenda was the expanded role it offered women, for O'Conner's feminism was just as authentic as her racism. And in certain ways the two were linked. O'Conner's "new role for women" in housing management was fully dependant on the continued production of inner-city clearance zones. In 1942–3 O'Conner was instrumental in establishing (and getting the Civic League to sponsor) a housing course for mostly female graduate students of Harvard and MIT, which included an internship with the Federal Public Housing Authority.[49] Its title was "Housing and the Police Power," and one focus was to be "the rehabilitation of tenants" by "sympathetic but unsentimental" female managers. Twice as many students applied as there were spaces. The Harvard/MIT course was nonetheless run by a male professor, the sociologist James Ford, though O'Conner personally taught another version at the all-female Simmons College. The Harvard/MIT course was the subject of an article by the *Christian Science Monitor* in 1942 which suggested that housing sites were ideally managed by women, for, "after all, they are essentially house-keeping projects on a large scale."[50]

Total war and total clearance

In most narrative histories of architecture, wars either are off-stage events in which construction gives way to destruction, or constitute time-outs in the game of theory and design. The *post-war rebuilding* with its promise of a *new era* are so much more common as sites or times in historical reflections on the creation of urban form. Yet war itself has arguably been one of the most productive forces shaping twentieth-century cities, and not just in terms of the clearances caused by aerial bombardment and ground invasion.

The war emergency of 1940–1 was treated by the architecture and planning communities as the huge professional opportunity it turned out to be. Some design professionals did not shrink from discussing aerial bombardment as a positive turn in urban planning – one that would quicken the physical break-up and dispersal of cities, which they viewed as desirable and inevitable. An anonymously authored article in MIT's *Technology Review* in January 1940, entitled "Decentralization by Bombing," began by quoting Sir Raymond Unwin that "military considerations now demand the rapid dispersal of many [urban] industries" because London and similar cities presented too easy a target to the *Luftwaffe*. The Housing Commission of the League of Nations had already encouraged dispersal, the article noted, as an element of "town and country hygiene." The *Technology Review* writer hoped that the war would be the "necessary spur to adoption of a similar policy by metropolitan regimes in this country" even if the results were "radical changes in the patterns of existing cities and regions." The writer illustrated the danger with an aerial photograph of downtown Boston, the type of image that was more normally captioned as a clearance project. "History may record that, in the era of enlightenment," the author concluded, "bursting bombs helped to make better cities for a better age."[51]

The author of the *Technology Review* article was most likely John Burchard, director of the Bemis Foundation, MIT's prefabrication think tank. Burchard was close to Unwin, and would go on record about the positive effects of aerial bombing the following year. "No Great Loss: Physical Destruction of Cities by Bombing May Mean their 'Ultimate Salvation' says John E. Burchard of MIT" was the *Lewiston (Me.) Journal* headline on March 16, 1941.[52] Such opinions were not restricted to technophiles and proponents of prefabricated housing. Writing in the architectural journal *Pencil Points* in March 1941, Konrad Wittman proved he was no modernist by celebrating the beauty of European cities (particularly their cathedrals) and decrying the trend toward standardization. But American cities, to Wittman, had far less value. They had never given him and other traditionally trained architects a sufficiently expansive stage for their talents. He thus agreed with Burchard and other modernizers that the emergency brought positive benefits:

> The spending of countless millions of dollars for defence, extension of resettlement of factories, construction of military highways, the carrying out of new principles for aerial defence, present problems of which alterations of whole cities and a new orientation of city-planning are the natural consequence . . . The development of motor traffic and the menace of aerial warfare speeds up what sociologists and hygienicists have been urging for a long time.

Although this was a "necessary evil," according to Wittman, it was the architects' duty "to turn the evil into the building of cultural values." More pointedly, these external threats could be used to "remove many hindrances of real estate omnipotence or speculative thinking" that had marginalized the architectural profession's impact on housing.[53]

In February 1941 the journal *Pencil Points* illustrated a series of posters from an exhibition entitled "Defense Housing: 1940" put together by the Washington, D.C. chapter of the American Institute of Architects (AIA). The posters had labels like "Housing: An Integral Part of Total Defence"; "Shape Community Futures while Meeting Emergency Needs"; "Preventing the Economic Waste of Blight and Slums"; and "Broad Gauge Rehabilitation of Blighted Areas." The AIA was attempting to leverage the new war emergency in order to transform the post-emergency landscape by providing what would be later be termed (during the Cold War) "dual use" rationales and strategies. It particularly called for the proliferation of local planning agencies, which were needed in "each critical defence area."[54]

The exhibition also featured an historical component, chronicling how planning had been intrinsically related to state declarations of emergency. One poster entitled "Two Recent Emergencies" showed pictures of "War, 1917" and "Depression, 1929," declaring that "each contributed to the nation's planning progress." Another poster on "War Emergency Communities, 1918" blamed the influenza epidemic on urban overcrowding, and the disinterest of "private capital" in housing. "After the War Emergency: The Twenties" contrasted "jerry-built" housing with the rational planning prematurely abandoned in 1918. "America after the Present Emergency" contrasted a grid-pattern aerial photo (present) with a free-form plan (future) in the shape of an artist's easel.[55]

Thus did the spectacle of a successfully conducted "total war" begin to make a "total solution" to America's urban problems seem more reasonable and less utopian. Indeed, after the tide of war had clearly turned in 1943–4, the stance of architects, engineers, planners, and industrialists toward cities became even more aggressive and uncompromising. All parties to the building process began to discuss plans and ideas that would have been considered radical (or *long-haired*) before the outbreak of hostilities. The transition from slum to blighted area, accomplished by the end of the economic emergency, was now extended by the war emergency to planning for total or near-total urban clearance. By 1944, the Committee on Civic Design and Development of the AIA could state that:

> contrary to the prevailing conception of the public, deterioration is not confined to the slums or to the blighted areas. The process affects all classes of structures. It extends to office and loft structures, and to docks, terminals, and warehouses . . . [even] many properties which are comparatively new [are caught up in] a strong trend towards premature economic obsolescence.[56]

The very language of architecture and city planning became more warlike. In July 1944, Alfred C. Williams, president of the San Francisco district of the

Association of California Architects, warned his profession of the need to "win the peace." "How? By keeping America on the march! By seeking out a new enemy and striking him whenever and wherever we find him, and with everything we have." The new target was located "in population concentrations – contagious diseases, juvenile delinquency, property blight, fire hazards, traffic hazards, noise, squalor – and if we choose to go all the way, prejudice, avarice, and cynicism." "Like any campaign," he pointed out, "it requires planning."[57] John T. Howard, director of the City Planning Commission of Cleveland, described himself and his fellows as "the front-line officials who have to act, one way or another, now" before "our cities rot and fester." Planning required not just skill and foresight, but "strategy" and "tactics."[58]

The contention that nearly all of built America was *obsolete* now largely replaced the earlier diagnosis of *blight*. The dazzling display of "wonder weapons" may have made the idea of rapid technological evolution more real than before to many writers, although they still crafted lengthy articles with detailed schemes of how to build obsolescence into the stubbornly long-lived house-product. Bernard Smith, attorney-member of the New York Building Congress, told the Massachusetts Postwar Construction Conference of 1943, for instance, that, in order to attract capital to construction and "regularize" it after the war, "we must find some means for increasing the rate of replacement of existing building structures." Clearance alone was not doing the job. What was needed, according to Smith, was a "system of obsolescence" like the one built into the automobile industry. The present average replacement rate of American houses, Smith lamented, was over 100 years. "We must find some formula for annually junking obsolete houses just as the automobile industry annually junks its obsolete cars," bringing the "useful life" of frame dwellings down to about 25 years. His practical solution was a "home replacement bond," which the owner would purchase through a 25-year mortgage (rather than the house itself) and which could only be redeemed toward construction of a replacement dwelling.[59]

World War II is rightly considered a period of booming domestic construction. Often overlooked, however, are government policies that contributed to the consolidation of the building industry and the de-skilling of its labor by giving priority to prefabrication. A committee studying the problems of American small business concluded in September 1945 that "construction is a war-time casualty." Over 100,000 small construction firms went out of business between 1941 and 1945, and 80 percent of the construction labor force was drained from the domestic market. With the war over, the committee found that "large-scale building organizations threaten to capture many construction markets. Increasing monopolization of land by large housing operators will make it more difficult for the small builder to compete successfully in the heavily populated large urban areas."[60]

Uncontrolled real estate speculation had already sent land prices skyrocketing, thus putting a greater premium on cost-cutting methods. "Builders see some hope of cutting construction costs by using techniques learned in the war," wrote one observer. "This would include the use of power saws, paint spraying guns, pre-cutting of lumber, and off-the-job assembly of accessories." The writer was worried about the response of the building trades unions, but noted that they had ceased to reproduce themselves during the war emergency. "No building-trades apprentices have been trained for the last four years." Moreover, the "little builder" of five to ten houses would take a year or more to get back into business, by which time the larger "operatives" would have consolidated the better suburban sights.[61]

In 1944, an American Forum of the Air debate involving Frank Lloyd Wright, housing reformer Dorothy Rosenman, the head of the National Real Estate Boards, and the mayor of St. Paul considered the question: "shall we rebuild the cities or shall the people be siphoned off into the hinterlands of the nation?" These were the only two choices the forum presented to urban listeners: rebuild or disperse. The mayor and real estate man mostly fought a rearguard action against Wright, who declared that "the city is an outmoded institution" and should be abandoned. This was no great loss, he said, as "they were never planned in the first place." Wright invoked "the new space scale," which, because of the automobile and telephone, "have made ten miles as one mile used to be." Rosenman held onto the concept of the city, but only if was made less dense through demolition. Responded Wright: "I believe in taking all the blighted areas and planting grass there," which would be "two thirds of the area." Wright advised radio listeners to "shake the dust of all this urbanism from our souls."[62]

Wright was attempting to be contrarian and provocative, but such ideas were already becoming mainstream. The president of the Celotex Corporation, Bror Dahlberg, had said much the same thing the previous year (1943) when addressing the American Society of Planning Officials. Under the title "Building Tomorrow," Dahlberg claimed that "homes can be placed in terms of flying time" because helicopters (a recently publicized military technology) will soon be as cheap and available as cars. Dahlberg believed that "few people really like city life" and referred to the "tendency of slum residents to drag substantial and healthful housing projects down to their own slovenly level." Too many urban residents spent money, when they got it, on "diamonds and nightclubs" rather than on homes and appliances. Mass production in building would be a "new frontier" for everyone, which "may spread out cities fanwise over large areas [and] may result in the decline of city living quarters in favor of rural islands of integrated manufacturing and housing units." As for existing cities, Dahlberg had "no sympathy with efforts to coddle the landowners and municipalities." If slums could be cleared, fine, but "if not, we must move to other fields and abandon the owners of property in such cities to their fate." Public housing, as he saw it, should be reserved for "the aged, crippled, the sick, and the destitute."[63]

Dahlberg's vision of "Usonia" (Wright's name for a fully de-urbanized America of prefabricated houses) may have had a sharper, Spencerian edge then that of most architects and planners, yet it did not diverge in fundamentals. Dahlberg – who was a major force behind *reclamation* of the Florida everglades – was among the first of a growing number of building materials manufacturers who, sensing the drift toward mass housing, were willing to abandon their traditionally urban markets for the promise of suburban development and a return to *frontier* conditions. The Celotex Corporation had been part of the Houses, Inc. syndicate in the early 1930s and, with its *cemesto* wallboard product, was able to take full advantage of government-directed cost-cutting methods in wartime building. True to Dahlberg's word, Celotex would soon abandon its corporate home in Chicago for a new headquarters in Tampa.[64]

Prefabrication, which had largely failed in the Depression-era marketplace, was revived and given a fresh start as a wartime technology. Almost 2 million permanent war-housing units were built in more than 1,000 localities for war workers, and many of these were prefabricated using a plywood panel method pioneered by the U.S. Department of Agriculture's Forest Products Laboratory in Wisconsin. This would become a critical technology in the coming post-war sub-urbanization. It also helped that local building codes were waived during the war emergency. Major General Phillip Fleming, administrator of the Federal Works Agency (FWA), noted in 1945 under the heading "Uncle Sam and the Local Building Code" that "what is considered appropriate and desirable for Bingville is totally rejected by Bingtown, over in the next county." Local restrictions "were wholly out of place in wartime" wrote the general, before implying that they were obsolete in peacetime too.[65]

The wartime campaign against *obsolete cities* reached perhaps its inevitable conclusion when, only a month before Hiroshima, the city of Toledo, Ohio became the first in the nation to raze itself to the ground, at least under its master plan. Norman Bel Geddes' sixty-one-foot-long, $250,000 model of "Toledo Tomorrow," similar in spirit and execution to his Futurama exhibit for General Motors at the 1939 New York World's Fair, was exhibited as a *fait accompli* to the citizens of Toledo on July 4, 1945. In Bel Geddes' city under glass, Toledo has been cleared of all its existing buildings (excepting a few office towers downtown) and even of existing street patterns. The very shape of the river has changed. Toledo, formerly dense, is now mostly open space. In Bel Geddes' terms the new city was "congestion proof." Unlike earlier, similar plans by Corbusier and other theorists (and Bel Geddes' own Futurama), this one was sanctioned by the Chamber of Commerce and paid for by the local newspaper. The Chamber of Commerce report that accompanied the model, entitled "What about Our Future?," was congratulated by a national architecture journal for its "dramatic, unflinching presentation of the Toledo slum picture." "All blight will be uprooted and replaced by clean structures set amongst greenery" was the verdict. Toledo Tomorrow had "a welcome and pleasant openness which is a far cry from the nightmare of the well-publicized Futurama."[66]

Toledo, just over the Ohio border from Detroit, was the headquarters of Owens-Corning, a major defense contractor desperate to find a peace-time market for its major product, fiberglass. Fiberglass – whose principal application was then in warships and airplanes – would find a major post-war market as building insulation, as would another Owens-Corning product, asbestos.

Spacious new *cities under glass* (and cities, towns, and houses filled with fiberglass) would soon become a standard feature of the post-war planning scene, particularly under the Fair Deal/Great Society program of *urban renewal*. Small cities like Toledo were particularly susceptible to such three-dimensional arguments. They longed to be *urban* in the renewed sense of the term, and the apparent key to urbanity, by 1945, was to tear your city down.

Notes

1 Catherine Bauer, "Social Questions in Housing and Community Planning," *Journal of Social Issues*, vol. 7, nos. 1 and 2 (1951), pp. 1–34, p. 4.
2 Franklin D. Roosevelt, Second Inaugural Address (January 20, 1937).
3 Quoted in Kenneth K. Stowell, "A Preliminary Plan for the Building Industry," *Architectural Forum*, vol. 55, no. 2 (August 1931), p. 125.
4 Thomas P. Hughes, "The Evolution of Large Technological Systems," in W. E. Bijker, T. P. Hughes and T. P. Pinch, eds., *The Social Construction of Technological Systems* (Cambridge, MA: MIT Press, 1987), pp. 51–82.
5 Albert Farwell Bemis, *The Evolving House* (Cambridge, MA: Technology Press, 1933).
6 "President's Conference on Home Building and Home Ownership," *Proceedings of the PCHHO* (Washington, D.C., 1931).
7 Ibid. Neither the conference planning committee nor its correlating committees, which issued recommendations based on the work of twenty-five subcommittees, included a single mayor. Only one city manager was included, from Rochester, New York.
8 Ibid.
9 A "Dymaxion Index" published by the Fuller Research Foundation in 1947 records every reference to the term "dymaxion" since 1928. It runs to twenty-six single-spaced pages with about forty references per page. The number of actual dymaxion houses, however – that is, houses that strictly conformed to Fuller's original design, including the requirement of factory production – is zero. For a synopsis of Fuller's Dymaxion House and the literature surrounding it, see H. Ward Jandl, John A. Burns, and Michael J. Auer, *Yesterday's Houses of Tomorrow* (Washington, D.C., Preservation Press, 1981).
10 John E. Burchard, "Needs for Research in the Building Industry," paper read before the SPEE Civil Engineering Conference on Construction Education, State College, PA, June 1939. Typed manuscript in Burchard Papers, MIT Archives, Box 4, Folder 21.
11 Kenneth K. Stowell, "Housing the Other Half," *The Architectural Forum*, vol. 56, no. 3 (March 1932), p. 217.
12 Knut Lonberg-Holm and Theodore C. Larson, "Trends in Building Production," *Real Estate Record*, April 18, 1936, p. 126.
13 The best record of this phenomenon is Editors of *Fortune*, *Housing America* (New York: Harcourt Brace, 1932). I am also drawing here on the large collection of publicity-related material from Houses, Inc. and similar corporations in the Bemis Foundation Papers, MIT Archives.
14 Ibid., p. 118.
15 Ibid., pp. 112–13.
16 Ibid., Appendix.
17 The establishment of the Albert Farwell Bemis Foundation at MIT in 1937, as well as the Purdue Housing Research Foundation (Indiana) and the Pierce Foundation (New York) in the same decade, signaled recognition by private industry that academic research was necessary to help it sort out unexpected problems of design, distribution, labor organization, marketing, etc.
18 The Bemis Foundation Papers in the MIT Archives provide a rather full picture of New Deal prefabrication research efforts, including correspondence between Arnold and the Foundation on the issue of "labor obstructionism" (Box 5, Folder "Low Cost Housing").
19 "Report on Housing" (January 6, 1938), typed manuscript in Joseph Hudnut Papers, Harvard University Archives, Box 5.
20 Bemis, *The Evolving House*, p. x.

21 Kenneth Kingsley Stowell, "Housing the Other Half," *Architectural Forum* (March 1932), pp. 217–20, p. 218.

22 A. Stephen Stephan, "Prospects and Possibilities: The New Deal and the New Social Research," *Social Forces*, vol. 13 (1935), pp. 515–21.

23 Vannever Bush, "The Scientific Approach to Our Housing Problem," in "Homes of Tomorrow," special issue of *The Technology Review*, vol. 39, no. 9 (July 1937), pp. 21–4.

24 Knut Lonberg-Holm and C. Theodore Larson, "Industrialization of Housing," in *Technical America*, March 1938.

25 K. K. Stowell, editor, "Housing – A National Issue," *Architectural Forum* (June 1932), pp. 565–6.

26 Quoted in Gail Radford, *Modern Housing for America: Policy Struggles in the New Deal Era* (Chicago: University of Chicago Press, 1996), p. 103.

27 Unwin raised a number of objections to the Wagner–Steagall Act at a 1938 conference in the United States. "Our municipalities [in the UK]," he said, "are not permitted to clear a slum until they are in a position to offer alternative accommodations for people in the slums . . . You cannot just pull down the dwellings and let people filter in anywhere" ["News in the Field," *Shelter* (March 1938), p. 108].

28 "Housing Comes of Age," *Architectural Forum* (November 1934), pp. 386–7.

29 Quoted in Bruce L. Melvin, "Emergency and Permanent Legislation with Special Reference to the History of Subsistence Homesteads," *American Sociological Review*, vol. 1, no. 4 (August 1936), pp. 622–31.

30 Quoted in H. Wright, "Housing Conditions in Relation to Scientific Machine Production," *Journal of the Franklin Institute*, October 1934, 487.

31 Clarence A. Perry, *Housing for the Machine Age* (New York: Russell Sage Foundation, 1939).

32 Wright, "Housing Conditions in Relation to Scientific Machine Production," p. 488.

33 "Housing Comes of Age," pp. 386–7.

34 Quoted in Mabel Walker, *Urban Blight and Slums: Economic and Legal Factors in their Origin, Reclamation, and Prevention* (Cambridge, MA: Harvard University Press, 1938), p. 143.

35 *Pencil Points* (March 1944).

36 Lawrence Veiller, "Housing and Health," *Annals of the American Academy of Political and Social Science*, vol. 37, no. 2 (March 1911), pp. 258–9.

37 Coleman Woodbury, "Land Assembly for Housing Developments," *Law and Contemporary Problems*, vol. 1, no. 2 (March 1934), pp. 213–31, p. 214. Woodbury served at various times as Assistant Administrator, National Housing Agency (NHA), and Executive Director, National Association of Housing Officials.

38 The Housing Committee of the Twentieth Century Fund, *American Housing: Problems and Prospects* (New York: Twentieth Century Fund, 1944), pp. 3–4.

39 Ibid, p. 36.

40 Walker, *Urban Blight and Slums*, pp. 4–7.

41 Ibid.

42 Draft manuscript for *Johnson O'Conner English Vocabulary Builder* (Boston: Human Engineering Laboratory, 1938), in the Howe, Manning, and Almy Papers, MIT Archive. The authorship of at least the architectural and planning terms is attributed to Manning based on their convergence with her own practice, and language elsewhere in her papers. It is likely that this draft was intended to be combined with a larger draft constituting the whole book, and edited by her husband. O'Connor was one of the inventors of the "aptitude test," and the related field of "psychometrics," beginning with work he did for the General Electric Corporation in the 1920s. A decade later GE would be a major promoter of prefabricated housing, beginning with American Houses' "moto-homes."

43 Howe, Manning, and Almy Papers, MIT Archive, Box 19, Folders 855 and 871.

44 Ibid., Box 31, Folder 937.

45 Ibid.

46 Undated report, *c.* 1940, by E. M. O'Conner in Howe, Manning, and Almy Papers, MIT Archives, Box 19, Folder 855.

47 C. W. Ferrier, "Prefabricated Buildings and Structures after the War," *Bay State Builder* (July 1944), pp. 7–14.

48 By 1943, the Housing Committee was the largest (with twenty-nine members, fourteen of whom were women). Howe, Manning, and Almy Papers, MIT Archive, Box 19, Folder 855.

49 By November 1941, according to the US Housing Agency, eighty courses were being offered at American colleges and universities specifically geared to housing, while "hundreds of others" dealt with the subject. Howe, Manning, and Almy Papers, MIT Archive, Box 19, Folder 855

50 *Christian Science Monitor*, December 17, 1942, p. 4.

51 Anonymous, "Decentralization by Bombing," *Technology Review* (January 1940), pp. 103–5.

52 Clipping in Burchard Papers, MIT Archives, Folder "Press Clippings, 1935–64."

53 Konrad Wittman, "American Architecture Viewed Objectively," *Pencil Points* (March 1941), pp. 199–202.

54 "Defense Housing: 1940," *Pencil Points* (February 1941).

55 Ibid.

56 "Master Plans and Rezoning Needed," *Architect and Engineer* (August 1944), pp. 27–8.

57 Alfred C. Williams, "In Support of Post-War Planning," *Architect and Engineer* (July 1944), pp. 23–4, 36.

58 John T. Howard, "Democracy in City Planning," *Bay State Builder* (July 1945), pp. 5, 18.

59 Bernard Smith, "Uneconomic Practices in the Construction Industry," *Bay State Builder* (October 1943), pp. 15–23.

60 "Preliminary Report of Special Committee to Study Problems of American Small Business," *Bay State Builder* (September 1945), pp. 5–17, pp. 5–6.

61 Joseph M. Guifoyle, "Home Building Lag," *Bay State Builder* (August 1945), pp. 3–5, 16–17.

62 "What are the Air Waves Saying?" (excerpts from American Forum of the Air broadcast, February 29, 1944), *Journal of the American Institute of Architects* (April 1944), pp. 176–82.

63 Bror Dahlberg, "Building Tomorrow" (address at 1943 Annual Meeting of the American Society of Planning Officials, New York), typewritten manuscript, Howe, Manning, and Almy Papers, MIT Archive, Box 19, Folder 869. Dahlberg's purchase of large tracts of the Florida everglades in the 1920s was to facilitate its replanting with sugar cane, whose waste product (once the sugar was drained) was the raw material for the Celotex Corporation's wallboard product.

64 Ibid.

65 Major Gen. Phillip Fleming, "Uncle Sam and the Local Building Code," *Bay State Builder* (April 1945), pp. 3–9.

66 "Model of Toledo Plan Opens New Dimension for Post-War Projects," *Pencil Points* (September 1945), p. 112. Bel Geddes' first design projects (outside his early work in theater) were of automobiles. He also designed a "house of tomorrow" in the early 1930s.

10 Concealment and exposure

Imagining London after the Great Fire

Li Shiqiao

A flood of designs followed the devastating fire destroying the timber City of London in September 1666, a fact that did not escape a contemporary theatrical expression; Sir Positive At-all, a character of Thomas Shadwell's comedy *The Sullen Lovers*, had seventeen of them all designed by himself. Five of these designs survive: John Evelyn's and Christopher Wren's vistas and nodes, Valentine Knight's and Robert Hooke's generic open-ended grids, and Richard Newcourt's hierarchical enclosed grid; together, they captured an intriguing moment in the history of urban planning ideas. The designs contested ideas of the city at the dawn of modernity; here, the consequences of science and trade are mixed together with visions of the Platonic revival of the Renaissance, Baroque verbosity and obscurism, and vestiges of traditions tracing back to much earlier periods. They contextualized and speculated on the possibility of a new kind of transparent city, largely grounded in market or scientific principles rather than those of centralized power. Through the inherent accessibility of the market or scientific principles as well as their implied hygienic and safety improvements, these speculations tentatively redefined London as a target; London changed from a traditional target of siege and pillage to a modern target of systemic damage. Perhaps the irony of London being wiped out twice in 2 years (the Plague and the Fire), not by enemy siege and pillage but by systemic damages in the forms of bacterial growth and chemical reaction, had finally inspired the thoughts that it was time to re-imagine the enemies of the city and its status as a target. This chapter builds a context of the development of urban thinking leading to this crucial moment in the history of cities, explains the design strategies of the five proposals for London and considers the implications of these designs and the fact that none of them was realized. The chapter argues that, in the Western urban tradition, city development has been driven by a unique force for exposure, a quality of urban space deeply connected to an intellectual formulation first established in the ancient Greek *polis*. These proposals captured a moment when the emergence of modern science gave the moral and aesthetic drive for exposure a new physical and urban reality. As a consequence, the elevated and exposed site of the acropolis was later replaced by a number of other city forms such as gridiron patterns and zoning that emerged as they contested with other demands of the city: defence, social hierarchies, landownership and security. For centuries, the imaginations of the 'exposed city' – visibility and speed as desirable urban traits – have shaped countless designs of cities. The edge of the city is one interesting space that embodied this change; traditionally, many cities took walls, moats and gates as their most powerful defences; over many centuries, the edge of the city has been modified from the hard walls and moats to soft signage and tollgates, and has recently transformed itself into interactive electronic screens, dramatically shifting our perception of fundamental concepts of space and time.[1] Here, the pedestrian, the horse, the motored vehicle and the electronic signal all shaped their own versions of transparency of the city.

Power, vulnerability and aesthetics

The primal drive for exposure, which is argued here to lie at the centre of a compelling form of urban imagination, could perhaps best be seen in its embryonic form in the ethical content and aesthetic expressions found in classical Greece. It was the achievements of classical Greece that gave rise to the reformulation of politics, literature, art and architecture since the Italian Renaissance. Richard Sennett, in *Flesh and Stone* (1994), described an astonishing rise of the extraordinary ethical content of the exposed male body in Pericles's Athens and the aesthetic expressions associated with it.[2] The exposed male body, in classical Greece, could be understood as one of the most important sites for the cultivation of a form of life founded on openness. The courage of taking off ones clothes served a set of complex goals; at the most obvious level, exposure of the body required a devotion to the constant toning of the body to attain its best form, sustained in gymnasia and academies. In a larger context, the tradition of competitive sports in ancient Greece, an element of life that we enthusiastically embrace today, underlines the strong attraction of such a body culture. Thucydides tells us that the Athenians and the Spartans 'were the first to play games naked, to take off their clothes openly'; while in ancient times during Olympic Games, 'the athletes used to wear coverings for their loins, and indeed this practice was still in existence not very many years ago'. Thucydides claimed that 'even today many foreigners, especially in Asia, wear these loincloths for boxing matches and wrestling bouts'.[3] A deeper reason for such views of the body perhaps lies in the ancient Green physiology of the body in which 'heat' was understood to be the vigor of life; an active and well-toned body is an outward sign of the balance of heat – a unique quality of the male body beyond the reach of the bodies of the female and the slave.[4]

Competitive sports, of course, served as a metaphor for war; it was in wars, more than any other arenas of life, that this body culture – freedom to express and courage to combat – was most profoundly celebrated as power. If Thucydides was right, it was precisely at the time of war in the winter of 430/1 that Pericles delivered one of the most influential orations in history: Pericles, in his Funeral Oration at the start of the Peloponnesian War against the Spartans, praised 'the way of life which has made us great'.[5] He claims proudly that 'we, when we launch an attack abroad, do the job by ourselves', whereas the Spartans often bring their allies with them. The body culture of the Athenians gave them an 'easy mind' not attainable through 'laborious training'; they were endowed 'with natural rather than with state-induced courage'.[6] Openness was seen to be both power and vulnerability, a form of domination and a magnified target. Power, in this light, is perhaps at its greatest when it is cultivated at its most vulnerable moments. This construct of openness and power has been one of the most enduring ideas in the formulation of the aesthetics in ancient Greece; Phidias's supreme skill to depict the idealized body is one extraordinary example of how an intellectual framework shaped the arts. E. H. Gombrich called the classical Greek art 'the greatest and most astonishing revolution in the whole history of art', noting how much the Greeks had moved away from the arts of the Egyptians.[7] We can see that the Greek imagination remains at the centre of the Western tradition of the arts, which has been driven by a desire to achieve ever greater definition and clearer structure (greater exposure); the Western intellectual and artistic traditions further flourished on the basis of studies in anatomy and perspectives, geometry and proportions, and techniques of realism.

As in many other things, the aesthetic ideal of the exposed male body functioned on the basis of what Kant would call 'aesthetic judgment' – arising from 'trivial meanings that open up a set of existential or transcendental meanings'[8] – that sustains a much larger set of qualities: Pericles continued in the Oration that 'each single one of our citizens, in all the manifold aspects of life, is able to show himself the rightful lord and owner of his own person, and do this, moreover, with exceptional grace and exceptional versatility'.[9] At the moment of conceptualization, the 'combatant body' was deeply intertwined with a 'debating mind', a form of intellect that privileged a deliberate cultivation of clarity of argument and effectiveness of delivery. Platonic dialogues, in this light, could be seen to be a ritualized form of intellectual combat, displaying the power of memory, strength of logic, and the elegance of form; both in war and in debate, bodily engagement is founded on that of combat: the contact of the eyes and the bodily composure in assertions and responses. Public virtues formulated in this context – courage, decorum, politeness, taste, etiquette – could be understood as mechanisms of the construct of openness as power. On this way of life, Karl Popper claimed that 'the Greeks started for us that great revolution which, it seems, is still in its beginning – the transition from the closed to the open society'.[10]

A necessary and significant consequence of the aesthetic ideal of the naked male body is its concealment of the female body (and that of the slave for that matter), which was constructed to fall short of the ideal; both the ideal and the condition of 'falling short' are part of the definition of this unique body culture sustained through an exclusion of other forms of beauties and intelligences.

Among all the ancient Greek cities, the city of Athens perhaps best exemplified the intellectual and aesthetic ideal of openness. We return to Pericles again:

> Our city is open to the world, and we have no periodical deportations in order to prevent people observing or finding out secrets which might be of military advantage to the enemy. This is because we rely, not on secret weapons, but on our own real courage and loyalty.[11]

The normative function of the defensive citadel of the acropolis, as Ictinus, Callicrates, and Phidias recreated it in Athens between 450 and 430 BC to celebrate their famous victory over the Persians, seemed to have turned into its reverse role of display. The Parthenon was designed and crafted with enormous attention to its anthropomorphic details; it stood in full view of the city, like a well-toned male body and a well-constructed argument. The city and the open body/mind may be seen to have become one and the same; Thucydides described this merging of the city and the body through the Corinthians, who described the way of life of the Athenians to the Spartans at the start of the Peloponnesian War: 'as for their bodies, they regard them as expendable for their city's sake, as though they were not their own; but each man cultivates his own intelligence, again with a view to doing something notable for his city'.[12] Here, the power/vulnerability of the body is reconstituted as that of the spatial construct of the city: its open agora, its amphitheatre, and its acropolis. Athens's defeat in the Peloponnesian War perhaps put an end to such an exploration of the conception of the city, but its civil values (freedom and equality) and imperial aspirations (domination), like its philosophy, politics, art, and architecture, left a huge legacy. From Alexander to the United States of America, successive military and cultural empires have attempted to build open societies; the Roman Empire, in particular, brought the Greek ideal to a much more extensive realization, achieving a genuine form of an open world through, like the Greeks, a deliberate cultivation of the body culture and suppression of other traditions.

It was these ideals of the classical Greek world that provided, from a hazy temporal distance, some of the most crucial conceptions of the Italian Renaissance, and left an indelible mark on our intellectual life today. While Europe re-urbanized itself after the collapse of the Roman Empire, the Greek and Roman conceptions of the city and architecture became once again persuasive to Italian intellectuals. The financial success of the Medici family in the fifteenth century contributed greatly to the revival of the Greco-Roman values and to a recovery of lost ancient manuscripts and their reconstitution. In this context, ancient Roman ruins were no longer evidence of pagan indulgence and immorality; they stood as testimony to a form of courage and beauty essential to a new level of empowerment. With Marisilio Ficino, Pico della Mirandola, and Angelo Poliziano, the ancient form of life generated tremendous excitement in Quattrocento Florence. The pleasures and pains of recreating the lost form of life in the Christian world had resulted in countless intellectual and artistic productions that spread rapidly to Rome and Venice, and then to the French and English courts in the seventeenth century.

The Great Fire of London

London in the 1660s stood on the periphery of the new imaginations of the papacy in Rome and the French court, but had every intention to attain the same degree of achievements. In the early seventeenth century, the court of James I and Charles I was beginning to rival those in Europe and Italy in its massive assembly of objects, paintings, sculptures, and architecture; the English monarch was surrounded by cultivated courtiers conversant with the cultural values underlying the artistic productions of the Italian Renaissance. At the same time, London also stood at the threshold of a new kind of city, a city that placed science and trade above all other hierarchies – characteristics that marked London as one of the first 'modern cities'. However, the new city of science and trade was still not very visible beneath its medieval walls and its chaotic urban life. Returning from Rome, John Evelyn commented in 1659 that London, in comparison, appeared to him to be an image of hell: 'the Buildings . . . are as deformed as the minds & confusions of the people', 'a very ugly Town, pestred with Hackney-coaches, and insolent Carre-men, Shops and Taverns, Noyse, and such a cloud of Sea-coal, as if there is a resemblance of Hell upon Earth'.[13]

Indeed, to him and many other well-travelled Englishmen, the devastating fire, which broke out on Sunday, 2 September 1666 and lasted for 5 days or so, must have seemed a divine intervention despite the horrific loss of lives and property. The fire destroyed an area of 1.5 by 0.5 miles, about 373 acres inside the city walls and 63 acres outside, 89 churches (including St Paul's Cathedral), 52 guild halls, and 13,200 houses (Figure 10.1).[14] An estimated 65,000 people were made homeless.[15] Samuel Pepys described the scenes on 2 September 1666 as 'the churches, houses, and all on fire and flaming at once; and a horrid noise the flames made, and the cracking of houses at their ruine'.[16] Evelyn, in his diary on 7 September 1666, recounted the horror of walking through the smoldering ruins of the city: 'in

Figure 10.1 Area of London damaged by the fire (Wenceslaus Hollar's engraving).

five or six miles of traversing about I did not see one load of timber unconsumed, nor many stones but what were calcined white as snow'.[17] In the mass hysteria and chaos, the fire was immediately perceived as the result of foreign military targeting. Evelyn saw London, like Troy, as a 'great city laid waste by a cruel enemy', and the rumours of the fire being started by the French and Dutch before their imminent invasion were widespread.[18]

Exposure through lines of sight: vistas and nodes

Lines of sight became a leading idea in the design of cities that grew in size and complexity in Europe since the medieval period. With this idea, the city could be imagined to be a series of important nodes linked with straight streets lined with impressive façades. Standing at these nodes, the city presents itself as 'transparent' and being 'seen through'. This opening up of the vistas – and access – of the city is an act contrary to the instinct of defence through obstruction and concealment; it created a 'city of façade' which may be seen to be a much denser and more compact version of the diagonal processional path in classical Athens that cut through the agora.

The idea of lines of sight was first tried out in Rome as a 'retro-fit' project. Sixtus V, during his 5-year pontificate between 1585 and 1590, and his architect Domenico Fontana (1543–1607) put the powerful idea of the 'long vista' in practice. In Rome, about 120 streets were repaved, and several key streets were straightened to connect between major nodes marked by important buildings, such as Piazza del Popolo and Piazza S. Maria Maggiore. More recently, Gianlorenzo Bernini (1598–1680) rose from the pontificate of Urban VIII (1623–44) and designed the piazza for St Peter's in Rome in 1657, using free-standing colonnades and a large oval-shaped piazza; the Piazza of St Peter's could be seen to be the crowning achievement of urban design beginning with Sixtus V. The visionary Counter-Reformation popes, together with their architects and planners, perhaps saw the Catholic Church much in the same light as the Roman Empire, only that the Catholic Church was more spiritual and more successful. Through the long vistas and the piazzas, Rome created its own version of an exposed city, and a kind of intellectual confidence that was founded in part on the ancient ideal of openness as power, in their real and spiritual wars against the Protestant reformers of the Church. The idea and practice of the long vista were to have a decisive impact on the urban planning of the seventeenth century; the significance of the magnificent results of a more open and transparent city certainly far outgrew the immediate agenda of Counter-Reformation propaganda.

Another extraordinary development of the long vista idea can be seen in André Le Nôtre's garden designs – the ambitious vision to conquer vast spaces with geometry and linear views. Because of its size and central administration, France emerged in the seventeenth century as one of the most powerful states in the central land mass of Europe, forming a tripartite power structure with Spain and the Holy Roman Empire. The deep intellectual connection between seventeenth-century France and the Greek intellectual and aesthetic ideal could in one way be seen in the reinvention of Louis XIV as the Greek god Apollo: *le Roi Soleil*. The French court enthusiastically embraced the architectural and urban explorations of the long vista in Rome; it was Louis XIV who began to transform the defensive city walls into tree-lined promenades in Paris in 1646. 'Boulevard', originally meaning bulwark or palisade, was created in the northeast side of the city; opaque defensive walls gave way to transparent pleasure parks.[19]

The first two proposals for the City of London to reach King Charles II, designed by Christopher Wren (1632–1723) and John Evelyn (1620–1706), came from this tradition. Evelyn saw some of these achievements while he was traveling in Rome and Paris; Wren met Bernini briefly in Paris in 1665 and saw Bernini's designs for the east façade of the Louvre. As members of a Royal Commission to repair the city's cathedral, St Paul's, Wren and Evelyn were already actively involved in the project of improving London's conditions; one week before the fire, on 27 August 1666, both Wren and Evelyn were at the site of St Paul's Cathedral, proposing a new and fashionable domed structure against the recommendation from Hugh May and Roger Pratt to patch up the old structure. Both Wren and Evelyn were close to the court and Charles II. Wren's family had been close to the royal circle; Wren's father, Dean of St George's Chapel at Windsor and Register of the Order of the Garter (a chivalric order highly valued by Charles I), brought his son up in the company of the royal children including the future Charles II. Matthew Wren, Wren's uncle, was a leading figure of the Anglican Church. When Charles II was restored to the throne in 1660 after the civil war, the young Wren was bestowed with royal favour in the form of the promise to revert the prestigious post of Surveyor General after Sir John Denham; in preparation for this important job, Wren was dispatched to Paris in 1665 to study the grand projects begun by Louis XIV, as well as to meet prominent Parisian scientists. Wren's visit to Versailles must have impressed him deeply; he was to return to the geometries and grandeur of Versailles, not just in Charles II's incomplete Winchester Palace (1682–5) but in a range of royal projects that demanded magnificence.

Evelyn had long been a keen scholar in art and architecture; his claim to authority in matters of architecture probably came with the publication of his translation of Fréart de Chambray's *A Parallel of the Antient Architecture with the Modern* in 1664. Evelyn had a deep interest in architecture and urban planning; while traveling as a young man with the Earl of Arundel on the Continent in the 1640s, Evelyn observed closely all the urban transformations taking place in Rome, Paris and the Netherlands since the Renaissance. He was an ardent proponent to improve the urban conditions of London. In 1661, Evelyn published *Fumifugium*, 'the Inconveniency of the Smoak of LONDON dissipated', describing a strategy of relocating polluting trades so that London's air and water could be clean again. Between 1662 and 1663, Evelyn was a commissioner for the repair of highways and sewers of London.

Wren's and Evelyn's designs, presented to Charles II on the 11 and 13 September respectively (Figures 10.2 and 10.3), share several similarities, both clearly influenced by the Baroque city planning in Italy and France.[20] Evelyn's design is dominated by four straight streets parallel to the Thames, and four

REFERENCES.

1 Temple Bar
2 Fleet Conduit
3 St Dunstans in the West
4 Ludgate
5 Newgate ...
6 The colledge of Physicians
7 Drapers Commons
8 St Pauls
9 ...
10 The two Sheriffs of London Houses
11 Mercers Chapel
12 Bow Church & the Sydus
13 The Fountain in ... Church Street
14 Fountaine in the East
15 Guild Hall
16 Greshos Hospital & Church
17 The Lord Mayors House
18 The Royal Exchange
19 The Custom House & Starrding court
20 The New Office
21 The Trinity House
22 Billinge-gate
23 The Fish Market
24 Queen Hithe
25 Pauls Wharf
26 The Place
27 Sessions House Newgate Prison
28 Bridewel Work House & Bridewell
29 The Church Yard & Inns
30 The Key
30a Black Fryers Church & Watling Street
31 The Tower
32 Now-Gate
33 Alders-Gate
34 Cripple-Gate
35 Moor-Gate
36 Bishops-Gate
37 Ald-Gate
38 Charing-Gate
+ The several Parish churches so in Number
• The Halls of the 12 Ancient Companies
o The Publick Fountains

Spital Fields

Moore Fields

West Smithfield

Turn-mill Stream

Regent

East Smithfield

RIVER THAMES

SOUTH WARK

The rest of the Openings are for the Markets &c. And as the intermedial Squares and Areas, what narrower Streets shall be thought fit.

Scale of Feet

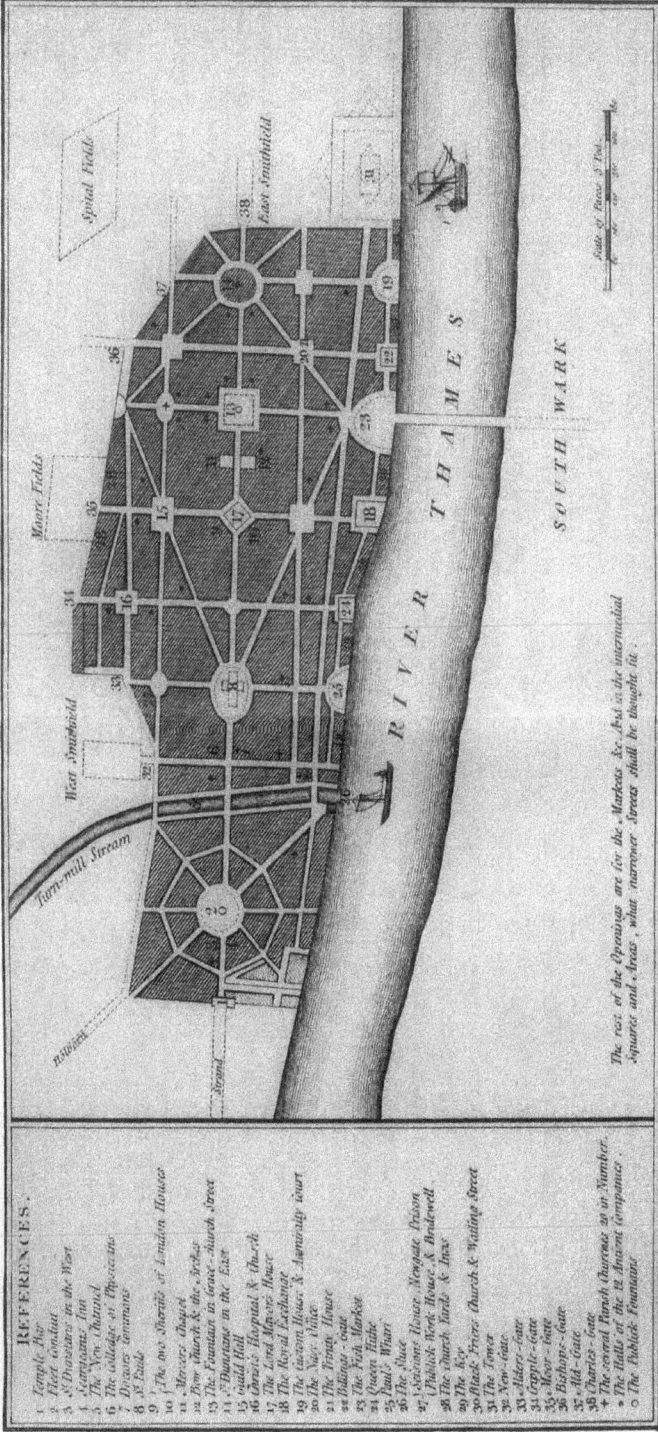

Figure 10.2 One of John Evelyn's plans, 13 September 1666 (use the version engraved by Wenceslaus Holler).

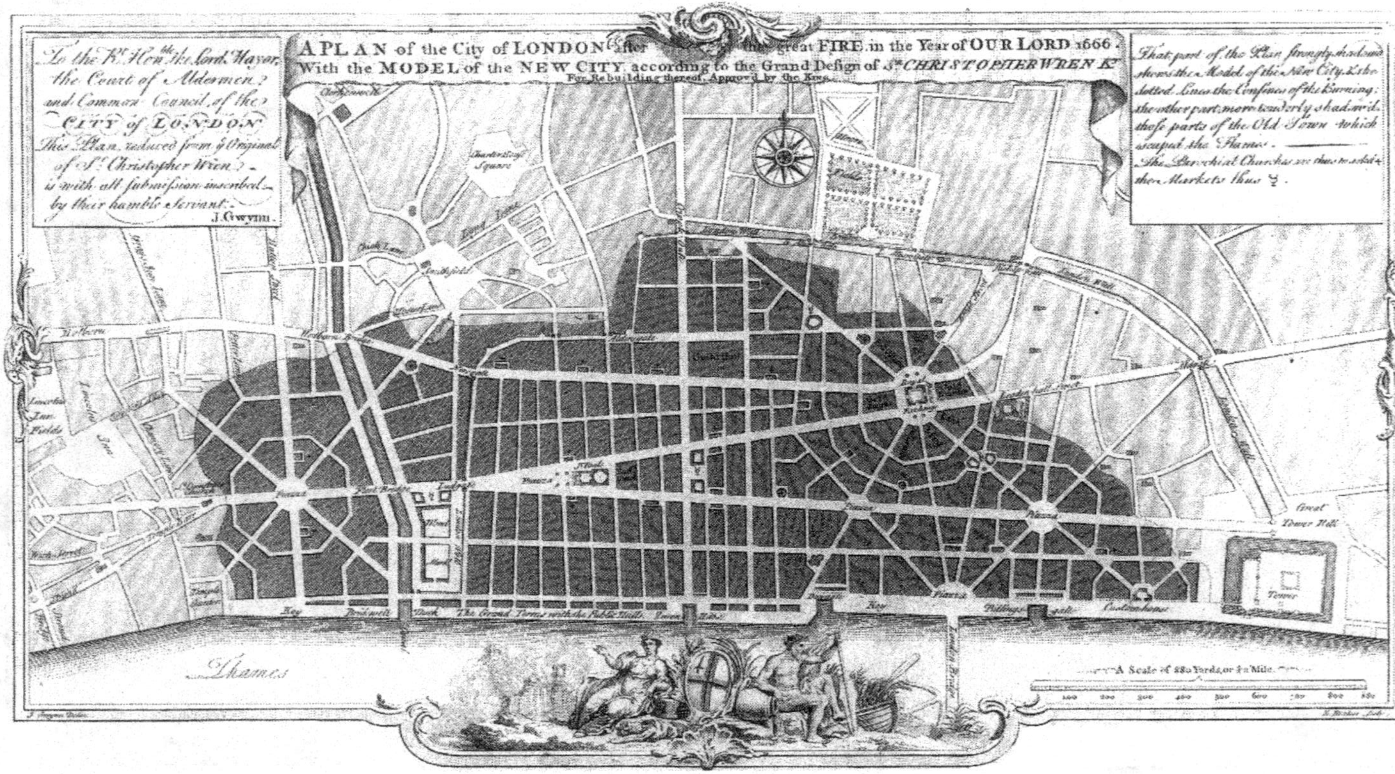

Figure 10.3 Christopher Wren's plan, 11 September 1666 (Guildhall Library).

radiating streets anchored at St Paul's, London Bridge, a northern entry point and a circular piazza in the east. At each major intersection of these major streets, piazzas are designed in 'oblong, circular, and oval figures, for their better grace and capacity'.[21] Functionally speaking, Evelyn's plans, particularly when placed next to that of Wren, appear more idealistic and amateurish due to the lack of sophisticated geometry rooted in the use and scale of buildings, and a degree of refinement of the pattern of the roads informed by the movement carriages and pedestrians.

Wren's design for London is dominated by four nodes – two piazzas, St Paul's Cathedral and the Exchange – from which a series of radiating streets were designed, forming the main framework of the urban pattern. St Paul's and the Exchange certainly have the greatest presence in the design; St Paul's is located at a uniquely open site, where Ludgate is connected with Aldgate and Tower Hill in two long, straight and converging streets; on the other hand, the Exchange is situated at the centre of a grand intersection of ten streets.

Although Wren and Evelyn probably understood that London was emerging as a new centre of science and trade, they did not hesitate to consider royal interest in Baroque magnificence as the first task in their proposals. The long vista, from the time of Sixtus V's Rome, embodied a hierarchical framework, which demanded the placing of the most important religious and civil structures as nodal points, from which the rest of the city formulated their subservient relationships. This strategy worked brilliantly from Rome to Versailles. This way of planning the city would have also worked well with the agenda of the Restoration; Charles II and the Anglican Church, after a decade of Puritan persecution and pillage, were culturally and politically eager to restore the importance of the monarchy and the Anglican Church. Charles II's restoration was never an easy task; Robert Filmer's advocacy of the divine right of the monarchy in his *Patriarcha* (1680) led to the publication of John Locke's refutation of the divine right and his idea of civil government in *Two Treatises of Government* (1698), a lasting monument of political liberalism. The centralised geometrical patterns devised by Wren and Evelyn, although derived from Italian and French sources, effectively embodied London's monarchical and religious restoration.

As in the case of the architects for Rome and Versailles, Wren and Evelyn gave their imaginary London a geometrical structure by which the city could become more accessible and visible – their versions of openness and transparency. The visibility of their city is anchored in the idea of continuous façades and landmark heights. As opposed to the medieval city, in which cloisters served as the key component of the city, the city of vistas and nodes celebrated the exposed exterior as the city of façades. The medieval and Renaissance expansion of the city had resulted not only in the increase of urban mass alone, but also in the invention of a planning technique which considerably reduced the opacity of that mass. The long shadows of this planning technique could be seen in Pierre L'Enfant's plan for Washington in the nineteenth century and Daniel Burnham's plan for Chicago in the twentieth century. The twentieth-century obsession with skyscrapers and cultural centres as landmarks, often with their existence far exceeding any real demand for spaces and facilities, continues to reinvent the openness of the city in its ability to project a system of façades that can be seen and understood quickly in a speeding car or on a tourist bus.

Wren's and Evelyn's designs reinvented the classical Greek vulnerability and power construct, shifting its central site from the male body to the city in the context of urban expansion and royal power; like the deliberate erasure of defensive walls in the cities of the Roman and the Ottoman Empires, and in the cities in Napoleon's Europe, Wren's and Evelyn's London flaunted confidence and security. It was Charles II who wished that the city walls of London not be rebuilt, as Clarendon, one of Charles's closest advisors, recalled:

> the walls and gates being now burned and thrown down of that rebellious city, which was always an enemy to the crown, his majesty would never suffer them to repair and build them up again, to be a bit in his mouth and bridle upon his neck, but would keep all open, that his troops might enter upon them whenever he thought necessary for his service, there being no other way to govern that rude multitude but by force.[22]

Exposure as systemic transparency: the open-ended grid

Meanwhile, the idea of exposure was going through a dramatic change. Adding to the crucial importance of the exposure of the corporeal (the male body and the monarchy) was the rise of the exposure of the systemic (the market and scientific knowledge). The 'Renaissance man' was supplemented with, and eventually surpassed by, the 'careful specialist'. Francis Bacon represented a leading advocate of such a shift; the Greek ideal of openness as power, instead of being embodied in the corporeally centred power of memory, strength of logic and elegance of form, was then recast as a new kind of systemic transparency – 'the experimental knowledge'. The means to achieve this new exposure took the form of the empirical 'scientific report', which, according to Bacon, is able to cut through opaque and meaningless disputations that were best exemplified by the works of Thomas Aquinas. The scientific report was pure exposure and transparency. It opens a different kind of line of sight between man and nature that allows man to reposition himself in the man/nature power relationship. Bacon argued that it was this experimental knowledge, not the Platonic dialogue, that would eventually lead us to genuine power. Bacon distrusted the mind and its inherent abilities to propagate mysteries and idols; to overcome these weaknesses, according to Bacon, we must rely on verified sense impressions. The Royal Society, established in 1662, with its strict adherence to observation, documentation, and verification of experiments, and its hostility to Cartesian speculations, explored the substance of the new scientific knowledge and provided a version of a scientific community that Bacon envisaged 50 years before. The new power founded in the transparent knowledge of the scientific report was rooted not only in freedom to express and courage to combat, but also in the creation of the machine in the painstaking construction of the 'scientific fact'. Experiments can be seen as 'sense machines', through which our physical senses and strengths could be infinitely amplified.

On the other hand, what germinated in the late seventeenth century and flourished in the eighteenth century was the rise of a consumer culture that was underlined by 'free competition' – the ritualized combat of commodities similar to that of the body in ancient Greece. The idea of 'free market' – an artificial construct like the notion of 'scientific report' – appears to have been formulated analogous to the idea of exposure. Increasing the exposure of commodities for competition through standardization, advertisement, mechanization and organized labour – traditionally known as capitalist expansion – can be seen to rehearse in the systemic, once again, the ethical values of the exposed male body in ancient Greece. After all, the standard rhetoric of the market has been focused on free and fair competition instead of monopoly and control.

One remarkable proposal for the City of London brought the reality of the market into sharp focus. On 20 September 1666, a captain named Valentine Knight published a proposal for the rebuilding of London. This was a bold design. Knight's idea for London depicted a single-minded vision of the City as a vast potential real estate (Figure 10.4); this is perhaps a fitting reflection of London's rise to become one of the most important financial centres in Europe. Knight's design is dominated by six major and four minor roads linking the city to the quays from north to south, and two major roads are laid out from west to east; within

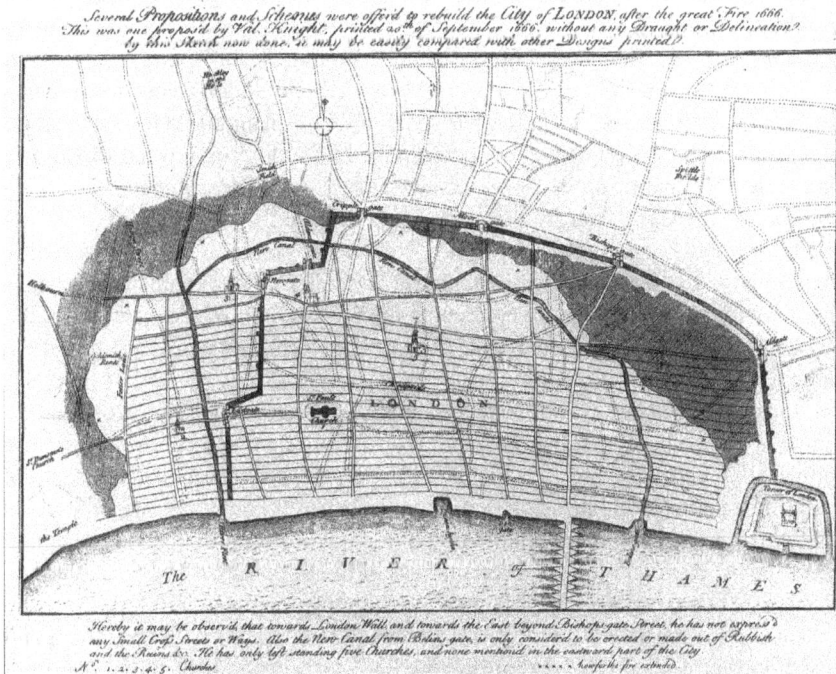

Figure 10.4 Valentine Knight's plan, published on 20 September 1666: 'the ground all put to the best profit' (Guildhall Library).

this general road pattern, small east–west streets divide the land into long and thin strips (500 feet by 70 feet on average) to accommodate two rows of houses.[23] All these streets are also connected to the Thames through a new canal of 30 feet wide. We could perhaps detect some Dutch influence in Knight's mercantilism and his use of the canal as a key element of urban design, which was a prominent feature in Dutch cities such as Amsterdam and in the urban speculations of Simon Stevin (1548–1620). Knight claimed that in his plan 'the ground all put to the best profit'; it would earn Charles II £372,360 and additional annual revenue of £223,517 in fees levied on the passage of the barges. Knight's idea did not please Charles II, who decided that he would not want to be seen to profit from the misery of his subjects; he ordered Knight to be put in jail for making such a suggestion.[24]

If Knight got off to a bad start for a new city for the era of science and trade, another design, attributed to Robert Hooke (1635–1703), put forward a distinctly more insightful and acceptable new vision (Figure 10.5).[25] Hooke presented a plan to the Royal Society on 19 September 1666, and Richard Waller, who compiled a collection of Hooke's works and lectures in 1705, claimed that Hooke's design was based on a rectangular grid of streets; this gridiron design for the City of London, reproduced by several Dutch map-makers, would seem to be a reasonable hypothesis of Hooke's intentions, until contrary evidence comes to light. Hooke was Wren's close colleague in their pursuit of scientific knowledge, but they lived a world apart when it came to their connections to the court. Born on the Isle of Wright, Hooke studied at Westminster College in London before moving to Oxford in 1653, where he began his career as an assistant to eminent scientists such as Thomas Willis and Robert Boyle, who gathered around John Wilkins at Wadham College, Oxford. Hooke built many sophisticated instruments for Boyle's experiments, including the much-publicized air pump for the creation of vacuum. The experiments conducted with Hooke's air-pump led to Boyle's first scientific publication, *New Experiments Physico-Mechanical, Touching the Spring of the Air and its Effects* (1660). In various gatherings of scientists in Oxford and London, Hooke displayed his great abilities to design scientific experiments that were both enlightening and entertaining. His talent in designing experiments propelled him to become the first Curator of Experiments of the Royal Society after it was given a royal charter in 1662, and a full member of the Society a year later.

Hooke's connections with the scientific circle did not bring him closer to the court. It was perhaps this distance from the royal circle that made Hooke a more radical (if slightly eccentric for his time) modernist both in conducting scientific experiments and in his proposal for London. Whereas Wren rushed his plan to Charles II in 1666 and bypassed the Royal Society, Hooke presented his design to a meeting of the Society and representatives of the Lord Mayor and the Aldermen of the City, who then decided that it should be shown to the king.[26]

The design for the City of London attributed to Hooke is both traditional and new because of his unique use of the universal instrument of planning, the grid. The grid has been employed in all kinds of urban traditions as an effective way to organize the spaces for the city,[27] but Hooke's interpretation of this technique

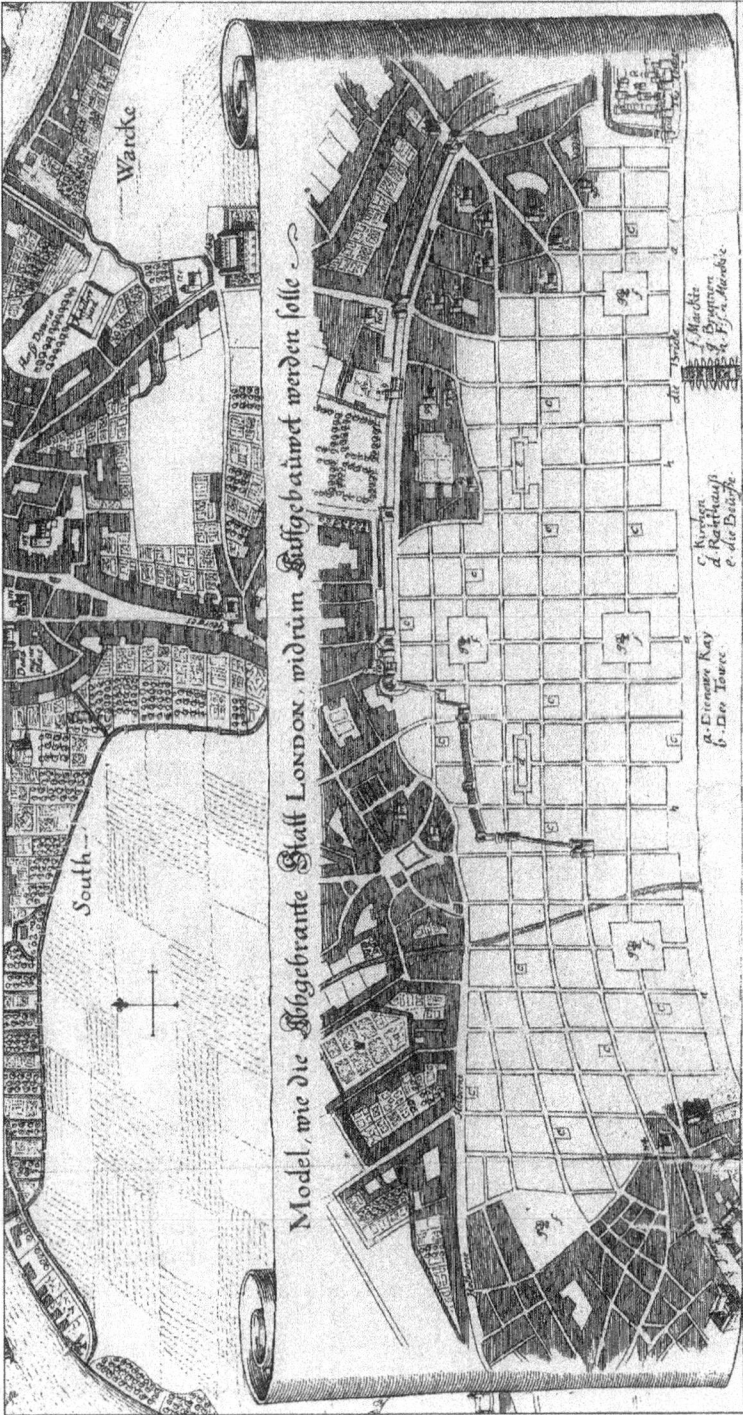

Figure 10. 5 Plan attributed to Robert Hooke, first presented to the Royal Society on 19 September 1666; detail from Marcus Willemsz Doornick's 1666 plan (Guildhall Library).

conveyed something radically new. Unlike Wren and Evelyn, Hooke gave more prominence to the institutions of the City; the Guildhall, the Exchange, the markets and the quays occupy strategic locations. The absence of St Paul's Cathedral in this plan is a curious feature, but one that would be consistent with the reduction of the number of parish churches. All of these components are subservient to a universal and open-ended grid of streets, propagating no particular spatial hierarchies. This gridiron layout brought a new degree of clarity and efficiency to the City of London, uncompromising and functional.

There seems to be no evidence to suggest that Hooke was familiar with the gridiron designs of Greek and Roman colonies; there is even less evidence to link Hooke with the regular grids in cities in other parts of the world such as the Chinese city of Chang'an in the tenth century. The earlier gridiron plans were instruments of political domination of the imperial administration, and of the settling aristocracy in the new colonies.[28] In Hooke's design, the geometrical relationships between the streets and the market squares, the guildhall and trading hall, and the parish churches, all suggest the idea of 'street as public space', which seems to be quite different from other gridiron cities before him. What seems to be clear is that Hooke was thinking ahead of his time – a typical trait of his intellectual production; he projected a vision of the city for the future, one that would flourish in North America in the nineteenth and twentieth centuries in eras when science and trade reached new heights. Although it might be different in reality, the gridiron plan of American cities was argued for on the grounds of democracy and egalitarianism.[29] Here, Hooke moved away from the designs of Wren and Evelyn, and gave a material form to the modern city long before the conditions of putting it in practice were developed. It was not surprising that Charles II preferred Wren's design, and the City of London, which initially supported Hooke's design, switched their backing to that of Wren.

As the crucial person in charge of experiments at the Royal Society, Hooke's views resonated deeply with those of Bacon, and he poured his energy into the conception, design and construction of instruments such as the ear trumpet, telescope, microscope, etc. His *Micrographia* published in 1665 – a collection of meticulous drawings of the details of tiny objects and insects previously concealed to the naked eye but exposed with the aid of the microscope – was both a record of a scientific experiment with the microscope, and a new form of visual art. Hooke was not without artistic aspirations; as a young man, he had apprenticed under Peter Lely, a well-established Dutch painter patronized by the royal circle.[30] *Micrographia*, perhaps for the first time, presented the possibilities of a new kind of aesthetic pleasure dominated by an 'over-exposure'. In this light, the inventions of photography, the cinema and the electronic screen in the twentieth century can be seen to have re-imagined Hooke's art with renewed energy. The scientific laboratory has since become one of the most enduring metaphors for places of artistic production.

Hooke's proposal for the City of London provided a physical manifestation of the free market, not only in the provision of markets, exchange building and the quays, but also in the symbolic 'leveling of the ground' through the generic and open-ended grid; London, in Hooke's design, looked to the future of the city of the free, equal and accessible market as one of the most profound shaping forces of urban development. The common use of the grid in seventeenth-century Dutch cities perhaps highlighted the same open market mercantile culture; it is interesting to note that Hooke's plan for the City of London was printed by several Dutch print makers.

Concealing the city: the enclosed grid

The proposal for the City of London by the map-maker Richard Newcourt (Figure 10.6) serves as a convenient reminder that the idea of an 'open city' is by no means all that was imagined after the fire. In this plan, Newcourt ignored the burnt-down area of the City of London (shown as dotted lines on the drawing), and enlarged the area of the City towards the north. The dramatically new city was to be enclosed by a continuous rectangular wall, with one side open to the Thames, and the other three sides punctuated by three gates on each side of the wall. The plan contains fifty-five uniform blocks, each measuring 570 by 855 feet, with churches at the centres. Each church is about 120 or 130 feet in length,

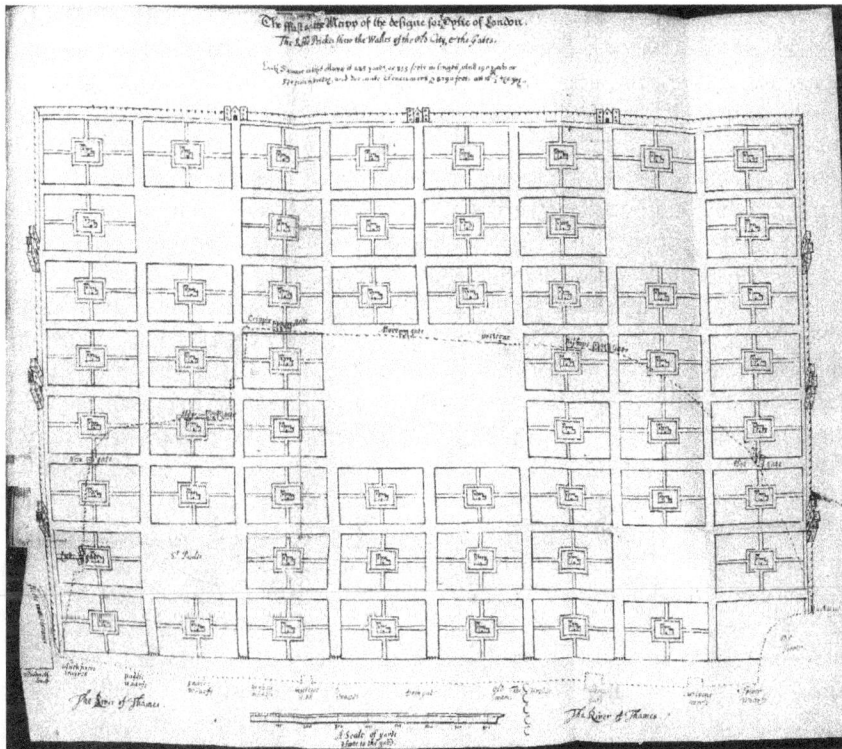

Figure 10.6 Richard Newcourt's plan (Guildhall Library).

and 50–60 feet in width. The rest of the uniform block is divided into four parts, regardless of the function and type of buildings. The city has a central open space, which is envisaged as a palace for the Lord Mayor, and four other open spaces, which are for either St Paul's Cathedral or other functions such as markets.

Newcourt's intervention was particularly heavy-handed as none of the existing features of the City of London was retained. In recreating the City of London as a walled city, Newcourt turned his back on much of the urban developments that had taken place since the Renaissance, and reinstated a form of the city dominated by defence and order. In this sense, Newcourt's enclosed grid had much in common with the Chinese city of Chang'an in the tenth century in which the extreme regularity of the rectangular grid served as an instrument of control. Newcourt's rectangular enclosed grid is certainly very different from Hooke's open-ended grid; they played completely different roles in the planning of the city. In stark contrast with Wren's and Evelyn's lines of sight and Hooke's gridiron street as public space, Newcourt reduced the city into smaller and orderly 'social units' unconnected with a larger (global) space and time. It certainly fell short of engaging with the new intellectual and economic conditions of London.

The return of the labyrinth

In the seventeenth and the eighteenth centuries, when the ideal of openness conquered vast spaces and gave rise to the Baroque garden, the labyrinth also appeared at the same time, like an artificial counterpoint to systemic transparency – an abstract sign of the impenetrable and the concealed that underlines the perceived triumph of openness as power. Like the blind spots of knowledge that return to haunt the scientific report, the concealed spaces continue to inhabit the city as ambiguities, as gated communities, as ghettos and shanty towns, and as yet-to-be-understood beauties and intelligences.

What happened to the City of London after the fire reinforces this point; it was nothing like any of the proposed designs. On 13 September 1666, Charles II issued a royal proclamation, detailing the broad principles concerning the materials and a framework for rebuilding London.[31] Charles II supported Wren's proposal at a Privy Council meeting shortly after receiving it, presumably discarding Evelyn's designs; the Lord Mayor Thomas Bludworth and the Court of Aldermen initially promoted Hooke's design, but switched their support to Charles II's choice. The House of Commons discussed the rebuilding of London on 27 and 28 September 1666, and rejected Wren's idea in favour of limited improvements. The improvements proposed by the Commons included the establishment of two broad streets: one links Temple Bar to Leadenhall, the other connects Bishopsgate to the Thames. Other measures included clearing the river banks for a continuous quay for trade, and relocating polluting trades such as brewers, dyers and sugar bakers.[32] Ironically, Wren's public quay as a signification of London's new openness became an aspect that attracted criticism; Wren's riverside quay – more symbolic than functional – would have shut out the enormous shipping and warehousing business that took place next to the river.[33] After the first round of consultations, Charles II decided to pass the matter to specialists; he appointed Wren, together with Hugh May and Roger Pratt, as royal commissioners to rebuild the City, and the City of London, in turn, appointed Hooke, together with Peter Mills and Edward Jerman, as their choices. In reality, Wren and Hooke dominated the rebuilding process; they did not build a new city, but worked hard to provide a better infrastructure such as roads, pavements and drainage, and to recreate the parish churches and St Paul's Cathedral. Further detailed rebuilding plans and the financial support were enacted by the Rebuilding Acts of 1667 and 1670: widening of major thoroughfares, taking in strips of land from the adjacent properties, which were paid for at 5 shillings per square foot by the Corporation of the City from a tax on coal.[34] Hooke's team carried out the survey. Markets were moved from the streets to dedicated sites, creating Honey Lane Market and the Stocks Market. All buildings were to be constructed with brick and stone.

All these would not have been completed had it not been for the establishment of a Court of Fire Judges by an Act of Parliament; it bypassed all established legal practices, and its decrees enabled those who could afford to build to build at the expense of those who could not, cancelling agreements and substituting others.[35] The City of London rose from its ashes very much following its previous urban pattern, a far cry from all the different visions of London presented by Wren, Evelyn, Knight, Hooke and Newcourt. On the other hand, the broadened streets, the towering dome of St Paul's and the inventive steeples of the parish churches brought a new but limited degree of clarity and visibility to London.

The new visions of Knight and Hooke failed to find their realization in London, but their reworking on the ancient planning technique of the grid in the era of market expansion and scientific investigation found much greater resonance in North America. Among many gridded layouts in North American cities, William Penn's Philadelphia, first publicized in Thomas Holme's *Portraiture of the City of Philadelphia* (1683), embraced the visions of Knight and Hooke; its influence is enormous. The city as it is realized has decidedly shifted from the opaque citadel to the transparent grid; this change is seen in both the methods of construction and the methods of destruction of cities. The traditional siege and pillage has long given way to calculated systemic damage, particularly in the age of wars dominated by 'air superiority'. The five proposals for the City of London after the Great Fire in 1666 marked a crucial moment of this process of change.

Notes

1 Paul Virilio, 'The Overexposed City', in Steven Redhead, ed., *The Paul Virilio Reader* (New York: Columbia University Press, 2004), pp. 83–99.
2 Richard Sennett, *Flesh and Stone, the Body and the City in Western Civilization* (New York and London: W. W. Norton, 1994), pp. 31–67.
3 Thucydides, *History of the Peloponnesian War*, trans. Rex Warner (New York and London: Penguin Books, 1972), p. 38.
4 Sennett, *Flesh and Stone*, pp. 40–4.
5 Thucydides, *History of the Peloponnesian War*, p. 145.
6 Ibid., p. 146.

7 E. H. Gombrich, *The Story of Art* (London: Phaidon, 1995), p. 77.

8 Scott Lash, 'Risk Culture', in Barbara Adam, Ulbrich Beck and Joost Van Loon, eds., *The Risk Society and Beyond, Critical Issues for Social Theory* (London: Sage, 2000), p. 53.

9 Thucydides, *History of the Peloponnesian War*, pp. 147–8.

10 Karl Popper, *The Open Society and its Enemies* (Princeton, NJ: Princeton University Press, 1950), p. 171.

11 Thucydides, *History of the Peloponnesian War*, p. 146.

12 Ibid., p. 76.

13 John Evelyn, *A Character of England* (1659), quoted in Adrian Tinniswood, *By Permission of Heaven, the True Story of the Great Fire of London* (New York: Riverhead Books, 2004), p. 11.

14 Paul Jeffery, *The City Churches of Sir Christopher Wren* (London: Hambledon Press, 1996), pp. 7–30. Also see Tinniswood, *By Permission of Heaven*; Walter George, *The Great Fire of London in 1666* (London: John Lane, 1920); Stephen Porter, *The Great Fire of London* (Gloucestershire: Sutton, 2001); Kevin Lynch, *What Time Is This Place* (Cambridge, MA: MIT Press, 1972).

15 Lisa Jardine, *On a Grander Scale, the Outstanding Life of Sir Christopher Wren* (New York: HarperCollins, 2002), p. 251.

16 Samuel Pepys, *The Diary of Samuel Pepys*, ed. Richard Le Gallienne (New York: The Modern Library, 2003), p. 189.

17 John Evelyn, *The Diary of John Evelyn*, ed. William Bray (London: Dent, 1973), p. 15.

18 Ibid., pp. 15–16. Pepys also recorded in his diary the rumour of a French attack on 5 September 1666, in Pepys, *The Diary*, p. 190. A rumour was circulating that 60,000 Presbyterians, with the French and Dutch forces, had been in arms; see Porter, *The Great Fire of London*, p. 47.

19 Spiro Kostof, *The City Assembled, the Elements of Urban Form through History* (London: Thames and Hudson, 1992), p. 33.

20 Evelyn mentioned that he and Wren discussed their ideas of London design, in John Evelyn, *London Revived: Considerations for its Rebuilding in 1666*, ed. E. S. De Beer (Oxford: Clarendon Press, 1938), pp. 45–6.

21 Evelyn quoted in Tinniswood, *By Permission of Heaven*, p. 206

22 Clarendon quoted in Tinniswood, *By Permission of Heaven*, p. 199.

23 Porter, *The Great Fire of London*, p. 82.

24 George, *The Great Fire of London in 1666*, p. 241.

25 This design was published by several map makers, Marcus Willemsz Doornick in 1666, and Jacob Venckel in 1667, and has been attributed to Hooke by Porter (2001) and Tinniswood (2004). The Guildhall Library catalogue attributes the design in Venckel's print to Hooke. But all of them seem to have failed to cite convincing reasons for their attributions. Michael Cooper, in *A More Beautiful City, Robert Hooke and the Rebuilding of London after the Great Fire* (Gloucestershire: Sutton Publishing, 2003), suggests that the different versions of published designs could be schematic representations of Hooke's original design, in Chapter 10, pp. 111–14.

26 Lisa Jardine, *The Curious Life of Robert Hooke, the Man Who Measured London* (London: HarperCollins, 2003), pp. 143–4.

27 Spiro Kostof, *The City Shaped, Urban Patterns and Meanings through History* (London: Thames & Hudson, 1991), Chapter 2, 'The Grid'.

28 Ibid., p. 99.

29 Ibid., p. 100.

30 Michael Cooper, 'Hooke's Career', in Jim Bennett, Michael Cooper, Michael Hunter and Lisa Jardine, eds., *London's Leonardo – the Life and Work of Robert Hooke* (Oxford: Oxford University Press, 2003), pp. 2–3; Jardine, *The Curious Life of Robert Hooke*, p. 53.

31 Tinniswood, *By Permission of Heaven*, pp. 191–4.
32 Ibid.
33 George, *The Great Fire of London in 1666*, p. 235.
34 Jeffery, *The City Churches of Sir Christopher Wren*, p. 22.
35 George, *The Great Fire of London in 1666*, pp. 243–58.

11 Moscow

Fortress city

Irina Aristarkhova

Quiet, quiet, quiet, my loud age!
By me, floods – and coming generations.   (Marina Tsvetaeva 1931)[1]

I am the place of your birth, the birth of the New World, the only world.
Writing is auto-bio-graphy, auto-matically, physically. Does a city have such auto-biography? Does it write? Does it leave marks? Has the place of your birth left marks on your body? Marked you out? Marked you inside out?

Is your mother a place . . .?

Desire to desire, forgetting and remembering, playing *fort/da* – you just know that you cannot take another step as soon as you have realised that you are THERE forever. Either UP there, or DOWN there, as they say. You can only confirm it. And you do. Just recollect your dreams . . .

I know I can help you to move, for I do it every day and every night. When I read that you are 'not able to return' from Moscow, Berlin, New York; from HOME/birthplace/mother tongue; that you are travelling, fleeing, running, writing, collecting – struggling – I tell myself: yes, you are still MINE, and mine forever. Do I have a choice in having you or freeing you? Yes . . . yes, I do.

Do I still want you? Want you inside myself? This question is with me, you know. If I leave you just for a while, just to give birth to you, just to teach you to take your first step, to walk, I know I leave you in-between birth and death. I even help you in teaching you how to substitute the word 'birth' with the word 'life', so that you are left between 'life' and 'death', and you think both belong to you. I made you think that way.

Always in place? In my body. Now . . . GO. Walk away. Find out for yourself. And by the way, call me not 'yours' or 'my birthplace'. Too many of you do it. I contain the army. I contain the nation. I contain all past and future heroes, the people, the matter, the air you breathe. If you want to be *special, different, not the same* – and this is what you have always asked for – if you want to be *the chosen one,* then this is the way to weave the words of the new world. 'New World': is there something more trivial for the Muscovite ear? Trust me: I've imagined this world for you, and each day you continue to rename me and yourself – anew, obsessed with the past.

Do not call me your 'Mother'. Do not call me 'Mother-Russia'. Do not call me 'Mother-land'. Do not call me 'Mother-earth'. Unlearn these words before coming back – to your senses. This is my last lesson as a mother. I am your first word and your last word; never mind what is written in your sacred texts. Calm down. Sleep. Eat, darling, eat. Sleep is good for you, food is good for you. *I* am good for you.

In Russia everyone wants to belong to Moscow. Everyone wants to be able to claim: 'I live in Moscow'. Even though after such claims some are as ready to disclaim the use of it, its importance, and try to 'purify' themselves of what I call *Moskvozentrism* (Moscow-centrism). How many times do you read: in 'Moscow, Russia'? Let's face it: Moscow = Russia. When you write of Moscow, you write of Russia by default. Many non-Muscovite Russians dislike this imperial attitude about Moscow and Muscovites. Until they become Muscovites themselves. However, here again birth is significantly different from life. It is true that those who live in Moscow already lay claim to rights to write about the city. But they are still only partly Muscovites. In Moscow these things mean a lot: whether you are *born* a Muscovite or you have only *become* a Muscovite. That is, which generation immigrant are you?

You must be already wondering: what about this author? Does she have the right to write about Moscow because her name sounds Russian? Because she *is* Russian? Let me assure you: I have the right to write about Moscow. I WAS BORN IN MOSCOW. I WAS BORN IN RUSSIA. I WAS BORN IN THE USSR.

Moscow is mine through and through. Full stop. Those who were not born in this place will always be haunted by a desire to possess it, *in one way or another.* Something that is given (as a birthright) is experienced differently from something that is conquered. It means that one and one's parents do not need 'to make it' to Moscow. One *has* Moscow. One has the Muscovite attitude. One does not need to learn it, to mimic it, to wear it. Performance is *natural*, given by and absorbed through the mother's milk. Muscovites can identify each other by gaze, by being the makers and the centre of the universe called the 'Russian empire'. Muscovites have that famous Muscovite accent that betrays me anywhere. Actually, that privileges me, marks me out as special, as some 'chosen one', as the lucky one. One cannot buy an accent, one can only spend years or hours of hard work on trying to speak (*with*) what Russians call '*without* accent'. That is, in the Muscovite accent, just as many Russian actresses and actors had to learn in order to work in Moscow. In order to call Moscow 'theirs'. However, it *is* mine. By birthright. Mother, thank you. Moscow is my Mother-land. It is my Mother-tongue. It is the place where I was born; the place I love.

Do not take me seriously. I am not expecting it. You know that when a *woman writes*, she writes from her heart; pure emotions and passions speak through her. Being Russian, woman doubles her lack. Lack of sense. Lack of reason. And if you want me/her . . . to remain 'Russian woman' – *as you know her* – let me destroy, let me sacrifice, or let me suffer. But remember: 'Russians do not surrender'. So you have to let me remain *certain*, remain *standing* in my holiness. Or I would lose my identity, therefore you would lose yours. Do you want that? Think again, how many hopes and pleasures would be lost. Do not give me your questions.

Just enjoy me, just experience me. I do not speak your language, and you cannot speak mine, even if both of us seem to speak the *same* language. Translations are strong aphrodisiacs. Let yourself go and do not feel guilty: I grant you permission.

Come to me, Moscow, Russia...

You must excuse me – I forgot another important part of my Muscovite existence, one that is becoming crucial in the next millennium. Let me introduce myself *properly* to ease our communication. I am Russian. I am not *just* a Russian citizen, not *just* Muscovite. I am ACTUALLY Russian. One hundred per cent. Although some of my Moscow friends claimed that my eyes are *a bit* Mongoloid, but much less than those of Yeltsin or Lenin, of course. Yet others were suspicious of my nose: it was suggested within earshot that my nose was *slightly* Jewish.

With the latest Chechen wars, this question has acquired a stronger meaning, and I am proud to assure you that I am not just ethnically Russian (I hope you believe me by now). I am . . . BLONDE. I am *naturally* blonde. Trust me – this is my *real* colour (I was asked many times). I am *really* white (or would you refer 'fair'?) though I am not using any whitening lotions. My skin is delicate, properly white, *naturally* white skin. To help you to understand, let me emphasise that my skin does not tolerate sun. As a test, observe yourself. If your skin does tolerate sun, you are not *completely* white by Muscovite standards. Among my school friends, those of not completely white skin were called 'Gypsy-likes'. My eye colour is grey-green; depending on the colour of my clothes and mascara it becomes greyer or greener. But of course the point about my eyes is that their colour is not dark; it is not brown.

When I was young and slim, I sometimes looked like Botticelli's Venus.

And you . . .?

I have often heard that 'logos' and rationality do not operate in Moscow, Russia, especially in our 'irrational' post-Soviet era. We are 'senseless', we are losing our sense! There are claims that we lack a tradition of metaphysics and 'proper' phenomenology. We are 'naturally' *not reasonable*. We do not make sense, we can prove this to you on demand. Hence we must urgently work on our reason, otherwise we could be completely consumed by our 'essential' passion for the 'strong hand', our love for terror, for blood, for power. That is why we do not have anything to deconstruct. No, no! We are *scared* to even think of doing so – isn't this obvious? We speak your language, we call ourselves your 'Great Other' (a child of the 'Big Brother'). We can deconstruct *you* – but take your hands off *us*! You cannot possibly understand what it means to live here, to experience it, to possess a 'Russian soul'. It is irrational, maternal, eternally feminine. Today, more than ever, it needs 'borders', 'reason', it needs a strong frame of metaphysics and rationality. At the end of the day, we say that the Soviet period was alien to great Russia, holy Russia. What those communists had committed was 'sin'. What can save us now? The God = the Russian Orthodox church and *solid, steady* thought. Thought that can stand for centuries.

However, the mode of steady thought needs 'a man', a hero, a thinker and a protector of Russian culture. All cultural aspirations today are directed towards exactly this: a great man, a new Russian hero. You just wait, wait, you will see.

He will be strong, he will be a genius, he will be Russian, and he, of course, will live in Moscow (perhaps I could be HIM if I were not HER?).

Before we can think through heterogeneity and diversity, before we can think *with* Chechnya, *with* Tatarstan, *with* Kolyma, *with* you, WE NEED ANOTHER RUSSIAN HERO.

See for yourself: it takes eight centuries to deliver into the world the Union of Soviet Socialist Republics. They will all see, I will show them what we can deliver. Finally they all saw. Moscow never felt more fertile and potent. It wanted more. It wanted to swallow the whole world. It was the mother of all poor and abandoned children. What's next? Today we, Muscovites, do not try to protect everyone, do not claim to love everyone who agrees with us. In the new millennium I want to protect *my own* children. They are in danger. We are in danger. The danger hovers at our threshold. She/death is dark skinned, she is fecund. Our kin might disappear. I must bear more children with my blood, with my skin, with my eyes. I must be a responsible citizen. Once again, my sons, my children: behind you – Moscow, behind you – Russia. Fighting, you defend your mother, your coming generations, your bright future.

Can you ever come back/to/from home, mother(land), Moscow, the USSR, Russia – from ME?

Fortress city

> in many places Moscow looks as tightly sealed as a fortress.
>
> (Walter Benjamin 1927)[2]

> The Kremlin is not like any other palace, it is a city in itself; a city that forms the root of Moscow, and that serves as the fortress between two quarters of the world. (Marquis De Custine 1839)[3]

Moscow acted out the primal scene of the twentieth century, the place where it all started. A womb or birthplace that citizens of the world will never be able to experience without some sort of reactive bowel movement. As an abject mother of the 'Soviet monster', an embodiment of the spectre of communism, totalitarianism, terror, etc., Moscow realised its dream of immaculate conception – of delivering the third Rome, the holy city, the New World.

From the early years of Moscow and its fortress the Kremlin, subsequent generations had been left with fortress consciousness. The Kremlin multiplied obsessively, expanding and enclosing in successive concentric circles, like a *matreshka* (the Russian doll), into the surrounding regions. Every major Russian city was striving to have a Kremlin, or one semblance of it. Fortification also became a primary operation in the domestication of conquered territory. For example, the Russian appropriation of the Siberian 'body politic' started in 1571 with Ivan the Terrible's system of fortifications. It was a series of southern *ostrogi* (forts) to defend from Tartar attacks, behind which Ivan the Terrible established peasant *slobody* (settlements). Fortifications were used to establish the boundaries of what was conceived to be Russia and Russian. Then, in addition to serving as places to deport 'the depopulated' of Russia, these fortification towns and villages helped to clarify spatially and politically what constituted Russia.

Catherine the Great's 'Russification' policy used the fortress logic to build up identifiable borders of the Russian national identity using the language of the French Enlightenment. It is noteworthy that in the first *ukaz* (edict) of 1764, this policy was articulated as a means of assimilating the Cossacks into the Russian population, and bringing them to 'acceptable cultural standards', as 'they lacked social discipline and intellectual sophistication'. At the same time, the issue of the protection and defence of Russians within an ever-growing Russian territory was addressed. It was estimated that the 'original' Russian state covered approximately 15,000 square miles in 1462, but had since then expanded at a rate of some 50 square miles a day over a period of 400 years, creating a vast empire of about 8,660,000 square miles (constituting one-seventh of the total land surface of the earth) by 1914. Inscribing the borders of the 'Russian way' or the 'Russian soul' meant that those who were incompatible with these were to be expelled from within fortress-Russia.

It is in the Kremlin that one finds the roots of the Gulag. To claim that the Gulag is the result of Bolshevism or communism, as argued by Solzhenitsyn among others, is to be blind to Russian history, and especially to the way in which Russian national identity has been historically implied in this process. Up to today, the expression *sotyi kilometre* (one-hundreth kilometre) remains familiar to Muscovites. It refers to the distance of 100 kilometres from the official borders of Moscow. A circle with Moscow in the centre, it is an area that former convicts and other officially prohibited citizens were not to enter. Russian identity with Moscow at its centre has been fortifying itself in many different ways, and it seems many of those practices and discourses have been utilised for building Russia and the USSR.

The fortification logic of Moscow, which has been essential for the constitution and territorial consolidation of the Russian nation, is of dual nature. On the one hand, it guards its borders and imagines itself to be in constant danger, ever vigilant to aliens of all sorts. On the other hand, Moscow propels itself outwards, feeding off its internal turbulence (after all, etymology of 'Moscow', *mosk*, translates as 'turbulent'). This momentum is realised in the centripetal expansion of Russia. Kremlin walls absorbed urbanisation in 1147, once and forever. The rest of Moscow, as many have insisted, is a 'big village'. No matter how many Stalinist stone buildings have been erected, and how eloquently Moscow parades its current construction work, it ultimately fails to be simply *a* city, one of the world's capitals. It is *the* city. The rest of Russia is destined to being a means of ensuring that *only* Kremlin embodies Russia as such. The rest of Russia, *as a whole*, is residue, excess, discharge, is 'the rest'. Today more than ever. Anyone who valorises excess and margins must feel suffocated in this territory: the space outside Kremlin is negative; it is a shadow. So many domains, so many cultures and civilisations, have been *systematically* swallowed for this one to claim a special destiny, to claim its red purity, to 'surprise the world'.

To let THIS go, in order to wake up from a thousand-year-old dream of wholeness and holiness, is in the Russian imaginary tantamount to treason. The dream clears all charges of responsibility.

Entrances into fortresses are always ambivalent, as any other *vkhod v ukrytie* (entrance to shelter): what makes a fortress a fortress is its simultaneous elicitation and frustration of the desire of those outside it. In Russia 'fortress' has been translated into mythology, into law, into language and culture, into *national identity*: most clearly exemplified by the fortress city, 'Kremlin'. Russians feel compelled to constantly *defend* themselves, being in a permanent state of anxiety of all sorts and kinds. However, to not be desirable any more is Kremlin's ultimate nightmare. If the fortress cannot sustain its attractiveness by all means at its disposal, those who belong within it lose more than those relegated outside. Defence of one's own 'way of life' does not know the boundaries of the word 'enough'. For this rationale, defence is the way to make sense of the world. It is not to say that somehow this siege mentality marks out Russia as a special case, but, certainly, in the 'Mother-land' it took on monstrous forms.

Anyone who lives in Moscow or comes into Moscow for more than 3 days knows this word: *propiska* or *registrastiya* (Figure 11.1). To be a Muscovite (temporarily or permanently) is to have *propiska* – best translated as *inscription* or '*writing through*'. This practice today has at least two dimensions: spatial and legal. The former is characterised by being allocated to a particular space, by being

Figure 11.1 Irina Aristarkhova's *propiska*. Courtesy of the author, 2011.

localised in a particular *home*, being fixed into a space and also being granted a space in which to place one's body. So it is a *spatio-corporeal inscription*. It provides control over the body and its movements in city space. To be a Muscovite in this sense is written through one's body; it is to have a *Muscovite body*.

It is well known that Russians – to sustain their identity as spatially and ethnically stable and homogeneous – have historically employed movings, re-movings, deportations and re-placements of peoples. In the early period, the main target of this activity was an 'exchange' of the wealthiest native people with Russian merchants and the deportation of conquered citizens to the interior of the Moscow principality. For example, in 1486 merchants from Moscow 'replaced' a few thousand people from Livonia. In 1656 'pro-Swedish' subjects from Ingria, Finland and Karelia (about 8,000 families from the last two countries) were driven out of their homelands. Peter the Great continued to use this policy in 1708 when, following his invasion of Dorpat in the Baltic region, its German citizens were forcibly relocated in long caravans to Vologda (their descendants are today known as 'Volgian Germans'). Russian national identity, based on the principle of homogeneity to be defended by fortification, found its earliest instantiation in such strategies of exile and deportation. *Propiska* is one of more modern means to keep *nezhelatel'nye elementy* (undesirable elements) from places of strategic importance, specifically Moscow.

Thus, those without *propiska* are to be constantly removed from Moscow, checked on, shifted around, deported, imprisoned, tracked, categorised and marked out in ethnic, racial, sexual and class terms: mainly prostitutes, non-whites (who are defined in contemporary Russia as 'persons with non-Slavic appearance'), vagrants, migrants and refugees. This topographic inscription has an embodied power only if it exists as a stamp in a valid identity document – for Russian citizens, this means their national passport. Identity papers, inscriptions, pictures and stamps within them discursively mark out the 'sexualised' and 'eth-nicised' bodies of non-Muscovites, and the exclusive bodies of Muscovites. It is also important to note that, from the time of the break-up of the Soviet Union and the introduction of the new Constitution of the Russian Federation, the practice of *propiska* has become unconstitutional. It remains in force primarily in Moscow, and is today defined as 'registration' instead of 'inscription', most probably with intent to neutralise the terminology. The Moscow municipal government continues with the practice, despite constitutional and court orders. Moscow protects its own privileged status of exclusivity and desirability, making sure that the rest of Russia remains THE REST.

Let's imagine that this bureaucratic bastion of Moscow, *propiska*, soon falls. Will it change things? Only to a certain extent: Muscovites (therefore, Russians) have learned that the only way to keep fortress identity alive and impregnable is to keep it expanding, innovative, to generate new 'others', 'them' as opposed to 'us'. Historically it was the West or Asia; today it is 'Islamic terrorism', 'blacks from the Caucasus', and even uncompromising sociological facts such as declines in the birthrate of 'white' Russians. Muscovites are *vsegda gotovy* (always prepared), like student-scouts in Soviet schools, to defend our Mother-land and

Fatherland, to defend our women and children, to defend ourselves. Fortress Kremlin-Moscow-Russia still guards its limits.

I dream: Moscow will lose its identity, it will fail holy Russia, it will fail to surprise, to protect, to attract, and deliver 'them'.

I am home. I am fortress.

That's all I am. *Da*?

Notes

1 Marina Tsvetaeva, *To the Wind: Selected Poems*, ed. H. B. Alekhin, Moscow: Letopis, 1998, p. 487 (translation mine).

2 Walter Benjamin, *Selected Writings, Vol. 2, Part 1: 1927–1930*, ed. Michael W. Jennings, Howard Elland and Gary Smith, Cambridge, MA: Harvard University Press, 1999, p. 43.

3 Marquis de Custine, *Empire of the Czar: A Journey through Eternal Russia*, New York: Doubleday, 1989, p. 400.

12 Unbombing the world, 1911–2011

100 years of aerial bombing of the human habitat – a proposal for an installation on the history and future of planned destruction and reconstruction

Tjebbe van Tijen, Imaginary Museum Projects (work in progress, 1999–2011)

The idea for the Unbombing Project came after I visited Tokyo in 1995. At first I could not understand why so few older buildings and landmarks could be seen, and I was shocked to learn that a great part of this huge city had been torched and burned down during aerial bombing campaigns of the US Air Force in March–July 1945. I was ashamed not to know that far over a hundred thousand people died, probably more than the death toll taken by the atom bombs dropped on Hiroshima and Nagasaki in August 1945. It prompted me to start a study on aerial bombing, and I discovered the Italian general Douhet (1869–1930), who formulated in 1921 his doctrine "*Il dominio dell'area*," "the dominion of the air," in which threats to bomb enemy cities were proposed to break "the will of a nation." Douhet, who had experienced the endless suffering in the trenches of World War I, hoped to evade such prolonged ways of warfare; he saw aerial bombing as a humanitarian way to cut a war short. It was also Italians who carried out the first aerial bombardment during the Italo-Turkish War in Libya in 1911, throwing grenades – by hand – from their fragile airplanes over the desert.

The Unbombing Project is an attempt to go beyond the dichotomized way of discussing war. It raises questions on the massive use of air power during World War II as a means to defeat Nazi Germany, fascist Italy, and imperial Japan (it certainly will not fail to document the indiscriminate and vicious attacks by the air forces of these Axis countries). It raises questions on the practice of "terror-bombing"; aimed not at military or economic targets, but at the morale and habitat of the population, and thus at their lives. The post-World War II international tribunals of Nuremberg and Tokyo failed to address the issue of aerial bombing and the hundred thousand victims it caused. Massive bombing as a military strategy continued during the Korean and Vietnam/Indochina wars.

Air power (aerial bombing from manned to unmanned airborne vehicles, and missile attack) remains essential. Non-western powers use it, such as the Soviet Union and its offspring in Afghanistan and Chechnya. "Third world" nations joined in: Angola, Columbia, Eritrea, Nicaragua, Sierra Leone, Sri Lanka, Sudan, and Zaire, as air power became also a tool for internal repression of "civil unrest" and rebellion. There is a decline in the number of bombardment victims, and massive and indiscriminate targeting of urban areas is no longer on the military agenda, as management of "public opinion" has become part of military operations. Nevertheless, the Gulf, Balkan, Afghan, Palestinian, Lebanese, and Libyan war theaters saw, next to taking out intended targets, many incidences of "unintentional killing," despite the praised "precision" of modern weaponry.

The aim of the "Unbombing the World" installation is to come to an understanding of the military–industrial complex and political decision-making that keeps this kind of warfare on the agenda. The project allows us to listen to those from the past who spoke against torching of cities and villages, the spraying of poison, and the casting of cluster bombs, and to those today who protest death delivered by drones. It makes us listen to the bomb victims on the ground and at the same time hear the voices of the air crews in the air and the military in command. The World War II air crews are displayed as a special category, who risked – and often gave – their lives in what was, for them, a fight against totalitarian and murderous regimes; a defense of their own nations. Unbombing is seen not as undoing the wrongs of the past, but as a stimulus for more peaceful resolution of conflicts in the future.

Tjebbe van Tijen, 25 August 2011
Full documentation at http://imaginarymuseum.org/UBW/ubw01a.html

Primordial air-power – shamans soaring through the sky – Zeus casting thunderbolts – Indra, keeper of the universe, striking with vajras – an archeological hot-air fantasy imagines Nazca Indians flying a smoked balloon (Peru, 500 bce–500 ce). Cyrano's trip to the moon with bottles of sun-heated dew 1655 – the mythical Chinese dragon becomes a war kite, a windsock with a smoking torch used by Mongols, Dacians, and Romans as a signaling device and to scare their enemies.

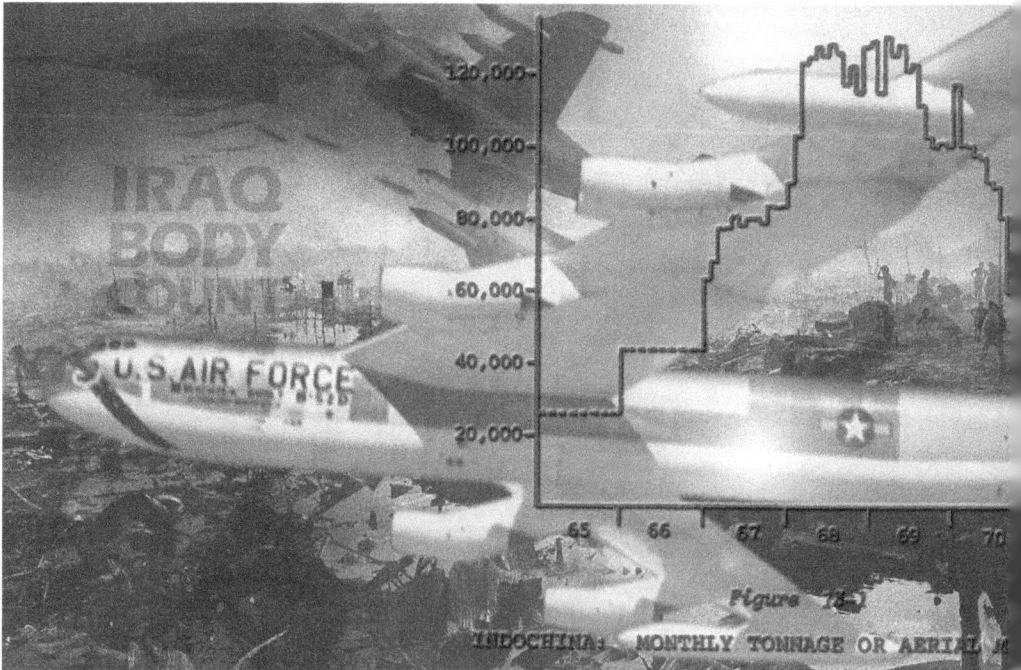

Since the year 2004, war fatalities – civilian and military – are tallied publicly on the Internet – often names of victims are mentioned, sometimes even their pictures shown. Iraq bodycount 11,000 (2004)/103,000 (2011) civilians. We still do not know whether we should count the bomb victims of the war in Indochina – 40 years ago – in the tens or hundreds of thousands – names of targeted villages and towns are hardly known – the deaths anonymous.

Then the Chinese dragon takes the shape of a two-stage gunpowder rocket, setting cities ablaze – Samurai warrior borne aloft by giant Wan-Wan kite, also used to enter or leave besieged cities. "Will You sweep away the righteous with the wicked?" asks Abraham – in the end only Lot and his daughters escape God's judgment of fire and brimstone that devastates Sodom and Gomorrah (Genesis 18:28).

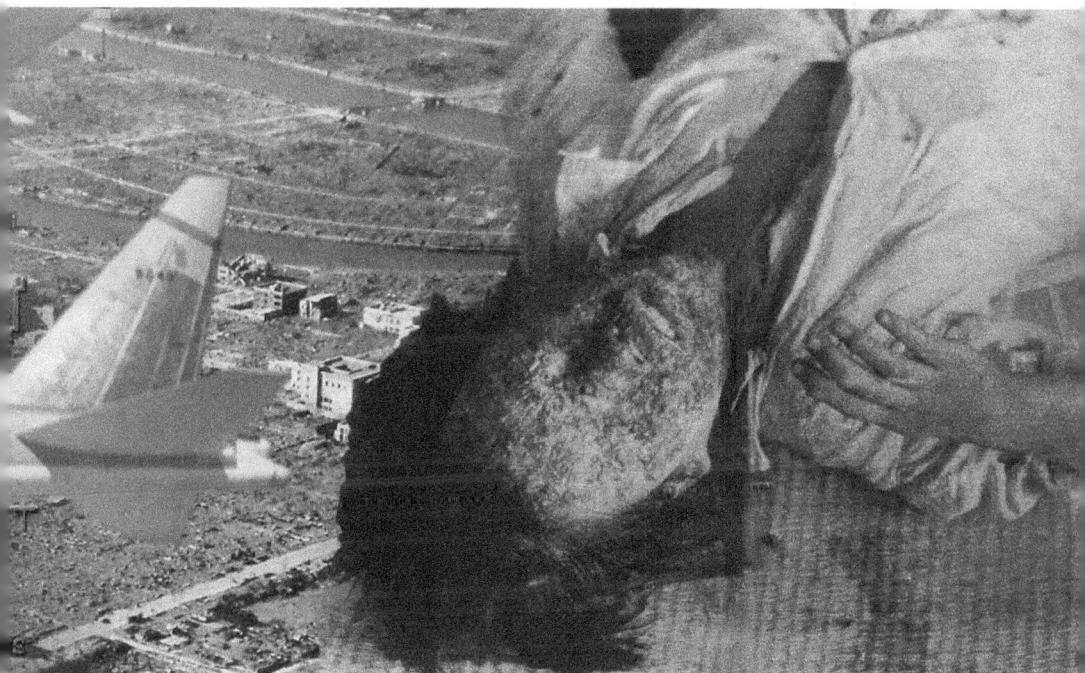

The Boeing B-29s of World War II are replaced by the B-52s of the Cold War, warriors in the third dimension, dropping death for more than half a century: dumb bombs, fire bombs, smart bombs, and . . . twice an atom bomb . . . "Water water!" cries the girl, until she stops breathing (1945) – a US study about the Atom bomb on Hiroshima, 20 years later, claims a total of 70,000 dead; the Japanese count double that amount.

The semi-devine monkey Hanuman destroys the corrupt city of King Ravana on Lanka with his lashing tail of fire: "The friendly wind conspired to fan the hungry flames that leapt and ran" (*Ramayana* book LIV). "The sun became black as sackcloth of hair, and the moon became as blood; And the stars of heaven fell unto the earth, even as a fig tree casteth her untimely figs, when she is shaken of a mighty wind" (Revelation 6:12).

An atom bomb on the heart of Hiroshima, where, afterwards, only white lines mark where streets once ran. The assembled plutonium core for the first atomic bomb at Trinity, New Mexico, and the only color photos of this test explosion – a huge plutonium-producing reactor and small blocks of uranium show the compact power of this apocalyptic device.

The Revelation of St. John becomes an apocalyptic human judgment when German Catholic troops bombard German protestants in Magdeburg in 1631: 20,000 dead (symbol of the horrors of war in its time). Leonardo da Vinci (1452–1519), painter of the Mona Lisa, was also a military engineer traveling with the armies of his warring patrons, producing "undiscovered inventions": ballistic machines and flying vessels.

The Underground proved the best shelter during the Blitz on London: platforms, rails, corridors, and escalators were full night after night – still 60 percent of Londoners preferred their own risky beds. "To this day I am still afraid of airplanes – for me an airplane means something evil that comes out of the sky": German woman (1992) talking about her youth.

Swift's flying island of Laputa (1727) casts stones or crushes earthly rebels – Jesuit priest Lana Terzi (1631–1687) decides – God forbids it – not to develop a vacuum- and wind-driven airship capable of bombing ships and cities. The hot-air balloon not just for pleasure cruises or scientific observations, but also imagined as a war machine, as in this British plan (1799) for the annihilation of the French fleet by timed self-exploding balloons.

"There it is, skipper – straight ahead. Keep her steady," Lawrence called, watching the indicators as they crawled up his sword-sight. "Eight seconds to go." Description from Campbell, "The bombing of Nuremberg". There was often no visibility at all and bomb loads were pretty much dropped blindly, or a vague contour on a flickering radar screen was the only indication.

Jules Verne's airship, the *Albatross* (1886), as intervention force against West African "barbarians" – US fleet bombards the Libyan pirate city of Tripoli (1810); beginning of interventionist American "Big Stick" naval policy. General Graf von Zeppelin (1838–1917) perseveres in his plan for an invincible imperial German air fleet and sows terror in Antwerp, Paris, and London during World War I: "Zeppelin kommt!"

Looking through a magnifying glass at an aerial photo in order to find and mark targets – to analyze the damage done. Double planning: destruction and construction – fleeing paths, signal points, incendiary zones, transport and industrial locations versus fire lanes, spreading, rearrangement of city structures that were virtually annihilated.

The Italian general Douhet (1869–1930) calls for bombardments on the "will of a nation" (*Il dominio dell'area*, 1921). Douhet finds supporters among strategists from all emerging air-power nations, though civil morale proved to be stronger than thought. The Japanese bombardments of Chinese cities such as Shanghai, Canton, Nanking, and Hankow in 1937 were condemned by British and American governments as "barbaric acts" against defenseless civilians.

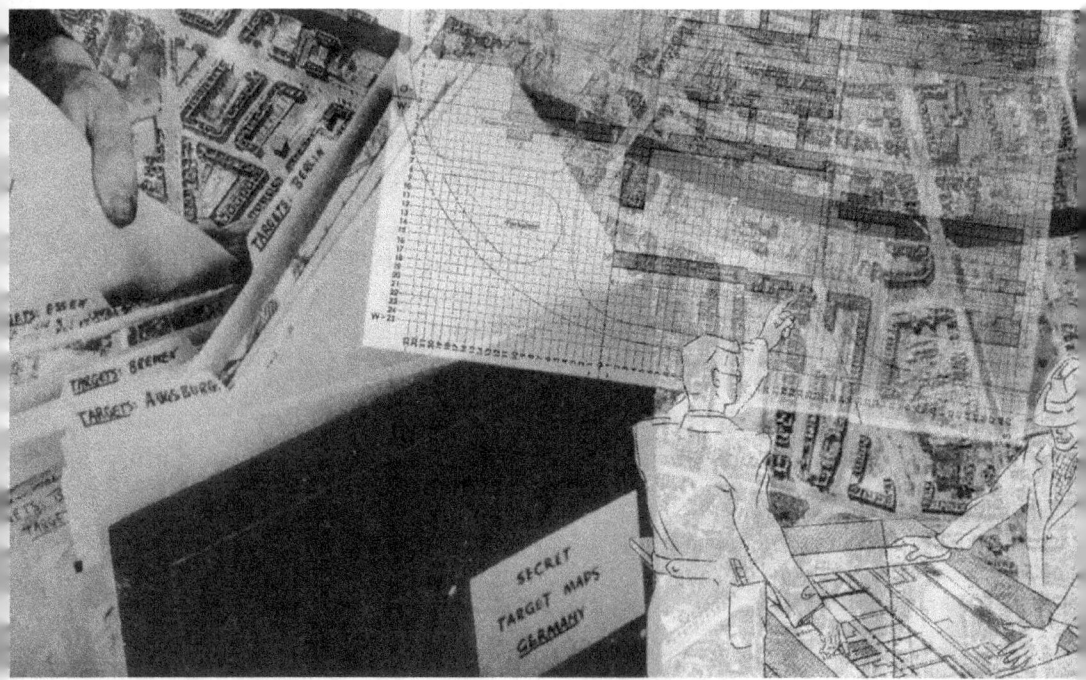

Rationalization, grids – a violent mirror image – planned destruction, planned reconstruction often with little reference to the past, resulting in social amnesia . . .

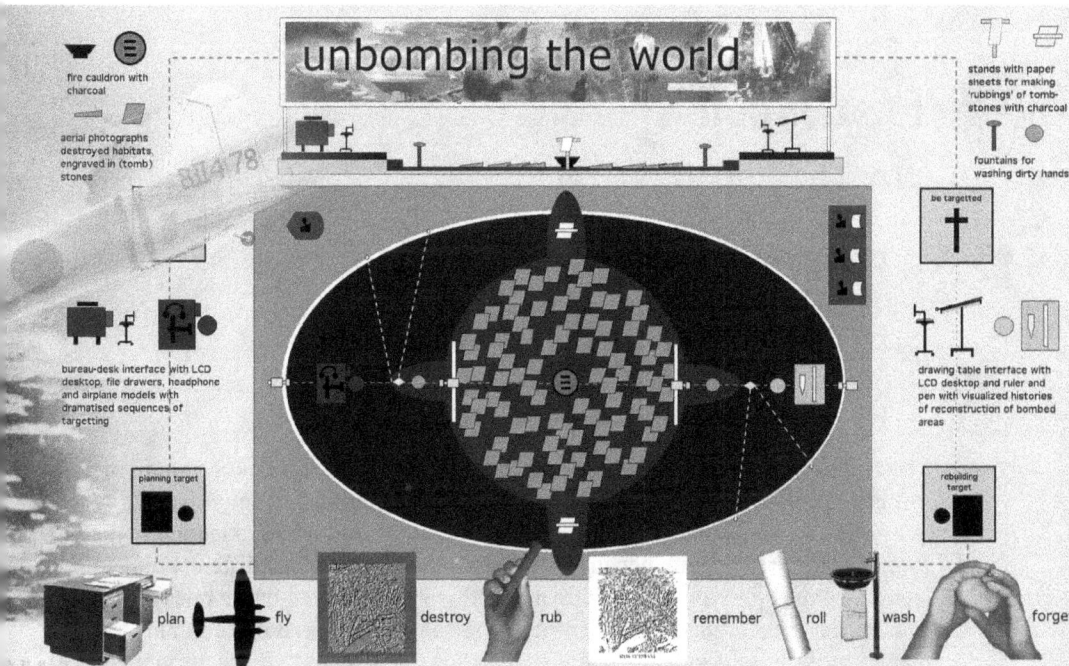

unbombing the world

fire cauldron with charcoal

aerial photographs destroyed habitats, engraved in (tomb) stones

bureau-desk interface with LCD desktop, file drawers, headphone and airplane models with dramatised sequences of targetting

planning target

plan · fly · destroy · rub · remember · roll · wash · forge

stands with paper sheets for making 'rubbings' of tomb-stones with charcoal

fountains for washing dirty hands

be targetted

drawing table interface with LCD desktop and ruler and pen with visualized histories of reconstruction of bombed areas

rebuilding target

The "Unbombing the World" installation – shown here – will dramatize "one century of aerial bombing of humans and human habitat," making the whole process understood. Plan, fly, bomb, die, remember, reconstruct, reconcile: politicians deciding, engineers and scientist designing, military strategists planning, industrialists producing, pilots and other aircrews flying and bombing, people below bombed and dying, architects and urbanists reconstructing, victims and heroes of destruction being remembered, next generations of different nations trying to overcome and reconcile . . .

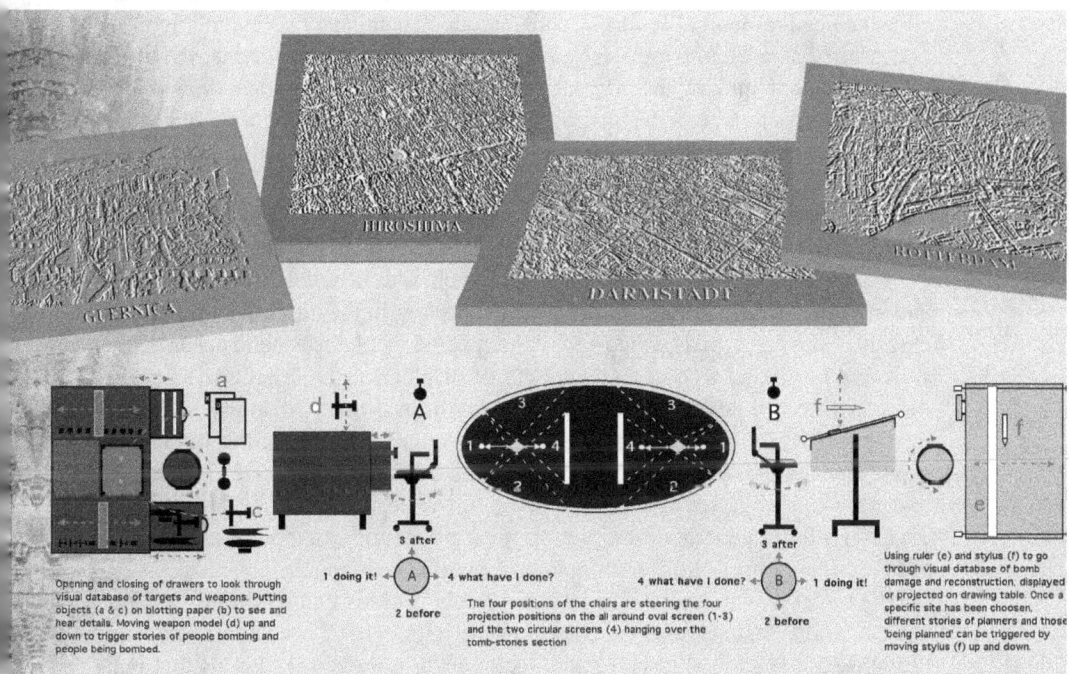

HIROSHIMA

DARMSTADT

ROTTERDAM

GUERNICA

Opening and closing of drawers to look through visual database of targets and weapons. Putting objects (a & c) on blotting paper (b) to see and hear details. Moving weapon model (d) up and down to trigger stories of people bombing and people being bombed.

1 doing it! → A → 4 what have I done?

2 before

The four positions of the chairs are steering the four projection positions on the all around oval screen (1-3) and the two circular screens (4) hanging over the tomb-stones section

4 what have I done? → B → 1 doing it!

2 before

Using ruler (e) and stylus (f) to go through visual database of bomb damage and reconstruction, displayed or projected on drawing table. Once a specific site has been choosen, different stories of planners and those 'being planned' can be triggered by moving stylus (f) up and down.

In the center of the Unbombing installation a graveyard of tombstones with aerial photographs of bombed cities engraved. The stones can be contemplated and visitors can make charcoal rubbings of stones to take home. Around, a huge panoramic projection screen showing documentary materials of bombing from a text and multi-media database that can be steered by the visitors seated behind a desk, symbol of the bureaucracy of destruction, opening drawers from the past . . .

13 London

The imperial target

Rajeev S. Patke

The notion of a target evokes several kinds of image: a shield, an arrow flying towards a bullseye, the cross hairs of a gunsight. Such images might appear to converge on a single meaning: the exclusivity of a target inviting attention in the form of force applied with penetrative intent; however, there is a different dimension to the metaphor in which a targeted entity is transformed but not destroyed. This mode of targeting isolates an object as the focus of vision: the thing that matters most. It is a form of penetrative attention that intends to reach the targeted entity, touch it, transform it, become one with it. To this form of attention, the target is a destination, or a point of arrival, or the projected fulfillment of desire. When cities become the function of such desire, we could say that the intention of targeting is not to hit an urban center, but to hit on it.

That is how migrants treat the Ithaca of their imagined desires. Migration is an endemic need for many life forms, and ubiquitous in human history. In migration, bodies are displaced into motion by a motive force whose locus defines the trajectory of diaspora, making the migrant a kind of missile. As individual or group, the migrant aspires to enter a destination as if piercing the eye of a needle or a storm, actions that require timing, instinct, steadiness of aim, and a willingness to live with the consequences of having taken a huge risk, from which there is no going back. But migrants as missiles also blur agency, dissolving the membrane that separates the willing from the forced, the intentional from the inadvertent.

Among willing bodies in motion, two treat cities as benevolent targets: tourists and migrants. In the former, targeting is temporary; in the latter, it is indefinitely extended; the first type is welcomed without being liked, the second needs neither welcome nor liking to make a home out of displacement. The tourist is a tame descendant of the adventurer and the explorer of past eras. Colonial history bred three other kinds of targeting traveller: the voluntary colonist, the involuntary slave, and the indentured labourer. Postcolonial history perpetuates that lineage under the altered guises of the migrant, the self-exile, and the exile. The notion of diaspora offers a generic description for their plight and experience, although the term conceals a host of differences that are worth clarifying.

The traveller who undertakes journeys freely is motivated by desire, and aims at destinations that serve as the reward of the journey. The involuntary exile and the self-exile leave home with regret, compelled to move for reasons that bully choice. They accept destinations that are not the end of the journey, and struggle to live from place to place while overshadowed by a sense of persistent displacement. The self-exile is permitted the illusion of choice; the true exile is denied even that meager luxury. Both are figures of disenchantment. The migrant swallows regret in order to embrace the target as an optional future; whereas the exile and the self-exile accept the future as a stock whose value is sunk past recovery (see further Patke 2006: 207).

Taking Kingston (Jamaica) and London as specific instances of urban centers linked by diasporic patterns of migration, one can approach the history of peoples on the cusp of the colonial/postcolonial as linked by the metaphor of a target, in which the missile also becomes a missive. Jamaica became independent in 1962. Since the *SS Empire Windrush* unloaded several hundred West Indians onto English soil in 1948, migrants and writers from the Caribbean made England their preferred target-destination for the next three decades. More was at stake in this diaspora than what is conveyed through Salman Rushdie's image of "The Empire Writes Back." The movement was more like an ironic Revenge of Empire. There are several paradoxes and ironies attached to this cultural targeting.

The Caribbean poet Eric Roach identified the ambivalence at the heart of the Caribbean targeting of London in the 1950s (soon after the German V2 rockets had done their explosive worst):

> We turn Columbus's blunder back
> From sun to snow, to bitter cities;
> We explore the hostile and exploding zones.

> (Roach 1992: 127)

The kinds of question migrants-as-missiles kept asking themselves have remained the same over half a century. Trinidad-born Amryl Johnson identified them as follows: "where are you going?," "how will you get there?," "what will you find there?" (Johnson 1985: 54). The logic of such imperatives acquires additional bite in Benjamin Zephaniah's "A Modern Slave Song," which ends with an explicit declaration of a hostile intent:

> Remember where I come from, cause I do.
> I won't feget.
> Remember yu got me, cause I'll get yu.
> I'll make yu sweat.

> (Zephaniah 1992: 52)

The average Caribbean migrant was not a writer drawn to London for reasons of richer cultural outlets. The average migrant left home in search of jobs and an alternative to the limitations of the Caribbean economy, a problem to which Britain provided a kind of answer from 1948 by absorbing West Indians into work "in hospitals, factories and railway and bus depots" (Dabydeen 2000: 64). Those who left the Caribbean were generally glad they did so, regardless of their problems with racial prejudice in the target metropolis. The poetry of Linton Kwesi Johnson, for instance, gets its permanent political subject matter in those problems: "the general conditions that black people were living under and what we were experiencing in British society" (Markham 1995: 259). A poem by Fred D'Aguiar calls this type of metropolitan inhabitant one of the "Throwaway People":

> The problem that won't go away
> people.
> ...
> The things have got to epidemic proportions
> people
> The we have no use for you
> people

> (D'Aguiar 1993: 10)

Several other poets demonstrate how the human missiles directed at the imperial center were less than welcome, as they produced results that brought the margins to the center almost like shrapnel seeding a field. This is how the Jamaican Creole poet Louise Bennett begins "Colonisation in Reverse" (1966):

> What a joyful news, Miss Mattie;
> Ah feel like me heart gwine burs –
> Jamaica people colonizing
> Englan in reverse.
> By de hundred, by de tousan,
> From country an from town,
> By de ship-load, by the plane-load,
> Jamaica is Englan boun.

> (Proctor 2000: 16–17)

Such poems illustrate the irony of an urban target forced to give in and make room for reverse colonization. Speaking for those who migrated to London from the Caribbean during the 1950s and 1960s, David Dabydeen is blunt in "The Introduction" to *Slave Song*:

> "England" is our Utopia, an ironic reversal, for Raleigh was looking away from the "squalor" of his homeland to the imagined purity of ours whereas we are now reacting against our "sordid" environment and looking to "England" as Heaven . . . Our desire for "white-ness" is as spiritual as it is banal. On one level it is a craving for mind and soul – the "savage" wants civilization of the renaissance kind; on a baser level what he wants is "civilization" of cars and fridges – a mere material greed.

> (Dabydeen 1984: 9)

A poem from Dabydeen's *Coolie Odyssey* evokes the world of the first-generation migrant through a letter in which the young son reports:

Englan nice, snow and dem ting,
A land dey say fit for a king
. . .
And I eating enough for all a-we
And reading book bad-bad.
. . .
Soon, I go turn lawya or dacta,
But, just now, passage money run out
So I tek lil wuk –
I is a Deputy Sanitary Inspecta,
Big – big office, boy! . . .

(Dabydeen 1988: 17)

The Jamaican Evan Jones captures the ambivalent experience of migration from a more insouciant perspective:

My yoke is easy, my burden is light,
I know a place I can go, any night.
Dis place Englan'! I'm not complainin',
If it col', it col'. If it rainin', it rainin'.
I don' min' if it's mostly night,
Dere's always inside, or de sodium light.
I don' min' white people starin' at me
Dey don' want me here? Don't is deir country?
You won't catch me bawlin' any homesick tears
If I don't see Jamaica for a t'ousand years!

(Figueroa 1982: 86–7)

At a more intimate level of interaction between the black and white races, a poem such as Dabydeen's "The Seduction" dramatizes an encounter in which the immigrant of color is unable to consummate a sexual relation in which he targets a white woman as the object of his colonial desire, only to be discomfited by the discovery that he carries more anxious baggage to the meeting than the girl expects or accepts. The weight of his history contributes to a failure of nerve that is psychic as well as physical. The sexual missile becomes a damp squib, and the poet has the objectivity to adopt a self-deprecatory stance toward the failure of his sexual targeting:

She said her name was really Jane
That she was sweet as sugarcane
Unblighted by colonial reign
That all he wanted was some pain
To wrap himself in mythic chain
And labour in his self-disdain.
. . .

Britannia it is not she cries!
Miranda also she denies!
Nor map nor piracy nor prize
Nor El Dorado in disguise
With pity gazed into his eyes
And saw he could not improvise

(Dabydeen 1988: 30–1)

This Caliban cannot get rid of his internalized guilt at the prospect of despoiling Miranda.

Throughout the latter half of the twentieth century, the relation between Caribbean writers and Britain has remained a curious mixture of need and resentment. It also allows for the kind of question that Merle Collins muses over in "Whose Story?":

Walking through the streets of this Britain
which you seek to save from the painful fate
of black invasion, I wonder
if mine had been the invading nation
would history just have shrugged
written the story upside down
left a different people clothed
in this distant arrogance?

(Kay *et al.* 1996: 94)

The angry and frustrated version of the relation between black and white communities in Britain finds expression in the 1970s and 1980s through Linton Kwesi Johnson, as in "Inglan is a Bitch," which ends:

Inglan is a bitch
dere's no escaping it
Inglan is a bitch fi true
is whe wi a goh dhu bout it?

(Johnson 2002: 41)

A more balanced recognition of what Britain can represent for its black minority can be sampled from Benjamin Zephaniah's work of the 1990s. He ends the preface to *Too Black, Too Strong* with the affirmation: "it is because I love the place that I fight for my rights here. If it were simply a case of hating the place and all that it stood for, then I would have left when I first got expelled from school" (Zephaniah 2001: 14). His work shows the fragile but genuine accommodation reached between missile and target, which we meet more frequently in the bland disguise known as multiculturalism. Another recent poem, "The Angry Black Poet," suggests that, after half a century in Britain, the tired typology of black frustration might afford some self-deprecatory laughter:

Next on stage
We have the angry black poet,
So angry
He won't allow himself to fall in luv,
So militant
You will want to see him again.
Don't get me wrong
He means it,
He means it so much
He is unable to feel,
He's so serious
If he is found smiling
He stops to get serious before he enters stage left . . .

(Zephaniah 1996: 29)

That is how the target and the missile hope, eventually, to become friends of sorts in contemporary London.

References

Dabydeen, D. (1984) *Slave Song*. Mundelstrup, Denmark: Dangaroo Press.
Dabydeen, D. (1988) *Coolie Odyssey*. Hertford: Hansib Publishing.
Dabydeen, D. (2000) "West Indian writers in Britain," in F. Dennis and N. Khan (eds) *Voices of the Crossing*. London: Serpent's Tail, pp. 59–76.
D'Aguiar, F. (1993) *British Subjects*. Tarset, Northumberland: Bloodaxe Books.
Figueroa, J. (ed.) (1982) *Caribbean Voices: Volume 1, Dreams and Visions*. London: Evans [first published 1966].
Johnson, A. (1985) *Long Road to Nowhere*. London: Virago Press.
Johnson, L. K. (2002) *Mi Revalueshanary Fren: Selected Poems*. London: Penguin Books.
Kay, J., Collins, M. and Nichols, G. (1996) *Penguin Modern Poets, Volume 8: Jackie Kay, Merle Collins, Grace Nichols*, London: Penguin.
Markham, E. A. (ed.) (1995) *Hinterland: Caribbean Poetry from the West Indies and Britain*. Newcastle-upon-Tyne: Bloodaxe Books [first published 1989].
Patke, R. (2006) *Postcolonial Poetry in English*, New York: Oxford University Press.
Proctor, J. (ed.) (2000) *Writing Black Britain 1948–1998*, Manchester: Manchester University Press.
Roach, E. M. (1992) *The Flowering Tree: Collected Poems 1938–1974*, Leeds: Peepal Tree.
Zephaniah, B. (1992) *City Psalms*. Tarset, Northumberland: Bloodaxe Books.
Zephaniah, B. (1996) *Propa Propaganda*. Newcastle-upon-Tyne: Bloodaxe Books.
Zephaniah, B. (2001) *Too Black, Too Strong*. Tarset, Northumberland: Bloodaxe Books.

14 Keizu to Nendaiki

Making and erasing history in Tsukuba Science City at the edge of empire[1]

Sharon Traweek

Finding Tsukuba: *mura to gakuen toshi*

I first visited Tsukuba in the summer of 1976; it was hard to find. The people at the main railroad station in Tokyo were not quite sure why a foreigner wanted to visit a small, old village (*mura*) near the top of a mountain with a modest Buddhist temple and Shinto shrines known, if at all, for a poem about the area written by Emperor Yozei (869–949):

Tsukuba ne no	From Tsukuba's peak,
Mine yori otsuru	Falling waters have become
Minano-gawa	Mina's still, full flow:
Koi zo tsumorite	So my love has grown to be;
Fuchi to nari nuru	Like the river's quiet deeps.[2]

After hearing this *waka* (thirty-one-syllable poem) many times from Tsukubans, finally I found Yozei's poem superimposed on an art photograph of Mt. Tsukuba, briskly sold as a postcard at the University of Tsukuba bookstore and at Seibu, the single upscale department store in Tsukuba Science City. A friend in Tokyo said he thought Tsukubans appreciated the poem's existence more than its content; that is, the mention of Mt. Tsukuba in the aristocratic form of a *waka* written by an emperor more than 1,000 years earlier reassured them: perhaps living and working in a government town placed in the economically depressed Ibaraki Prefecture, unfortunately located in the always inauspicious northern direction from Tokyo, was not as *déclassée* as they feared.

From Tokyo Station I was sent to Ueno, another train station in the "downtown" (Shitamachi) working-class section of Tokyo, and told to take a train north to Tsuchiura City in Ibaraki Prefecture. From there I was to change to a small branch line for Tsukuba-mura. In Tsuchiura, near Lake Kasumigaura where *kamikaze* pilots had been trained during WWII, a conductor looked at me, a tall, then auburn-haired woman who did not look the least bit Japanese, and asked what I was going to do in Tsukuba-mura; when I replied that I was looking for a physics laboratory he laughed and suggested I take a bus to the new Tsukuba town (*machi*).

"Tsukuba academic new town," as it was first called, was launched by an official national governmental initiative on September 10, 1963.[3] Within 3 years, over 70,000 acres (nearly 30,000 hectares) had been purchased, and the ground-breaking ceremony was held on November 6, 1969.[4] The first few students were admitted to the new University of Tsukuba in April 1974. Construction of the physics laboratory with the new high-energy accelerator began that year; the facility officially opened 2 years later, just before I arrived.

For over 30 years I have been studying how international collaborative research has been conducted in Europe, Japan, and the United States.[5] By now I have spent several years at that lab, the first built in what is now called Tsukuba Science City (*Tsukuba Kenkyu Gakuen Toshi*); the town now includes nearly fifty national research institutes and laboratories, four colleges and universities, two medical schools, six foundations for the advancement of research, and about fifty private research and development laboratories and institutes.[6] That number represents almost 30 percent of Japan's national research institutes.[7] As the area has grown into an important international research center, histories of the region have flourished.[8] Nonetheless, most professional historians would say that almost no history of Tsukuba has been written.

Basic research and patents

By the 1960s Japan was becoming rich enough to afford and want basic research based in Japan. Following the well-worn and widely known path of other successfully industrialized countries around the world, Japan's industrial sector had become so proficient that paying royalties on patented processes from other countries had become a significant expense. Eventually, "reverse engineering" had given them their own patents on improved manufacturing procedures.[9] Japan already had embarked on the third stage: generate the new applied knowledge locally in order to get patents so that companies in other countries must pay royalties to them. They knew, of course, that the following stage is to invest in basic research from which most applied knowledge is thought to flow. By the mid-1960s Japan began to plan for that stage.[10]

Instead of distributing the new research facilities throughout the existing national university system, it was decided to concentrate all the new facilities in one place. The site selected was in the middle of an economically depressed agricultural region. The project had been coupled with a 1962 decentralization agreement to relocate national governmental facilities outside Tokyo.[11] That agreement, in turn, was part of a plan to redistribute throughout the country the resources that had become concentrated in a narrow corridor along the Pacific Ocean between Tokyo and Osaka. (Even now, 50 years later, 10 percent of Japan's population is still concentrated in the Tokyo region.)[12] Eventually, governmental planners also thought that they could use basic research not only to increase the knowledge base for industry, but also to trigger economic development in rural areas and redistribute the population. The idea came from many sources: their own colonial practices in China, as well as the former Union of Soviet Socialist

Republics, the United States, and the United Kingdom. That is, part of Tsukuba's history can be found in the USSR, the United States, and the United Kingdom.

Science cities, science parks, and garden cities: a century of planning and administration

"Technopole" is the term now used to describe cities whose key industries are scientific and technological, often with close ties to military funding, although the cities themselves predate the industries, unlike science cities and parks.[13] Los Angeles, California, and Houston, Texas, are two examples.[14] Technopoles are established cities that have multiple knowledge industries based on science and technology with multiple links among them. By contrast, science cities and science parks are two names for related patterns of settlements around new scientific and engineering facilities. Science cities are usually developed in areas away from traditional urban, intellectual, and economic centers; they have facilities for research and community life. Science parks are clusters of laboratories, public and private, that might have a synergistic effect and stimulate neighboring, local economies. Garden cities are planned and developed in rural areas not far from traditional cities; they include extensive open, "green spaces" along with housing and sectors for business, cultural activities, and local activities. Three ways of developing these settlements emerged by the 1950s: national government planning, university initiative, and local/state government planning. In all three examples there had been significant population increases and economic development for the region, regardless of the country.

Los Alamos in the United States and Novosibersk in the former USSR are said to be the first science cities.[15] They were designed and built by national governments during wartime in what were thought of as isolated places for the purpose of designing weapons in secret. They included laboratories, fabrication facilities, offices, administrative buildings, housing, and some entertainment facilities. They survived both WWII and the Cold War, and they have continuously expanded. Settlements near Richland, Washington, and Oak Ridge, Tennessee, have similar histories, developed for producing plutonium for weapons at sites in then relatively undeveloped parts of the United States.[16]

In 1953 Stanford University opened an industrial park on its extensive campus lands in a primarily agricultural region near San Francisco, California, that also included many military-related industries.[17] Eventually, the park focused on "high technology" tenants.[18] Now called the Stanford Research Park, it is seen as an essential ingredient in the development of "Silicon Valley" as the region from Palo Alto to San Jose came to be called in the early 1970s.[19] A consortium of universities, private companies, and local and state governments established the Research Triangle Park (RTP) in North Carolina near Duke, the University of North Carolina, and North Carolina State University in 1959.[20] It developed slowly until 1965 when IBM and the National Institute for Environmental Health Science opened offices there; they were followed by more than 100 other groups and companies. Much later, a similar consortium developed an area in the far western suburbs of Boston, Massachusetts, for computer companies that came to be known by a highway through the region called "Route 128."[21]

Those seven earlier cases proved so successful that national, regional, and urban planners wanted to replicate them. "Green" science cities and parks can now be found in all rich and developing nations, including Japan.[22] In fact, a special law was passed in Japan to facilitate such development.[23] The International Association of Science Parks (IASP) had nearly fifty members by 1999, half of which were in Europe; the Association of University Related Research Parks (AURRP) had 410 members.[24]

By now there is a vast body of applied research in many languages on "science cities" and "science parks." Faculty teach many courses in university public policy programs and public administration programs internationally and train planners in how to implement that research in designing, funding, building, operating, and evaluating such cities and parks. Professional associations, research journals, and newsletters unite the worldwide practitioners and keep them informed of developments in the field.[25] The field's theories and methods at any given time are imbedded in the cities and parks worldwide that were designed then.

Tsukuba and its sister city of Irvine in southern California were conceived and constructed within a few years of each other. In 1963 the cabinet of the Japanese government decided "to build an academic new town in Tsukuba" and ground breaking took place in 1969. In 1959 the private Irvine Company decided to sell the University of California 1,500 acres for a new campus; a "master plan" for a city of 50,000 with industrial, residential, and recreational and commercial areas, as well as green belts, was designed by the university architects and the Irvine Company planners. The first facilities and infrastructure were completed in 1970. Tsukuba and Irvine became sister cities in 1989.[26] The two cities also show a remarkable physical resemblance to each other with broad boulevards providing the major arteries linking neighborhoods with curving streets; both have extensive parks and green belt areas.

Bringing scientists and engineers to a remote site does not always turn a depopulated, impoverished site into a nice place for middle-class people to live and work, nor does it always create many service jobs for displaced farmers and agricultural workers.[27] Urban historians and anthropologists have just begun to study science cities beyond the early stereotypic lamentations about the supposedly dreary institutional aesthetics and artificial economies of planned cities. Yet others have found a long history of what has come to be called "colonial" or "imperial" science.[28] These researchers have argued that national governments have transformed whole regions, such as the American west, into vast scientific or engineering research sites.[29] Such regions are usually far from centers of power and sparsely populated, or, at least, the number of powerful people who might successfully resist these developments is sparse.

Just as certain terrains are mapped by those in power as sites useful only for the extraction of raw materials, other sites are mapped as useful for the extraction of raw data, often to be processed elsewhere, at the metropolitan centers of knowledge-making and documentation. Many cultural historians, cultural geographers, and cultural anthropologists have limned these new cultural spaces.[30] Of course, many colonialists have planned and built administrative centers. The Japanese are no exception. Aaron Moore has argued that Japan's "comprehensive industrial and land planning (*kokudo keikaku*) helped shape Japan's total war mobilization system and later, post-war reconstruction and high-speed development."[31]

Generating documents: planning and managing science cities

Because most science cities, like Tsukuba, have been meticulously planned, budgeted, and managed by government agencies, it might seem that documentation for their histories is nicely assured. That is, the very act of planning and getting approval of those plans by bureaucrats who are often highly skilled and intelligent generates a stunning array of bureaucratic documentation, particularly in highly centralized countries such as Japan, France, and the former USSR. Some of those documents become available when they are produced; these would include the "eminent domain" laws enabling the purchase of the needed lands, the construction of facilities, and administrative policies.[32] Many are made public in order to announce new policies and laws that require public compliance; in Tsukuba these take the form of websites, newsletters, and inserts in the local newspapers.[33] Yet others are part of an effort to enroll public opinion in support of developing policies. For example, at one of the Tsukuba City websites there is now a document on the policies for the next stage of developing the science city.[34] These already published documents provide the source materials for many of the histories generated by local governmental agencies.[35]

When the government archives reveal the remaining documents to historians in the customary 30–100 years I have no doubt that we will find a vast quantity of information about the kinds of topics that interest governments, especially administration and legislation. Both the content and the structure of such documents, like all documents, can be studied for their cultural, political, economic, social, intellectual, etc. assumptions, motivations, and intentions. Reading a set of documents we can look for patterns in those practices. The patterns include the modes and categories of inquiry, as well as the forms of interpretation in use at the time they were generated. We will be able to study those structures and how they shaped the content. Such documents are already being used for studies of Los Alamos, Novosibersk, Richland, and Oak Ridge, during the 1940s and the Cold War.[36] They are not yet available for Tsukuba Science City.

However, the design and decision process itself may never have been documented. That is, there may be no trace of the myriad informal conversations (face-to-face meetings, emails, telephone calls) in which policies and designs were drafted. The few documents from such encounters (sketches, drafts, appointment books, log books, memos, electronic tapes) may have been discarded. Increasingly, historians are encouraging participants in such activities to archive such documents for the sake of future historical interest in their work. Of course, they might well want such documents kept confidential for some period of time.

Ethnographic historians can study the government documents that are distributed to citizens about both the past and the present and how the citizens respond. We can interview bureaucrats, politicians, and other community leaders. We can study the local practices of remembrance, such as festivals, celebrations, memorials, and ceremonies. We can notice what people work to preserve. We can listen and watch as people teach the next generation about the past. Each wave of newcomers generates another layer of "locals" who remember earlier times and like to tell their stories. Advocates and critics of current practices sometimes invoke histories of the origin and etiology of what they like or dislike. We can attend to discussions and debates about the future, as each plan for the future usually invokes a history as a supporting argument. (Fortunately for this ethnographer, the scientists in Tsukuba are very interested in the future, both in the near and long term, and they do invoke a past in support of their plans.) From these I can cull some patterns in how Tsukubans make histories and what they ignore. In turn those patterns display the themes that concern Tsukubans.

Ignoring the past

Ibaraki, the prefecture in which Tsukuba is located, is the traditional home of the Mito family, one of the three branches (*go-sanke*) of the Tokagawa dynasty that ruled Japan for 250 years before the civil war of the 1860s. (The Mitos were on the losing side in that civil war; resources for the management of the new prefecture of Ibaraki were less than what would have been found in friendlier domains.) Some historians have argued that two particular Mito lords (*daimyo*), Mitsukuni Tokugawa (1628–1700) and Nariaki Tokugawa (1800–60), provided exemplary models of governance and economic management, as well as advanced education, including mathematics and science, for the managerial samurai.[37] The *Kodokan* housed the samurai school; after the civil wars the school was closed, but in 1872 (Meiji 5) it was reopened as the first office building for the new prefectural government of Ibaraki. Its history is noted in some of the Mito City and Ibaraki tourist brochures, and the building is now open to the public.[38]

The *Kodokan* could have been invoked as an historical precedent for the advanced education now pursued in Tsukuba. I have asked this question in Tsukuba several times over the last two decades to various people involved with developing new kinds of educational institutions and programs in Tsukuba and beyond. Most had never heard of the school building or its role in the history of science education in Japan; of those who knew that such a school existed no one thought it worth invoking in current debates. The Mito *daimyo* loomed large in the Japanese public imagination during the late twentieth century, and I thought that connection might be useful for Tsukuba. There is an extremely popular weekly Japanese TV series called *Mito no Komon* that has been running since the 1970s; the show is only slightly younger than Tsukuba Science City.[39] It is based on the Mito *daimyo* Mitsukuni Tokugawa. He is represented in the television series as a kind, wise, modest, and very smart elderly man known as Mito-no-Komon-sama who travels around his domain *in cognito* with two strong retainers, alleviating poverty and fighting injustices, usually perpetrated by incompetent or corrupt government officials. *Mito no Komon* is an allegory about a wise man challenging bad government on behalf of a weak people. When I came to understand the extremely powerful and ongoing role in Tsukuba of bureaucrats from the central government, I began to grasp why invoking the important Mito history in education might not be a useful strategy for scientists in Tsukuba to strengthen their position with the government.

I had another interest in Mitsukuni Tokugawa: in 1657 he began to compile what eventually became the 397-volume *Dainihonshi* (*History of Great Japan*), generally regarded as one of Japan's most important official histories.[40] That compilation came to be invoked as a foundation for national identity. I was intrigued that a study made at the northern margins of Tokugawa power and at the northern margins of the Kanto plain could have become so significant in a society that eventually came to disparage those margins in particular. I was also interested in how Mitsukuni had amassed the documentary sources for his compilation in the marginal site. I wondered what people in Ibaraki thought of that history today.

In his retirement Mitsukuni Tokugawa had moved to a modest house he called Seizan-so, near Hitachi Ota, a village about 15 kilometers north of Mito City, the capital of Ibaraki Prefecture. From 1691 until his death 10 years later he worked there on the *Dainihonshi;* Seizan-so is now a tourist attraction.[41] The Tokugawa Museum in Mito City also has some displays on Mitsukuni Tokugawa, as does the Ibaraki Prefectural History Museum, also in Mito; both contain documents on the *Dainihonshi* as well.[42] Each is mentioned in many tourist brochures, but during various visits there during the 1980s and 1990s I have not seen many tourists, although I have seen school children visiting the displays of material culture at the prefectural museum.[43]

Most of the *Dainihonshi* materials are now located at the National Archives of Japan.[44] The Tsukuba Annex with its state-of-the-art storage facilities is at the northern border of KEK, the High Energy Accelerator Research Organization; I had heard often of the negotiations involved when that part of KEK land had been taken for the National Archives storage facilities. Physicists told me that they could not refuse, especially since the National Archives were part of the Prime Minister's Office. They knew they might need good working relationships with that office if they were to get funding for the new, "global" laboratory they wanted. (It is extremely difficult for me to imagine that a major scientific laboratory in the United States would find it prudent to abdicate land to a national archive facility.)

Since 2002 I have been working with some physicists to establish an archive at KEK for documents concerning the development of the laboratory. We have visited the neighboring National Archives to learn about their facilities and procedures, as well as to see their limited exhibition areas devoted to the history of the area. The physicists were curious about the old documents, but did not see a connection between those historical documents and the kinds they wanted to collect, nor did they want to reproduce the archiving practices used at this national facility.

Now that we have established the KEK archive, we hope it will eventually serve as an archive for much Japanese research in particle physics, as well as for the various international research collaborations based in Japan. The eminent retired physicist leading the KEK archives project has been working on labeling and classifying a large collection of photographs of old equipment, no longer in use, but quite important in the early work of the laboratory. He often comments on the determination required for this particular project, but he has resolved to complete the task. I have mentioned that perhaps we should name his office Seizan-so; I also suggested that we invoke the *Dainihonshi* in the funding proposals we are now writing by calling the project *Daikagakushi* (*History of Big Science*). My colleagues clearly found this suggestion odd, but amusing. They are much more interested in seeing the KEK archive as a part of the international history of science than as part of the national history of Japan.

Forgetting the founders

One Japanese physicist told me that the idea of Tsukuba began with the University of California at San Diego.[45] He said that he was very impressed with how scientists in the United States had imagined the best sort of university for educating scientists and then just got it built.[46] The Japanese physicist said that in the 1960s he had become intrigued by the American higher education system and particularly the liberal arts colleges where so many of his American scientist friends had been undergraduates. Eventually, he traveled by car across the United States, visiting many of those schools. He said he was especially impressed that students on those campuses had, simultaneously, active intellectual lives, active social lives, and even active athletic lives, all centered on the college as a community; it seemed so very healthy to him. The fact that students did not chose a specific area of study before enrolling in college, but took a general course of study and majored only in the last 2 years, impressed him. He noticed too that the physics professors at those American schools were not isolated within their departments, and that they tended to have many interdisciplinary discussions. It became his dream to build a school in Japan like the ones he saw at UCSD and on his trip.[47] Eventually, he became the vice-president of the new University of Tsukuba.

I asked this senior physicist how he managed to build his dream school in Tsukuba. We had been talking in the lobby of a Tokyo hotel and he had been so expressive and even cheerful up to this point in our conversation; I was surprised that he suddenly became taciturn and withdrawn. I felt that inadvertently I must have deeply offended him. Since 1976 I have heard many stories in Japan about this man. Several physicists in Tsukuba told me they believe that only a person with a very forceful personality could have built Tsukuba and its laboratories; they acknowledge that having a forceful personality in Japan and being willing to use it to accomplish self-defined goals certainly leaves that person open to scrutiny, gossip, isolation, and perhaps hostility. (Some disliked his conservative domestic politics and his putative religious views.) Most physicists seem to think that the largeness of vision and creativity of this man easily compensated for any errors in his judgment, while pointing out that many Japanese feel much less sympathetic to such people than Americans would.

In various public materials introducing the University of Tsukuba I expected
to find some reference to this man who had worked so hard to establish Tsukuba
Science City and the University of Tsukuba, but I have found none. Recently, a
senior physicist explained that he had heard from an official at the University of
Tsukuba that this founding figure had established a regulation at the university:
there would be no memorial rooms for any individuals, although that is a customary remembrance practice in Japan.

In all the histories and chronicles of Tsukuba Science City and its laboratories
that I have collected, none of the official ones mention individuals, other than listing mayors, governors, and directors. Even those are not easy to find. Certainly,
various laboratories and research institutes could invoke the names of inventors,
engineers, and scientists who made discoveries and inventions while living in
the area. Two important examples are Takao Doi, the astronaut once based at the
National Space Development Agency (Uchu-kaihatsu Jigyodan) in Tsukuba, and
Hideki Shirakawa, professor at the University of Tsukuba, who won the Nobel
Prize in Chemistry in 2000 for research on conductive polymers.[48] However, no
reference to these people can be found in their home universities' websites or any
other brochures introducing their laboratories and universities. In fact, it is quite
difficult to find any public information about the faculty and research staff at the
various laboratories and universities.

This is in sharp contrast to similar brochures and websites for laboratories
and universities in other parts of the world where individuals who have carried
out significant work are figured prominently and where the regular faculty and
researchers usually are required to have web pages that give considerable information about their education, funding, and publications. University buildings and
campus roads are named for individuals who have made important contributions
to the campus. For our nascent KEK archives I have mentioned that it is important
for us to at least collect data on all scientists who have worked at KEK, either as
staff members or as visiting researchers. My Japanese physicist colleagues have
expressed considerable surprise at this idea, saying that in Japan such individual
work histories (curriculum vitae) are considered very personal. They agreed that
the Ministry of Education, Culture, Sports, Science and Technology that manages
the laboratory would have this information, but they assumed that such records
were destroyed when the person stopped working at the laboratory or retired. I
have suggested that we set up a restricted, confidential file with no access for a
few decades, and then ask the laboratory's scientists to voluntarily provide this
sort of information; I added that such data would be available at every other
archive at laboratories for high energy physics. I also mentioned that for our
funding proposals to U.S. government agencies I would need such information
from each of them. All these comments have led to much discussion and visible
consternation; I received the same response asking about this issue from scientists
in various laboratories and universities around Tsukuba and Japan.

Later I showed my archive colleagues how I had been collecting data on who
worked on which projects at KEK and how that fluctuated. I collect the lab's
telephone books; they include several modes of cross-referencing people, offices,

and telephone numbers, including maps of offices with the names of the occupants and the phone/fax numbers associated with that room. My colleagues were surprised that so much could be learned from a collection of phone books. I suggested that the archives get a complete set of the books; they then learned that the books have not been saved, either by the lab's library, or by the government bureaucrats who manage the lab.

Often I have asked why so few prominent individuals' names are invoked at Japanese universities and laboratories; one physicist said that the government bureaucrats think they are the ones who have made those organizations strong, not the faculty. Informally, scientists do sometimes use the name of a person to refer to a certain institute or laboratory. I was surprised to learn, for example, that what I had always heard of as the Yukawa Institute for Theoretical Physics (after Hideki Yukawa, the 1949 Nobel Prize-winning theoretical physicist) in fact has a different, official name, even though the name I had heard is now used on its website.[49]

Missing technicians

At Japanese government laboratories it is difficult to find machine shops and other kinds of workrooms for building and modifying research equipment. The Japanese government agencies that sponsor research laboratories rarely allocate budgets for such staff positions, space, or equipment. Instead, scientists and engineers collaborate with engineers at private companies to supply all their equipment needs. This arrangement might be adequate in fields using standardized research equipment that can be purchased from catalogues; however, in many other fields the design of a first-rate experiment requires developing new research equipment, new kinds of software, and new computing hardware. In those fields it is customary for the scientists and engineers to design and develop prototypes in their own laboratories. Private companies then manufacture more of the items to the scientists' specifications.[50]

Japanese high energy physicists in Tsukuba design their one-of-a-kind research equipment and commission its construction from private industry. Consequently, over nearly three decades those researchers have developed very strong, long-term working relationships with the engineers at the companies they choose to supply their laboratories. The companies have been selected because they have been willing to have their employees participate in this process with researchers at the government-sponsored laboratories. For the companies these activities represent a "research and development" (R&D) project; after they acquire knowledge about how to develop and manufacture an esoteric product, they then use their new knowledge to develop new products. Several of these companies are based in Ibaraki Prefecture.

The only material trace of this complex process is in the laboratory procurement records, the company work orders, and the equipment itself. Future historians of the knowledge made in Tsukuba will have no way to understand the processes used to design materials for making that knowledge. I have recommended that

KEK's retired scientists at one laboratory hold "reunions" of their research teams along with their colleagues from their supplying companies. We could then tape their conversations about their past projects and deposit these oral histories in the laboratory archive. We could also ask those companies to contribute their documents on older programs to the new KEK archives.

Keizu to Nendaiki: genealogies of organizations and chronicles of machines

One pattern of remembrance quite popular in Tsukuba is genealogy (*keizu*); some of the local governmental brochures give a history of Tsukuba Science City that reads like a biblical list of "begats." However, these genealogies are not for people, but for organizations. The Tokugawa Shogunate, Japan's first centralized nation-state, in the early seventeenth century combined six small domains into two: the Mito and Kasama *han* (domains). Following Japan's civil war of the 1860s the new national government began a policy of erasing the borders of former fiefdoms, especially those that had been on the opposing side in the civil war, as had the Mito *han*. On July 14, 1871 the Mito and Kasama *han* were abolished and sixteen prefectures established; 4 months later those sixteen were combined into three prefectures, Ibaraki, Niihari, and Inba. In 1875 those were united into the new Ibaraki Prefecture.

Since the early seventeenth century the national government demarcates the boundaries of local governmental districts, such as villages, towns, cities, counties, and prefectures. Policies of rewarding smaller groups for aggregating into larger units have been revived periodically in the 1880s, 1930s, 1950s, and 1980s, as well as the current decade.. Several current brochures for Tsukuba Science City show inverted genealogy charts marking the merger of twenty villages and towns in the Tsukuba area over four generations or stages since 1953. In the penultimate generation there were eight villages and towns that gradually were folded into Tsukuba Academic New Town and Tsukuba Science City; they merged in 1988.[51] Some of the five colleges and universities in Tsukuba are about to merge. Consequently, over time maps of the area routinely show differing boundaries and names for the same areas as this process of mandated convergence continues apace and the old names are erased. Usually new towns and new schools are represented as the result of a merger of existing towns and schools, as is the case for Tsukuba Science City and the University of Tsukuba, officially represented as the merger and relocation of the campuses of the Tokyo Kyoiku Daigaku (Tokyo Metropolitan University of Education) in 1973.

These lists of mergers and erasures are not unlike the family registers (*koseki*) kept in local government offices throughout Japan. Women are added to their new husbands' family register (*seki o ireru*) at marriage and deleted from their parents'. (With divorce the process would be reversed.) Traditionally, new registers (*bunseki*) are initiated when younger sons are allowed to establish a cadet branch of the family elsewhere; more recently, some nuclear families have set up their own *koseki* for other reasons. Nonetheless, some families never separate from the paternal register, even if their residence has been separated for many decades. Formal records on Japanese people are kept only as part of a family register, not under an individual's name.[52] A genealogy is of a family, not an individual. Japan and South Korea are the only countries in the world that use such a family registration system for its citizens. Japan's dates from the early Meiji period (1870s); Korea's was imposed by Japan during its colonial rule.

The extrapolation of that household form to Tsukuba City is not surprising if the government regards cities as an aggregate of households. Indeed, populations of Japanese villages, towns, and cities are routinely given in numbers of households, as well as numbers of men and women: there were 63,455 households in Tsukuba as of July 1, 2001 according to its Japanese language newsletter.[53] The English language newsletter does not include these numbers; it does provide the total population and lists the number of foreign residents by the top twenty nationalities.[54]

Another pattern found in many Tsukuba Science City publications, as well as those of many national laboratories, is the chronology (*nendaiki*) of machines.[55] One list foregrounds the first local instances of transportation and communication devices: public clock 1822, the Tsuchiura to Mitsukaido highway 1890, taxi 1911, bus 1913, electricity 1918, railway 1918, telephone 1923, cable car 1925, radio broadcasting 1925, Yatabe airfield 1932, West Tsukuba airfield 1940, expressway 1985, closing of Tsukuba railway 1987, express bus to Tokyo 1988, express bus between Mt. Tsukuba and Tokyo 1991, heliport 1991, first homepage in Japan at KEK 1992, cargo terminal 1992, express bus to Narita airport 1994, Tsukuba Science City homepage 1997, etc.[56]

At KEK, a similar chronological list is called a history of the laboratory. A page at the laboratory website lists the dates at which various accelerators and detecting devices became available for physics research.[57] A similar list appears each year in KEK's annual report.[58] Within those annual reports there are several graphs labeled "histories," where time is plotted on one axis and many different variables are on the other axis, such as "operation hours," "average intensity of the 12 GeV Proton Synchrotron," and "average intensity of the Booster."[59] Another laboratory document called a history lists the dates at which an accelerator reaches higher energies and greater precision in focusing. The Science Museum of Map and Survey at the Geographical Survey Institute (Kokudo Chiri-in) includes many lists of devices itemizing the dates that they were first used in Japan.[60]

Another interesting pattern among histories in Tsukuba Science City is that they keeping getting older, much more so than the mere accumulation of time. As the city grows in population and incorporates more land, the origin of Tsukuba is getting earlier and earlier; the shadow of the present gets longer and longer. Current city brochures are now pointing out that people began living in the area "circa 20,000 to 10,000 BC" and paddy rice farming started "circa AD 100 to 400." Various historical sites in the area are now being claimed by Tsukuba Science City: the site of the local Oda Castle, designated a "national cultural asset" in 1935, the Otsuka residence that gained the same designation in 1976, and the remnants of the Hirasawa Public Office (1980) are all mentioned in the same 1999 brochure.[61] Various contemporary studies of communities' efforts to get listed in the U.S. National Register of Historic Places have noted the same phenomenon.[62] That is, for various kinds of strategic reasons community leaders will begin to invoke different elements of an area's history, especially when competing with other communities for scarce resources, such as relocating businesses, retirees, tourists, or film-makers use of the area as a film site. In the mid-1980s Tsukuba Science City finally had a competitor: the new Keihanna Science City in Kansai, located in the triangle between Osaka, Kyoto, and Nara, which was established in June 1986. From the beginning the leaders of Keihanna invoked Tsukuba as a failed, culturally arid site because of its lack of any important cultural history in its local area. Recently, I counted forty-nine references to "culture" on the Keihanna website.[63]

Furosato Monogsatari: hometown tales

The last few years there has been an effort to define Tsukuba as a "hometown" (*furosato*). It has begun to hold an annual festival (*matsuri*) characteristic of established neighborhoods and villages; for the first time it held a traditional memorial ceremony to honor the area's war dead. In November 1997, on the tenth anniversary of the shift in Tsukuba's designation from town to city, a logo, flower, bird, and tree were selected, along with street nicknames and thirty scenic sites. During the last few decades the national government has had a policy of offering funds to depopulated rural areas for developing tourist sites; many have also designated flowers, birds, and trees as emblems.[64] All this has created a flurry of advertisements for travel to Japan's "hometowns." Tsukuba Science City chose to announce these "hometown" emblems on the same day that it announced the opening of the city's new website.

In a recent policy statement on the future of Tsukuba Science City the government announced that "Tsukuba should pass down traditional festivals and folk entertainment from generation to generation, and promote cultural exchanges with foreign residents."[65] Tsukuba Science City has begun to celebrate its own summer festival each year, as villages, towns, and urban neighborhoods have done for centuries. At a certain point in its development the focus of government planners shifted away from relocating educational and research facilities to Tsukuba from Tokyo into a sort of "science park"; the emphasis changed to building a "science city" with all the resources needed for community life. It was not to be dependent any longer on its neighbors, such as Tsuchiura City and Mito City, for crucial transportation links or branches of national government offices.[66] With that shift came a need for a past, a past to pass to the next generation. History-making became part of the policy-making.

Over the last few years many examples have emerged of commercialized nostalgia for the peasant life that once filled the area now called Tsukuba Science City.[67] There is a huge wooden farmhouse near the top of Mt. Tsukuba that has been turned into a restaurant serving the peasant food that has become so fashionable in the big Japanese cities among the urbane, internationally minded young people. Not far from Tsukuba Center there is a traditional rustic Japanese teahouse serving peasant foods, run by Japanese artists, refugees from Tokyo. Tsukuba's internationalization and urbanization has generated the conventions of nostalgia for simplicity found all over the rich industrialized world.[68]

Meanwhile, some of the villages and towns that were melded into the new administrative unit of Tsukuba Science City, as required by the national government, have found ways to maintain and redefine their distinctiveness. All the traditional summer festivals are still held in the old neighborhoods and villages; the established shrines and temples still hold their traditional festivals. What is new is the widespread advertising, often attracting many tourists, some of them foreign. A few of these festivals are even listed on the internet web pages of the government's national tourist organization.[69] Of course, all over the world tourism has become a huge business and the marketing of traditional cultural sites and events has become crucial to attracting that business.[70]

The year after they lost their own municipal government because it was melded into Tsukuba City, the town of Oho (Oho-machi) where KEK is located published its own history.[71] The large committee that wrote the elegantly bound 447-page history included four people from the University of Tsukuba: a geologist and three people from the Department of History and Anthropology.[72] The book covers the history of the earth at Oho and the full history of human settlement at Oho, including the archeological artefacts that have been found in the area though excavations of the local ancient burial mounds. The area's various religious sites are mapped and their histories traced, along with their many engraved stone markers. In addition, the book includes extensive political, economic, demographic, educational, and social histories of Oho, as well as the distinctive products for which Oho has been known throughout the Kanto region, including its special brooms for the 10-centimeter-thick brocade-bound *tatami* rush floor mats used in traditional Japanese rooms. It also incorporates a brief history of the establishment and accomplishments of KEK.

Missing persons

None of the official Tsukuba Science City's lists, genealogical charts, and emblems of *furosato* have mentioned the local people who lived in the area before the national government decided to "develop" it. They have not introduced us to the people who felt forcibly relocated to Tsukuba when their research institutes and universities and company laboratories were moved there as part of the price of expansion and funding increases. In these charts and lists and emblems we have not found the people who chose not to relocate to Tsukuba, who stayed in the universities and companies that were denied new resources at the old sites.

We have not encountered the people who learned about the government plan to buy 4,000 hectares of their land in 1963; the first contracts were signed with the Japan Housing Corporation on December 28, 1966.[73] [Eventually, 28,401 hectares (over 70,000 acres) was sold.] Shortly before the national government announced its plans for Tsukuba City in 1963 a group of developers bought land in the Oho Town area, ostensibly to build a golf course and country club. By the time land was being purchased for laboratories, the course was not yet finished; the National Laboratory for High Energy Physics was built on that site. The *Oho Cho Shi* (*Oho Town History*) published by the town merely states that there was no opposition among the town's citizens to the purchase of the golf course for the laboratory.[74] The history adds that the several cities that later were merged into Tsukuba Science City banded together to negotiate collectively with the Nihon Jutaku Kodan (National Land Trust) to that end.[75] We do not learn about that negotiation process.

We have not found the locals who stayed and adapted to the waves of scientists and engineers and their families from all over Japan and even the world. In total, 167,338 people lived in Tsukuba as of July 1, 2001; new policies project that the future population will be 350,000. We know that less than 4 percent (6,329) were registered as foreigners (and that included me). Nearly 75 percent of those foreigners were from other Asian countries, and 8 percent (520) were from countries around the world that are conventionally labeled "western; the remaining 18% of the foreigners came from over 100 countries."[76]

We do not know how many families currently living in Tsukuba have been here for more than a generation, although we do know that in 1970 the population was 71,649, including 15,999 households.[77] All the chronologies and emblems ignore them. I have begun a project to interview many people who have lived in this area for generations. One part of the project is to study the history of land title transfers and to study land use in those 28,401 hectares that are not occupied by research institutes, universities, and public offices. Another is to study the women who work as secretaries, clerks, and cleaning staff at the various research institutes.

The past few months I have been organizing an academic workshop with three colleagues, two from Japan.[78] We received funding from UCLA, my university, and the Japanese Society for the Promotion of Science (JSPS). In discussing the program for the two-day workshop with the deputy director of the JSPS San Francisco office we all were shocked when told about a regulation that JSPS must be listed at the organizer of the workshop and that our names could not be listed. When we protested that in fact we four were the organizers, not JSPS, we were told that we would forfeit our workshop funding if we insisted on listing our names. I was in the midst of revising this paper on erasure when I found my own name and those of my colleagues were being erased from a project we had conceived and brought into being. Then I remembered the name of the Yukawa Institute surviving on the website of the officially named Research Institute for Fundamental Physics, and found a strategy for keeping our names on our project.

Figure/ground

Maps of the Tsukuba area published over the last 30 years show two distinctive patterns of settlement.[79] The streets in the areas developed by the national government generally follow a grid plan of rectangles with a few diagonal lines; the streets in the other areas are mostly curvilinear. The two patterns are contiguous.

The maps published by Toshi Kaihatsu Kodan (Housing and Urban Development Corporation), the government agency that plans Tsukuba, show the new Tsukuba Science City districts, streets, and buildings in vivid colors (such as sun yellow, sky blue, lime green, emerald green, lavender, and bright pink); the older streets are delineated in pale grey.[80]

None of the local villages and towns is located in a first rough sketch of the new city, although two nearby cities are mentioned (Ushiku and Tsuchiura), as are two lakes (Kasumigaura and Ushikunuma), two highways (6 and 125), and Mt. Tsukuba. The text accompanying the sketch states that: "The development of the Science City focused on the flatland forests and, out of consideration for the local farms and people's daily lives, existing villages and farmlands were avoided as much as possible."[81] Yasuhiro Naruse, Director of Urban Designer Atelier, wrote:

> I think that the city [was] intend[ed] to be a completely "different world" . . . hardly concerned about the geological features and harmony with the nearby garden scenery. That is to say, Tsukuba is a city [like] the architecture of *"Rokumeikan"* in the period when Japan [was] open[ed] to foreign trade and diplomatic relations. . . . the city looks like . . . the government feel[s] sorry [for] construct[ing a] science city apart from [the] Tokyo metropolitan area.[82]

Rokumeikan was constructed in the Hibiya district of Tokyo in 1881 as directed by Kaoru Inoue, the foreign minister, and designed by Josiah Condor, a British architect and *oyatoi* (foreign teacher/expert) who taught Japan's first generation of architects who designed buildings using European styles.[83] *"Rokumeikan"* means "House of the Cry of the Stag," a literary reference to a Chinese classic, which, as any learned Japanese would have known, referred to "a place of convivial gatherings."[84] It included a ballroom, a reading room, a billiards room, and a music room; its purpose was to provide a place for "westerners" and Japanese to socialize in "western" dress and "western" style.[85] By linking Tsukuba with the *Rokumeikan*, Naruse is claiming derisively that Tsukuba is a foreign forum in which Japanese try to act like foreigners.

Arata Isozaki, the Pritzker Prize-winning and internationally prominent Japanese architect of Tsukuba Center, had a related but more complex interpretation of Tsukuba and defended his deliberately dislocated and ironic re-rendering of the *Capitoline piazza* in his designs for Tsukuba.[86] He noted that while Tsukuba City Center was being built it did not exist, administratively speaking; the center was sited within the boundaries of Sakura village. Isozaki argued that "if I were to say that Tsukuba Center Building is the expression of the absence of something, I would not be taken seriously. Yet actually, the central concept of the design is that very absence."[87]

Naruse implied condescendingly that the impulse to build *Rokumeikan* and the desire to participate in the Victorian entertainments within it generated pale imitations of a culture based elsewhere. By contrast, the architectural historian Carter Horsely argues that "Japan's architects have dominated the architectural world since the mid-1960s and . . . its 'team' of great architects would easily better those of the rest of the world," claiming that "Japan's incredible design creativity . . . has been pre-eminent in the world for more than a third of a century."[88] I would respond to Naruse by saying that Japanese architects have taken an international genre and inflected it with a vernacular Japanese sensibility. Their international prominence suggests that they have moved the center of the international architectural world to Japan.

Entrepreneurs from the edge

One man who was born in Ibaraki developed a new business around the visiting foreigners and their desire for automobiles: he rents us cars.[89] Now in his sixties, he shifted from repairing farm equipment and farmers' cars to renting to foreigners some older, dented cars most Japanese would not use. Registering, insuring, and getting the regular official auto inspections are both complex and very expensive. Only recently have many foreigners begun to do this for themselves. Some of them have purchased the cars they once rented and continue to get their cars serviced and get advice about the bureaucratic procedures from the same man. Tsukuba now has the highest automobile-to-resident ratio in Japan and the highest automobile accident rate. The man who once rented just to foreigners now sells, leases, and repairs cars with his son.

He has built a very large, new, traditional-style house for his extended, multi-generational family next to his old house and the garage; it is lovely with a great deal of fine woodwork. He has also acquired a new hobby: flying small planes with his old friends, one of whom has a nearby sushi shop, decorated with a large propeller. Most of the foreigners at KEK have visited this man, his family, and his friends, some on many occasions, and he visits them; I have met only one Japanese physicist at the lab who knew him.

Some years ago I found a notice on a lab bulletin board of a tutor specializing in teaching foreigners Japanese, mentioning that the tutor had received a degree at an institute in London for teaching Japanese as a second language. I called and made arrangements for studying with the tutor. Over the next several months I learned that she and her family had been in the Tsukuba area for generations. She was a child when Tsukuba Science City was under construction; as a high school student she and her family realized that she could earn a good living providing language lessons to the foreigners coming into Tsukuba. They decided she would need some kind of certification to attract students and they located the program in London where she then studied for a few years.

The International Institute for Management Development, located in Switzerland, issues world competitiveness rankings: "of the 47 nations covered, Japan lags behind all of them in 'entrepreneurship' and 'creation of firms.'"[90] The two people I have described etch an entrepreneurial history of Tsukuba, traced among all the service businesses that have emerged here in this knowledge-making city. They need to be interlaced with the stories of those who come to Tsukuba from around the world and from the rest of Japan.

KEK might well qualify as entrepreneurial. About 35 years ago a group of Japanese high energy physicists, some of them in diaspora, decided to get funding from their government, build world-class research equipment in Japan, carry out first-rate experiments there, and become active participants in deciding the next generation of research goals for the field internationally. Almost none of their colleagues outside Japan thought that they would be able to do this, even if they could get the funding. No other country's scientists had moved from the periphery of a field to the center since those from the United States and the former USSR had done so during World War II, benefiting from massive wartime budgets and migrations of eminent scientists from Central Europe.

There was no guidebook, and there were no professional planners to help them. However, those Japanese scientists accomplished all their goals within 25 years. In the process they reversed the "brain drain" from Japan in their field and modified Japanese graduate education in the sciences, Japanese basic research funding procedures, Japanese research institute organization and administration, and the Japanese infrastructure for basic research, as well as the Japanese hiring and promotion procedures for researchers. Along that path they also revised the international standards and strategies for accelerator design and the organization of their international field, along with winning two Nobel prizes. That is another story, one apparently missed by that world competitiveness ranking in entrepreneurship.

An imagined lab requires a past

High energy physicists around the world have reached a consensus that they need a device that they call a global linear collider (GLC) in order to pursue and answer the new questions in their field; the machine will cost several billion dollars. They know that no one government will build such an expensive machine. In some sciences the research facilities have been so expensive and complex over the last 50 years that each country could afford to build only one. In my field we call those fields "big sciences"; they include astrophysics, plasma physics, particle physics, and physical oceanography. Whether the facility is an observatory, an accelerator, or a ship, all the scientists in a big science need to come together in one place to use the special device.[91] Examples include the KEK laboratory in Tsukuba and the Super Kamiokande laboratory in Gunma-ken.

The successors to those research devices are now being designed; they will be so expensive and complex that no one country can afford the money and human resources to build them. National governments and scientists are beginning to call these facilities "global laboratories." Existing labs are controlled by one nation or one region, but they welcome scientists from many countries. However, these new labs must be a joint project of at least several regions of the world; these labs will not be controlled by any one country or any one region. The Japanese high energy physicists at KEK want that lab built in Japan.

Although scientists from around the world have been working together at the national labs for the last 50 years, they realize that a genuinely global lab will require a different kind of organization to facilitate the work of scientists there, something like a "united nations" lab. At least five international committees of particle physicists are working now on the organizational design for such a laboratory in their field of high energy physics.[92] Most of the existing major national and regional labs are in Japan, Europe, and North America. How can those national models be adapted for global laboratories? The Japanese physicists have to convince their international colleagues that a lab built in Japan can accommodate a global project. Part of that argument, they realize, will be based on their history over the last 35 years of transforming their Japanese accelerator lab into one that welcomes foreign participation. To that end KEK's director general and the laboratory executive council authorized the development of an historical archive of KEK's development and its international relations. Documenting that past is one strategy for building the future they want.

Tohoku haiku to Tono Monogatari

If it is built, that new global scientific laboratory will be built in some very specific local site, of course. Many potential sites for the GLC are now being investigated in at least three different countries: Germany, Japan, and the United States. Aside from the necessary space and the required geological features, what would be the right kind of place for one to two thousand scientists and engineers from around the world to work and live with their partners and their children? Because so much land would be needed, it is most likely that those world labs will be built somewhere that is now rural. No matter where this world lab might be built, if it is built, it will be in or near someone's hometown.

Who would want a global laboratory nearby? Probably some economically depressed area with serious depopulation problems would be eager to host the GLC. A few years ago one such prefecture in the Tohoku region of northern Japan that might well be interested in hosting this global lab asked me to visit and speak with them about the characteristics of the people who would come to such a lab and what kind of settlement they would build. I think it will be more like a global village than another science city like Tsukuba. No one knows yet how to design a global village; nonetheless, some things are obvious: it will become a hometown with a past and a future. Children and other newcomers will soon be told stories about what makes the place special.

One potential site in Tohoku, part of the Kitakami River Basin Technopolis Project, is one of the areas designated under the Technopolis Law of 1983.[93] It is located near Hiraizumi City, a capital of northern Japan during the twelfth and thirteenth centuries whose wealth was drawn from gold mining in the region. The very impressive historical temples of Motsuji and Chuzonji are now major tourist sites with brochures printed in Chinese, English, and Korean, as well as Japanese.[94] Basho, an influential seventeenth-century poet from Iga-Ueno, near the ancient capital of Nara in western Japan, traveled throughout northern Japan dressed as a pilgrim. When he toured the elegant, then bucolic Hiraizumi in 1689 he composed a *haiku* in which Yoshitsune, a famous Minamoto warrior, had been killed 500 years earlier by his half-brother, Yoritomo:

Natsu kusa ya   A thicket of summer grass
Tsuwamono domo ga   Is all that remains
Yume no ato   Of the dreams and ambitions
          Of ancient warriors."[95]

I would add that a thicket of summer grass is all that can be seen, as yet, of the dreams and ambitions of the world's particle physicists.

The site is also near an interesting old village called Tono. A folklorist named Kunio Yanagida visited Tono nearly 100 years ago, compiled stories told about the place by Kizen Sasaki, and published them.[96] The book was read by generations of Japanese school children. In the public imagination Tono has come to represent the old Japan and Tono became Japan's hometown. Now it is a successful tourist site with an open air museum of village life, an anthropological museum of traditional Tono, and assorted restaurants and shops. Something similar has happened to Yanagida's birthplace. Yanagida was born in Hyogo Prefecture in 1875. The house where he and his well-known brothers were born has been renovated and turned into a museum; it is in West Harima, now part of Harima Science Garden City, another planned city developing around another "big science" physics laboratory called "Spring 8."[97]

Takayuki Tetsumi has argued that Yanagida was not generating yet another piece of nostalgia during Japan's rapid industrialization: "Yanagida attempted to radically question the modern western distinction between science and literature, . . . fact and fiction, and the actual from the imaginary."[98] In more ways than either Yanagida or Tetsumi could have imagined, Tono is again at the confluence of science and stories, the future and the past. The physicists from KEK are fully aware of the multiple cultural associations of Tono and Tohoku. After all, they read those books as school children. Many of the KEK physicists also spent their childhoods in small towns and villages. They like the idea of bringing the world's best science to Tono, of linking their future with their past.

Two mayors and two physicists

When I visited the historic temples in Hiraizumi I was escorted by prefectural officials, a KEK physicist, and a resident monk who discussed the history of the buildings and the sophisticated art within them. I also was able to meet the young mayor of the town. On the wall in his office was a very large artist's drawing of a big new industrial facility he had just lured to the town; I asked him about it and he spoke enthusiastically for at least fifteen minutes, describing the process of bringing it to his hometown and how it would help the local people. His open and optimistic language and posture would not be surprising in a young, successful American mayor. In fact, his manner was an almost exact match to that of the KEK physicist who hoped that the GLC would be built nearby. The two of them, shoulders rolled back with their elbows out and hands resting on the arms of their chairs, chatted quite amiably for about 30 minutes as the far more restrained bureaucratic officials in our party watched these convivial men discuss their hopes and plans.

The mayor of Hiraizumi and the KEK physicist reminded me of two men important in launching Tsukuba Kenkyu Gakuen Toshi. The late Kembei Fujisawa (1901–94), from a major land-owning family in the area, had been a leading proponent for the establishment of Tsukuba while he served as the mayor of Sakura-mura (1959–79). That village served as the administrative base for Tsukuba Academic Town before it was officially established; it is now a part of the Science City where there is a statue of him in Doho City Park. (His son, Masakazu Fujisawa, became the mayor in 1996.) The late Nobuyuki Fukuda was a physicist who had dreamed of a new kind of university in Japan.

Both wrote autobiographies, a rather unusual practice in Japan.[99] Fujisawa described in considerable detail a long trip he took in the summer of 1964, study-ing "new towns" and "garden cities" throughout Europe and the United States.[100] Accompanied by two people from the Ibaraki Prefectural government, they visited England, the Netherlands, France, Spain, Italy, Germany, and Sweden, before traveling to the United States. He also describes their trips to nightclubs, resorts, and Disneyland. Just as enthusiastically Professor Fukuda had told me of his peregrinations across the United States in the late 1960s to see the liberal arts colleges he wanted to emulate in Tsukuba. Neither of these men's names can be found in the historical chronologies so widely circulated in Tsukuba Kenkyu Gakuen Toshi.

Controlling territory and defining history

Since the publication of *The Invention of Tradition* (edited by Eric Hobsbawm and Terrence Ranger) and *The Invention of Culture* (by Roy Wagner) over 25 years ago many, many studies have emerged on how certain versions of history and definitions of culture have shaped and been shaped by specific powerful interest groups, usually national and colonial governments.[101] Often professional anthro-pologists and historians have colluded in this process, however unwittingly; many examples have been studied, most famously by Edward Said in his *Orientalism*.[102] Some have argued meticulously, if controversially, that the very interpretive strategies and the modes of inquiry in the professional disciplines of history and anthropology (among many others) themselves have been constrained, at a mini-mum, by the same processes.[103]

These three lines of argument have generated an enormous body of scholarship in many countries and in many fields of inquiry, including studies of Japan.[104] Interestingly, very few works in the history, philosophy, or sociology of science have explored how those fields themselves have been influenced by such forces.[105] Similarly, many prefer to confine their studies of science to the activities found only in labs, classrooms, and seminar rooms. Unlike many of my colleagues, I think that our studies of research practices must include the whole cultural, social, political, and economic environment in which the practitioners live and work. Fortunately, there is a growing body of research showing how laboratories are not citadels isolated from the rest of the world by a moat of "neutrality" crossed only by funding and commuting scientists and engineers. Many now argue that the sciences and the technologies generated in those laboratories and the worlds where the scientists and engineers live are mutually constituted.[106] That is worth studying.

Kaidan to Kanryou: ghost stories, bureaucracy, and power

Looking for Tsukuba's history I found that it is not in Ibaraki, or even in Japan, but in New Mexico, San Diego, Siberia, Italy, and the United Kingdom. Although the past of Tsukuba is distributed all over the world, the villages and towns that once occupied the local site are disappearing from Tsukuba's historical accounts. As they disappear, we find Tsukuba newly claiming the historical and archeological record of the whole area while neglecting much of its own recent history. Tsukuba's historical and contemporary links to its remaining neighbors are unexplored. Even Tsukuba's center was once elsewhere, in Sakura-mura. Its future appears to lie elsewhere, too, well to the north in Tohoku. The place is both powerful and displaced.

The founders cannot be found in the official histories of the city, the university, or the laboratories. Some of these have written memoirs, regaining a voice, but not a place. Many of the region's people are missing, having left the area three or four decades ago after selling their land. Many people stayed in Tsukuba, but their stories remain missing. As I have discussed this point with many scientists in Tsukuba, many tell me that it is culturally unacceptable to call attention to one's self in Japan. They add that for others to name some individual in an official institutional history would elicit much conflict within the institution about why that person is mentioned and not some other. They know that I am well aware of those two cultural practices; nonetheless, I counter that their conversations and their oral histories are chock full of stories about individuals and conflict, as are the many histories of Japan written by Japanese, as well as the accounts of contemporary events in newspapers and on television. The reluctance of the local historians to name even the former directors of their labs, the former university presidents, and the Nobel prize winners at the local university must have another source.

I have found many, many authoritative chronicles and genealogies. Reports from government agencies tell us about building machines, organizations, and a city. There are powerful genealogies of converging villages, towns, and cities. There are important chronicles listing the appearance of technologies past and present. Successions of designs, decisions, laws, plans, regulations, and maps show that a huge construction project has remade a vast site of 70,000 acres. Itemized lists of these projects are everywhere, but the only names on those lists are for cities, organizations, events, laws, offices, laboratories, and machines. A quick glance into the 1930s and 1940s shows that Ibaraki was then too the site of many large military projects, remaking the landscape into sites for the production of empire.

Looking for histories in Tsukuba I have found origin stories, ghost stories (*kaidan*), and heroic tales of building; much was missing. I found no historical narratives (*koudan*) that take all these presences and absences into account. What do these official stories and their silences do for the people of Tsukuba? Why is there no history that brings them together into the same story? Outside the official governmental histories there is lively storytelling, beginning with television tales about *Mito no Komon*, his travels, and his retreat at Seizanso. Another old building, the *Kokodan*, bears witness to another time when science and technology were powerful in Ibaraki Prefecture. Nobel prizes and awards from the emperor and others, as well as important arts, elegant crafts, and a stunning fireworks festival bring national and international renown to exceptional people. Why is it so difficult to find these stories in the official accounts of Tsukuba's history?

I would argue that all these missing names and stories are not merely marginal details of local, folkloric interest. Their very absence creates a large presence. Paraphrasing that comment by Arata Isozaki I quoted above, "the central concept of [these histories] is that very absence."[107] Deleting the names accomplishes something. Against these receding places and missing persons we can easily find the authoritative presence that writes the histories of Tsukuba in all those chronologies of projects, organizations, and machines. The author is the bureaucracy (*kanryou*) of the national government. After coming to this conclusion I began to search for the specific authors of those chronicles I have found in so many places. It has not been easy for me to find the simple answer. At KEK scientists had assured me that the KEK annual reports and the KEK website were written and composed entirely by scientists. Upon pressing them to help me locate the authors of the history pages, they began to concede that perhaps those history pages were written by the government bureaucrats administering KEK.

Kanryou: bureaucracy authorizing science

It is difficult for Americans to grasp the pervasive power in Japan of the centralized government bureaucracy; there is nothing comparable to it in the distributed and decentralized governmental agencies in the United States, no matter how concentrated they sometimes seem to us, even during wartime. For well over 100 years, at the very least, the bureaucracy in Japan has dominated the executive, judicial, and legislative branches of the government at every level, from the prime minister's office to the local town hall. For example, almost every piece of legislation debated in parliament is conceived and written by bureaucrats. Put differently, Japanese politicians rarely propose legislation; they merely debate and vote upon bills that begin within various government bureaucracies. The other players in the government intervene in the bureaucracy only occasionally; although their displays can be dramatic, they are rarely effective, sometimes to the vast relief of the populace. Many observers (Japanese and foreign) over most of the twentieth century have pointed out that the Japanese government is essentially government by technocrats and bureaucrats, independent of the political turn of the moment.

These bureaucrats can be stunningly effective, as only a highly centralized organization can be. Ever since the formation of a centralized nation-state in Japan during the seventeenth century the bureaucracy has only grown stronger through all the fluctuations in the form of government. We can find parallels only in the 400-year-old bureaucratic histories of three other equally centralized nation-states: China, France, and Russia.[108] Certainly, bureaucrats in those four countries usually are well educated, sometimes far better than the politicians. In some cases the politicians are retired bureaucrats who reinforce the power of the bureaucracies.

The ministry that oversees KEK and several other laboratories in Tsukuba is called Monbukagakusho (briefly, Monkasho) in Japanese and Ministry of Education, Culture, Sports, Science and Technology in English. It administers not only many national research laboratories, all national and public universities, and their affiliated research institutes, but also the equivalents of the National Science Foundation (NSF), Social Research Council (SSRC), National Endowment for the Humanities (NEH), and National Institutes of Health (NIH), as well as every public archive and museum, not to mention the entire K–12 educational system and all non-professional sports (including the 2000 Winter Olympics and the 2002 World Cup competition in soccer). Its day-to-day and long-term role in universities and research institutes far exceeds anything I have ever witnessed in Europe and North America, except in France and the former Soviet Union.

The entire administrative, clerical, financial, and facilities staff at universities and research institutes are directly supervised by the Monkasho senior people at each site. That is, everyone from the director's, president's, dean's, or department chair's secretary to the accountants managing all the purchases and the library staff and so on are all hired and supervised and evaluated and promoted (if at all) by the Monkasho people, not the academics/researchers. Furthermore, all administrative, clerical, financial, and facilities maintenance procedures are Monkasho procedures. It is extremely difficult to change any of those procedures at local sites.

At any given level in the organization the top four or five people would each be circulating to other Monkasho sites at least every 3 years. All universities and research institutes/labs have senior Monkasho people working on site, looking carefully at every policy decision, reporting that back to the central office in Tokyo, and then giving the academic leaders their "advice"; when the advice is ignored or directly challenged, the academic leader is called to Tokyo for consultations. Of course, some academics have been intimidated by this process, but others are not. Some of these might form strategic alliances among themselves or with politicians.

Sometimes the Monkasho people assigned to a specific site can become very interested in the actions and policies initiated by the academics or researchers; and for a while they can serve as effective go-betweens with their home ministry. However, any ministry employee on a "career" track is rotated around different Monkasho sites at least every 3 years; obviously that works against the formation of any long-term alliances between local academics and ministry representatives. For example, a previous senior Monkasho administrator at KEK was then sent to manage the Winter Olympics at Nagano, after which he became the senior administrator for a university in western Japan. That is, whatever special expertise a Monkasho person happens to gather about the activities at any one site, those skills are not likely to be used or developed at the next site. It is clear that a bureaucrat's career success is tied to executing Monkasho practices adroitly, not "going native."

Furthermore, most Japanese academics and researchers working within this system do not realize that universities, research institutes, or funding agencies around the world are not structured in the Japanese fashion. That includes even people who have spent considerable time working abroad as researchers or as visiting faculty members who might now be in leadership positions in Japan, negotiating collaborations with foreigners.

The University of Tokyo was established to educate the government's upper echelon of bureaucrats, and it still serves that purpose. The ministries are sufficiently powerful that many of the "best and the brightest" students from the best universities have as their greatest ambition to have a career in one of the ministries. Most people in Japan see the power of the ministries as ranked, with the Ministry of Finance at the top. Monkasho is around number seven or eight. That is, among those "best and brightest" students, they would hanker first after a job in the Ministry of Finance, and then so on, down the line. The bureaucrats are generally quite well educated in a specific mode; they formulate plans, they design, they implement, and they manage. They expand, but rarely contract.

To get into an important ministry position graduating undergraduate students begin by taking a ministry's exam; based on the results they would be assigned a post. (People with graduate degrees are not sought by the ministries. They like to train their own, on the job, although they may choose to send one of their members to a graduate management program abroad.) For the rest of their career in the ministry everyone around them would know their ranking on that exam. Heads of ministries would be selected only from among those who had done well on that entry exam. After entering a ministry there is no shifting around to other ministries. That is, someone who does a truly exceptional job at Monkasho at any level never moves "up" to higher ranked ministries.

Meanwhile, within the ministries there is a three-track system. At the top are all the people who took and passed the difficult entry examination. Next are the well-educated people who joined the ministry, but did not take the examination. Some of those people will work at one site their whole careers, never having the chance to circulate every 3 years; no matter how effective, they will never be promoted into the jobs reserved for the top layer of employees. At the bottom are the "*arbeito*" workers (from *arbeit*, the German word for work), which in Japan is used to refer to so-called "part-time" workers. Many such *arbeito* employees work 40 hours a week for several decades; they are called part-timers because they can make only trivial advancement, they have no security of employment, and they receive few, if any, employment benefits. Almost all working women in Japan are *arbeito* workers.

Nendaiki to Suji: chronicles and narrative threads

Clearly, Monkasho is far more pervasively influential within Japanese universities and research institutes and laboratories than most American academics could imagine. It is easy to see how its enormous power to either resist or deliver change could have strongly influenced any group of academics or researchers in Japan. So what do such massive, hierarchical, extensive, highly centralized, and very powerful national bureaucracies accomplish with their genealogies of convergence, their construction chronicles, and their erasure of names? They affirm that they, and they alone, have built Tsukuba. People outside the organization remain unmentioned in their lists. Their policies against allowing the names of individuals on events, designs, projects, and buildings means that stories about the role of those outside their group will not survive. As it is the bureaucracy's lists that will be archived and become the historical documents of the future, we will have only a history of how the bureaucracy made Tsukuba. It will seem that the bureaucracy was the only effective player in making its history.

Why does the bureaucracy avoid historical narratives? Why doesn't it figure heroically in stories of its own making? Why does it avoid any public display of agency? The Japanese bureaucracy has had many difficulties with historical narrative. The documents of Japan's twentieth-century imperial history are suppressed. According to the bureaucracy there is no evidence to substantiate the efficiently organized and devastating Nanjing massacres, POW camps, medical experiments, and sexual slavery.[109] Many of Japan's neighbors and allies, including the United States, have learned to live with Japan's loss of historical memory, and have their own tales to tell about their complicity in this erasure.

Why are Tsukubans complicit in this project of historical erasure, multiplying genealogies of mergers and chronicles of emerging machines, buildings, and events? Why are they themselves generating the very forms of history that deny their own agency in making the past, present, and future of Tsukuba? I claim that it is a very strategic response to the bureaucracy's power. The locally generated genealogies and chronicles are submitted to the bureaucrats as reports of itemized accomplishments in a structure the bureaucracy welcomes. The people in Tsukuba need the bureaucracy's resources to make their history, present, and future. The cost is the erasure of their names in the historical documents.

Of course, they tell stories; there is a lot of lively storytelling in Tsukuba. Finding those stories, we can locate the names and tales that are not included in all those chronologies and genealogies, in all those official public documents of Tsukuba Science City and the national research institutes, or in the planning and evaluation documents of the officials who manage science cities in Japan and around the world. In those stories we will find the missing narrative thread, and find their other strategies for making knowledge and making their world.

Finally, we have learned how most public histories are made in Tsukuba, who makes them, and why. These histories take the form of *nendaiki* (chronicles), but not of people and their events; instead, they feature the assembly of machines and organizations. Such chronicles, along with the names they have erased, argue that the only agency capable of such stupendous construction is the bureaucracy of the national government. The bureaucrats alone, as these histories display, can create and destroy. Any other form of history would require names, events, and *suji*, some narrative thread that would explain why all the names are missing. I have tried to locate some of those *suji*.[110]

Notes

1 Copyright held by Sharon Traweek, Women's Studies and History Departments, UCLA, Los Angeles, California, USA 90095–1473. An earlier version of this chapter appeared in Jesus Valero de Matas, ed., *Social Study of Science: An Interdisciplinary Context* (Auckland: Auckland University, 2004).

2 Poem 13 in Clay MacCauley, *Single Songs of a Hundred Poets and Dominant Note of the Law* (Yokohama: Kelly and Walsh, 1917). The canonical translation into English is MacCauley's.

3 This date is cited in various histories, for example *Nihon no daigaku kakumei [Vol. 1: University Reforms in Japan]* (Tokyo: Nihon hyoronsha, 1969); Fukuda Nobuyuki, *Hirakareta gakuen Tsukuba daigaku [Open University Tsukuba University]* (Tokyo: Gendai johosha, 1974); and Fukuda Nobuyuki, *Tsukuba daigaku no bijon [The Vision of Tsukuba University]* (Tokyo: Zanponsha, 1983).

4 Keiko Yuasa, ed., *Guide for Tsukuba Science City: Institutes and Organizations of Tsukuba Science City*, prepared by the Public Relations Committee, Tsukuba City Liaison Council for Promotion of Research Exchange, Shin-ichi Kurokawa, Chairperson (Tsukuba: Tsukuba Press, 1997; distributed by Maruzen), published in Japanese as *Kagaku no Machi: Tsukuba Kenkyu Gakuen Toshi Gaidobukku* (Tsukuba Shoten, 1996).

5 Sharon Traweek, "*Kokusaika* (International Relations), *gaiatsu* (Outside Pressure), and *bachigai* (Being Out of Place)," in Laura Nader, ed., *Naked Science: Anthropological Inquiry into Boundaries, Power, and Knowledge* (New York: Routledge, 1996); "*Bachigai* (out of place) in Ibaraki: Tsukuba Science City, Japan," in G. E. Marcus, ed., *Technoscientific Imaginaries* (Late Editions, vol. II) (Chicago: University of Chicago Press, 1995); "Border Crossings: Narrative Strategies in Science Studies and among High Energy Physicists at Tsukuba Science City, Japan," in Andy Pickering, ed., *Science as Practice and Culture* (Chicago: University of Chicago Press, 1992), pp. 429–65; "Big Science as Colonialist Discourse: Regional Differences in Japanese High Energy Physics," in Peter Galison, ed., *Big Science* (Stanford, CA: Stanford University Press, 1992), pp. 100–28; and *Beamtimes and Lifetimes: The World of High Energy Physicists* (Cambridge, MA: Harvard University Press, 1988), pp. 92, 95.

6 Keiko Yuasa, *Guide for Tsukuba Science City*.

7 See http://www.info-tsukuba.org/english/index.html and http://www.info-tsukuba.org/english/educate/main.html.

8 See Hiroshi Dohi, "38 Years of Tsukuba: The Short History of Planning and Construction of Tsukuba New Town," presentation at the New Garden City International Conference at Kobe Design University, Japan, 2001: http://www.kobe-du.ac.jp/env/g-city/newgc/abstract/eng/t_sess1.html; Tetsuo Sakitani, *Sekai saidai no haiteku kichi Tsukuba gakuen kenkyu toshi [Tsukuba Research University Town, the Largest High-Tech Base in the World]* (Tokyo: PHP kenkyujo, 1985). The following are by Nobuyuki Fukuda, one of the founders of Tsukuba and Tsukuba University: *Hirakareta gakuen Tsukuba daigaku [Open Tsukuba University]* (Tokyo: Gendai johosha, 1974) and *Tsukuba daigaku no bijon [Vision for Tsukuba University]* (Tokyo: Zanponsha, 1983). Kambei Fujisawa (1901–94), former mayor of Sakura-mura (1959–79) and a leading proponent for the establishment of Tsukuba Science City, wrote an autobiography: *Kano Jiden* [Tsukuba: Seiyo (Santosha Insastu), Heisei 2, 1990]. Fujisawa was from a leading landowning family in the region; his son is now mayor of Tsukuba. See also the following local, regional, and national governmental publications: *Oho Cho Shi [Oho Town History]* (Oho Machi, Tsukuba Shi, Ibaraki-ken, Japan, 1989); *Tsuchiura Tsukuba Science City Japan* (Tsukuba City Office, Tsuchiura City Office, Kukuzaki City Office, Tsukuba Tourist Information Center, 1992); *Tsukuba: '95 Comprehensive Guide of Tsukuba City* (Tsukuba City, Japan: International Division, Tsukuba City Office, 4711 Yatabe, Tsukuba City, Japan 305: 1995) [also in Japanese: *Tsukuba: Shi Sei Gaido (Condition of Municipal Life)* (same publisher, 1995)]; *Tsukuba: Tsukuba*

City Handbook (Tsukuba: Tsukuba City Office, 1999); *Tsukuba Daigaku Junenshi Henshu Iinkai, Tsukuba daigaku sono junen [The Past 10 Years of Tsukuba University]* (Tsukuba: Tsukuba Daigaku Somubu Somuka, 1983).

9 For statistical data on the introduction of foreign technologies to Japan, contract terms, cross-licensing, and patents see Kagaku Gitsu Cho Kagaku Gitsu Seisaku Kyokuhin, *Kagaku Gitsu Yoran 2000 [Indicators of Science and Technology 2000]*, compiled by the Bureau of Science and Technology Policy at the Science and Technology Agency (Tokyo: Printing Bureau, Ministry of Finance, Heisei 12, 2000), pp. 96–111. The trend is clearly away from reliance on technologies developed outside Japan.

10 Stuart Leslie and Dong-Won Kim, "Winning Markets or Winning Nobel Prizes: KAIST and the Challenges of Late Industrialization," *Osiris*, vol. 13, no. 2 (1998), pp. 154–85.

11 Reference to the December 1962 "verbal Cabinet understanding" to relocate national governmental facilities outside Tokyo is in English at http://www.info-tsukuba.org/english/what/history/indes.html.

12 The population of Japan increased more than 50 percent from 1950 to 2000 – from about 83 million to nearly 130 million; it was about 45 million in 1900. For population projections from the National Institute of Population and Social Security Research see http://www.ipss.go.jp/English/ppfj02/top.html.

13 Manuel Castells, *The Informational City: Information Technology, Economic Restructuring, and the Urban-Regional Process* (Blackwell, 1989); Manuel Castells and Peter Hall, *Technopoles of the World: The Making of 21st Century Industrial Complexes* (New York: Routledge, 1994); Doreen Massey, Paul Quintas, and David Wield, *High Tech Fantasies: Science Parks in Society, Science, and Space* (London: Routledge, 1991); Hilary Sunman, *France and Her Technopoles*, in the series "The Economics of Technology Change: the European Experience" (Pentyrch, Cardiff: CSP Economic Publications, 1986). See also Anne Theodore Briggs and Stephen Watt, website on Technology and Research Parks, 2001: http://www.american.edu/carmel/ab5293a/techparks.htm.

14 Houston, Texas: http://www.cityofhouston.gov/abouthouston/economytrade.jsp. Los Angeles: http://www.ci.la.ca.us/lacity19.htm; Mike Davis, *City of Quartz: Excavating the Future in Los Angeles* (London: Verso, 1990); Carey McWilliams, *Southern California: An Island on the Land* (Salt Lake City, UT: Gibbs-Smith, 1973, 8th edn, 1990); Zena Pearlstone, *Ethnic L.A.* (Beverly Hills, CA: Hillcrest Press, 1990); Allen Scott, "The Technopoles of Southern California," *UCLA Research Papers in Economic and Urban Geography* (no. 1, July 1989); Allen Scott, *Technopolis: High-Technology Industry and Regional Development in Southern California* (Berkeley: University of California Press, 1993); Allen Scott and Edward Soja, *The City: Los Angeles and Urban Theory at the End of the Twentieth Century* (Berkeley: University of California, 1996); John D. Weaver, *Los Angeles: The Enormous Village 1781–1981* (Santa Barbara, CA: Capra Press, 1980).

15 Los Alamos National Laboratory (LANL), New Mexico, USA: http://www.lanl.gov/worldview/; Lawrence Badash, Joseph Hirschfelder, and Herbert Broida, eds., *Reminiscences of Los Alamos, 1943–1945* (Dordrecht: D. Reidel, 1980); Lillian Hoddeson, Paul W. Henriksen, Roger A. Meade, and Catherine L. Westfall, *Critical Assembly: A Technical History of Los Alamos During the Oppenheimer Years, 1943–1945* (Cambridge: Cambridge University Press, 1993). Akademgorodok, Novosibirsk in Russia: http://www.nsc.ru/other/akadem/; Paul Josephson, *New Atlantis Revisited: Akademgorodok, the Siberian City of Science* (Princeton, NJ: Princeton University Press, 1997).

16 Hanford Laboratory near Richland, Washington: http://hanford-site.pnl.gov/. Oak Ridge Laboratory on Tennessee Valley Authority (TVA) lands: http://www.ci.oak-ridge.tn.us/oakridge.htm; Tennessee Valley Authority (TVA): http://www.tva.gov/; Richard Berkman and W. Kip Viscusi, *Damming the West* (New York: Grossman, 1973); North Callahan, *TVA: Bridge over Troubled Waters* (New York: A. S. Barnes,

1980); William Chandler, *Myth of TVA: Conservation and Development in the Tennessee Valley, 1933–1983* (Cambridge, MA: Ballinger, 1984); Terry Reynolds, *Stronger than a Hundred Men* (Baltimore: Johns Hopkins University, 1983).

17 On patents and stages of industrial development see Stuart Leslie and Robert Kargon, "Selling Silicon Valley: Frederick Terman's Model for Regional Advantage," *Business History Review*, vol. 70, no. 4 (Winter 1996), pp. 435–72. On Stanford Industrial Park (renamed Stanford Research Park in 1974) see http://www.stanford.edu/dept/ SMC/researchpark/ and the Silicon Valley Archives, Special Collections of Stanford University Libraries: http://lib.stanford.edu/stanford-silicon-valley-archives.

18 Stanford Linear Accelerator Center (SLAC), California: http://www.slac.stanford.edu/ history/; on Frederick Terman, see http://www.pbs.org/transistor/album1/addlbios/ terman.html; on Varian, Inc. see http://www.varianinc.com.

19 AnnaLee Saxenian (http://www-dcrp.ced.berkeley.edu/Faculty/Anno/Index.htm), *Regional Advantage: Culture and Competition in Silicon Valley and Route 128* (Cambridge, MA: Harvard University Press, 1996) and "Silicon Valley's New Immigrant Entrepreneurs" (San Francisco: Public Policy Institute of California, September 1, 1999). Silicon Valley, California, USA, and Moffett Field, Mountain View, California, USA: http://www.nasa.gov/centers/ames/about/history.html; Silicon Valley Archives Project: http://lib.stanford.edu/stanford-silicon-valley-archives.

20 Research Triangle Park in North Carolina: http://www.rtp.org/.

21 Anna Lee Saxenian, *Regional Advantage*.

22 Examples include Eura-Lille, the communications and distribution center near the Euro Tunnel, Eura-Sante, a health center, and Villeneuve-D'Ascq, an education and research center, all near Lille, France: http://www.mairie-villeneuvedascq.fr/english/ present/present.htm; Sophia Antipolis, linked to the University of Nice, on the Cote d'Azur in France, which was launched in 1974; the King Abdulaziz City for Science and Technology (KACST) established in Saudi Arabia in 1977: http://www.kacst. edu.sa/about_kacst/about.htm; Keihanna Science City, which began in 1986 between Nara, Kyoto, and Osaka: http://www.kri.or.jp/ and http://www.keihanna-plaza.co.jp/ KRI/gaken/zaidan_e.htm

23 Technopolis Law of 1983, Japan (Law for Accelerating Regional Development Based upon High-technology Industrial Complexes): http://www.japanlaw.com/lawletter/ may83/ahw.htm. US National Science Foundation report on the Technopolis Law: http://www.cs.arizona.edu/japan/www/atip/public/atip.reports.93/regional.nsf.html

24 Association of University Related Research Parks (AURRP): http://www.aurrp.org/; International Association of Science Parks (IASP): http://www.iaspworld.org/.

25 American Planning Association: http://www.planning.org/. The Association of Collegiate Schools of Planning (ACSP) provides links to thirty-seven UK, US, and Canadian doctoral programs in planning: http://www.acsp.org/. Planning Utopia is an independent clearing house for information, links to other websites, publications, and essays on land use planning, growth management, smart growth, and new urbanism: http://planneronline.homestead.com/NewPlanningMeridian.html. Internet Planning Media lists almost 100 different electronic and print planning publications and websites: http://www.planning.org/info/editors.htm.

26 See *Tsukuba: Tsukuba City Handbook*, p. 15, and http://www.city.tsukuba.ibaraki. jp/english/inter/sister.htm. Irvine is also sister cities with Taoyuan, Taiwan, near the Hsinshu Science-based Industrial Park, which opened in 1981; by 1998 there were 272 companies there: http://www.sipa.gov.tw/seconde/index1.htm.

27 http://www.laidoffinsv.com/statistics.htm; http://www2.ucsc.edu/cgirs/publications/ cpapers/leuthje.pdf; http://www.secretsofsiliconvalley.org/; http://www.ppionline.org/ ppi_ci.cfm?knlgAreaID=107&subsecID=297&contentID=949.

28 Itty Abraham, *The Making of the Indian Atomic Bomb: Science, Secrecy and the Postcolonial State* (London: Zed Books, 1998); Roy MacLeod, "On Visiting the 'Moving Metropolis': Reflections on the Architecture of Imperial Science," *Historical Records of Australian Science*, vol. 5, no.3 (1982), pp. 1–16.

29 See, for example, Richard Berkman and W. Kip Viscusi, *Damming the West* (New York: Grossman, 1973); Bruce Hevly and John M. Findlay, eds., *The Atomic West* (Seattle: University of Washington Press, 1998); Scott Kirsch, *Experiments in Progress: The AEC's Project Plowshare and the Geography of Science and Technology* (Berkeley: University of California Press, 2000); Gerald D. Nash, *The American West in the Twentieth Century: A Short History of an Urban Oasis* (Albuquerque: University of New Mexico Press, 1973); Allen Scott and Edward Soja, *The City: Los Angeles and Urban Theory at the End of the Twentieth Century* (Berkeley: University of California, 1996).
30 See, for example, Scott and Soja, *The City*; Edward Soja, *Postmodern Geographies: The Reassertion of Space in Critical Social Theory* (London: Verso, 1989), and Alexander Wilson, *The Culture of Nature: North American Landscape from Disney to the Exxon Valdez* (Cambridge, MA: Blackwell, 1992).
31 Aaron Moore, "Total War, Colonial Engineers and the Precursors of Postwar 'Comprehensive National Land Planning'," presentation at the workshop on Dis/continuities: Nation-State Formation in Japan with Science, Technology, and Medicine during Imperialism, War, Occupation, and Peace, 1932–1962, UCLA, May 29–30.
32 Tsukuba Science City Construction Act, May 1970: http://www.info-tsukuba.org/english/what/descript/index.html. Technopolis Law of 1983, Japan (Law for Accelerating Regional Development Based upon High-technology Industrial Complexes): http://www.japanlaw.com/lawletter/may83/ahw.htm. NSF report on the Technopolis Law: http://www.cs.arizona.edu/japan/www/atip/public/. Kansai Science City Construction Promotion Act June 9, 1987 (law 72–1987): http://www.kri.or.jp/.
33 Tsukuba Science City (Tsukuba Kenkyu Gakuen Toshi), Ibaraki-ken, Japan: http://www.city.tsukuba.ibaraki.jp/index.htm; *Tsukuba Newsletter* is published monthly in both hard copy and at the city's website by the International Affairs Section, Tsukuba City Office, 1979 Konda, Sakura Branch Office, Tsukuba City: http://www.city.tsukuba.ibaraki.jp/english/news/back.htm. *Koho Tsukuba*, a larger newsletter in Japanese, is published bimonthly in both hard copy and at the city's website by the Design Section, Public Relations Bureau, Tsukuba City (Kikabu, Kohokocho, Tsukuba Shi): http://www.city.tsukuba.ibaraki.jp/cgi-bin/news2.pl.
34 "The Future of Tsukuba Science City: Tsukuba Science City Information": http://www.info-tsukuba.org/english/index.html.
35 See note 8.
36 Reynal Guillen, "Sicentific Colonialism: Chicano/a Identity and Scientific Practice in an American Southwest Technopole," Dissertation, History Department, University of California at Los Angeles, 2004.
37 The three branches of the Tokugawa shogunate were the Owari in Nagoya, the Kishu in Wakayama, and the Mito.
38 Ronald Dore, *Education in Tokugawa Japan* (London: Athlone Press, 1984), Andrew Gordon, *A Modern History of Japan: From Tokugawa Times to the Present* (New York: Oxford, 2003), H. D. Harootunian, *Things Seen and Unseen: Discourse and Ideology in Tokugawa Nativism* (Chicago: University of Chicago, 1988), and Herman Ooms, *Tokugawa Ideology: Early Constructs, 1570–1680* (Princeton, NJ: University of Princeton Press, 1985). Ibaraki government brochures in English referring to the *Kodokan* include "A New Wave: Mito/A City with History," prepared by the Section for Commerce, Industry, and Tourism, Mito City, Ibaraki Prefecture, April 1994, p. 16; and "Ibaraki Travel Information," compiled by the Ibaraki Prefecture Tourism and Local Products Division in Mito (no date), p. 14.
39 Commentaries on the *Mito Komon* television series aired by the Tokyo Broadcasting System (TBS) abound; see, for example, http://www.concentric.net/~Budokai/chambara/mitokomon.htm. As a form of public entertainment the samurai genre, of which the *Mito Komon* show is one example, has waxed and waned in popularity, much like the "Western cowboy" genre. The last several years the genre has not been as popular as in the past, so there are relatively few such shows on television or films; however, the *Mito Komon* show has survived these fluctuations.

40 On the 397-volume *Dainihonshi* (1657–1906) see http://www.meijigakuin. ac.jp/~pmjs/trans/trans02.html.

41 On Seizan-so see http:/www.tokugawa.gr.jp/seizan-so.htm and the following tourist brochures, both in Japanese: "Ibaraki Destination Campaign Event Guide Book," compiled by JR (Japanese Railways) Group (1999), p. 36, and "Hitachi Ota," *p.* 2, combined with "Hitachi Ota Map for Sightseeing," compiled by the Hitachi Ota City Tourism Division (no date). See also, for example, these brochures, available in both Japanese and English, compiled by the Ibaraki Prefecture Tourism and Local Products Division in Mito: "Ibaraki Travel Information" (no date), pp. 1, 11, and "Travel Information on Ibaraki: Tourist Guide to Ibaraki Prefecture" (no date), p. 12.

42 On the Tokugawa Museum (Tokugawa Bijutsukan) see http:/www.tokugawa.gr.jp.

43 See "Ibaraki Destination Campaign Event Guide Book," pp. 2, 32. See also "Travel Information on Ibaraki: Tourist Guide to Ibaraki Prefecture, p. 6, and Ibaraki Travel Information, p. 15.

44 National Archives of Japan (Kokuritsu Kobunshokan): http://www.archives.go.jp/ index_e.html. Archives of prefectures and designated cities in Japan can be found at http://www.archives.go.jp/index_e.html.

45 Much of this and the next paragraph are excerpted from my "*Bachigai* (out of place) in Ibaraki."

46 I have heard this version of the establishment of both UC San Diego and UC Irvine from several American physicists and biologists. While a visiting faculty member at UCSD in 1990 and actively participating in a seminar at UCI, I realized that many faculty at UCSD and UCI find these "origin stories" ludicrous; the scientists are not fazed by the incredulity of their colleagues in the humanities and social sciences.

47 Since the Meiji Restoration in 1868, many Japanese scholars have established schools according to some model found in North America or Europe; in fact, there is an even older history in Japan of building schools based on models found in China.

48 More recently Takao Doi has been the director of a new Museum of Emerging Science and Technology in Tokyo called Mireikan. On Hideki Shirakawa see http://www. nobel.se/chemistry/laureates/2000/shirakawa-autobio.html.

49 For a biography of Hideki Yukawa see the Nobel Prize website at http://www.nobel. se/physics/laureates/1949/yukawa-bio.html; for information on the Kiso Butsurigaku Kenkyujo (Research Institute for Fundamental Physics) at Kyoto University see http:// www.yukawa.kyoto-u.ac.jp/.

50 Because of the Japanese government's funding restrictions this has been nearly impossible. This problem was recognized in the "Science and Technology Basic Law," passed in 1995 to develop scientific and technological knowledge. This "basic law" outlines ways that the "creativity" and "autonomy" of researchers and engineers should be respected and encouraged; in part, this is to be accomplished by supporting the infrastructure needed for their work. See bilingual text of Kagaku Gitsu Yoran 2000, pp. 115. See also: The Science and Technology Basic Law (Unofficial Translation) (Law No. 130 of 1995. Effective on November 15, 1995), provided by the Council on Science and Technology Policy, Cabinet Office, Government of Japan. Article 12, page 4. Access English translation at http://www8.cao.go.jp/cstp/ english/law/law.html. See also "Preview of the Second Science and Technology Basic Plan," Report Memorandum #00-18, Tokyo Regional Office, [U.S.] National Science Foundation, December 4, 2000. Access at http://www.nsftokyo.org/rm00-18.html. The Science and Technology Agency (STA) was disbanded in 2001; its various functions have been distributed into other government ministries, including the former Ministry of Education, Culture, and Sports (Monbusho) which has been renamed the Ministry of Education, Culture, Sports, Science and Technology (Monbukagakusho, or, more familiarly, Monkasho); it also now has an acronym: MEXT. The subsequent "Science and Technology Basic Plan" was approved by the Japanese government cabinet in March 2001. See Arimoto Tateo, "Research and Rescue," *Look Japan* (March 2002): 32–4. This clearly indicates that such support had been missing in the past.

Unfortunately, in general, the proposed "solution" was only to increase the resources available under the existing system of using support staff from private corporations. It has been about 15 years since the Science and Technology Law was passed and 10 years since the Science and Technology Basic Plan was decided, but that law and those policies have had no noticeable effect on the number of technicians/craftspeople at KEK as far as I have been able to determine. I have heard that the Finance Ministry that controls the budget for all ministries has interpreted another government policy on reducing the number of government employees as taking precedence over the Science and Technology Law and Basic Plan.

51 See, for example, *Tsukuba: Tsukuba City Handbook*, p. 14.
52 As of fall 2002 each person will be assigned a number (*sebango*) as part of a new computerized registration system.
53 *Koho Tsukuba*, August 2001. Access back issues of the Tsukuba Newsletter (*Koho Tsukuba*) in seven languages at http://tsukubainfo.jp/Photos/Photos; Japanese http://www.city.tsukuba.ibaraki.jp/13/1729/3998/4012/index.html; English http://www.city.tsukuba.ibaraki.jp/13/1729/3998/4012/index.html.
54 *Tsukuba Newsletter*, August 2001, no. 120, p. 8.
55 Hiromi Mizuno, *Science for the Empire: Scientific Nationalism in Modern Japan* (Stanford, CA: Stanford University Press, 2008).
56 *Tsukuba: Tsukuba City Handbook*, pp. 10–17.
57 KEK's "History" page: http://www.kek.jp/index.html.
58 High Energy Accelerator Research Organization (KEK), *Annual Report 2000* (Tsukuba, Ibaraki-ken: KEK, 2001), p. 12.
59 Ibid., pp. 60–1.
60 Science Museum of Map and Survey at the Geographical Survey Institute (Kokudo Chiri-in): http://www.gsi-mc.go.jp/.
61 *Tsukuba: Tsukuba City Handbook*, pp. 12, 15.
62 Terri Casteneda, "The Politics of Memory in Galveston, Texas," PhD Dissertation, Rice University.
63 Keihanna Science City website: http://www.kri.or.jp/gaken/.
64 Jennifer Robertson, *Native and Newcomer: Making and Remaking a Japanese City* (Berkeley: University of California Press, 1991).
65 "The Future of Tsukuba Science City: Tsukuba Science City Information," Chapter 4: "Basic Plans for Tsukuba Science City," Section 4: "Comfortable Living Environment and Beautiful Scenery," Part 3: "Scenery and Culture Worthy of Tsukuba Science City": http://www.info-tsukuba.org/english/what/after/chp4.html.
66 Ibid. See also Hiroshi Dohi, "38 Years of Tsukuba."
67 See, for example, Maurizio Peleggi, *The Politics of Ruins and the Business of Nostalgia* (Bangkok: White Lotus Press, 2002); Dean MacCannell, *Empty Meeting Grounds: The Tourist Papers* (London: Routledge, 1992). See also Arata Izosaki, "Of City, Nation, and Style," in Masao Miyoshi and H. D. Harootunian, eds., *Postmodernism and Japan* (Durham, NC: Duke University Press, 1989).
68 Elsewhere I have written about the internationalization of Tsukuba and the urbanization of the area: "*Bachigai* (out of place) in Ibaraki."
69 Japan National Tourist Organization: http://www.jnto.or.jp/; see also *The Japan Times'* festival page: http://www.japantimes.co.jp/.
70 See Peleggi, *The Politics of Ruin*, and MacCannell, *Empty Meeting Grounds*.
71 *Oho Cho Shi* (compiled and published by Ohomachi, Tsukuba Kenkyu Gakuen Toshi, Ibaraki-ken, 1989).
72 The geologist is Atsushi Onodero and the historian is Hiroyuki Iwasaki; both are faculty at the University of Tsukuba. Two graduate students assisted Professor Iwasaki on the project.
73 *Tsukuba Science City* [Ibaraki, Japan: Toshi Kaihatsu Kodan (Housing and Urban Development Corporation, formerly Japan Housing Corporation), Ibaraki Regional Branch Office, 1997], p. 22.

74 *Oho Cho Shi*, p. 310.
75 Ibid., p. 235.
76 *Tsukuba Newsletter*, August 2001, no. 120, p. 8. Projections are in "The Future of Tsukuba Science City: Tsukuba Science City Information," Chapter 4, Section 3, Part 2 at http://www.info-tsukuba.org/english/what/after/chp.4.html.
77 "Tsukuba: My Town," published by International Affairs Section, Citizen's Activities Division, Tsukuba City Office 305–0018, April 2000, p. 1.
78 The topic is "Dis/continuities in Nation-State Formation in Japan with Science, Technology, and Medicine during Imperialism, War, Occupation, and Peace, 1932–62."
79 *Tsukuba: '95 Comprehensive Guide of Tsukuba City* (Tsukuba City, Japan: International Division, Tsukuba City Office, 4711 Yatabe, Tsukuba City, Japan 305, 1995) [also in Japanese: *Tsukuba: Shi Sei Gaido (Condition of Municipal Life)* (same publisher, 1995)].
80 *Tsukuba Science City*, pp. 12–13.
81 "Tsukuba Science City Information: Outline of Town Building Scheme" at http://www.info-tsukuba.org/english/what/descript/index.html.
82 Yasuhiro Naruse, "Comparison of Letchworth Garden City and Tsukuba Science City in Terms of 'the City Environment Design,'" presentation at The New Garden City International Conference at Kobe Design University, Japan, 2001: http://www.kobe-du.ac.jp/env/g-city/newgc/abstract/eng/t_sess1.html.
83 On Josiah Condor see David Stewart, *The Making of Modern Japanese Architecture: 1868 to the Present* (Tokyo: Kodansha, 1987). A bibliography on *oyatoi* can be found at http://www.oriental.cam.ac.uk/jbib/For2–10.html; see also a brief historical description of *oyatoi* at http://www.dentsu.com/MUSEUM/meiji/index1.html.
84 John H. and Phyllis G. Martin, *Tokyo: A Cultural Guide to Japan's Capital City* (Rutland, VT: Charles E. Tuttle, 1996), p. 41.
85 Ibid., pp. 40–1. The very terms "western" and "eastern" as used in this context are based on English colonial discourse from the nineteenth century: "near east" and "middle east" referred to various parts of West Asia; the "far east" meant East Asia. From that standpoint, Europe, being west of Asia, was called "the West" and Asian countries to the east of London were named, collectively, "the East." It is very interesting to see this language used by people who eagerly dissociate themselves from colonial discourse in other ways.
86 Arata Isozaki, "Of City, Nation, and Style." The Japanese version appeared in *Shinkenchiku* (November 1983). On the heritage of Condor and the inheritance of Isozaki see Carter B. Horsley, "Review" of Botond Bognar, *The Japan Guide* (New York: Princeton Architectural Press, 1995), pp. 3–5: http://www.thecityreview.com/bognar.html.
87 Arata Isozaki, "Of City, Nation, and Style," pp. 49, 60.
88 Horsley, "Review," p. 1: http://www.thecityreview..com/bognar.html.
89 This and the next paragraph are excerpted from my "*Bachigai* (out of place) in Ibaraki," p. 336.
90 Motoya Kitamura, "Management Buyouts Find Favor as Restructuring Tool," *The Japan Times*, December 3, 2001, p. 16.
91 For a history of some of these projects see Peter Galison, "Introduction: The Many Faces of Big Science," in Peter Galison and Bruce Helvy, eds., *Big Science* (Stanford, CA: Stanford University Press, 1992).
92 The five include a subcommittee of the International Committee on Future Accelerators (ICFA), a globalization committee at KEK, a subcommittee of the High Energy Physics Advisory Panel (HEPAP) to the United States Department of Energy, a subcommittee of the European Committee on Future Accelerators (ECFA), and a subcommittee of the Organisation of Economic Co-operation and Development (OECD).
93 See D. K. Kahaner, "Regional Science and Technology Development in Japan," prepared for the U.S. National Science Foundation (May 15, 1993).
94 Mimi Hall Yiengpruksawan, *Hiraizumi: Buddhist Art and Regional Politics in*

Twelfth-Century Japan (Cambridge, MA: Harvard University Press, 2001). See also http://www.pref.iwate.jp/~hp3501/english/hiraizumi/index.html.
95 Matsuo Basho (1644–94), *Oku no Hosomichi*, translated by Nobuyuki Yuasa as *The Narrow Road to the Deep North and Other Travel Sketches* (Harmondsworth: Penguin, 1966). See the translated text, along with commentaries and alternative translations of the *haiku*, at http://www.uoregon.edu/~kohl/basho/23-hiraizumi/index.html.
96 Kunio Yanagida, *Tono Monogatari* (1910). The book was published in English as *The Legends of Tono* (trans. Ronald A. Morse, Lanham, MD: Lexington Books, 2008). For a brief biography of Yanagida, an analysis of the book, one of the films based upon it, and its influence see Takayuki Tatsumi, "Deep North Gothic: A Comparative Cultural Reading of Kuno Yanagita's *Tono Monogatari* and Tetsutaro Murano's *The Legend of Sayo*," *The Newsletter of the Council for the Literature of the Fantastic*, vol. 1, no. 5 (1998): http://www.uri.edu/artsci/english/clf/n5_a1.html. For a study of Yanagida's role in the development of anthropology in Japan see Miriam Silverberg, "Constructing the Japanese Ethnography of Modernity," *Journal of Asian Studies*, vol. 51, no. 1 (February 1992), pp. 30–54.
97 On the Kunio Yanagida Matsuoka Kenshokai Museum see http://web.pref.hyogo.jp/kankou/travel/e3/31/travel31b.html; on Harima Science Garden City (Harima Kagaku Koen Toshi), Hyogo-ken, Japan, see http://web.pref.hyogo.jp/harima/index-e.htm; on Spring 8 see http://www.spring8.or.jp/.
98 Takayuki Tatsumi, "Deep North Gothic," p. 1.
99 Fujisawa Kambei, *Kanou Jiden* [Tsukuba: Seiyo (Santosha Insastu), Heisei 2, 1990]. Fukuda Nobuyuki, *Hirakareta gakuen Tsukuba daigaku (Open University Tsukuba University)* (Tokyo: Gendai johosha, 1974), and Fukuda Nobuyuki, *Tsukuba daigaku no bijon (The Vision of Tsukuba University)* (Tokyo: Zanponsha, 1983).
100 Fujisawa Kambei, *Kanou Jiden*, pp. 238–71.
101 Eric Hobsbawm and Terence Ranger, eds., *The Invention of Tradition* (Cambridge: Cambridge University Press, 1992); Roy Wagner, *The Invention of Culture*, revised and expanded edition (Chicago: University of Chicago Press, 1981). See also Benedict Anderson, *Imagined Communities: Reflections of the Origin and Spread of Nationalism* (London: Verso, 1991) and Akhil Gupta and James Ferguson, eds., *Anthropological Locations: Boundaries and Grounds of a Field Science* (Berkeley: University of California Press, 1997).
102 Edward Said, *Orientalism* (New York: Vintage, 1979) and *Beginnings: Intention and Method* (Baltimore: Johns Hopkins University Press, 1975). See also Talal Asad, ed., *Anthropology and the Colonial Encounter* (Amherst, NY: Prometheus Books, 1995); George E. Marcus, and James Clifford, eds., *New Directions in Anthropological Writing: History, Poetics, Cultural Criticism* (Madison: University of Wisconsin Press, 1988); Renato Rosaldo, *Culture and Truth: The Remaking of Social Analysis* (Boston: Beacon, 1989).
103 Johannes Fabian, *Time and the Other: How Anthropology Makes Its Object* (New York: Columbia University Press, 1983); Donna Haraway, *Primate Visions: Gender, Race, and Nature in the World of Modern Science* (London: Routledge, 1989); Henrika Kuklick, *The Savage Within: The Social History of British Anthropology, 1885–1945* (Cambridge: Cambridge University Press, 1992); Adam Kuper, *Anthropology and Anthropologists: The Modern British School*, 2nd edn (London: Routledge, 1983); Hayden White, *Metahistory: The Historical Imagination in Nineteenth-Century Europe* (Baltimore: Johns Hopkins University Press, 1973) and his *Tropics of Discourse* (Baltimore: Johns Hopkins University Press, 1990); Raymond Williams, *Keywords: A Vocabulary of Culture and Society*, revised edition (New York: Oxford, 1983).
104 Harry Hartoonian and Harumi Befu have examined the Japanese nativist discourses on identity; see H. D. Harootunian, *Things Seen and Unseen: Discourse and Ideology in Tokugawa Nativism* (Chicago: Chicago University Press, 1988); Harumi Befu, *Hegemony of Homogeneity: An Anthropological Analysis of Nihonjinron* (Melbourne: Trans Pacific Press, 2001): http://www.transpacificpress.com/befu/htm. See also

258 *Sharon Traweek*

Dorinne Kondo, *Crafting Selves: Power, Gender, and Discourses of Identity in a Japanese Workplace* (Chicago: Chicago University Press, 1990), Tessa Morris-Suzuki, "Race," in *Re-Inventing Japan: Times, Space, Nation* (New York: M. E. Sharpe, 1998), and Michael Weiner, "Discourses of Race, Nation and Empire in pre-1945 Japan," *Ethnic and Racial Studies*, vol. 18, no. 3 (July 1995), pp. 433–56. Miriam Silverberg has studied how the formation of Japanese anthropological knowledge was imbedded in its historical political economy; see Miriam Silverberg, "Constructing the Japanese Ethnography of Modernity," *Journal of Asian Studies*, vol. 51, no.1 (February 1992), pp. 30–54. Andrew Gordon and others have developed similar arguments about history, and Hiromi Mizuno has done the same for the history of science field in Japan; see Andrew Gordon, ed., *Postwar Japan as History* (Berkeley: University of California Press, 1993) and Hiromi Mizuno, "Science, Ideology, Empire."

105 See Sharon Traweek, "How Modern Became Retro: An Historical Political Economy of Knowledge," in Sharon Traweek and Roddey Reid, eds., *Cultural Studies of Science, Technology, and Medicine* (New York: Routledge, 2000) and my *Who Knows? Crafting Cultural Studies of Physics, History, and Anthropology*, unpublished manuscript. See also Miriam Silverberg, "Constructing the Japanese Ethnography of Modernity" and Hiromi Mizuno, "Science, Ideology, Empire."

106 See, for example, Laura Nader, ed., *Naked Science: Anthropological Inquiry into Boundaries, Power, and Knowledge* (New York: Routledge, 1996); Gary Downey and Joseph Dumit, eds., *Cyborgs and Citadels: Anthropological Interventions in Emerging Sciences and Technologies*, School of American Research Advanced Seminar Series (Santa Fe, NM: SAR Press, 1997); Anne-Jorunn Berg and Margrethe Aune, eds., *Domestic Technology and Everyday Life: Mutual Shaping Processes*, Proceedings of the COST A4 workshop in Trondheim, Norway, October 1993, edited by Tarja Cronberg and Knut Sorensen (Luxembourg: European Commission, Directorate-General XIII, Science, Research and Development, Office for Official Publications of the European Communities, 1994); Wiebe Bijker and John Law, eds., *Shaping Technology/Building Society: Studies in Sociotechnical Change* (Cambridge, MA: MIT Press, 1992); and Weibe Bijker, Thomas Hughes, and Trevor Pinch, eds., *The Social Construction of Technological Systems: New Directions in the Sociology and History of Technology* (Cambridge, MA: MIT Press, 1987).

107 Arata Isozaki, "Of City, Nation, and Style," pp. 49, 60.

108 For a different position see Peter Drucker, "In Defense of Japanese Bureaucrats," *Foreign Affairs* (September/October, 2002), 68–80. He first claims that bureaucracies are uniformly strong the world over, and that the United States is the anomalous case. That claim is the preamble to his primary assertion that, absent the bureaucracy, no other element of Japanese society (politicians, military, academia, religious groups, business world) is capable of leading or governing Japan. Obviously, both arguments are weak. However, such arrangements seem to have served U.S. interests since the occupation of Japan under General MacArthur; hence, I would accept Drucker's remarks as valid assessments of U.S. policy. No doubt these are the reasons his essay was published in *Foreign Affairs*.

109 See, for example, Yuki Tanaka, *Japan's Comfort Women: Sexual Slavery and Prostitution During World War II and the U.S. Occupation* (London: Routledge, 2002).

110 For several years I have chosen to write in what some call the middle voice: "The middle voice is in the middle of the active and the passive voice because the subject cannot be categorized as either agent or patient but has elements of both": http://en.wikipedia.org/wiki/Grammatical_voice#The_middle_voice. I do this for strategic epistemological reasons discussed in some of my other works. In ethnographic research we account for what the people we study make of us, thereby providing the reader with an additional indicator of our subject positioning in the research process. In this practice we are being resolutely empiricist. As some of the physicists I study have said: you are a detector and you calibrate the effects of the detector on the data you collect.

15 The city and the economy of "losing"

Targeting competitive bodies in an era of global competition

Robbie B. H. Goh

Sports and warfare can trace their affiliation at least as far back as classical Greece: Plato in *The Republic* refers conflatingly to "warrior athletes" whose conditioning in the "military gymnastic" was crucial for their specialization as the state's "dogs" of war (Jowett 1969: I, 334). The intensity and motivatedness of this association has, if anything, only increased in recent years: Mrozek (1980: 178–9) shows that an American creed of "toughness," characterized as an "aggressive, action-oriented attitude," intensified in the wake of World War II and in the Cold War period. Thus, the "Football is Violence" culture that flourished in Cold War America and after has its roots in a militarism which associated America's military successes with the broad inculcation of an aggressive toughness such as was fostered by painful physical training. Similarly, Chick and Loy (2001: 6, 14) show how "combative sports" – those that "involve actual or potential contact between opponents with the object of inflicting real or symbolic injury on opponents, gaining playing field territory, or are patently warlike" – play a significant role in socializing values of aggressiveness associated with "warfare."

There are obviously differences between sports and warfare in terms of operational modes, equipment and results, and to a certain extent scale: among other things, the incidence of permanent disability, and certainly of fatality, is incomparably higher (per incident) in military conflicts than in even the most violent contact sports, and military conflicts operate much more closely in response to ideologies and discourses of "national interests" than do the more complexly tribal and often shifting loyalties and identifications operating in sports. Yet the similarities, particularly in an age of global capital, global cities competition, and digital communications, are structurally significant: footage from military campaigns has been screened regularly on cable television and web pages since "Operation Desert Shield" in 1991 – a campaign that was also renowned for introducing a new generation of "smart" bombs and other offensives using remote optical sensing. The rite of passage of this phase of war-as-spectator-sport into popular cultural consciousness is perhaps marked by a scene from the action movie *Patriot Games*, directed by Phillip Noyce (1992), in which the protagonist Jack Ryan (played by Harrison Ford) together with a room full of CIA and other intelligence personnel watch a screen on which a covert operation halfway around the world is being relayed in astonishing detail (down to individual kills) by satellite. Terrorism, the fate of the body, surveillance, gladiatorial contests, violence, and the cult of the spectator all come together at this point in time under the aegis of the global capitalist system as much as of the actual technology and security issues.

In much the same way, the gladiatorial clashes of American football, rugby union and league, soccer, and other sports are broadcast and replayed on cable television and webpages, with highlights and controversial moments reviewed by "video referees" and replayed on large stadium screens. From "electronic eye" technology used to judge tennis serves to computer-based camera technology used to judge offside rulings in soccer (Martinelli 2004: 8), the face (or, more appropriately, the structured body) of popular sports has been changed significantly by surveillance technologies. Furthermore, the growing dominance of cable sports providers such as ESPN and Star Sports has shaped viewing habits by creating a (more or less, and growing) global viewership that has become very much a part of the game itself, involving an elaborate economy of commentators and pre- and post-game shows, merchandising, promotional sequences, and other segments which have become part of the spectatorship ritual, creating complex fan bases that are as much to do with the marketing of the athletic bodies on display as they are about older national or regional loyalties and identifications. "Combative sports" such as American football and rugby have capitalized on both game surveillance and broadcast technologies to expand their domains, combining the technologies to create new rituals of viewership and display; thus, the higher-level rugby games featured on cable television have in recent years incorporated a "TMO" (television match official) whose job is to referee and adjudicate footage of game action that for various reasons cannot be caught by the primary referee. Large screens installed in the stadia broadcast this questionable footage (which is also broadcast to television viewers) while the TMO deliberates. The same process of blowing up, replaying, and perpetually highlighting the action is of course enacted with all the significant episodes, especially the try scoring, jarring tackles, and sudden accelerations that are so much a part of the game of rugby. The result is a heightened scrutiny of athletic bodies that becomes normalized as part of the game, but also economized as the domain of a global marketing strategy and the creation of a larger consumption base.

Here again, "combative sports" and the military employ similar disciplines and displays (the two are interwoven) of the body. Combat technology not only images the offensive target, but in the process also contributes to a popular image of the soldier (as well-trained, successful, a winner not only in battle but in social terms as well) that feeds into the recruitment of soldiers and more funding for military equipment. The analogous process in sports is more familiar, in which increasingly sophisticated training techniques, monetary inducements (including all-important endorsement deals), and competitive leagues produce elite professional athletes who become images of the winning athlete for a younger generation with targets of a successful career in sports. Occasionally the two sets of images converge particularly closely, as in the media coverage of former Arizona Cardinals safety Pat Tillman who quit the NFL in order to become an army ranger, and was subsequently killed in Afghanistan in April 2004. Predictably, Tillman is glowingly held up as the image of the athlete–warrior–patriot, a role model as much for his physical prowess as for his military zeal, and has helped fuel the post-9/11 consciousness targeted at national security and patriotic sentiment.

In both warfare and sports, this technological-capitalist targeting of winning bodies is closely associated with the global city. As Bishop (2004: 61–3) observes, military C³I (Command, Control Communications, and Information) and other technology has made its impress upon the shape of the global city, creating a "vertical city" in which a strategic "high ground" is used to survey, discipline, and control the various elements of the urban order. This is combined with various broadcast technologies that, in their "unidirectional" and mechanical methods of issuing information and images, have something of the "ballistic" nature of military projectiles (Bishop 2004: 63, 72–6). To this we might add that urban control is both a capitalistic and a corporeal project – technologies of surveillance and control, if initiated by the military for nationalist agendas, have quickly been incorporated into multinational capitalism, not only as the measures of military-like security and enforcement required to safeguard corporate interests on a large scale, but also to scrutinize and regulate individual employees to prevent the compromising of production and marketing targets. The "corporation" not only is an abstract embodiment of financial interests, but also has physical manifestations, in the concrete space of buildings and plants and their organization of human behaviour, and also in the selection, discipline, and manipulation of human labor resources to fit the corporate goals.

As Sassen (1996a: 187, 193) observes, the "internationalization of capital" finds its corollary in the "internationalization of labour" and the way that this is shaped in the space of the global city: beyond the older racial–social segregations seen in slums and ghettos is the spatial logic of a "corporate culture" that "devalues" low-level workers even as it espouses an ethos of apparent "neutrality"; its very pursuit of "technological development and efficiency" marginalizes and contains low-value workers in a space of insignificance. The persistence of such military and corporate technology-spaces and their organization of bodies is a sober corrective to cosmopolitanism with its emphasis on the unconstrained movements and privileges of global elites (Holston and Appadurai 1999; Pollock *et al.* 2002). Although it is certainly true that cosmopolitanism reveals itself not as "a circle created by culture diffused from a center," but instead reveals that "centers are everywhere and circumferences nowhere" (Pollock *et al.* 2002: 12), the real force of technologies in operation in global capital and global cities competition continues to structure bodies and sites around competitive centers that are proclaimed (with perpetuating results as much as mere fanfare) "winners" in this race.

One such form of targeting (of both cities and bodies) is the "rugby economy" for which a number of Pacific cities (Sydney, Melbourne, Brisbane, Auckland, Christchurch) compete against each other and against larger (particularly West European) cities with a range of other strengths and attractions, at the same time that they impose their "vertical" organization upon the surrounding territories and cities of the Pacific region. Like other professionalized contact team sports that attract large and often fanatical followings (American football, basketball, soccer, and to a lesser extent Australian rules football and rugby league), rugby union is a capitalist mechanism that structures and organizes bodies, paying high salaries, bonuses, and signing fees to attract ever bigger and more powerful athletes (Bathgate *et al.* 2002: 268), and uses a range of broadcast strategies (print and media advertising, merchandise marketing, cable and internet telecasts of games, the highlighting of game segments on large stadium screens) to project the image of winning athletic bodies onto spectators, viewers, and fans. The organization of spectator and fan bodies goes beyond merely the identification with a favourite player through the wearing of (a replica of) the player's jersey, the collection of memorabilia, or other forms of imaginative identification with the player; it also involves the attraction and organization of fans to fill the increasingly large sporting arenas in which the main games are held – a major logistical exercise in itself when it is considered that one of the premier sites such as Sydney's Telstra Stadium (subsequently renamed ANZ Stadium) can hold 83,500 spectators, and for the year ending June 30, 2003, reported a total revenue of A$35.6 million, although in recent years the income has been more modest (Telstra Stadium n.d.).

It is a fairly well-established fact that the global marketing of major sporting and cultural events (not only sporting events like the Olympics or the FIFA World Cup, but also major arts and cultural festivals like the Edinburgh Arts Festival and the New Orleans Mardi Gras celebrations) not only promises to contribute a major boost to the city's revenues (in accommodations and other knock-on spending), but also fosters the city's general standing as a desirable place to visit and live and do business in. In the case of Sydney, for example, its niche targeting of a gay and lesbian community pays dividends not only in terms of the revenues from recurring events such as the Sydney Gay and Lesbian Mardi Gras and the Gay Games, but also in terms of "defining and projecting the identity of Sydney" as being essentially "tolerant" and "stylish" and thus also an attractive place for investment purposes (Marsh and Levy 1998: 4, 15; Blundell 2000: 12, 16). Similar to the targeting of gay bodies in the niche marketing of gay and lesbian events, Sydney's rugby economy also involves the formation and promotion of a specific image (the competitive warrior-athlete) that forms the bulls-eye of a broadening series of circles of other targets and goals (spectators, television viewers, advertisers, merchandise marketing, sports-related investments, tourism, and a more general publicizing of the city's sporty culture and lifestyle). According to organizers' estimates, the 2003 Rugby World Cup, hosted by Australia, attracted more than 1.8 million spectators to the host cities, of whom about 40,000 were visitors to Australia; 31.5 million television viewers watched the various games in the tournament, and the official website had 495 million hits during the tournament (International Rugby Board 2003). For the upcoming 2011 Rugby World Cup in New Zealand, it is estimated that some 85,000 visitors will each stay an average of 23 days, and will purchase NZ$268 million (about US$210 million) of RWC match tickets (Rugby World Cup 2011). This amounts to not only a considerable economic gain for the major city venues and to the country as a whole, but also a significant image-producing industry reaching out to a wide base of interested fans and spectators.

In this respect the rugby economy is a useful paradigm of the kinds of targeting strategies aimed by professional contact sports at the receptive bodies of spectators, and which also impact the space and culture of the city. At the same time, rugby – as a smaller, newer, and less professionally developed economy and technology than soccer, American football, or some of the other contact sports – is also useful as an example of an emerging targeting technology, in the context of the highly competitive Pacific-area cities competition, rather than of the older competitions among "global cities" such as "New York, London and Tokyo" that have by and large already concretized their targeting strategies into the landscape of the city (Sassen 1996b: 23–5). As a sport that was only professionalized relatively lately (in 1995), rugby union has had to catch up (as it were) with sports with much longer histories of professional development, with the result that its adopted strategies and technologies tend to stand out for the rapidity and forcefulness with which they have been introduced, and the developmental inequalities that then often starkly emerge. In addition, because of its highly physical and competitive nature – within which discourses and images of the warrior, collisions (involving the hard body, as well as its necessary corollary, the soft and impacted body), anthropophagism (or, more accurately, corpophagism), and similar tropes abound – the example of rugby reveals ideological bases in common with both military targeting and urban survival that lie much deeper than the merely surface, analogical level.

Thus, the 2003 Rugby World Cup in Australia reveals in its territorial, logistical, and competitive organization the essential elements of competitive targeting, even as the controversies stirred by that event reveal the attendant problems and discontents. As with similar global sporting competitions, such as the FIFA World Cup, the highly competitive nature of the event is publicized and everywhere evident: the twenty teams involved had either reached the world cup by competing against sixty-six other national teams in various regional qualifying pools, or else had won an automatic qualification by virtue of their having reached the quarter-finals of the previous world cup (International Rugby Board 2003). The eliminative nature of the competition is constantly highlighted in publicity material and press coverage, with special attention being paid to casualties among star players, humiliating defeats of lesser teams, and the occasional upset elimination of the top teams. Thus, the fact that Tana Umaga, the vice-captain and one of the star players of tournament favourites New Zealand, was ruled out of the remainder of the tournament after injuring his knee in their very first game becomes one of the ingredients of the world cup Greek tragedy in a similar logic to that which gleefully celebrates humiliating losses such as Namibia's 142–0 defeat at the hands of Australia – to which was just as gleefully appended the trivia item that the record defeat in a rugby world cup qualifier match was Singapore's 13–164 loss to Hong Kong in 1994 (AFP 2003b,c/out of order).

Injury, incapacitation, and elimination become blown up to tragic proportions not only because of the "tribal" identifications fostered by spectator sports – identifications that have been accelerated by television broadcasts of games (Voigt 1980: 128, 132), and more recently by demand-responsive media technologies such as cable television, pay-per-view events and webcasts – but also because of the specifically martial nature of rugby. As one of the quintessential "combative sports" in which possession and territory are very much tied to the amount of physical pain each team is prepared to endure and inflict (Chick and Loy 2001: 6), with elaborate rituals (the "scrum" and the "lineout") marking particular contests of territory, rugby enacts territorialization and the body–territory–victory substitution logic in dramatic ways. Rugby has one of the "highest risk per player-hour of injury" among contact sports (Garraway and Macleod 1995: 1485); the advent of professionalism in 1995 has not only dramatically increased the rate of incapacitating injuries suffered by players, but has also propagated a new image of bigger and better-conditioned players (Bathgate *et al.* 2002).

The attention that is paid not only to players of exceptional physical attributes (such as the New Zealand winger Jonah Lomu, renowned in his peak not only for his speed and skills but also for being one of the largest wingers in the game, at 1.96 meters and 125 kilograms), but also to players renowned for their hard hits on other players (such as the veteran Samoan back Brian Lima, who is nicknamed the "chiropractor" for his bone-jarring tackles, New Zealand back Sam Tuitupou who has been hailed as Lima's heir-apparent, and English fullback Josh Lewsey's crunching tackle on Australia's Mat Rogers in a June 2003 match that has made the rounds of media and internet discussions) is an indication of this normalization of the hard-hitting body and its logical corollary, the target body that is dented and damaged by the impact. The targeting of size, impact, and collisions has stepped up in recent iterations of the rugby world cup: after the precedent-setting appearance of giant winger Lomu, many other teams have started to feature huge players in the backline (positions hitherto reserved for smaller and more nimble players), such as France centre Mathieu Bastareaud (1.83 meters, 110 kilograms), Scotland wingers Sean Lamont (1.88 meters, 102 kilograms) and Nikki Walker (1.93 meters, 106 kilograms), New Zealand centre Sonny Bill Williams (1.91 meters, 108 kilograms), and others of that build. Smaller and highly skilful backs continue to feature in international games, even in top teams, but they are increasingly targeted, not only by the big hard men of opposing teams as potential weak points in the defense, but also by a media and public who increasingly buy into this norm of the big hard-hitting game. This has been the recent fate of the Australian rugby team, who late in 2010 had a string of disappointing performances, for which its critics were quick to blame the "lack of physicality" of its skilful and experienced but comparatively small backs such as Quade Cooper and Matt Giteau (All Blacks 2010).

In the same vein, the signs, rituals, and discourses of warfare abound, and are regularly broadcast to fans and viewers. One of the top teams, the New Zealand All Blacks, have made their pre-game ritual – a Maori *haka* known as the "Kama Te," a ritual challenge to their opponents – a household sight. A cable television advertisement for the 2003 Rugby World Cup carried the slogan "Some Warriors Don't Need Armour" (a reference to rugby's particular boast that it is a game which is as violent as American football, if not more so, but without any of the padding and protection of the latter, thus interposing body to body) above a still of two clashing rugby players. This accentuation of hard bodies was taken to another level in the 2003 Rugby World Cup, which saw a number of the top teams (including England, France, and New Zealand) introduce a new style of rugby jersey, thin and extremely form-fitting in contrast to the thick and relatively shapeless jerseys previously popular. Ostensibly intended to provide a technological edge (by being "lighter" and "stronger" than the old heavy cotton jerseys, and offering little purchase for opposing players to grip), they also offer the muscular body typical of the modern top-level rugby player on evident display; England forward Richard Hill was quoted as saying that "when you wear it you feel you have not got a shirt on" (Lawson 2003; AAP 2003). England's version of the skintight jersey, in particular, with its collarless design and prominent red streaks (in contrast to the white of the rest of the jersey) around the region of the latissimus dorsi muscles, accentuated the V-shaped musculature of the players' bodies, reinforcing the game's image as a clash between muscled and powerful bodies. To connect the military-like technology displayed in the jersey design with the speed and power emphasized in the game, it might be said that the players' bodies come to resemble the streamlined shape of missiles, which in the course of the game are launched at the opposing targets in order to inflict maximum damage and gain the most territory.

The targeting of bodies logically leads to the tropes of anthropophagism or corpophagism that feature prominently in rugby. Many teams are named after predatory beasts – the Argentina Pumas, the US Eagles, the Super 15 teams the Cheetahs, Lions, and Sharks, Australian rugby league teams the Panthers, Wests Tigers, and Sharks, and many others – not only to propagate and market an image of fierceness, but also to emphasize the underlying eliminative logic inherent in professional rugby. Just as, at the level of individual play, the spoils (scoring points or winning territory, earning star player status and all the monetary rewards this brings) are won only by impacting the hard victor's body over the broken loser's body, so too, at the top competitive levels, survival as a team depends on targeting (the recruitment of) the best grouping of such hard bodies, and using that team to drive down the opposition. Although relegation to a lower division is a possible fate in a huge sporting league such as soccer's English Premier League, in smaller leagues the fate of losing teams is to be broken up and consumed, bought over in a corporate deal, with parts (players and staff) sold off or assimilated into a different organization. Anthropophagism in the media coverage of rugby games – such as in the wire report on the 2003 world cup game between Argentina and Namibia titled "Argentina's Pumas Devour Namibia" (AFP 2003a) – is thus an unconscious echo of the logic of rugby economics, in which losing teams ultimately face the danger of being destroyed and cannibalized, while the cohesion and identity of winning teams are preserved.

Territorialism and corpophagism are not merely confined to the playing field, but are writ large upon the landscape as well, targeting cultures and spaces to create the desired power structure. The logistics of the 2003 Rugby World Cup is illustrative: matches were played in a number of venues throughout Australia, including a number of relatively small and isolated towns sucuh as Townsville in Queensland and Launceston in Tasmania, with the big matches all played in the three major cities of Brisbane, Melbourne, and Sydney. The last four games were all played in Sydney's colossal showpiece, the Telstra Stadium (as it was then called), which has a capacity of 83,500 (in contrast, York Park in Launceston, one of the smallest venues, has a capacity of only 20,000, only half of that seated; International Rugby Board 2003). The concentric urban targeting of this arrangement becomes clear: at the periphery are smaller venues in lesser cities, in which the lesser teams meet in less important games. The periphery is nevertheless deliberately structured into the overall event, for of course the larger venues and cities are logistically capable of hosting the smaller games as well, and if it is not viable to operate so far under capacity, then an alternative organization featuring only major events in the major cities is possible. The value of the periphery, in the organization of the event as it stands, is the favourable light that it casts on the center by its contrast: the attractions of Sydney, that "cosmopolitan and vibrant metropolis" with its "state-of-the-art" Telstra Stadium, gain in attractiveness and value in contrast to the rather more makeshift and humble facilities of Launceston (International Rugby Board 2003).

The locational strategy of targeting (top sites and teams) and marginalizing (peripheral ones) was even more evident in the 2007 Rugby World Cup, hosted by France, but which, in an evident deal with rugby nations who had supported France's bid (or at least refrained from competing with it, as England has done), involved a small number of games played in Cardiff and Edinburgh as well. These, once again, were the less important pool games, although one quarter-final was also played in Cardiff. Within France, the lesser games were played in smaller stadia in peripheral towns such as Montpellier and Lens, while the bigger games (all the semi-finals, the bronze finals and the final) were all played in Paris's big stadia, the Parc des Princes and Stade de France. Metonymically, teams and players (as well as their supporters) also attach greater importance to winning an advance to a later round of competition, as this is reinforced by the ritual movement from the peripheral city to the central one – a movement that, in obvious eliminative and corpophagic logic, comes via impacting on, breaking, and consuming a rival team, its players, and supporters. For its part, the periphery hopes to benefit from excess consumption capacity, that is, from the demand (for match tickets, hotel rooms, tourist sites, retail goods, and so on) that is not fully met by the target cities and events.

If cities cannot eloquently speak of the pains of being at the periphery of such targeting structures, certainly players and staff can. The 2003 Rugby World Cup saw numerous complaints and controversies regarding logistical and other arrangements that were seen as favoring the top teams and disadvantaging the weaker ones. Tonga, Namibia, and Samoa were among the teams protesting against what they perceived as referees' biases that advanced the causes of the top teams, draw fixtures which clustered the games of weaker teams close together (thus hampering their recovery from the preceding game and preparations for the following one) while spacing out the top teams' games more generously, and general "second-class citizen" treatment on behalf of organizers (Reuters 2003a,b). Not just the sour grapes of less successful teams, some of these charges have been reinforced by the admission of International Rugby Board (IRB) chairman Syd Millar that the 2003 Rugby World Cup fixtures were arranged in such a way that the leading teams got more rest between games than the weaker teams in order to maximize media display of the top teams (which have larger fan bases) for revenue reasons (Reuters 2003c). In addition, the automatic world cup qualification of the top teams (which coincidentally happened to have been the eight teams to reach the quarter-finals of the previous world cup) also means that they have the luxury of longer and better-funded campaigns designed specifically to prepare for their assigned places in the competition, whereas weaker teams have to find the players, funding, and other resources to go through an attritional qualifying campaign without any certainty of reaching the goal of the world cup. Thus, the existing and continuing successes of top teams, their economic resources, the extra media attention paid to popular (i.e. successful and rich) teams, the organizing body's awareness of and conformity to the inequalities between teams, and the ways in which these measures get broadcast to viewers and supporters and translated into differing attitudes towards teams all constitute targeting strategies that perpetuate the strengths and attractions of top teams at the expense of their weaker opponents.

Inevitably, such technologies and economies have eroded the older sporting economies that were more closely aligned with national peoples and cultures. In an epoch in which emigration and working abroad are becoming much more common, and labor often moves internationally to take advantage of economic opportunities, the international rugby economy has accordingly facilitated the movement of talented players from their country of birth to play in and for other countries that offer them better opportunities. The IRB's regulations on player eligibility permit a player to represent a country other than that of his birth, provided he has one parent or grandparent born in that country, or has completed 36 consecutive months of residence there (International Rugby Board n.d.a). This effectively means that any player may be "adopted" (or, to put it less delicately, "poached") by another country, even without parental or grandparental ties, if he can be induced to ply his trade in the adoptive country for 3 years and then don that country's national colours.

The IRB's "One Union" rule, which prohibits a player from playing for more than one country if he has already played at one of the highest two levels for a country, is really intended to place some form of restriction on a player's national allegiances; what it effectively does, however, is to foster a system of targeting promising young players from other countries, and making them attractive offers to play in the adoptive country before they have been selected for higher national duties in their country of birth. This very strategy has been alleged in major rugby powers such as Australia, New Zealand, and England: Australian loose forward Radike Samo was born in Fiji but by virtue of having played in Australian club rugby since 1998 became eligible to represent Australia. His selection for the Australian national team in 2004, despite his having played for Fiji's under-19 team and after he had apparently indicated his desire to represent Fiji at the top level, caused a furor, with some critics seeing this as a cynical move by Australia whose result, among other things, would be to deny resource-strapped Fiji one of their more promising players. Another Australian squad member, South African-born winger Clyde Rathbone, played for South Africa's under-21 squad but was claimed by Australia on the grounds that his grandmother was Australian by birth. New Zealand also have a number of national players who were born in neighbouring Pacific Island nations: 2003 captain Tana Umaga is of Samoan origin, as is his cousin and teammate Jerry Collins, and fullback Mils Muliana; star winger Joe Rokocoko was born in Fiji; and other players are also of foreign origin and might have chosen to play for other countries. It is certainly difficult to distinguish between players who chose (or whose families chose) to come to New Zealand for reasons other than rugby, and those for whom the prospects of playing top-level professional rugby in a relatively resource-rich country like New Zealand was a significant consideration. However, it remains true at a structural level that the vastly superior developmental resources, competitive scenes, financial prospects, and general quality of life of countries like Australia and New Zealand are so far in advance of their Pacific Island neighbors that they naturally form the attractive hub for players of any ability and ambition. In the first place, the superior employment and salary prospects in general in countries like Australia and New Zealand (with 2009 GDPs of US$924 billion and US$126 billion respectively), compared with their rugby-playing Pacific Island neighbors Fiji (US$2.9 billion), Samoa (S$0.5 billion), and Tonga (US$311 million), are themselves inducements for emigration for players and their families who are assured of backup jobs if a career in rugby does not work out, or of jobs for members of the family other than the athlete himself.

Top rugby academies (which are especially well conceived and well supported in New Zealand) that train promising young children for professional careers in rugby also form an inevitable consideration in attracting and developing top players who might otherwise have to run many risk-laden years in poorly developed countries before getting a chance at a professional career. The New Zealand Rugby Union identified as one of its strategies for success "the maintenance of an accurate database to track progress" of promising players, and the maintenance of "outstanding identification and development programmes and systems . . . to generate quality players, referees, coaches and administrators" (NZRU 2009: 5, 8). The nature of the economic investment required to maintain such an accurate tracking and the development of promising players is sobering: the NZRU's 2009 expenditure was NZ$106 million (about US$80 million), which is about 16 percent of the entire GDP of Samoa, and more than 26 percent of that of Tonga (NZRU 2009).

Ultimately, there is no getting past the fact that rugby is a game in which bodies – the bigger/stronger/faster the better – matter a great deal, and there is only so much that talent development can do in countries where the majority of players come from racial stocks with smaller physiques. Such is the lot of countries like Japan, the most successful of all Asian countries in rugby terms, and one with all the economic resources and a reasonably well-developed domestic rugby arena, but whose national team still suffers from their huge physical disadvantage to the top teams. The increasingly global market for rugby bodies will mean not only that talented players may move from low-economy, low-development nations like Tonga, Samoa, and Fiji toward centers like Auckland and Sydney, but also that a "spillover" of players born in New Zealand and Australia who fail to win the top competitive places in their countries of birth will be induced to move to less successful rugby countries. Caucasian and especially Pacific Island rugby bodies are in demand not only in Japan, but also in contender rugby nations like Italy and Wales. The Japanese squad for the 2003 Rugby World Cup had several players born in New Zealand, including its star stand-off Andrew Miller, centers George Konia and Ruben Parkinson, and lock Adam Parker. Italy was coached by former New Zealand winger John Kirwan, and its squad was augmented by flankers Scott Palmer and loose forward Matthew Phillips from New Zealand, and fullback Gert Peens from South Africa. Even leading teams like Wales (with New Zealand-born centre Sonny Parker, and Australian-born lock Brent Cockbain) and France (which has featured New Zealander Tony Marsh in the center position) have had occasion to target and import select players from the southern hemisphere rugby giants.

Once again, the economy of "losing" plays a support function to the select targeting of top athletic bodies. It might be said that the consolidation of places such as Auckland and Sydney as the main targets of attraction for rugby stars and events depends upon the existence of significantly less successful and less competitive economies such as Japan to take up the spillover of those players who lose out in the competition for the top national places – this includes many players with stronger national and cultural ties to their respective countries of birth or domicile than the players who ultimately take their place. Losing, in this sense, is a structural and self-perpetuating feature of the world-system, rather than an occasional experience against an equal team that may be overturned in the near future; as shown in the 2003 Rugby World Cup, in which minor teams played in decidedly minor venues as a kind of secondary festival to the main event centered at the Sydney Telstra Stadium, and in which the predictability of wins by the major teams had to be palliated by a BBC listing of "world cup's unlikely losers" (a listing of star players from the weaker teams who "could give this year's eventual world champions a run for their money"; BBC 2003), losing is a distinct category of participation, with its own well-defined parameters and roles.

The international rugby economy, as an echo of global capitalism displaced onto the arena of competitive bodies and their fanatical supporters, reveals certain characteristics that cast perhaps a clearer light on the mechanisms of global capital than is evident within the realm of abstract financial symbolism. In the first place, the hierarchical and self-perpetuating order is organized not chiefly by any historical, physical/racial, and cultural advantages a nation may have in the sport: Scotland and Wales are examples of nations with long and proud rugby histories, but which have at times fallen short in terms of modern technologies of elite tracking, performance, and planning. Scotland currently ranks seventh in the world and Wales ninth, just ahead of economically poorer countries such as Fiji (tenth) and Samoa (eleventh). More significant than historical pedigrees are the advanced technologies of tracking and targeting of top players (both domestically and abroad) from an early age, economic inducements for players and coaches, the media and marketing focus that broadcasts the winning image of a particular team (thus enhancing fan identification with the team and generating several sources of revenue), and other means of perpetuating a large and highly competitive pool from which "winning" players are selected for the highest honours while "losing" players seek employment in lower-level nations. The cumulative and self-reinforcing benefits of such technologies and economies – competitive successes feeding media revenues that in turn reinforce popular support and merchandising revenues, all of which ensure the best developing and tracking programs and salaries to attract the best players – mean that inequalities and hierarchical organizations are likely to be perpetuated, at least in the medium term.

What is true of teams follows in many ways for cities as well: rugby and other highly competitive sporting economies confirm and perpetuate the positioning of winning cities vis-à-vis losing ones, in part by predatory and corpophagic strategies that weaken athletic competition (and thus also revenues) by targeting competitive bodies. If cities such as Sydney, Melbourne, and Auckland have comprehensive attractions for tourist revenues, high-value immigrants, and multinational corporate investments compared with Asia-Pacific neighbours such as Suva, Apia, Nuku'alofa, or even Christchurch and Townsville, this is in part due to the cumulative and reinforcing effect of sporting economies that enhance the winning image of such major cosmopolitan sites. Targeting, in this sense, reinforces targeting: as information management gathers data in order to outplay potential competitors (at the level of individual players, teams, cities, and events), this leads to the winning of attractive broadcast contracts that display winning images of successful cities, which become imprinted upon a global viewership and influence future investment and event-planning decisions by predisposing the repeat targeting of winner cities.

Territory, in this sense, is still very much a physical and specific reality, despite the seemingly abstract nature of space in a global economy. Yet the winning territory is no longer the national space, as was the rhetoric of nationalist imperialism in the late nineteenth to mid-twentieth centuries, but the one or two leading cities in the nation that are in a winning competitive situation in relation to their other compatriot cities. The strategic economies of global cities do not merely mean the weakening of national boundaries, as Holston and Appadurai (1999: 3) observe; they also mean a foregrounding of the leading cities at the expense of a kind of corpophagic dematerialization of the national space. National rugby teams now draw (often with the flimsiest of excuses) on the bodily resources of talented players born in other countries (and often with the most glaring racial and cultural contrasts, as with the New Zealand players in the otherwise very homogeneous Japanese team), in the process diluting or confusing the parameters of the "national"; their successes, merchandising, and bodily images are projected upon an identifying audience and fandom drawn from a global pool much wider than the national populace; and arguably the greatest benefit of their athletic successes, in terms of longer-term strategic targeting, is not the nation but the leading cities in which their events will inevitably get played. If national spaces and territories are indeed becoming increasingly abstract and shadowy in an age of global media, capital, and communications technologies, winning global cities seem to become more specifically targeted and more concretely benefited as a result.

Yet "losing" bodies and cities do not simply disappear, but are also strategically perpetuated within this strange competitive economy. Despite many grumbles and boycott threats from "losing" rugby nations, many of them grounded in the harsh realities of unequal targeting strategies by winning nations, such teams continue to play their assigned roles of perpetual also-rans. Media and organizational structures ensure that even the occasional upset (of a leading team by a second-tier one) does not substantially overturn the established hierarchy: the inertial body of large-scale marketing and merchandizing campaigns and media exposure supporting the leading teams buffers such teams from major dips in popularity and support in the event of upset losses, while the IRB's complicated system of calculating world rankings is intended, among other things, to ensure that rankings do not "over-react" to "freak results," effectively protecting leading teams from too sharp a dip in the event of an upset loss (International Rugby Board n.d.b). At the same time, predatory targeting by winning teams means that weaker teams continue to be weakened by losing their most promising players to the leagues and national teams of winning countries. The strategic perpetuation of hierarchies in rugby means that losing teams cannot overturn their assigned place merely by hard-won occasional victories on the pitch itself; any consolation for their place must come from picking up the revenue crumbs from playing against winning teams, and from the spillover strategic benefits that come from the athletic contest with such teams. There is a similar strategic perpetuation with second-tier cities, which are structurally better placed to play a supporting role to winning cities and pick up spillover business from major events such as the 2003 Rugby World Cup, than to hope for the major structural change that will permit them to leapfrog over the winning cities and their strategic advantages. Despite some shocks (relatively poor showings by New Zealand and Australia), the 2007 Rugby World Cup results showed little change from the 2003 ones in terms of top and bottom teams, with the likes of perennial powers such as South Africa, England, France, Australia, and New Zealand all reaching at least the quarter-finals, and perennial whipping boys such as Japan, Namibia, Romania, and Portugal all being eliminated after being defeated by typically large margins. The upcoming 2011 Rugby World Cup in New Zealand is hardly expected to dramatically reverse these habitual patterns.

In terms of global people movements and the fate of labor within global capital, the rugby economy reveals the underlying fate of common bodies, which is to be impacted and bruised for the sake of raising elite bodies whose pre-eminence is perpetuated and justified by corporate and competitive strategies. The targeting and tracking of promising rugby players through junior leagues and weaker teams to their eventual confirmation as winning athletes in top nations and the media system is in this respect analogous to the targeting and tracking ("headhunting") of promising MBA graduates or young professionals through the myriad organizations and positions available in multinational capital to their eventual confirmation as the top management of the major corporations. Although for these elite bodies (who are subjected to a corporate image-making machinery as much as are winning athletes and their fans) a kind of "cosmopolitan" ease of movement across the abstract space of nations and cultures is indeed facilitated, this comes at the cost of the common bodies in lower management and certainly in front-line labor whose efforts contribute significantly to the corporate successes claimed by elite CEOs, but who do not share significantly in the rewards paid to the latter, instead constituting a kind of statistical mass against which the CEO's salary is contrastively distinguished. Losing groups – the uneducated masses of lesser-developed nations, racial minorities whose socio-economic progress is systematically slowed by prejudicial popular images and competitive disadvantages, women in general, and others – may occasionally produce the rare individual who breaks into the ranks of the elite, but whose structural role is to fulfill the target role of mass labor and non-elite management whose existence highlights the contrastive "winning" ways of the elite.

Winners and losers – individuals, cities, laborers, athletes – constantly converge in variations of strategic targetings and organizations, but in hierarchical roles that are perpetuated by those strategic competitive and image-producing mechanisms. In the process, they constitute a different kind of battlefield from the frontal massing of opposing national and alliance armies familiar from the World War II conflict that signaled the end of nationalist imperialism. Global sporting economies and cities competitions are indicative of the ways in which competitive affiliations and sides ("nation," "culture," "race," even "the side") have become increasingly ill-defined and mutable. The army, as an "organized force" (*Oxford English Dictionary*) expressing the national (encompassing race, in "ethnos") will or interest, gives way to covert surveillance and intelligence-gathering units whose function is to track individual potential threats. In this sense (and in the sense, too, that certain kinds of surveillance emphases and patterns can themselves create a threat), the contemporary military is not dissimilar to global media and capital. In this simulacrum of competition produced by global capital, targeting precedes not only nation and other associative groupings, but also notions of evenness and openness in the movement and flow of bodies and resources.

References

AAP (2003) "England design no-grip shirt," nzoom.com, August 30. Available at http://onesport.nzoom.com/sport_detail?0,1278,217158-2-26,00.html (accessed July 29, 2004).

AFP (2003a) "Rugby: Argentina's Pumas devour Namibia," *The Straits Times*, October 15, 2003.

AFP (2003b) "Numb-Mibia," *The Straits Times*, October 26, 2003 .

AFP (2003c) "Have-nots mauled," *Today*, November 3, 2003.

All Blacks (2010). "Wallabies take three steps forward, five backwards," November 15, 2010. Available at http://www.allblacks.com/news/14881/Wallabies-take-three-steps-forwards-five-backwards (accessed January 25, 2011).

Bathgate, A., J. P. Best, G. Craig and M. Jamieson (2002) "A prospective study of injuries to elite Australian rugby union players," *British Journal of Sports Medicine*, 36, 265–9.

BBC (2003) "World cup's unlucky losers," November 3, 2003. Available at http://news. bbc.co.uk/sport1/hi/rugby_union/rugby_world_cup/3230845.stm (accessed November 24, 2003).

Bishop, R. (2004) " 'The vertical order has come to an end': the insignia of the military C³I and urbanism in global networks," in Ryan Bishop, John Phillips and Wei-Wei Yeo (eds) *Beyond Description: Singapore Space Historicity*, London: Routledge, pp. 60–78.

Blundell, G. (2000) "Insight into Sydney," in *Insight – Sydney, Australia 2000*, Spring Cape: Pacific Coast Publishing, pp. 6–28.

Chick, G. and J. W. Loy (2001) "Making men of them: male socialization for warfare and combative sports," *World Cultures*, 12(1), 2–17.

Garraway, M. and D. Macleod. (1995) "Epidemiology of rugby football injuries," *The Lancet*, 345(8963), 1485–7.

Holston, J. and A. Appadurai (1999) "Cities and citizenship," in James Holston and Arjun Appadurai (eds) *Cities and Citizenship*, Durham, NC: Duke University Press, pp. 1–18.

International Rugby Board (2003) "Rugby World Cup 2003 official website." Available at http://www.rugbyworldcup.com/EN (accessed July 13, 2004).

International Rugby Board (n.d.a) "Regulation 8: eligibility to play for national representative teams." Available at http://www.irb.com/laws/Regulations (accessed July 15, 2004).

International Rugby Board (n.d.b) "Rankings explained." Available at http://www.irb.com/WR/RankingsExplained/ (accessed August 2004, 5).

Jowett, B. (1969) *The Dialogues of Plato*, four vols., trans. and ed. B. Jowett, Oxford: Clarendon.

Lawson, A. (2003) "Discovery," *Sun Herald*, October 12, 2003.

Marsh, I. and S. Levy (1998) *1998 Economic Impact Statement: Sydney Gay and Lesbian Mardi Gras*, Sydney: Sydney Gay and Lesbian Mardi Gras.

Martinelli, N. (2004) "Technology: keeping an eye on the ball," *Newsweek*, July 12, 2004, p. 8.

Mrozek, D. J. (1980) "The cult and ritual of toughness in Cold War America," in Ray B. Browne (ed.) *Rituals and Ceremonies in Popular Culture*, Bowling Green, OH: Bowling Green University Popular Press, pp. 178–91.

Noyce, P. (dir.) (1992) *Patriot Games*.

NZRU (2009) "Annual Report 2009." Available at http://files.allblacks.com/comms/New_Zealand_Rugby_Union_2009_Annual_Report.pdf (accessed January 25, 2011).

Pollock, S., H. K. Bhabha, C. A. Breckenridge and D. Chakrabarty (2002) "Cosmopolitanisms," in Carol A. Breckenridge, Homi K. Bhabha, Sheldon Pollock and Dipesh Chakrabarty (eds.) *Cosmopolitanism*, Durham, NC: Duke University Press, pp. 1–14.

Reuters (2003a) "Coach won't back down," *The Straits Times*, October 22, 2003.

Reuters (2003b) "Tongans irked by early flight home," *The Straits Times*, October 30, 2003.

Reuters (2003c) "World cup draw fixed to maximise profits," *Straits Times*, November 4, 2003.

Rugby World Cup (2011) "News." Available at http://www.rugbyworldcom.com (accessed January 25, 2011).

274 *Robbie B. H. Goh*

Sassen, S. (1996a) "Analytic borderlands: race, gender and representation in the new city," in Anthony D. King (ed.) *Re-presenting the City: Ethnicity, Capital and Culture in the Twenty-First Century Metropolis*, Houndmills: Macmillan, pp. 183–202.

Sassen, S. (1996b) "Rebuilding the global city: economy, ethnicity and space," in Anthony D. King (ed.) *Re-presenting the City: Ethnicity, Capital and Culture in the Twenty-First Century Metropolis*, Houndmills: Macmillan, pp. 23–42.

Telstra Stadium (n.d.) "Telstra Stadium events and news." Available at http://www.telstrastadium.com.au/index.aspx?link_id=5.161 (accessed July 27, 2004).

Voigt, D. Q. (1980) "American sporting rituals," in Ray B. Browne (ed.) *Rituals and Ceremonies in Popular Culture*, Bowling Green, OH: Bowling Green University Popular Press, pp. 125–40.

16 Between targeting and display

Absorptive affiliations

Jordan Crandall

I am interested in the sense of wanting to be "in" something: the desire to be connected, synchronized, or bound up with a galvanizing *event*, in a way that mere visual possession cannot allow. The desire to be attuned to something that is happening, or that might happen at any moment – not necessarily as a conscious thought, but as a vaguely felt expectation. The desire to move toward the incipient *event* in order to absorb its force, touch it, taste it, submit to it – rather than simply to observe or capture it.

This immersive dynamic stands in contrast to analytical models based on the organizational paradigm of the apparatus. It challenges the dominance of a foundational condition of spectatorship or voyeuristic separation, and the understanding of media in terms of its capacity to produce a spectatorial relation. It

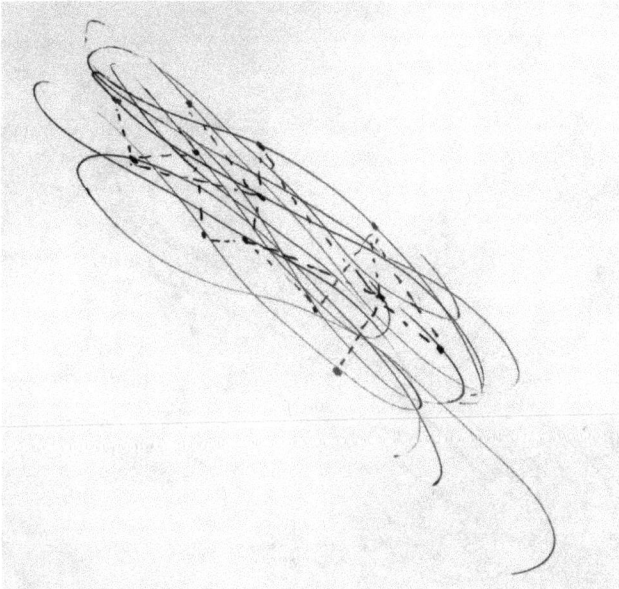

Figure 16.1 Image no. 1. Courtesy of the author/artist, 2011.

is an absorptive ecology that is less about acquisition than about divestiture. Its connection with "otherness" involves unconventional relational configurations, promiscuous and circuitous rather than directed. Its acts of (visual) mastery or possession are those that also cultivate their own (bodily) relinquishment, evacuating the primacy of distance and containment.

It is not about difference, repression, or voyeuristic enclosure.

Spectatorship is diffused within the absorptive arena. It unfolds within a condition of exposure.

A subject–object relational structure is distributed into shared networks of distance and connection – shared *events* within an ontological community that includes all manner of actors both human and nonhuman. No longer based in the unique personality central to modern notions of individualism, its *inclinations* are not necessarily based in *identifications*. They are not necessarily based in discrete positionality or the detection, classification, and constitution of behavior that has not been previously defined.

The challenge is to meet an external agency without reducing it to an object – to cultivate anomalous behavior as *event* rather than simply detecting, classifying, and targeting it.

To transform the *event*, however actual or incipient, immersive or extensive, into a *practice*.

The *event* is constituted as an object of fascination or concern through the stabilization and destabilization of a web of action.

It conforms to what you expect, yet it manifests an exceptionality.

It interrupts and assembles: it confounds expectations and categories, yet it also perpetuates them.

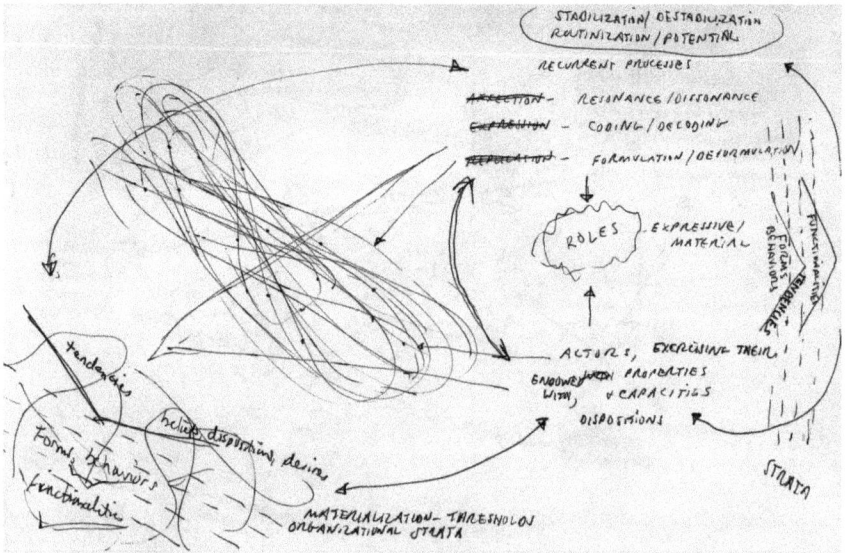

Figure 16.2 Image no. 2. Courtesy of the author/artist, 2011.

It is immanent, yet also transcendent: a dynamically stabilized, cumulative pattern, a discrete eruption or exception against a normalized field, or a threshold gradually attained or crossed.

I may seek to avoid detection, but I also seek to cultivate it: appearing yet hidden, disruptive yet screened in.

However configurative or fleeting my presence; however singular, multiple, or scalar my agency,

I position *myself* as a potential *event*.

In my movement, coding, and manner, I signal my availability for affiliation.

In this *practice of eventing*, I make contact with a stranger, an actor that I do not *know*, and in that moment I relate to that which transcends relations and inclinations. I cultivate an "inadequate" encounter that exceeds the known: the *event* that should not be sought, the *event* that one should not endeavor to *become*.

Detachment and visual mastery give way to an intimate, *excessive proximity* that functions at the level of body, time, and space, intertwined with urban configurations that it both structures and responds to: densities of the city that engender a mixture of closeness and distance, fascination and danger. An excessive proximity is achieved through scalar accumulation: the reproduction of impersonal, extensive correspondences and conductive affinities, in affiliations that may programically *calibrate* but not spatially or temporally *coincide*. The space in which this activity occurs is not a container but a generative mechanism.

The foundational structure of desire is not based in difference and alienation, polarized between lack and possession, as apparatus-driven theories would have it: an imperiled, incomplete subject, characterized by a primary absence, seeking its future completion as a coordinated form.

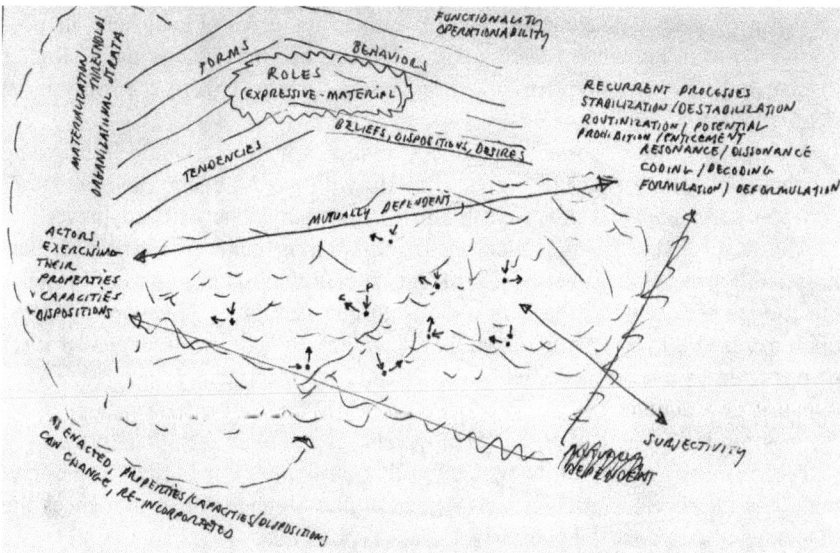

Figure 16.3 Image no. 3. Courtesy of the author/artist, 2011.

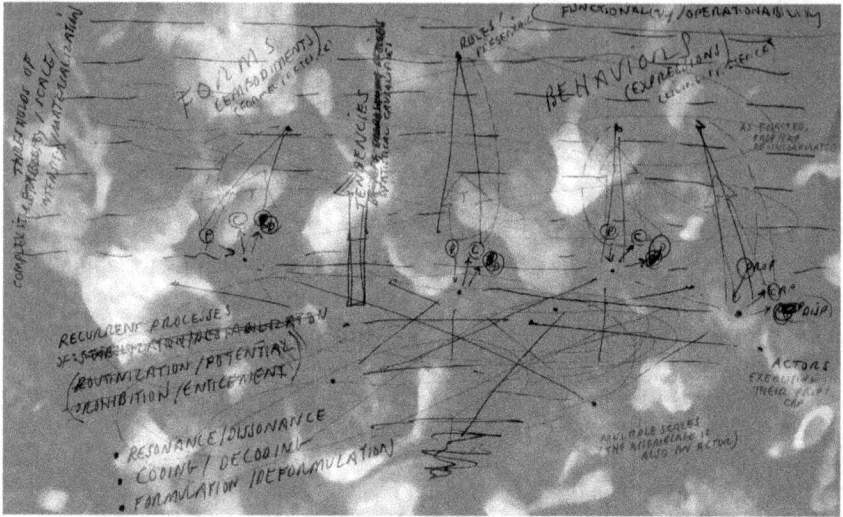

Figure 16.4 Image no. 4. Courtesy of the author/artist, 2011.

My object of desire does not even receive my desire, let alone complete it; rather, it extends it, modulates it, and attends it.

It is not an object *of* desire, but an object *in* desire – awash in transmissions among agencies, rife with affect and rhythm, in performative, open-ended circuits.

Actors are gathered and constituted within these immanent, extensive circuits of transmission, congealed in accordance with their *programs*, entrained in their conditions of affiliation.

If it is a "loss" – a relinquishment of self and its logics of enclosure, its possessive bases of knowledge-accumulation – it is a one that enacts "gain." Rather than seeing where an actor is not, in *reduction*, it shows where it already is, in *dissemination*.

My desire is not to possess my object, in such a way as it would fulfill some fundamental lack; rather, this extension, rife with excess energy and potential, activates the abundance already within me: it shows me what I already have.

The absorptive affiliation facilitates a compelling unknowable-ness. It harnesses the absorptive power of knowledge, fueled with its promises of mastery, but it does not deliver: it harbors not a truth but a *program*. It cannot be relied upon to resolve to a specific outcome, but, rather, to continually engender a set of possibilities whose outcomes we anticipate. Its absorptive power is the very dynamic of seduction.

Program is a vehicle of obscene enjoyment, in you more than you know.

Program has no body of its own, but rather exists in terms of the energies and materials that it channels. Yet it has agency: like a conductor, it influences the outcomes of the phenomena that it carries.

Program is a field of organized energy that always exists in or as a moving population of actors, at whatever scale, galvanizing its actors like a weather system.

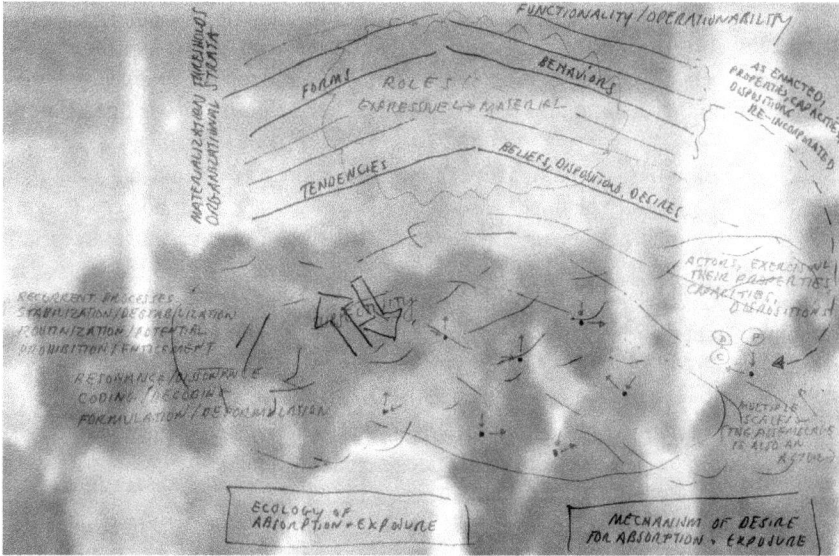

Figure 16.5 Image no. 5. Courtesy of the author/artist, 2011.

Program harbors compositional forces and delineations. It sets forth a dynamic of form. It contains codes and formulas, organizational principles and procedures, which are able to influence the timing, movement, and composition of actors and parts (human or nonhuman), to the extent that spatial, social, and somatic effects are generated, however illusory or fleeting.

A techno-scientific semiotics, embedded in an organizational form – combined with a dynamic of affective resonation that always undermines these logics, prompting readiness more than reading.

Programs give permission, while sustaining an undercurrent of prohibition. In this way they maintain both enticement and anguish: the anguish of temptation.

Program does not program in a determined way. Rather, it sets the stage. It is a string of enactable capacities that does not produce specific actions and forms so much as shape object/action tendencies. It conjures up space, engendering protocol and social conduct, but in such a way that unforeseen qualities, objects, and actions will emerge.

Programs are time-bound, providing calibrating infrastructures through which things move, or beat, rhythmically. They have a spacing function, which involves rhythm and temporal alignment, or calibration – the calibration of desires. Yet they also signal and modulate through a dynamic of intensification and discharge: they stabilize, accumulate and strengthen, lock in resonance with one another; they also discharge excess energies, as well as diverge or differentiate, generating new openings and fields of tension.

Programs exist at multiple levels of organization and stability. When they intensify – cross a certain threshold of organization – and are enacted in practice, they can eventualize forms.

Program generates excitations and teases out material objects indirectly. It agitates entities or parts until they are overcome with their own abundance, prompting accumulations and discharge-forms. It also generates appeals: libidinous attractions that solicit resonation-lockings, erotic groupings as quasi-forms, wet and sliding.

Within this appeal is bundled an element of horror: concealed death.

Programs are partly planned, partly emergent. They are generated collectively and polyrhythmically – emerging from the interactions of various forces and practices, and out of individually and collectively acquired patterns of response. Program "cooks" structuration in a weak or strong way, depending upon the libidinous energies that fuel it, and the material forces and parts that it is able to mobilize.

When programs reach a certain degree of stabilization, they can be formulized – replicated or applied as templates. This often happens in an emergent sense, as when a certain move or gesture propagates across a community, gaining strength and adhering in a dance move or social protocol. It entails a form of knowingness that is not necessarily the same as knowledge: a critical mass of affective transmissions that begin, over time, to bond a community and set the stage for a shared practice, intensifying the accumulation of knowledge, technology, and materials.

Program mobilizes carnal secrets – enticing combinations of calibrated sensation.

Programs are strings of distributed energies, channels, points, which have the potential to stabilize, differentiate, and pattern such that they can be "read," but this is only one of the apprehension modes that they solicit. They contain intelligible order but, more primarily, they modulate flows. They maneuver between the affective and symbolic registers, or between sensation and concept. They involve resonance as much as representation; living presence as much as formal presence.

Programs traverse the body, trafficking between the intensive and extensive realms of experience. They are structural-sensorial phenomena, erotically fueled, that act as motors and motivators for knowing.

Ultimately, no one can control the program's manifestations and effects: its formulas seem to take on a life of their own, like the silly pop tune that you can't get out of your head, propagating across a community and, at least at some level, developing social bonds. Program takes root to the extent that it resonates with something "in you": that potential excess of the self that always has the possibility of spilling over its bounds. It is something like a sensorial motif, a propagating pattern that generates excitations and structures disposition, yet at its core is meaningless.

Programs are trajectives that go nowhere in particular. They do not represent so much as engender. They operate through transversal mixings, redistributions of energy and meaning. They modify potentials (whether intentional or emergent) and reconfigure them in ways that might result in amplification or dampening.

To glimpse the workings of the program, one does not look to it as an object, but rather looks to the things with which it functions in combination, and to the things with which it transmits intensities. One looks at compositions (aggregates, assemblies); transformational processes (transmissions, flows); and the ongoing translations between multiple levels of organization, or higher-order and lower-order states. One avoids the form/content bifurcation and the signifier/signified duality, as well as the oppositions real/artificial, nature/culture, body/other. What emerges instead is something like a distinction between form and substance – or matter, content, and expression.

Program offers a primordial, animal thrill, though always infused with a cultural prohibition: a volatile, time-bound cocktail consumed with restraint, intoxicating and alerting. We drink but we can drive.

If there is a politics of program, it exists in the realm of competing formats and rhythms, embroiled in the struggles for systems compatibility. One works with it, additively, taking a compositional rather than oppositional approach.

Program is not operational, not algorithmic, yet it passes through computation and its logics. Or, rather, computation passes through it. Because it can always be disrupted and transformed by way of its instantiation in practice, it is not a mechanism of control. A phenomenon that can exist only within open-ended, emergent forms of space, sociality, and governance, it exists at the close of the panoptic paradigm.

17 "The target is the people"

Representations of the village in modernization and national security doctrine

Nick Cullather

"Why do you have to blow up so many of our fields and homes?" a farmer from the Arghandab district asked a top NATO general at a recent community meeting. Although military officials are apologetic in public, they maintain privately that the tactic has a benefit beyond the elimination of insurgent bombs. By making people travel to the district governor's office to submit a claim for damaged property, "in effect, you're connecting the government to the people," the senior officer said.[1]

Defenseless villages are bombarded from the air, the inhabitants driven out into the countryside, the cattle machine-gunned, the huts set on fire with incendiary bullets: this is called *pacification*.[2]

An often-heard criticism of American strategy in Vietnam was that it was conceived and implemented by a generation of men versed in tactics more suited to Omaha Beach or Bastogne than to the jungles and paddyfields of Southeast Asia. The reverse could, of course, be said of the architects of Operation Iraqi Freedom. Although General Ricardo Sanchez insists that there is no Vietnam analogy, he and most members of the military leadership up to Colin Powell and Donald Rumsfeld were schooled in combat in Vietnam. If there is a chain of concept and memory linking targeted cities from Hiroshima to Falluja, it runs most recently through the paradox-strewn villages of Southeast Asia.

During the formative decades of U.S. counter-insurgency doctrine, Asia was the primary Cold War battleground, and, outside of Japan, Asia was almost entirely agricultural. Its rurality constituted the principal strategic problem for American planners. Intelligence reports portrayed a roadless, censusless continent thickly inhabited by peasants who were untouched by the state or capitalist markets and liable, as China's revolution showed, to sudden and decisive shifts of allegiance. The collapse of imperial domination left the entire region without effective systems of intelligence or authority – in Dean Acheson's phrase, "an unknown world."[3]

U.S. officials were disturbed most by their powerlessness in Asia to steer or even anticipate social processes that had troubling implications for security. James F. Byrnes, the first postwar secretary of state, saw "Asia as a great smoldering fire" in which "a huge mass of humanity, the majority of the people of this earth," were combusting "from the middle ages into the era of atomic energy."[4] Although the Soviets had a plan for transforming peasant societies that appealed to Asian nationalists, the Americans had no safe answers to poverty or revolution. The United States was limited not just in its capacity to intervene but also in its capacity to imagine useful interventions. The vast social gulf separating an urban, industrial United States from Asian ways of life, George Kennan warned, called into question the entire concept of U.S. leadership: "We are deceiving ourselves and others when we pretend to have answers to the problems which agitate many of these Asiatic peoples."[5]

It was in the midst of this postwar "knowledge panic" that the term *village* came to encapsulate the problems of comprehending and controlling the Asian social environment within the logics of counter-insurgency doctrine and modernization theory. Rather than a place or species of social organization, it represented a schematic view of the human obstacles impeding the smooth operation of U.S. power. The village was defined by its paradoxes: it was both isolated and thickly populated, physically bounded but also a state of mind, unknowable but uniform, self-contained yet vitally important to the fate of nations. In its historical and anthropological construction, as David Ludden has observed, the village was the antipode of the state, "a destination for historical forces moving out and down from the centers and pinnacles of progress," in short, a target.[6]

This chapter aims, first, to investigate this abstract village, the object of U.S. counter-insurgency and reconstruction efforts for two decades, as a counterpoint to the city targets discussed in this book; second, to describe how this conceptualization structured military and political action in Asia (and especially Vietnam); and, finally, to suggest ways in which this conception persists in the "lessons" of the American counter-insurgency and nation-building experience.

The darker face of self-reliance

In the postwar policy lexicon, the village represented an explosive combination of poverty, population, and isolation that threatened the security of Asia. The policy makers' fear of isolated community derived from an interpretation of the causes of World War II that they projected onto contemporary conditions. In this view, the breakdown of global trade caused by the Depression had led to the creation of autarkic centers of power – the Soviet Union, Germany, the Japanese Co-Prosperity Sphere – that vied for resources and manpower necessary to make their economic self-sufficiency complete. Animated by ideology, relatively small and undeveloped powers swiftly assembled the ingredients of a modern war machine capable of challenging the United States.[7]

The autonomous village represented the early stages of this cataclysmic process, as Isidor Lubin, Harry Truman's foreign aid adviser, warned in 1952. In densely inhabited Asia "the so-called rural population is packed into what virtually constitutes an endless village . . . a breeding ground for violent revolution." The Chinese civil war revealed the hazard of this vast sea in which Maoist fish could swim, but the threat would persist even without communism. "Even if

Soviet totalitarianism came to an end," Lubin believed, the endless village could germinate "a series of ideologies that in the light of the next century might make the totalitarianisms of this century seem pale."[8] The rural landscape was an island, cut off from mechanisms of taxation and control, an unknown terrain inhabited by Naxalites, Hukbalahaps, Viet Congs, and other violent indigenes. Asian elites shared the Americans' dread of this closed sphere. "Many of us are two generations removed from the villages," an Indian official confided to Ambassador Chester Bowles. "The villages appall me."[9] The village was thus prefigured as the site of future conflicts that would finalize the ascendancy of the nation within a global system dominated by superpowers.

Scholars examining American identity at mid-century concurred with Kennan's view that the United States perceived Asia's troubles across an unbridgeable divide of history, affluence, and knowledge. With only 11 percent of Americans working in agriculture, David Potter noted, the dominant influence on the national character was now the city.[10] To David Reisman the city-bred American was two stages of personality development removed from the "tradition-directed" type personified by the peasant, making meaningful communication all but impossible.[11] This, coupled with the ideological appeal of communist models of collectivization and land reform, had distressing implications for the future of Asia. Reinhold Niebuhr warned that "Communism has a tremendous original advantage as a destructive force in the dying sleeping cultures of the Orient" where Western ideas of religion, democracy, and social science could gain no purchase. "We are in danger, therefore of facing the international 'class struggle' with an uncomprehending fury or complete dismay."[12] Arthur Schlesinger held hope that "American study of village sociology could help us to understand how we may most effectively release the energies so long pent up in the villages of Asia," but the sense that Americans were marooned on the wrong side of the urban–rural divide persisted.[13] As of 1958, the authors of the bestselling policy novel *The Ugly American* beheld "an Asia where we stand relatively mute, locked in the cities, misunderstanding the temper and the needs of the Asians."[14]

Social science rose to the challenge, generating a new set of conceptual tools for understanding rural Asia. Modernization theory, which gained policy authority in the mid-1950s, has often been regarded as a reassertion of colonial hierarchies and typologies under a new guise, but, although modernizers inherited some terms and categories, they self-consciously refashioned them to fit what they saw as the unprecedented, dynamic circumstances of an unstable era. Among "the pillars of the imperial constructs of India," Ronald Inden has noted, the village was constituted as justification for British rule.[15] Charles Metcalfe informed the Commons in 1830 that "village communities are little republics, having nearly everything they want within themselves . . . Dynasty after dynasty tumbles down, revolution succeeds to revolution . . . but the village communities remain the same."[16] The authentic, unchanging village stood in contrast to the artificiality and instability of the Indian state, justifying British succession to a long line of alien rulers while excusing the Raj's unconcern for the general welfare. U.S. social scientists accepted the characterization of the village as a distinct culture, unchanged for centuries, in opposition to the state, but they believed these attributes, which lent

Asian society a reassuring simplicity, were disappearing. The village's historic seclusion was rapidly, violently breaking down.

Academic, journalistic, and intelligence reports uniformly depicted an Asia in ferment, its traditional cultural bonds ruptured by the infiltration of modern ideas and technology. A 1950 CIA report noted "the particular susceptibility [to communism] of those abler individuals who, released by the weakening of customary social mechanisms, seek expression, status, and power."[17] Modernization theorist Lucian Pye explained this type of political restlessness as the product of an "expectation gap" arising when the villager acquired aspirations "which his society is as yet incapable of supporting."[18] The strength of the village bond intensified the social explosion at the moment of its release. "Just because village life is so all-inclusive," Barbara Ward explained in 1955, "the impact upon it of an evolving industrial system is cataclysmic."[19] Rural Asia's partial initiation to modern influences made it unpredictable and dangerous. "The region must be . . . regarded," the CIA warned in 1949, "as in dispute sociologically as well as geographically."[20] The village was presumed to be the social unit that would mediate the individual's encounter with modernity. Although social scientists acknowledged that the village had been an administrative unit of the colonial state, they continued throughout the 1950s to study it as a "natural system" to which inhabitants owed a "prime" loyalty, equivalent to the bonds of family.[21]

Both Orientalist typologies and the newer categories of social science ranked peoples on a civilizational scale with rural and urban forms of social organization at opposite ends of a continuum. While "tribe" represented a pure, traditional form, village represented a society on the first step of the civilizational ladder. In its Cold War construction, "the village" thus denied villagers the dignity accorded to the unspoiled savage, as well as the cunning and imitative aptitude of the urbanized *effendi*.[22] Unlike the nomadic Bedouin or Pashtun, the villager was sedentary, lacking in martial qualities, apathetic, and resentful. Suspended between two worlds, helpless to assert its own values or realize those of the city, the village greeted the future and the outsider in a vengeful mood. Village autonomy meant, Lewis Mumford observed in 1961, "isolation, jealousy, suspicion of the stranger, parochialism – the darker face of self-reliance and self-sufficiency. This independence too easily became quarrelsomeness, opposition for the sake of opposition, a willingness to cut off one's nose to spite one's face."[23] The frustrations of arrested development were as apt to erupt in directionless rage as in purposive activity.

Lacking the codes of blood and honor that kept tribal aggression in check, the village was innately violent. Field studies conducted in Turkey in 1963 by Ithiel de Sola Pool of the Massachusetts Institute of Technology confirmed that "all through human history, intimidation, brutality, and violence have been endemic in most of the village societies in which men have lived."[24] Violence was neither political nor ideological but rooted in psychological isolation. Roger Hilsman, an architect of pacification policy for Vietnam, observed in 1963 that the:

> strategic concept for South Vietnam was . . . based on the assumption that villages in Southeast Asia are turned inward on themselves and have little or no sense of identification with either the national government or

Communist ideology – that the villages are isolated, physically, politically, and psychologically.[25]

Elections, religious festivals, familial feuds, even war were simply occasions for bouts of irrational bloodletting. Frances Fitzgerald, writing in Vietnam in 1966, underscored the aimless, apolitical violence of guerrilla war: "When there are casualties, the injured must take revenge, as must any family in the hill towns of Sicily."[26] The Viet Cong succeeded, De Sola Pool argued, by connecting this instinctive thuggery with a political cause.

It was the distinctive violence of communalism that Marshall McLuhan pinpointed in 1968 in his conception of the "global village." Networked communications had universalized the villagers' rage against the discrepancy between the information they were given and the material things they couldn't have.[27] The Vietnam War itself was an example of the village's goal-less violence on an international scale, but the global village aimed its primary resentment at the global city. Citing the Detroit and Newark riots and campus takeovers at Columbia and Berkeley, McLuhan assured a *New York Times* reporter that the insurgents "won't hesitate to end the existence of cities either. They hate cities and machinery."[28] He offered this judgment as a compliment; the darkness of the villager's anger was a measure of the city's advancement.

Pacification strategies presented technology as a psychological projectile that could shock the villager out of his sullen inertia. Several leading economic theorists, including Walt W. Rostow, Charles P. Kindleberger, and Carl Kaysen, spent World War II as bombing targeters tasked with disrupting a modern industrial complex by "taking out" discreet parts. Modernizers imagined bringing the village out of the stone age through a reverse process, dropping in ingredients of change.[29] Flying over India in 1952, Rockefeller Foundation officials noticed that villages were "as uniform as so many anthills. Indeed, from the air, where a number of villages may be seen simultaneously, they have the appearance of structures built by creatures motivated largely by inherited animal instincts."[30] They speculated that the "village complex" comprised three interdependent elements, man, cattle, and plants, and "a change in any one will inevitably affect the entire system" by cutting the restraints of apathy and custom that held the village back.[31] Although peasants distrusted outsiders, social scientists saw them as hungry for technologies and methods that produced visible, dramatic results. Through repeated exposure to new techniques, villagers would exercise their powers of rational decision and, in spite of themselves, steadily advance toward modernity.

Because the psychology of the village was rooted in its material conditions, small changes were expected to produce profound transformations in moral and political outlook. By "adding to the material things in a community, improving the water supply with a new well or pump, drainage for the streets, a generator for village power," Edward G. Lansdale told graduating Green Berets in 1962:

> the community finds itself becoming linked up closely to the nation, a real part of something bigger. As it does so, the political life of the community

grows also, demanding more meaning in answer to the question: What is worth risking a man's life to defend?[32]

But although the Americans could add "material things" to the village, they were incapable of subtracting. The village was an irreducible particle of community, and so could not be destroyed but only displaced. Jonathan Schell raised this point with an air force sergeant selecting targets for Operation Benton, which was depopulating Quang Ngai province in 1967. "That's the way it was in Korea, too," he replied. "The villages got wiped out there, too, and everybody just picked up their stuff and went somewhere else. Those aren't houses. They're just huts."[33] Because in the abstract the village was indestructible, it was eligible for repeated destruction.

The village was thus reified as an assortment of pathologies that, by definition, could not be solved without turning the village into something else. The semantic trouble was skirted by rechristening villages that had undergone pacification or social engineering – they became hamlets or model communities – but the practical quandary remained: if the village was the problem, how could it be saved? The Vietnam War's domestic opponents recognized that to extricate their country from the war they needed first to extricate themselves from the definitional paradox of the village. Frances Fitzgerald's anti-war bible *Fire in the Lake* begins by redefining the Vietnamese village in relation to the city. Although urbanized Americans were accustomed to transient, rootless, disposable forms of society, the village was profoundly permanent, a community as much of the dead, buried in its fields and honored in its shrines, as of the living. Its permanence derived from the village's unbreakable connection to the land. "As the source of life," she explained, "the earth was the basis for the social contract between the members of the family and the members of the village."[34] The generational consciousness of this romantic counterimage, with its nurturing, ecological, and nostalgic connotations, is suggested by the names given to new-urbanist suburbs, a high-camp disco group "The Village People," and Hillary Clinton's book, *It Takes a Village*. But these associations would be attached later. In the 1950s and 1960s, modernizers were stuck with the village of their own creation.

Implementation and attitude

The United States and its Asian clients employed a variety of tactics against the linked problems of underdevelopment and insurgency in the countryside, but two of the more prominent schemes illustrate how the conception of the abstract village influenced actions and outcomes. The strategic hamlets deployed in Vietnam as well as the community development programs undertaken by the Ford Foundation in India aimed to reconstruct the village minus its defining attribute, its cultural isolation, but "model" villages could furnish only a demonstration of the village's antithesis, a connected, rationalized community dependent on outside markets and power.

Refined over three decades, "community development" was among the most studied and imitated nation-building techniques. India's massive Community

Development Programme, launched in 1952, was copied throughout the developing world. The United Nations created an agency to promote community development, and Indonesia, the Philippines, and other newly independent governments acquired community development ministries. Community development "was the key to the future of India and Asia," Ambassador Chester Bowles explained, "an administrative framework through which modern scientific knowledge could be put to work for the benefit of the hundreds of millions of people who have long lived in poverty."[35] Pioneered by Albert Mayer, an architect and real estate developer from New York, at Etawah in Uttar Pradesh beginning in 1948, the scheme expanded into the massive Ford Foundation "package program" in the 1950s, and became the operational doctrine of the Peace Corps in the 1960s. The process began with the remapping of a political district into "blocks" of forty or more villages, and sub-blocks assigned each to a *gram sevak*, a village social worker. The subjects' first indication of their imminent redevelopment was the arrival of this observer, whose modern vantage allowed him to discern and catalog "deficiencies" in village life that could be referred to specialists for study and recommendation. As an outsider, the *gram sevak* could expect only hostility from the villagers until he could demonstrate tools or techniques that aroused their curiosity. The aim was to "improve the land by improving the people."[36] The project would rationalize the functions of village life, breaking it down into constituent tasks and applying technological levers to magnify the value of effort. This, in turn, would produce a revolution in outlook, causing the peasant to view his political and physical condition through the eyes of a detached observer. Ultimately, the village itself would become a demonstration for peasants in the surrounding villages to see and imitate.[37]

Community development transferred the aesthetic of modernist urban planning to the village. Mayer had come to India as an Army lieutenant colonel in 1943 to design airfields for the Corps of Engineers. In 1945, shortly after Nehru was released from jail for the last time, the Congress Party leader invited Mayer to his home in Allahabad where their conversations over several days led to a request that Mayer draw plans for reconstructing Bombay and other cities and produce a scheme for village housing. Mayer returned to New York but on annual visits to India that continued through 1954 he elaborated on the philosophy and procedures of the project, launched at Etawah in 1948. He aimed to formulate a wholly original approach to rural modernization that would bring progress without the paternalism of colonial improvement, the bloodbath of Soviet collectivization, the scale or expense of the Tennessee Valley Authority (TVA), the disruption of land reform, or the austerity of Gandhian *swaraj*.

Educated as a civil engineer, Mayer went into the family business of constructing Manhattan apartment towers. His personal wealth (his mother was a Guggenheim) gave latitude to his architectural and philanthropic pursuits. In the 1930s, he joined Lewis Mumford, Henry Wright, and Clarence Stein in the Housing Study Guild, a group whose advocacy of large-scale, planned public housing projects led to the Wagner–Steagall Act and a national program of slum clearance and planned public housing. The Guild warned that the modern city was under threat from decay, overdevelopment, and competition from suburbs. Before the war and after, Mayer advocated an urban design strategy mixing green belt towns and high-density "tower in a park" urban housing, to solve problems of congestion and nuclear civil defense.[38] Cities had become "unpleasant to do business in, wasteful of people's time, and a strain on their nerves," and the decline could be reversed only if planners restored a sense of small community by creating self-contained neighborhoods with distinctive character.[39] Stuyvesant Town and Knickerbocker Village in New York, Thorneycroft in Queens, Pittsburgh's Chatham Village, and Baldwin Hills Village in Los Angeles expressed these principles.

As an urban planner, Mayer brought an original perspective to the problem of rural reconstruction. To economic planners and social scientists the city represented the terminal stage of social development, the model to which the village should aspire. The American city, especially New York, represented modernity's ultimate achievement. Mayer, who had already spent much of his career demolishing parts of New York to make way for neighborhood "villages," held a contrary view. He forecast a "revalidation of rural living" and regarded the Indian village as demonstrating "a revitalization of the small community which we in the West are now trying to create even in our own cities through planned 'neighborhood units.'"[40] In his designs for New York high-rises, he sought to steer modernism toward reconnection with nature and face-to-face community. His iconic apartment tower at 240 Central Park South, completed in 1941, compromised modernist austerity with curvilinear enclosures, gathering spaces, and rooftop conservatories to create a sense of seclusion and belonging within the city.[41] But his designs for Indian cities contain Mayer's most explicit statements about the permanence of the village in the modern world. In 1949, as work on Etawah was still under way, Nehru commissioned Mayer to draw the master plan for the new Punjabi capital at Chandigarh.

Along with Brasilia, Chandigarh is considered one of the preeminent manifestations of high modernism in urban design. Nehru intended it as an aesthetic expression of the new India, an administrative capital to replace Lahore, a dazzling imperial city detached by Partition. It was planned from scratch. Nehru chose a site at the foot of the Himalayas, a broad plain from which farmers had been forcibly removed, allowing Mayer to "start with just a blank sheet of paper."[42] Chandigarh is identified with the utopian modernist Edouard Jeanneret, known as Le Corbusier, who designed its monumental structures, but as a condition of his contract Corbusier accepted Mayer's master plan, making refinements to enhance its principal features, which emphasized segregation of the city's constituent functions (living, traffic, work, retail) and continuous green valleys running between walled neighborhood "superblocks" that Mayer felt "perpetuate[d] the Indian village community."[43] Houses and schools within each sector turned inward toward plots of green space rather than toward thoroughfares.

The diversity of Mayer's achievements has led historians to subdivide him into three historiographical properties. He figures prominently in studies of urban housing policy, and in a separate literature on urban planning and Chandigarh.

Still another literature on community development credits his work at Etawah, but what is seldom recognized is that the three projects progressed simultaneously, and, as Mayer suggested, they engaged a single theme: an effort to uncover universal principles of a functioning "human scale" community. His work in Chandigarh, New York, and Etawah each reflected a belief that the village composed an authentic, natural unit of human society, the building block of cities and nations. The city was conceived as a symmetrical arrangement of modular superblocks, each constituting, in Corbusier's phrase, a "vertical village."[44] Both the modernist city and the model village performed an instructional function in reforming the traditional habits and mentalities of their inhabitants. Because India's city dwellers were "still villagers and small community people at heart and fairly recently by origin," Mayer accommodated their lingering need for enclosed social space, but the infrastructure of the city would also discourage "traditional" habits and encourage new forms of interaction. Chandigarh's apartments, for instance, were built for a "modern" nuclear family of two adults and two children, with no room for storing *charpoys*, the lattice beds on which visitors and members of the extended family slept, or for cooking with a charcoal *tandoor*.[45] Written into the design of Chandigarh, three unreconciled assumptions about the essential nature of the village – its authenticity, modular reproducibility, and didactic function – informed the practices of community development as well.

At Etawah, as in Chandigarh, administration was carefully segregated from the functions of the village; crops and structures were reduced to a few uniform types; and emphasis was placed on the visual aspect of the community, particularly as viewed from outside.[46] Standardization, spatial order, and permanence had been hallmarks of model villages in the colonial period, but Mayer rejected physical reconstruction as insufficient.[47] The mental awakening of villagers was to be accomplished through "nonmaterial elements," processions, general meetings, technology demos, games and sports, and dawn tours (*prabhat pheris*) in which development bureaucrats paraded into a village at 5 AM with flags, placards, songs, and chants "to rouse the villages from their slumber."[48] Under the benevolent eye of the planner, the village and the capital were transformed into stages for enacting the spectacle of modernity.

The ambiguity of the word "model" elided tensions inherent in the model village, for Etawah was to be, simultaneously, (1) a representation of a typical village, (2) a reproducible prototype, and (3) an exemplar. The emphasis on display ruled out the choice of a village typical enough to possess all of the deficiencies that could be catalogued. Mayer selected Etawah for its modern infrastructure; it was a market center on the main road with primary and high schools, a clinic, and a veterinary hospital.[49] The model was to be presented as a starting point of a modernization process, but it was a product of earlier improvement schemes. Mayer chose also not to address structural problems, such as land tenure, and to concentrate instead on problems that could be addressed by "reproducible" methods. Democratic governance was carefully separated from planning, which was placed under professional project directors, but Mayer believed that an accessible process, involving approachable officials, village councils modeled on neighborhood associations, and public gatherings and ritual, created an "inner democracy" that was a substitute for the formalities of representation.[50] From the vantage of their more "advanced" society, Americans were better positioned than Indians themselves to anticipate the future aspirations of Indian villagers and urbanites. He admonished the planners of Chandigarh to "develop the city as modern, self-confident Indians would, if there were such a group."[51]

Community development gained global attention in 1952 when USAID and the Ford Foundation underwrote a $50 million program to create 35,000 model villages. Etawah's ideals were lost amid expansion and high expectations, Mayer felt, and the goal of spiritual regeneration yielded to the demands of quarterly performance targets.[52] The 1957 Balvantray report, which signaled the end of the honeymoon for community development in India (though not for USAID and its beneficiaries), exposed the gap between the perceptions of real villagers and Mayer's assumptions about the indivisibility of the village, the reproducibility of methods, and the effects of modeling. Wealthy, high-caste villagers dragooned powerless villagers into doing most of the work. The diversity of climate, terrain, village size, and customs foiled attempts to reproduce models, and villagers resented the streams of official visitors trooping through.[53] At about the same time, William Whyte and Jane Jacobs were demolishing the modernists' urban theories on the same grounds: that people simply didn't behave in the way they were supposed to in the plans.[54] When Horace Holmes, who worked with Mayer on the original project, revisited India in 1967 he was heartened by what he found at Etawah ("The little villages have grown. Many have become towns. . . . Certainly no one was hungry . . . Not one was critical of the government."), but the ruins of model villages he saw in other districts confirmed that India remained stubbornly unchanged.[55] After 8 years and $10 million, the Ford Foundation abandoned community development. "After you give a lot of young Indians a six months course in village development," foundation chairman Henry Heald complained, "you really haven't got much."[56] Community development returned to the United States in a variety of forms. The "inner city" programs of Lyndon Johnson's Great Society, such as the Office of Economic Opportunity, applied community development strategies. Mayer, who continued to plan cities in the United States and around the world, incorporated lessons learned in India, most notably in the design of Reston, Virginia (1965), a "master planned community" in which suburban "villages" were constructed around cultural focal points, such as a bandshell or a golf course.[57]

The "strategic hamlet" program, launched as a solution to Vietnam's insurgency, represented a militarized version of community development. The objective was to guide the village through the emergency of modernization. As a 1962 directive on counter-insurgency operations explained, "the revolution of modernization can disturb, uproot, and daze a traditional society. While the institutions required for modernization are in the process of being created, this revolution contributes to arousing pressures, anxieties, and hopes which seem to justify violent action." An infusion of agronomists, clinics, housing construction, and security assistance could alleviate the pressure of rising expectations. "The *ultimate and decisive target is the people*," the statement concluded (italics in original). "Society itself is at war and the resources, motives, and targets of the struggle are found almost wholly within the local population."[58] By centralizing peasants for defense, as well as to bring them within reach of government services and administration, the strategic hamlet pushed the village up the historical ladder at least as far as the middle ages. Beginning in 1962, the United States and the Saigon regime removed peasants into enclosures surrounded by moats, bamboo stockades, and watchtowers. One reporter considered the structure, which "brings to mind a frontier outpost of the American West," appropriate as "this is basically an Indian-type war with the Viet Cong cast as Indians."[59]

The strategic hamlet, according to Larry Cable, was "a grail, a powerful fetish with which to banish the discouraging prospect of prolonged and potentially fruitless conventional military operations against the Viet Cong."[60] Its aim was to fabricate a "front" in a frontless war; just as the model village manufactured a line of contrast between the modernity within and the underdevelopment without, the strategic hamlet worked by twinning images of the abstract village with its opposite. Because the village was isolated, strategic hamlets would be built around a radio transmitter and a helipad. The village was ephemeral, and movable, so concrete would be the construction material of choice. Villagers were anonymous, so occupants of the hamlets were endlessly polled, surveyed, and asked for identification. But doctrine also acknowledged that the village existed primarily as mentality, and so would the "front." The U.S. pacification command (USOM) stressed that the:

> essential, unique attribute of the true strategic hamlet is the commitment of the majority of its residents to resisting the communist guerrilla . . . This commitment is essentially a state of mind to be fostered and strengthened, to be reinforced by every physical and psychological means.[61]

Unlike the "combat village" of the Viet Cong, in which defenses (mines, traps) were passive and invisible, the strategic hamlet required ritualistic displays of allegiance, the daily reporting on the radio, the mustering of guards, the mending of barbed wire, and the turning of a wooden arrow, atop a watchtower, to steer helicopter pilots to the location of Viet Cong attackers. Officially, it was the Diem government's inability to inspire such displays that led to the abandonment of the program. Although it ended disastrously, accelerating the deterioration of government control in the countryside, USOM could still contend that these were not failures of the "true" strategic hamlet. Failure "does not necessarily invalidate the concept of the hamlet program," one province rep explained. "Its shortcomings like in implementation and attitude, not in theory."[62]

The collapse of Operation Sunrise and the successor "New Life" strategic hamlet program by the end of 1964 meant that by the time U.S. forces entered the war in strength counter-insurgency had been reduced to procedures for systematically depopulating the countryside. Operation Farmgate identified areas of Viet Cong control and tasked fighter bombers to eradicate enemy "structures" that consisted of any shelter visible from the air. Isolation defined the enemy. Orville Schell travelled with Farmgate air spotters in 1966 and observed that houses on the main roads and surrounding U.S. outposts remained intact while others had been almost totally eliminated. These were largely peasant homes. The Viet Cong avoided structures, recognizing that dike walls, treelines, and underground bunkers offered better shelter, but it took years before close air support tactics adapted.[63] Although the targeting of cities in World War II led to increasingly indiscriminate bombing patterns and weapons, it was the targeting of villages that sent the Defense Advanced Research Projects Agency (DARPA) in quest of "smart" techniques and weapons that could destroy with precision. The application of those techniques to Belgrade and Baghdad completed the targeting dialectic that fatally joins village and city.

Strategic hamlets in reverse

That the Cold War conception of the village persists in counter-insurgency and nation-building strategies is evident in tactics applied after 2003 in Iraq at Falluja and at Auja, a town that has been described as "a reverse strategic hamlet." "Instead of forcing peasants into new villages surrounded by barbed wire to separate them from the insurgents," the *Washington Post* reported, U.S. forces "encircled an existing village with barbed wire to keep its wealthy insurgents inside and under control."[64] U.S. forces claimed for themselves the favorable territory once dominated by the Viet Cong – the countryside, the night – but their conception of threat echoes Lubin's nightmare vision of 1952.

The village as an object of fear and reprisal, dormant for two decades, was revived by the war on terror. Even as the Vietnam War ground on, the city was replacing the village as a locus of apprehensions. After the wave of ghetto riots, environmental crises, and overpopulation, the enemy started to look like a city boy. When a 1972 USOM report identified urban Vietnam as a "forgotten front" for pacification, U.S. forces actually began resettling the countryside.[65] Apart from the Central American counterinsurgencies, in which client troops did the work, U.S. air operations and deployments in the 1980s and 1990s were primarily to urban combat zones: Lebanon (1982), Tripoli (1986), Manila (1989), Panama City (1989), Kuwait (1991), Los Angeles (1992), Mogadishu (1994), etc.[66] In the wake of the Green Revolution, development strategies likewise targeted urban economies with export processing zones, structural adjustment, and the creation of national stock exchanges, even as the promises and precepts of modernization theory lost credence in both academic and policy circles. Iran, Henry Kissinger noted, buried the supposition that development provided any "automatic stabilizing factor."[67] But the attack on two American cities on September 11, 2001, returned nation-building, counter-insurgency, and modernization to the policy discourse, and redefined the enemy as an isolated society, arrested in its development, and resentful of the dominance of metropolitan culture.

In a reversal of the discourse of globalization, academics and strategists have rediscovered isolation as a persistent and dangerous foe. In the late 1990s, as Ulan

Bator acquired a stock exchange and Tuaregs wore Chicago Bulls sweatshirts, the very possibility of seclusion from the global market seemed an anachronism. Globalization assumed "the immense enlargement of world communication, as well as the horizons of a world market," Fredric Jameson explained, such that the particular had become universal and the universal particular.[68] Collisions along the fortified boundary between universal and particular have returned policy discourse to the concerns and conceptual schemes of modernization theory. Bernard Lewis, the preeminent interpreter of Islam, explains Arab resentment against the West as the natural temper of an inert culture unable to match the developmental pace of its rivals.[69] The Pentagon's grand strategist, Thomas P. M. Barnett, has delineated a frontier between the world's "functioning core" and its "non-integrating gap," where most U.S. deployments can be expected to take place in the next century. "[S]how me where globalization is thinning or just plain absent, and I will show you regions plagued by politically repressive regimes, widespread poverty and disease, routine mass murder, and – most important – the chronic conflicts that incubate the next generation of global terrorists," Barnett explains. "Disconnectedness defines danger."[70]

Although at the highest levels the Bush administration has steadfastly refused to indulge in theorizing about the root causes of terrorism (which it would then be obliged to address), the National Commission on Terrorist Attacks, known as the 9/11 Commission, moved to fill this interpretive gap in its widely read report. It, too, found underdevelopment and social isolation to be the focal point of danger. Distinguishing between the urban, married, educated "entrepreneurial terrorists" such as Mohammad Atta and Osama bin Laden, and the uneducated, fanatical, single, and predominantly rural "muscle hijackers," the report claimed that this latter group personified the social condition that allowed Al Qaeda to thrive. All came from villages along the Saudi–Yemen border, a "weakly policed area . . . sometimes called 'the wild frontier.'"[71] These remote areas, untouched by oil wealth, harbored "a large, steadily increasing population of young men without any reasonable expectation of suitable or steady employment – a sure prescription for social turbulence."[72] The report emphasizes the need for a "balanced modernization" that would secure employment and marriage for these young men thereby changing their outlook and that of the region.

In Afghanistan, NATO forces have once again adopted a "population-centric" counter-insurgency model that seeks to lure – or, if necessary, to drive – rural folk into the administrative embrace of the city. In late 2010, General David Petraeus advocated the introduction of heavy armor partly because tanks would destroy fields and homes, thus clarifying the costs of continuing the insurgency. By forcing villagers to travel to the district capital to file a claim for damaged property, a senior officer explained, "in effect, you're connecting the government to the people."[73] Perhaps without knowing it, the unnamed senior officer echoed with eerie exactness Samuel P. Huntington's 1968 claim that the squalid camps into which Vietnamese refugees were driven were "a gateway to a new and better way of life."[74]

"The common image of the country is now an image of the past," Raymond

Williams observed, "and the common image of the city is an image of the future."[74] This leaves an undefined and perilous present. Like an earlier generation, today's nation builders regard progress as a journey from country to city. Many writers still celebrate the depopulation of the countryside as a natural and desirable outcome of development.[75]

In our conception of progress, agriculture is an inherently pre-modern or anti-modern activity, and, although it can be endlessly modernized, it can never be modern. Consequently, the way for rustics to enjoy full economic and social citizenship in a modern state is to move to the city. Nation-building was a process of encouraging that migration. But unlike liberal internationalists of the 1960s, neo-modernists subject their targets to a narrower range of interventions possible in the present. Between structural adjustment and rolling in the tanks there is a yawning gap in the modernizing repertoire where the clinics, dams, and planned villages used to be.

Notes

1 Rajiv Chandrasekharan, "U.S. Deploying Heavily Armored Battle Tanks for the First Time in Afghan War," *Washington Post*, November 19, 2010, p. A1.
2 George Orwell, "Politics and the English Language," *The New Republic*, June 17, 1946, pp. 872–4.
3 Dean Acheson, *Present at the Creation* (New York: Norton, 1969), pp. 4–5.
4 James. F. Byrnes, *Speaking Frankly* (New York: Harper, 1947), p. 204.
5 George F. Kennan, "Review of Current Trends: U.S. Foreign Policy," PPS 23, February 24, 1948, in Thomas H. Etzold and John L. Gaddis, eds., *Containment: Documents on American Policy and Strategy, 1945–1950* (New York: Columbia, 1978), p. 226.
6 David Ludden, "Subalterns and Others in the Agrarian History of South Asia," in James C. Scott and Nina Bhatt, eds., *Agrarian Studies: Synthetic Work at the Cutting Edge* (New Haven, CT: Yale, 2001), p. 217.
7 For a succinct statement of these perceptions, see Melvyn P. Leffler, *The Specter of Communism* (New York: Hill and Wang, 1994), pp. 60–3.
8 Isidor Lubin, "The World's Awakening Peoples and their Demand for Human Betterment," *Department of State Bulletin*, vol. 26 (June 9, 1952), pp. 935–6. There's more than a passing resemblance between Lubin's forecast and Mike Davis's recent depiction of the endless slum. See Mike Davis, "Planet of Slums," *Harpers*, June 2004, pp. 17–22.
9 Quoted in Donald K. Faris, *To Plow With Hope* (New York: Harper, 1958), p. 107.
10 David M. Potter, *People of Plenty* (Chicago: University of Chicago Press, 1954).
11 David Riesman, *The Lonely Crowd: A Study of the Changing American Character* (New Haven, CT: Yale, 1950), pp. 43, 113.
12 Reinhold Niebuhr, *The Irony of American History* (New York: Charles Scribner's, 1952), pp. 120, 125.
13 Arthur M. Schlesinger Jr., *The Vital Center* (New York: Riverside Press, 1962), p. 223 [original 1949].
14 William J. Lederer and Eugene Burdick, *The Ugly American* (New York: W. W. Norton, 1958), p. 283.
15 Ronald Inden, *Imagining India* (Oxford: Basil Blackwell, 1990), pp. 131–61.
16 Quoted in David Ludden, "Orientalist Empiricism: Transformations of Colonial Knowledge," in Carol A. Breckenridge and Peter van der Veer, eds., *Orientalism and the Postcolonial Predicament* (Philadelphia: University of Pennsylvania Press, 1993), p. 251.

17 CIA, "Comprehensive Production Plan for National Intelligence on the Far East," June 1950, CIA Research Tool (CREST), RDP79–01082A0002000100008–0, National Archives and Records Administration, College Park, MD.

18 Lucian W. Pye, *Guerrilla Communism in Malaya: Its Social and Political Meaning* (Princeton: Princeton University Press, 1956), p. 355. On the implications of the expectation gap for counter-insurgency, see D. Michael Shafer, *Deadly Paradigms: The Failure of U.S. Counterinsurgency Policy* (Princeton: Princeton University Press, 1988), p. 81.

19 Barbara Ward, "The Challenge We Neglect in Asia," *The New York Times Magazine*, February 13, 1955, p. 203.

20 CIA, "Review of the World Situation," January 19, 1949, DDRS, ck3100371129.

21 See Robert Redfield, "Societies and Cultures as Natural Systems," *Journal of the Royal Anthropological Institute*, vol. 85, no. 1/2 (1955), pp. 19–32.

22 On colonial rural/urban dichotomies see Toby Dodge, *Inventing Iraq* (New York: Columbia University Press, 2003), pp. 63–81. For the state of sociological thinking in the 1960s, see R. E. Pahl, "The Rural–Urban Continuum," *Sociologia Ruralis*, vol. 6, no. 3/4 (1966), pp. 299–326; and Eugen Lupri, "The Rural Urban Variable Reconsidered: The Cross-Cultural Perspective," *Sociologia Ruralis*, vol. 7, no. 1 (1967), pp. 1–17. For the application of the dichotomy to modernization, see Edward Shils, "Centre and Periphery," in *The Logic of Personal Knowledge* (Glencoe, IL: Free Press, 1961), pp. 117–30.

23 Lewis Mumford, *The City in History* (San Diego: Harcourt Brace, 1961), p. 132.

24 Ithiel de Sola Pool, *Village Violence and Pacification in Viet Nam* (Urbana: University of Illinois Department of Political Science, 1968), p. 4.

25 Hilsman to Rusk, "South Vietnam," undated 1963, Declassified Documents Reference System, available online at http://galenet.galegroup.com/servlet/DDRS, doc. ck3100392511.

26 Frances Fitzgerald, "The Long Fear," in Milton J. Bates, ed., *Reporting Vietnam: American Journalism, 1959–1969* (New York: Library of America, 1998), 1, p. 317.

27 Marshall McLuhan and Quentin Fiore, *War and Peace in the Global Village* (New York: McGraw Hill, 1968).

28 John Leo, "M'Luhan Weighs Aimless Violence," *The New York Times*, May 26, 1968, p. 72; This was hardly an original point. A year earlier, Jerome Cavanagh, the mayor of Detroit, then occupied by the 82nd Airborne, stated that "we may be able to pacify every village in Vietnam . . . but what good does it do if we can't pacify the American cities." "Federal Riot Police Urged by Cavanagh," *The Washington Post*, July 31, 1967, p. A5.

29 W. W. Rostow, *Pre-Invasion Bombing Strategy: General Eisenhower's Decision of March 25, 1944* (Austin: University of Texas Press, 1981), pp. 21–3.

30 J. G. Harrar, Paul C. Manglesdorf, and Warren Weaver, "Notes on Indian Agriculture," New Delhi Field Office papers, RG 6.7, series II, Box 26, folder 147, Rockefeller Foundation archives, Tarrytown, New York.

31 Ibid.

32 Edward G. Lansdale, "Soldiers and the People," Lecture, Special Warfare School, Fort Bragg, August 30, 1962, in United States Operations Mission to Vietnam, Office of Rural Affairs, *Provincial Representative's Guide* (Saigon: USOM, January 1963), p. 11.

33 Jonathan Schell, "The Military Half," in *Reporting Vietnam*, 1: 463; Roger Hilsman also noted that destruction was of little use, as "to bomb a village, even though the guerrillas are using it as a base for sniping, will recruit more Vietcong than are killed." Hilsman testimony in the House Subcommittee on the Far East and the Pacific, United States Policy toward Asia, 89th Cong., 2nd sess., pt 1, 1966, p. 143.

34 Frances FitzGerald, *Fire in the Lake: The Vietnamese and the Americans in Vietnam* (Boston: Little, Brown, 1972), p. 10; Fitzgerald's later portrayal of the village is

strikingly different from the characterizations in her earlier journalism, which was generally supportive of the military effort.

35 Chester Bowles, *Ambassador's Report* (New York: Harper, 1954), pp. 197–8.

36 J. C. Kavoori and Baij Nath Singh, *History of Rural Development in Modern India* (New Delhi: Impex India, 1967), p. 117.

37 Albert Mayer, *Pilot Project, India: The Story of Rural Development at Etawah, Uttar Pradesh* (Berkeley: University of California Press, 1958); on the technique of community development, see Michael Latham, *Modernization as Ideology* (Chapel Hill: University of North Carolina Press, 2000), pp. 128–9.

38 Albert Mayer, Henry Wright, and Lewis Mumford, *New Homes for a New Deal* (New York: The New Republic, 1939); Albert Mayer, "Attacking the City's Slum Problem: A New Approach," *The New York Times*, February 18, 1934, p. xx3; Albert Mayer, "New Towns and Defense," *The Survey*, February 1951, pp. 64–5.

39 Albert Mayer and Julian Whittelsey, "Horse Sense Planning," *Architectural Forum* 79 (1943) 5: 59–74, p. 60.

40 Mayer, *Pilot Project*, p. 333.

41 Christopher Gray, "A Model of High-Density Residential Development," *The New York Times*, February 9, 1997, p. 47.

42 *Time*, "Architect's Dream," June 19, 1950, pp. 37–8.

43 "American to Plan New City for India," *The New York Times*, January 25, 1950, p. 4.

44 Russell Walden, ed., "Foreword," in *The Open Hand: Essays on Le Corbusier* (Cambridge: MIT Press, 1977), p. x.

45 Christopher Rand, "City on a Tilting Plain," *The New Yorker*, April 30, 1955, p. 44.

46 Le Corbusier referred to the capitol, separated from residential neighborhoods by a moat constructed by damming a branch of the Sukna River, as the "head," and the surrounding village superblocks as "l'ennemi." Sunil Khilnani, *The Idea of India* (New York: Farrar Straus, 1999), p. 134. Mayer's plan is illustrated in *Time*, "Architect's Dream."

47 On the ordering and enframing of colonial model villages, see Timothy Mitchell, *Colonising Egypt* (Berkeley: University of California Press, 1988), pp. 44–5.

48 Mayer, *Pilot Project*, pp. 113, 200. Mayer explained that "the fact that something like 100 improved plows have been sought out by them and sold in the last few weeks is not only an agricultural index, it is a social and spiritual index. He not only believes in this new plow, he begins to believe in us, and to be believe in his own and our further potentialities." Mayer, "Etawah Pilot Development Project, Second Interim Report," August 13, 1949, Box 2, folder 19, Albert Mayer Papers, Regenstein Library, University of Chicago, Hyde Park, IL.

49 Kavoori and Singh, *History of Rural Development in Modern India*, pp. 118–19.

50 Mayer to Shri M. S. Haq, December 12, 1951, Mayer papers, Box 2, folder 2.

51 Albert Mayer, "The New Capital of the Punjab," *Journal of the AIA*, vol. 14 (October 1950), p. 173. Mayer was not alone in thinking that this kind of temporal displacement defined leadership. Walter Lippmann had written in *A Preface to Morals* in 1929 that modern statesmanship "consists in giving people not what they want but what they will learn to want." Quoted in Ronald Steel, *Walter Lippmann and the American Century* (New York: Little Brown, 1980), p. 518.

52 Albert Mayer, "Working with the People," Cooper Foundation Talk at Swarthmore, February 24, 1952, Box 35, folder 11; Albert Mayer, "Community Development in India's Villages," Lecture at Southern Illinois, July 7, 1960, Box 35, folder 32, Mayer papers.

53 India, Team for the Study of Community Projects and National Extension Service, *Report*, three vols (Delhi: Coronation Printing Office, November 1957).

54 Jane Jacobs, *The Death and Life of Great American Cities* (New York: Vintage, 1961); William F. Whyte, *Street Corner Society: The Social Structure of an Italian Slum* (Chicago: University of Chicago Press, 1955).

55 Horace Holmes, "Trip Report," October 10, 1967, State Department Central Files, AGR 10 India, SNF 67–69, RG 59, Box 420, US National Archives, College Park, MD.

56 Heald oral history, January 7, 1972, Ford Foundation archives, New York; Hill, "Notes on Economic Development," December 10, 1958, Report 010459, Ford Foundation archives.

57 Albert Mayer, *The Urgent Future: People, Housing, City, Region* (New York: McGraw Hill, 1967); Kermit C. Parsons, "British and American Community Design: Clarence Stein's Manhattan Transfer, 1924–1974," *Planning Perspectives*, vol. 7, no. 2 (1992), pp. 181–210, p. 204.

58 Quoted in Latham, *Modernization as Ideology*, pp. 169–70; this doctrine was altered surprisingly little by the experience of Vietnam. A 1980 Marine Corps counter-insurgency manual described "population allegiance" operations in similar terms: "Regardless of means, the target is always the same – the people." U.S. Marine Corps, *Counterinsurgency Operations* (Quantico: Marine Corps, January 1980), p. 54.

59 Keyes Beech, "Strategic Hamlet Plan a Key to Viet Victory," *The Washington Post*, February 9, 1963, p. A7.

60 Larry E. Cable, *Conflict of Myths: The Development of American Counterinsurgency Doctrine and the Vietnam War* (New York: New York University Press, 1986), p. 197.

61 Quoted in William A. Nighswonger, *Rural Pacification in Vietnam* (New York: Praeger, 1966), p. 60.

62 George K. Tanham, *War Without Guns: American Civilians in Rural Vietnam* (New York: Praeger, 1966), p. 54.

63 Neil Sheehan, *A Bright Shining Lie: John Paul Vann and America in Vietnam* (New York: Vintage, 1988), pp. 114, 226.

64 Vernon Loeb, "U.S. Isolates Hussein's Birthplace," *The Washington Post*, November 17, 2003, p. A14.

65 Chester L. Cooper, Judith E. Corson, Laurence J. Legere, David E. Lockwood and Donald M. Weller, *The American Experience with Pacification in Vietnam* (Arlington, VA: Institute for Defense Analyses, March 1972), p. 48.

66 Although there was a trend, evident in the 1990s, to target specific neighborhoods as functionally, ethnographically, or politically distinct, a village within a city, e.g. the El Chorillo neighborhood of Panama City, the Black Sea district of Mogadisu, and Sadr City in Baghdad.

67 Quoted in Edward H. Berman, *The Influence of the Carnegie, Ford, and Rockefeller Foundations on American Foreign Policy* (Albany: SUNY, 1983), p. 123.

68 "Preface" to Fredric Jameson and Masao Miyoshi, eds., *The Cultures of Globalization* (Durham: University of North Carolina Press, 1998), p. 18.

69 Bernard Lewis, "The Roots of Muslim Rage, *Atlantic*, September 1990, available online at http://www.theatlantic.com/issues/90sep/rage.htm.

70 Thomas P. M. Barnett, "The Pentagon's New Map," available online at http://www.nwc.navy.mil/newrulesets/ThePentagonsNewMap.htm.

71 National Commission on Terrorist Attacks upon the United States, "9/11 Commission Report," Washington, 2004, available online at http://www.9–11commission.gov/report/911Report_Ch7.htm.

72 Ibid., available online at http://www.9–11commission.gov/report/911Report_Ch2.htm. The threat from remote, rural "ungoverned areas" is one of the cardinal constructs of the global war on terror. The Pentagon has identified areas in South America, Belize, the Philippines, Somalia, and northern Bangladesh where they seek to cultivate "friendly militias." Maxom Kniazkov, "US Wants to Build Network of Friendly Militias to Combat Terrorism," Agence France Presse, August 11, 2004.

73 Rajiv Chandrasekaran, "U.S. Deploying Heavily Armored Battle Tanks for the First Time in Afghan War," *The Washington Post*, November 19, 2010, p. A1.

74 Samuel P. Huntington, "The Bases of Accommodation," *Foreign Affairs* (July 1968), pp. 642–56, p. 649.

75 Raymond Williams, *The Country and the City* (Oxford: Oxford University Press, 1973), p. 297.
76 See Doug Saunders, *Arrival City: The Final Migration and Our Next World* (Toronto: Random House, 2010).

Index

and 155; protests in Seattle (1999) about
51; reversal of discourse of 293–4
Goankar, Dilip 121, 129
Gobineau, Arthur de 21
Goh, R.B.H. xi, 15–16, 259–72
Golan, Brigadier General Yair 71, 87n27
Gombrich, E.H. 182, 198n7
Google Earth 17
Goonewardena, K., Kiepfer, S., Milgrom,
    R. and Schmid, C. 145n6
Gordon, Andrew 253n38, 257n104
Gordon, Neve 66, 85n11
Gough, S. 115
Goyette, C. 107
gradualism 2
Graeber, D. 51
Graham, S. xi, 11–12, 18n1, 18n11, 27,
    92–117
Gray, C.H. 45, 46, 53, 59, 60, 297n41
Great Depression 4, 156–7, 158, 164, 173,
    176, 283
Great Fire (September 1666) in London
    183–5
Green, W. 106
green spaces, historical gardens and 151
Green Zone in Baghdad 108
Gregory, Derek 94, 95, 105, 115
Gropius, Walter 162
Gross, Aeyal M. 90n70
Grossman, Lt. Col. David 104
Grozny 1, 111
The Guardian 108
Guattari, F. 144, 146n24
Guggenheim family 288
Guifoyle, Joseph M. 179n61
Guillen, Reynal 253n36
Gulag 204
Gupta, A. and Ferguson, J. 257n101

Habermas, J. and Derrida, J. 121
Habermas, Jürgen 122
Hagan, Steve 104
Halutz, Dan 72, 83, 84, 84n7, 88n35, 88n37
Hamed, Sheikh Ibrahim 74
Hamilton, W. 103
Hammes, Colonel Thomas 94
Hanchard, M. 128
Haniyeh, Ismail 75
Haq, Shri M.S. 297n50
Haraway, Donna 59, 257n103
Hardt, M. and Negri, A. 58, 61, 145n15
Hardy, Thomas 31
Harel, A. and Isacharoff, A. 90n63, 90n66
Harel, A. and Regular, A. 88n45, 89n51
Harel, Amos 89n52, 89n53, 91n73
Harel, Israel 88n36

Harootunian, H.D. 253n38, 255n67,
    257n104
Harrar, J.G. *et al.* 296n29
Harris, Air Chief Marshall Sir Arthur
    "Bomber" 70
al-Hathim, Ibn 17
Haussmann, G.E., Baron 13, 136
Hayner, H. 105
Heald, Henry 291, 298n56
Hegel, G.W.F. 9, 10, 14, 121
Heines, Major Greg 110
Heinrich, J. *et al.* 28
Heller, A. 97
helping-hand construction work *(otasuke
    fushin)* 150
heritage renewal 151
Herz, J. and Macedonia, M. 104
heterogeneity in Moscow 203
Hevly, B. and Findlay, J.M. 253n29
Hezbollah 67, 69
Hill, Richard 265
Hilsman, R. and Rusk, D. 296n25
Hilsman, Roger 285, 297n33
Hiroshima 4, 176, 282
Hobsbawm, E. and Ranger, T. 244, 257n101
Hoddeson, L. *et al.* 251n15
Holler, Wenceslaus 187
Holloman Air Force Base, New Mexico
    107–8
Hollywood stagecraft 101
Holme, Thomas 197
Holmes, Horace 291, 298n55
Holmes, R. 37
Holston, J. and Appadurai, A. 261, 270
home-builders 157
Home Building and Home Ownership,
    President's Conference on (1931)
    158–9, 165
homeland security: imaginist city and 52;
    military–entertainment nexus and 111
hometowns: clearance, de-urbanization
    and 157; hometown *(furosato)* in Japan
    236–40
Hong Kong 263
Hooke, Robert 192, 193, 194, 195, 196,
    197, 198n25
hooks, b. 131
Hoover, Herbert 158
hope and pessimism, line between 20
Höpfl, H. 59
Hopkins, Johns 257n103
Horsely, Carter B. 239–40, 256n86, 256n88
hospitality 121–2
housing: emergency measures on
    156–7; estate management 170;
    house (and housing) in American

assortment of pathologies 287; village social workers, assignment of 288; Wagner-Steagall Act (1937) 288–9
Rushdie, Salman 219
Russia: national identity in, construction of 204; Orthodox Church in 202–3
Rwanda, aftermath of genocide in 122
Ryan, Jack 259

Said, Edward 124, 130, 244, 257n102
Sakitani, Tetsuo 250n8
Salecl, R. 41n12
Salim, Jamal 74
Samhadana, Jamal Abu 74
Samo, Radike 267
Samoa 264, 266, 268, 269–70
Sanchez, General Ricardo 282
Sarandon, Susan 139, 144
Sasaki, Kizen 243
Sassen, Saskia 261, 263
saturation bombing 53
Saunders, Doug 299n76
Saxenian, Anna Lee 252n19, 252n21
Schell, J. 50, 296n323
Schell, Orville 287, 293
Schlesinger, Arthur M. 284, 295n13
Schmitt, G. 40n4, 45
Schneider, J. and Susser, I. 27
Schopenhauer, A. and Stirner, M. 31, 41n15
Schulman, Zvi 90n65
Schumacher, E.F. 58
scientific machine production 165
Scotland 264, 269–70
Scott, A. and Soja, E. 251n14, 253n29, 253n30
Scott, Allen 251n14
Scott, J.C. and Bhatt, N. 295n6
Seal, C. 116
security service autonomy 73–4
"The Seduction" (David Dabydeen) 221–2
Segall, Stu 101
Segoli, Ephraim 64, 84n1, 84n5
segregation 170, 261; of city functions 289
seismic reinforcement (and anti-seismic reinforcement) 153
self-exile 219
self-fulfilling worlds 112–13
self-reliance, darker face of 282–7
Sennett, R. 34, 181, 197n2, 197n4
sense and reason in Moscow 202
September 11 2001, events of 135
Shachtman, N. 102, 109
Shadwell, Thomas 180
Shafer, D. Michael 296n18
Shaffer, Mark 96

Shahin, Rahmeh 67
Shakedy, Eliezer 77
Shamas, Charles 87n31
Shanab, Ismail Abu 75
Sharon, A. 72, 73, 76, 88n46
Shawer, Mahmoud 74
Sheehan, Neil 298n63
Shehadeh, Salah 68, 74
Shelah, O. and Limor, Y. 88n37
Shils, Edward 296n22
Shinjuku 7
Shirakawa, Hideki 232, 254n48
Shnayderman, Ronen 87n28
Shoten, Tsukuba 250n4
Sia, R. 52
Siboni, Gabrial 85n7
signs, discourses and rituals of warfare 264–5
Silverberg, Miriam 257n104, 258n105
sim cities 111–12
Simon, Sir Ernest 167
Simone, Abdou Maliq 86n17
Singer, P. 55
Sixtus V 185, 189
skopos 6, 13, 16
slave markets 125–6
Slave Song (David Dabydeen) 220
slums and blighted areas 164, 166, 167–9
small achievements, politics of 37
Smith, Bernard 174, 179n59
social capital 27, 36, 37
social change, large-scale projects for 21
social depletion (or conservation) 170
social interaction, modes of 38
social orders, biological constitution of 21
sociality, assumption of 28–9
societies of control 137
Soja, Edward 145n1
Solzhenitsyn, Aleksandr 204
Sorel, G. and Schmitt, G. 21, 31
South Africa 268, 269
spaces: Eurocentric control of 131; green spaces, historical gardens and 151; place, habitation and 129–31, 132; reappropriation through spatial practices 136; spatio-corporeal inscription 206
Special Operations Forces (SOFs), deployment of 44, 48–9, 60
spectacular government 44
spectatorship 276
spiritual gatherings 51
spontaneity 123
sports and warfare, differences between 259–60
Stahl, Roger 103, 104, 110, 113, 116

For Product Safety Concerns and Information please contact our EU
representative GPSR@taylorandfrancis.com
Taylor & Francis Verlag GmbH, Kaufingerstraße 24, 80331 München, Germany

www.ingramcontent.com/pod-product-compliance
Lightning Source LLC
Chambersburg PA
CBHW050457270326
41927CB00009B/1794